Takaharu＋Yui Tezuka　Architecture Catalogue
手塚貴晴＋手塚由比　建築カタログ

Takaharu + Yui Tezuka
Architecture Catalogue

First Published in Japan on March 15, 2006
Twelfth Published on September 30, 2017
by TOTO Publishing (TOTO LTD.)
TOTO Nogizaka Bldg., 2F
1-24-3 Minami-aoyama, Minato-ku
Tokyo 1070062 JAPAN
[Sales] Telephone: +81 3 3402 7138 Facsimile: +81 3 3402 7187
[Editorial] Telephone: +81 3 3497 1010
URL: http://www.toto.co.jp/publishing/

Author: Takaharu Tezuka, Yui Tezuka
Publisher: Toru Kato
Book Designer: Rie Amaki
Printing and Binding: Tosho Printing Co., Ltd.

This publication is released in time for the exhibition TAKAHARU + YUI TEZUKA
held at TOTO GALLERY.MA in Tokyo from March 15, 2006 to May 20, 2006

Except as permitted under copyright law, this book may not be reproduced, in
whole or in part, in any form or by any means, including photocopying, scanning,
digitizing, or otherwise, without prior permission. Scanning or digitizing this book
through a third party, even for personal or home use, is also strictly prohibited.
The list price is indicated on the cover.

ISBN978-4-88706-267-2

Takaharu + Yui Tezuka Architecture Catalogue

手塚貴晴+手塚由比
建築カタログ

Photography: Katsuhisa Kida

It has been eleven years since we returned home from London. Starting with small houses, we have continued to produce projects more-or-less randomly, yet looking back now, we finally feel an awareness of what we are trying to achieve. What we have noticed from our long period living overseas is that architecture should support society and exceed its era. Following the passion of the architect, architecture that continues to survive across several centuries will mature due to the affection it receives from people. All architecture is an extension of the house, and at the same time, the house is a miniature of the relationships between all of architecture and society. Regardless of size, our design process hardly changes. Architecture is a device that triggers the activities of people and society. Easily understood. Comfortable. And able to propose hitherto unknown values. These are all obvious responsibilities for an architect, but we wish to continue to make them the direct concerns of our work.

Takaharu + Yui Tezuka

ロンドンより帰国して11年。
小さな住宅から始まりやみくもに作品をつくり続けてきましたが、
いま振り返ってみるとようやく我々のやりたいことが
見えてきたような気がします。
長い海外暮らしで気がついたことは、建築は時代を超えて
社会を支えていく要であるということ。
数世紀を経て生き残った建築は、建築家の熱い想いの上に
人の愛着を身にまといつつ成長してきたということです。
すべての建築は住宅の延長線上にあると同時に、
住宅はすべての建築と社会の関係の縮図でもあります。
大小に関わらず我々の設計プロセスはほとんど変わりません。
建築は人や社会に行為を引き起こす仕掛けです。
わかりやすいこと。居心地の良いこと。
そして今までにない価値を提案できること。
いずれも当たり前の建築家としての務めですが、
それらをあえて真っ直ぐに構えて作品をつくり続けていこうと思います。

手塚貴晴＋手塚由比

Contents 目次

Preface 序文

01_ Soejima Hospital 副島病院

02_ Cherry Blossom House 花見の家

03_ Wood Deck House 鎌倉山の家*

04_ Light Gauge Steel House 辻堂の家*

05_ Kawagoe Music Apartment 川越の音楽マンション

06_ Machiya House 八王子の家*

07_ Megaphone House 腰越のメガホンハウス*

08_ Roof House 屋根の家*

09_ Balcony House バルコニーの家*

10_ Wall-less House 壁のない家

11_ House to Catch the Sky　空を捕まえる家*
12_ Step House　熱海のステップハウス*
13_ House to Catch the Sky II　空を捕まえる家II*
14_ Anthill House　蟻塚の家*
15_ Thin Roof Sukiya　薄い屋根の数寄屋*
16_ Thin Wall House　薄い壁の家*
17_ Hounancho "L" Condominium　方南町L*
18_ Canopy House　軒の家*
19_ Saw Roof House　のこぎり屋根の家*
20_ Skylight House　天窓の家*
21_ House to Catch the Sky III　空を捕まえる家III*
22_ Echigo-Matsunoyama Museum of Natural Science
　　 越後松之山「森の学校」キョロロ*

23_ Toyota L&F Hiroshima　トヨタL&F広島本社*
24_ Engawa House　縁側の家*
25_ House to Catch the Sky IV　空を捕まえる家IV*
26_ Floating House　フローティングハウス*
27_ Five-Courtyard House　ファイブコートヤードハウス*
28_ Thin Wall Office　壁の薄いオフィス*
29_ Clipping Corner House　隅切りの家*
30_ Double Courtyard House　ダブルコートヤードハウス*
31_ House to Catch the Forest　森を捕まえる家*
32_ Observatory House　展望台の家*
33_ Jyubako House　重箱の家*
34_ Big Window House　大窓の家*
35_ Shoe Box House　大箱の家*

36_ Floating Roof House　山すその家*

37_ Roof Deck House　屋上の家*

38_ Fuji Kindergarten　ふじようちえん*

TIME-LESS　変わらないもの

Project Data　作品データ

Publications　掲載誌一覧

Credits　クレジット

Biography　略歴

*Collaboration with MASAHIRO IKEDA co., ltd
　共同設計　池田昌弘 / MASAHIRO IKEDA co., ltd

Soejima Hospital

副島病院　1996

In this hospital, all patients can view the city from their bed. 4m x 80m louvers protect the patients' privacy and shield them from direct sunlight.

ベッドの上の患者から、街が見える病院。
庇とテラスが、患者を日差しと外の視線から守る。

01 _

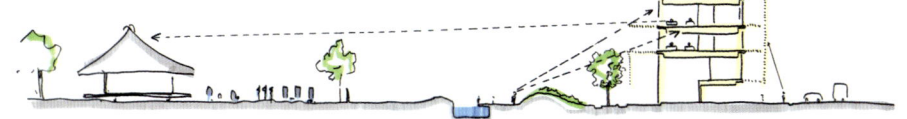

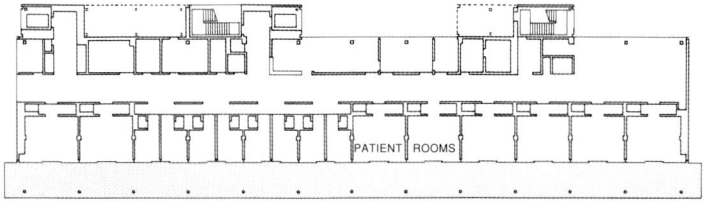

4F 1/800

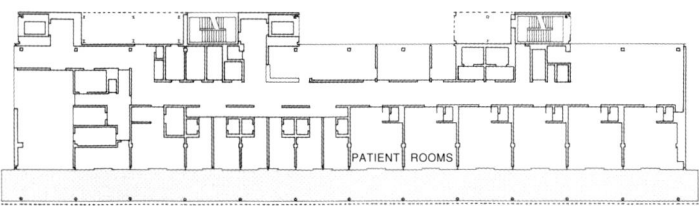

3F 1/800

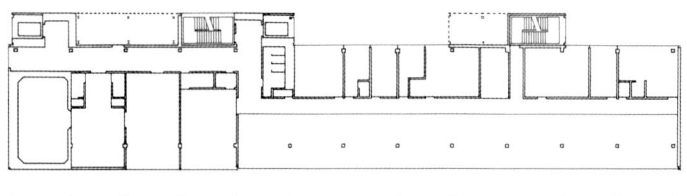

2F 1/800

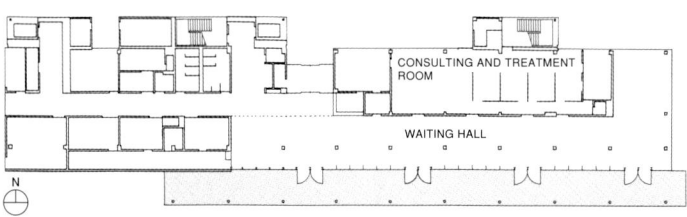

1F 1/800

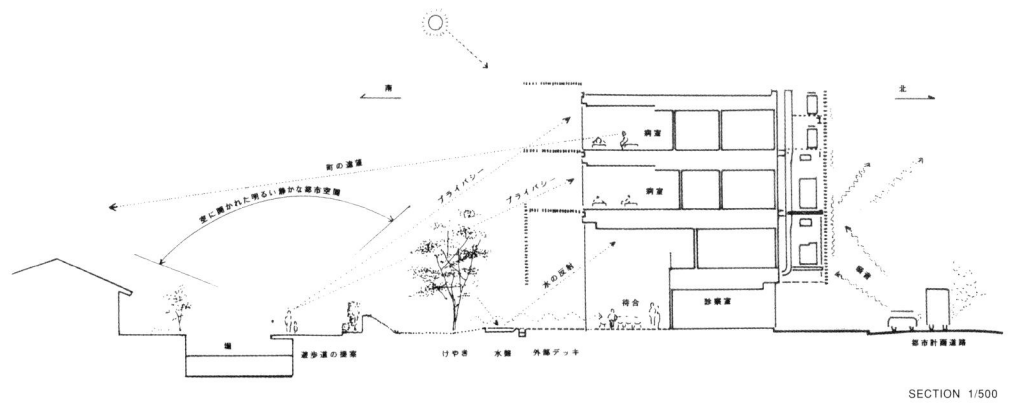

SECTION 1/500

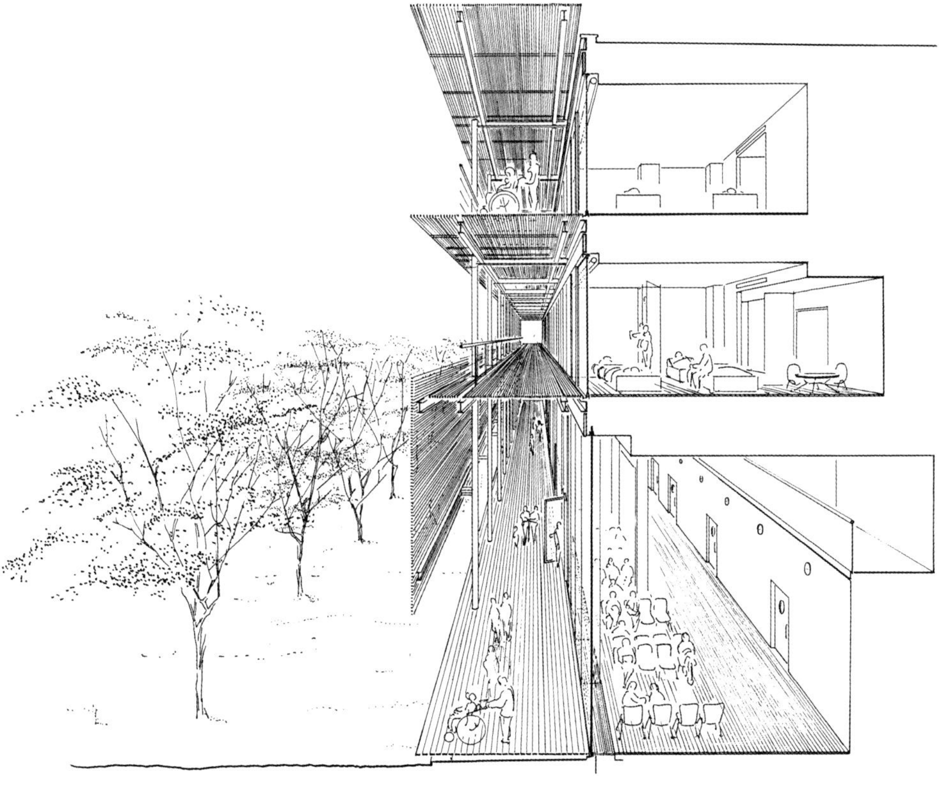

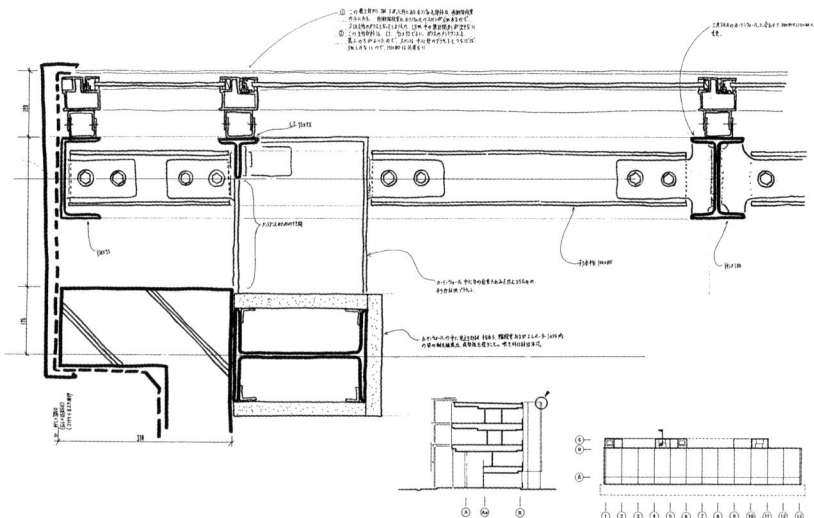

西側階段室カーテンウォール詳細図1

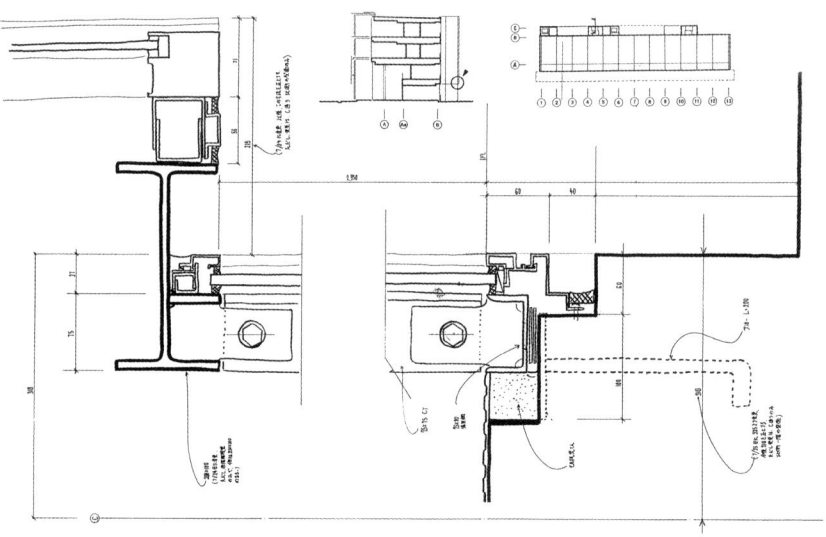

西側階段室カーテンウォール詳細図2

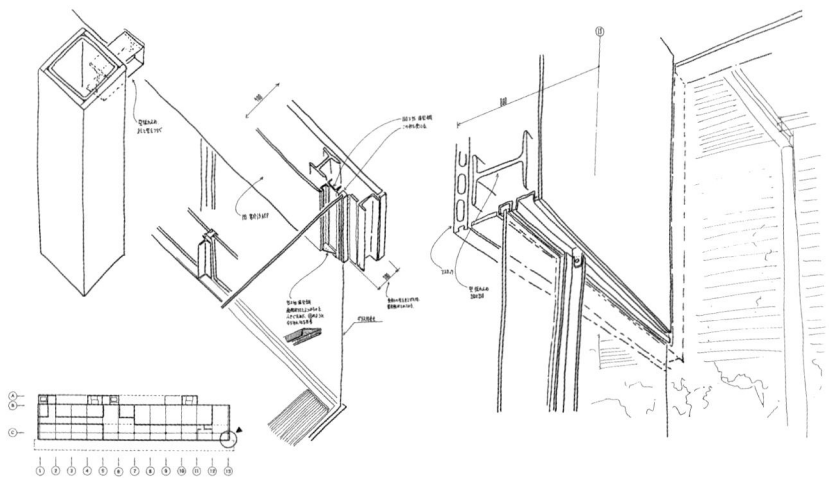

東側外壁グラザード取り合い説明図

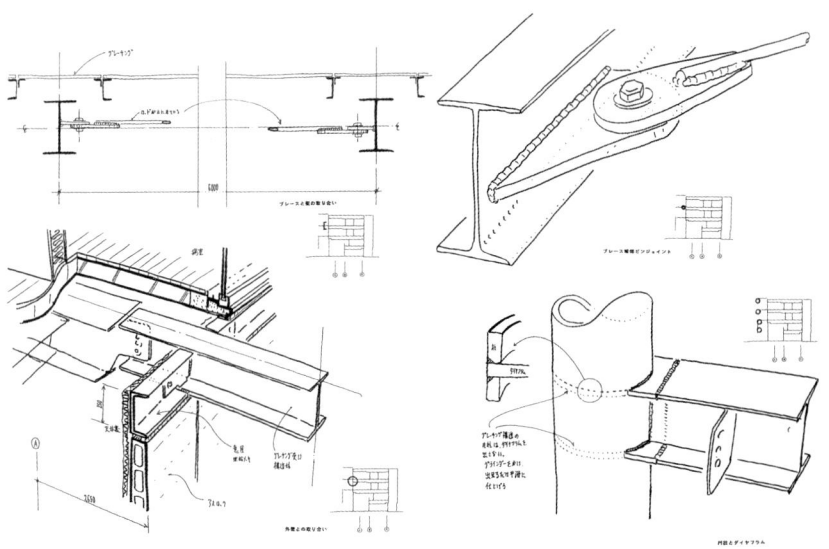

ルーバー支持部材詳細図

Cherry Blossom House

花見の家　1996

House designed for "Hanami" parties, the Japanese custom of drinking under cherry blossoms.
A cherry tree with a 2.5m trunk occupies most of the site. The house windows are inclined to look up at the blossoms against the background sky.

大きな桜の下の小さな家。
春には桜が咲き誇り、夏には茂みが涼しい影を落とす。
真ん中のミラーの箱はキッチンとバス。

02

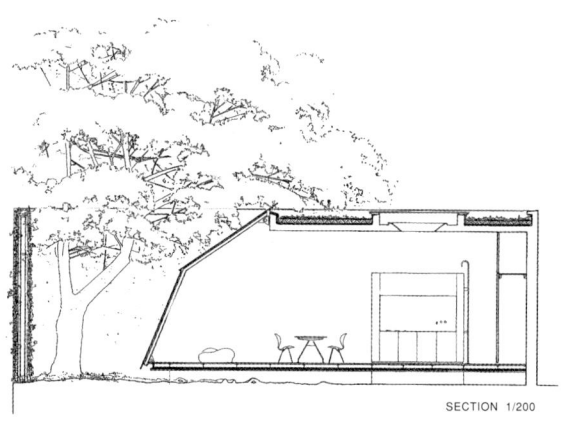

SECTION 1/200

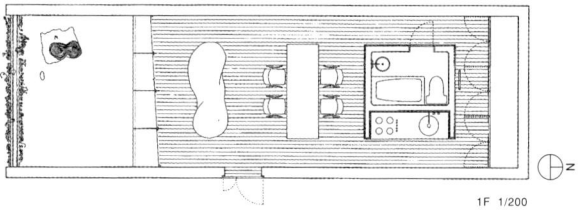

1F 1/200

Wood Deck House

鎌倉山の家　1999

This house on the Kamakura Mountain ridge overlooks the natural forest and the Pacific Ocean.
The space can be extended out to a 4m cantilevered deck and the surrounding forest by completely opening glass sliding doors on both sides.

江ノ島と雑木林の両方を望む峠の家。
森の上に4m突き出したデッキに向かって、二面が完全に開いている。

03

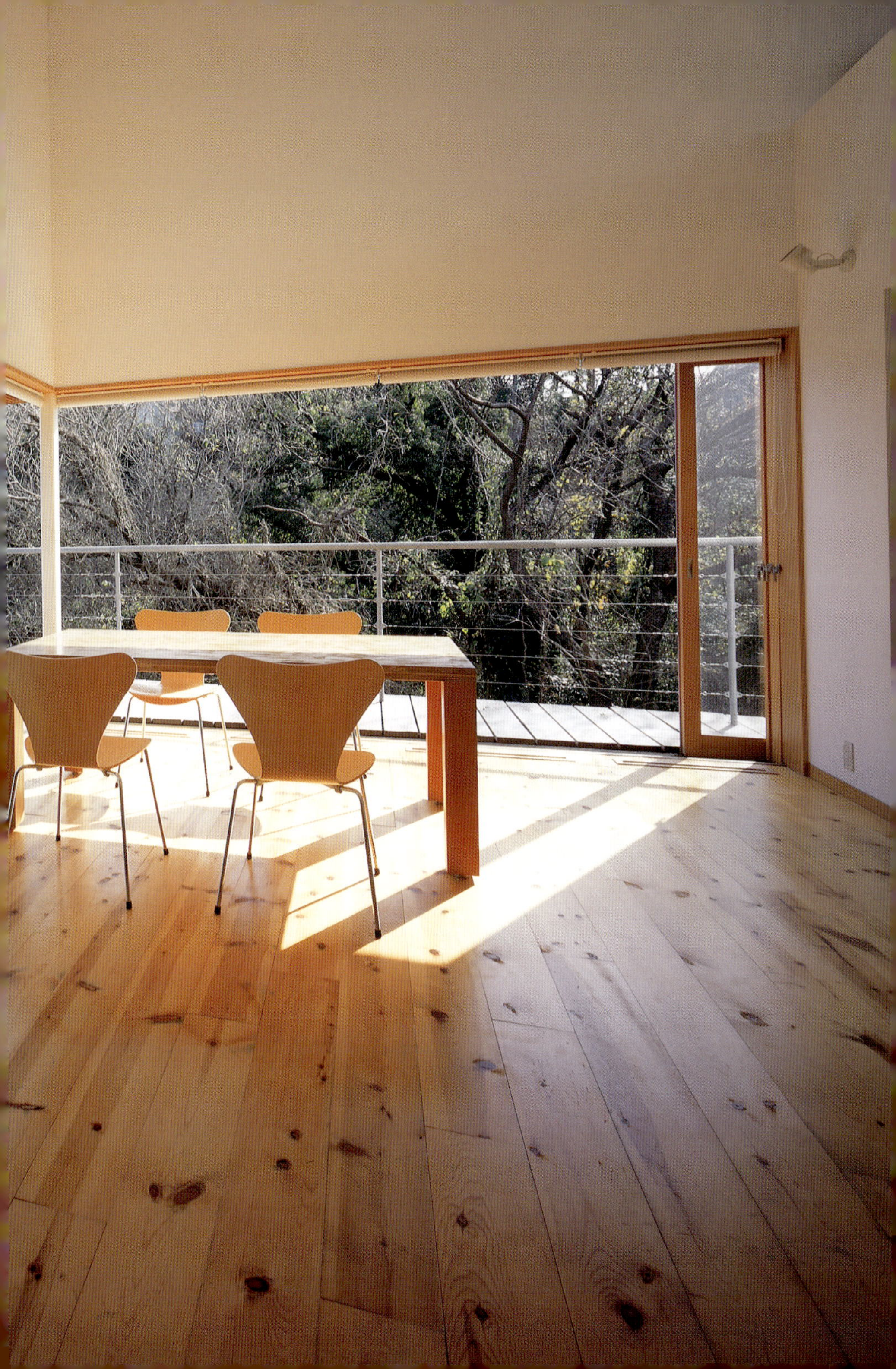

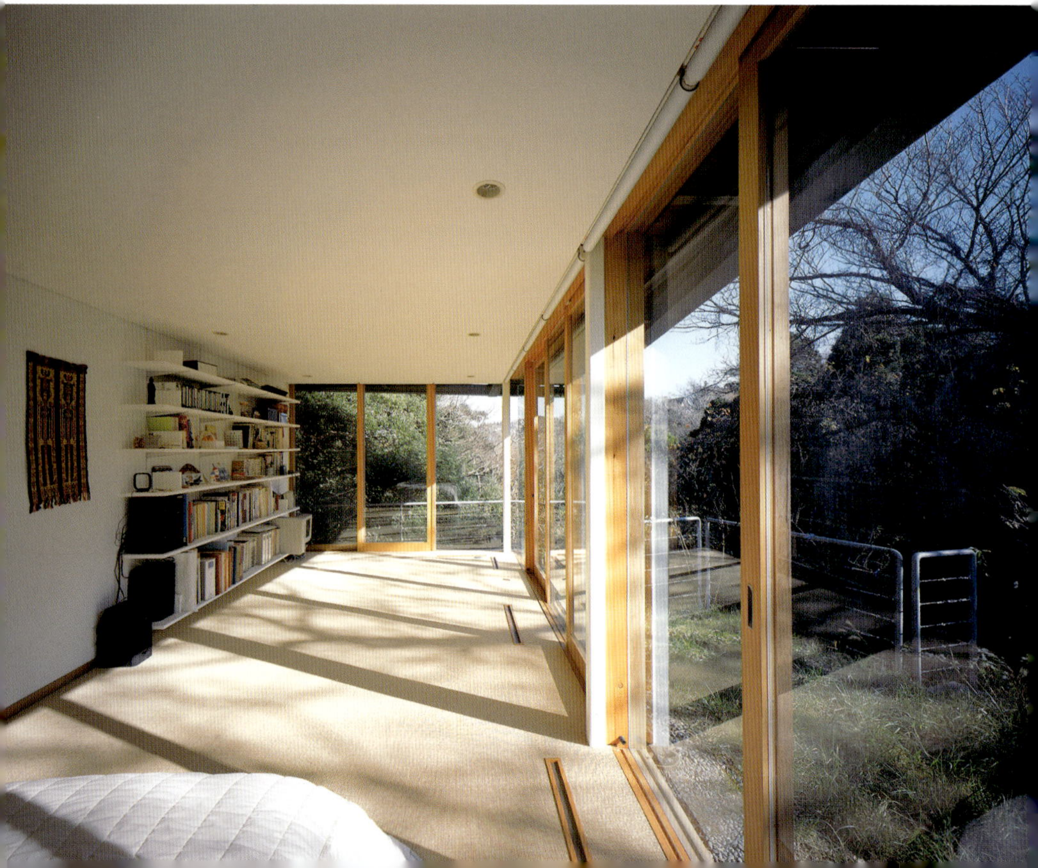

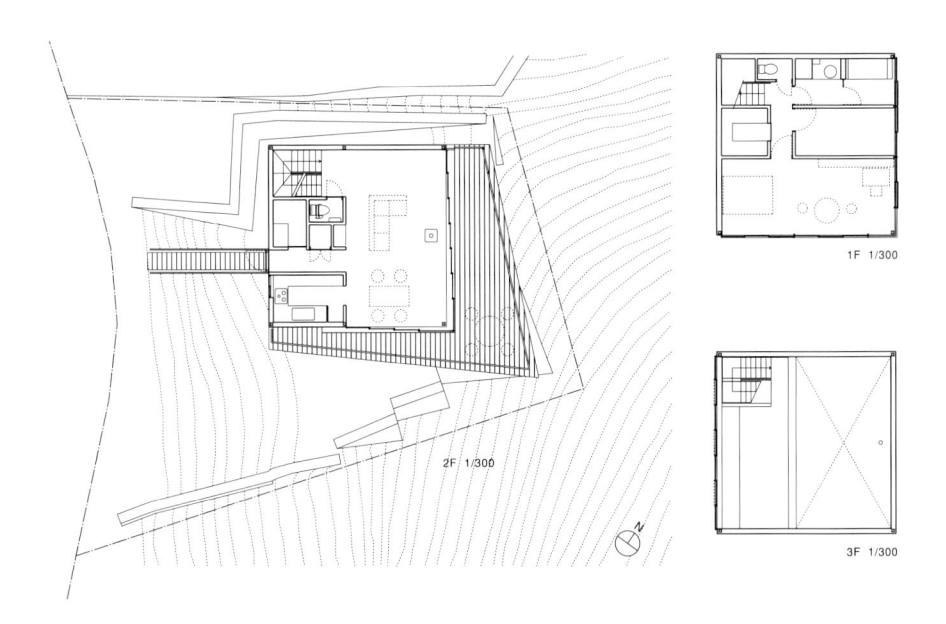

2F 1/300

1F 1/300

3F 1/300

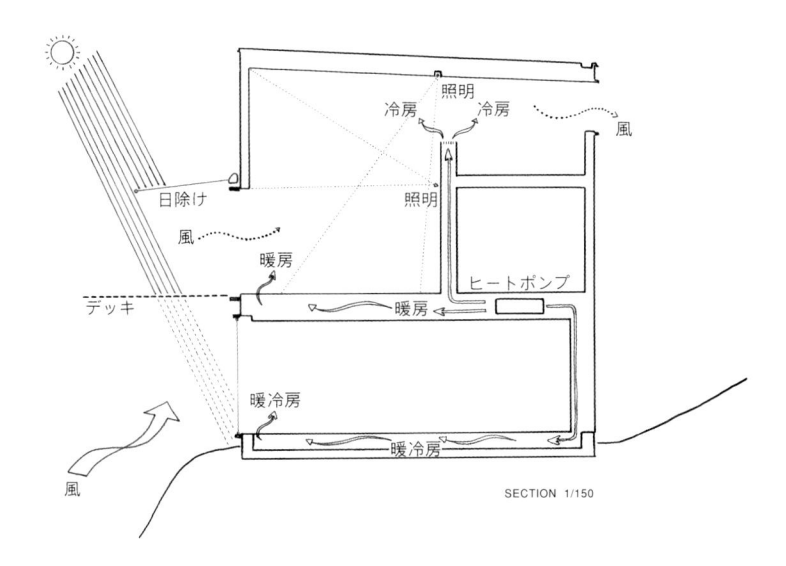

照明
冷房　冷房
風
日除け
風
暖房
照明
ヒートポンプ
デッキ
暖房
暖冷房
暖冷房
風

SECTION 1/150

Light Gauge Steel House

辻堂の家　1999

The Light-Gauge Steel House was designed for a site inaccessible to cranes.
The steel beams were light enough to be carried by hand.

LGSを使った新しい工法の家。
前面道路の狭い矮小地に適する。

04

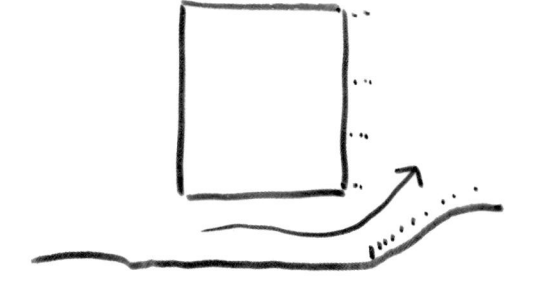

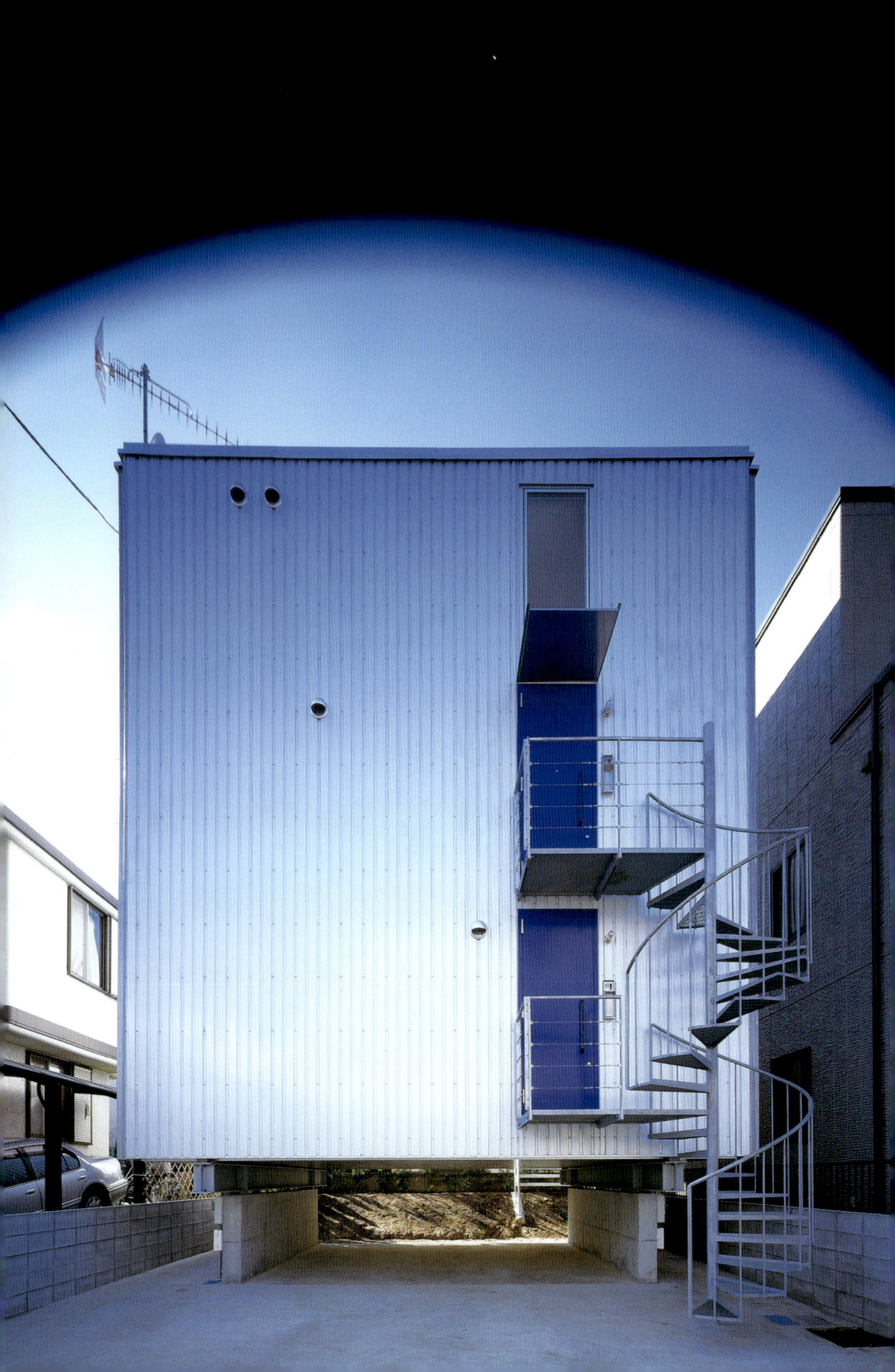

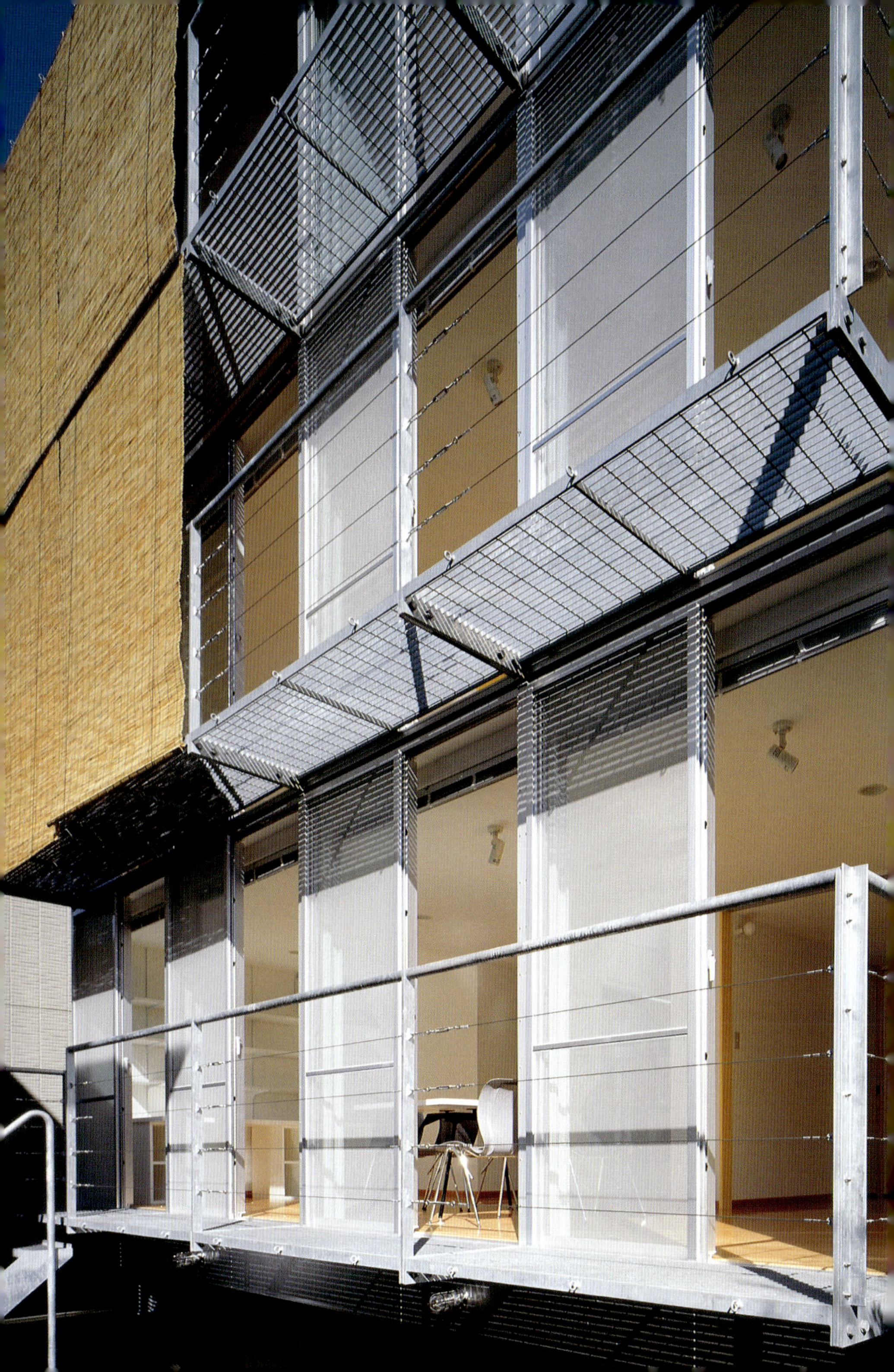

3F 1/200

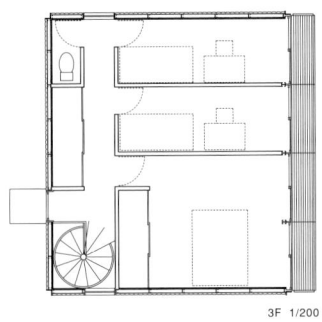

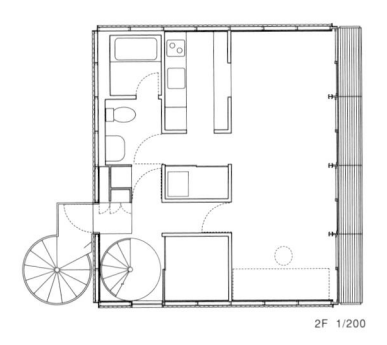

2F 1/200

1F 1/200

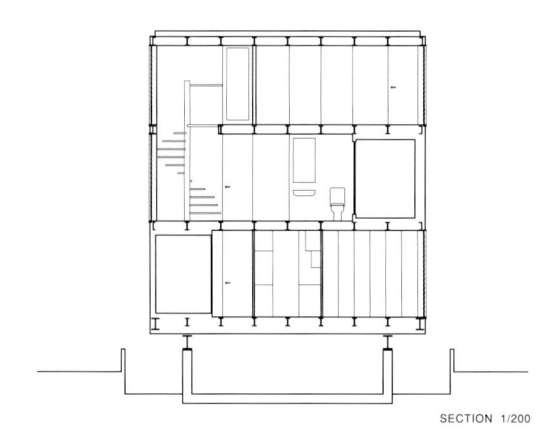

SECTION 1/200

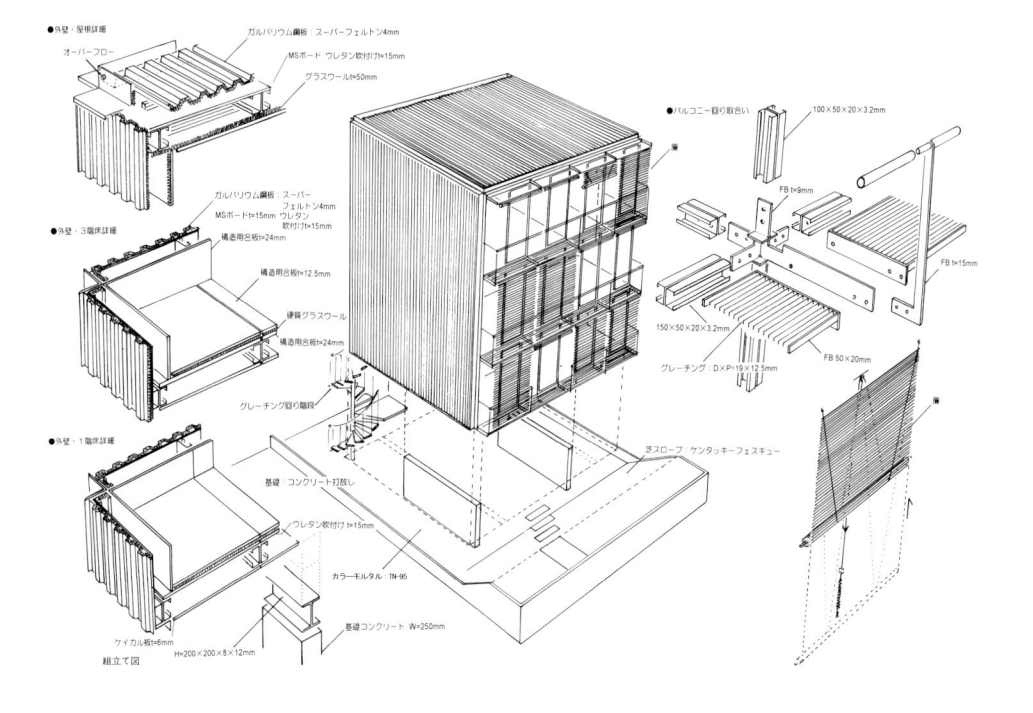

●外壁・屋根詳細
ガルバリウム鋼板：スーパーフェルトンt=4mm
オーバーフロー
MSボードウレタン吹付けt=15mm
グラスウールt=50mm

●外壁・3階床詳細
ガルバリウム鋼板：スーパーフェルトンt=4mm
MSボードt=15mm ウレタン吹付けt=15mm
構造用合板t=24mm
構造用合板t=12.5mm
硬質グラスウール
構造用合板t=24mm
グレーチング廻り階段

●外壁・1階床詳細
基礎：コンクリート打放し
ウレタン吹付けt=15mm
カラーモルタル：TN-95
基礎コンクリートW=250mm
ケイカル板t=6mm
H=200×200×8×12mm
組立て図

●バルコニー廻り取合い
100×50×20×3.2mm
FB t=9mm
150×50×20×3.2mm
グレーチング：D×P=19×12.5mm
FB t=15mm
FB 50×20mm
芝スロープ：ケンタッキーフェスキュー

Kawagoe Music Apartment

川越の音楽マンション　2000

Colorful, soundproof apartments with 4m-high ceilings. All rooms cantilever out 7m from a central corridor.

高遮音性能ワンルーム賃貸マンション。
隣のピアノの音はほとんど聞こえない。
4mの天井高と、天井いっぱいの大きな窓。

05

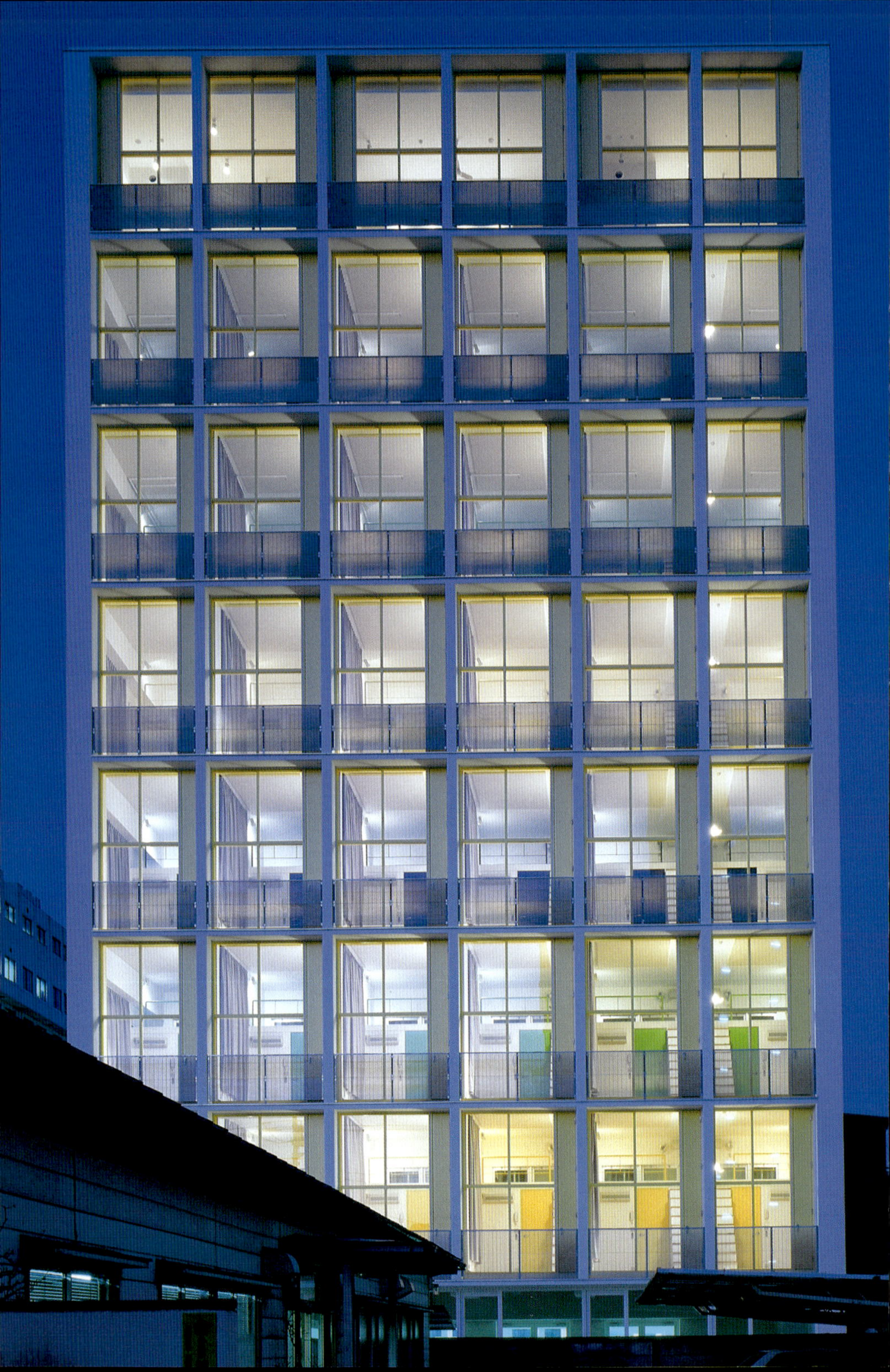

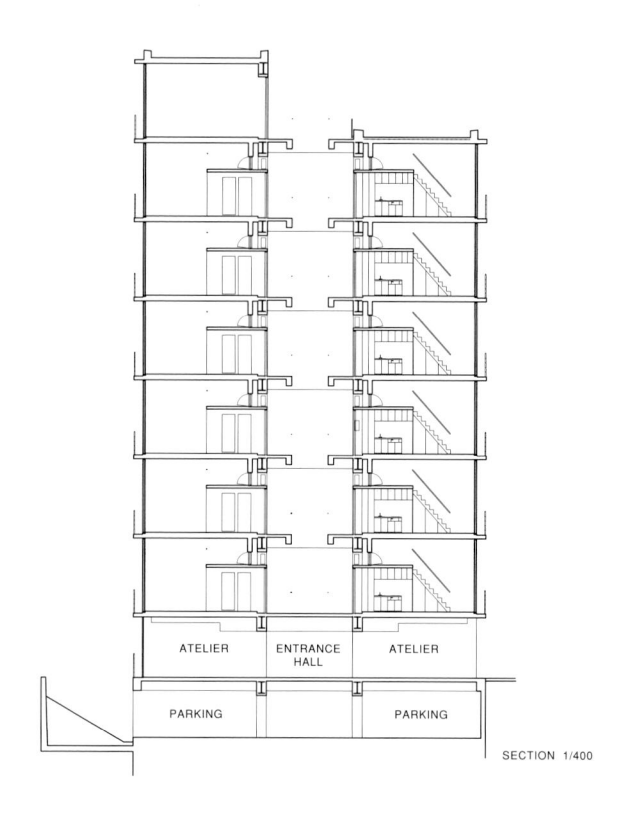

ATELIER	ENTRANCE HALL	ATELIER
PARKING		PARKING

SECTION 1/400

PLAN 1/400

Machiya House

八王子の家　2000

A reinterpretation of the Japanese courtyard house. Once the sliding doors are open, the boundary between the inside and the outside disappears. The courtyard space extends out to the next courtyard and again to the next.

町屋のダイアグラムの再解釈。
すべての空間が二方向に開けている。
プライバシーと開放された空間の両立。

06

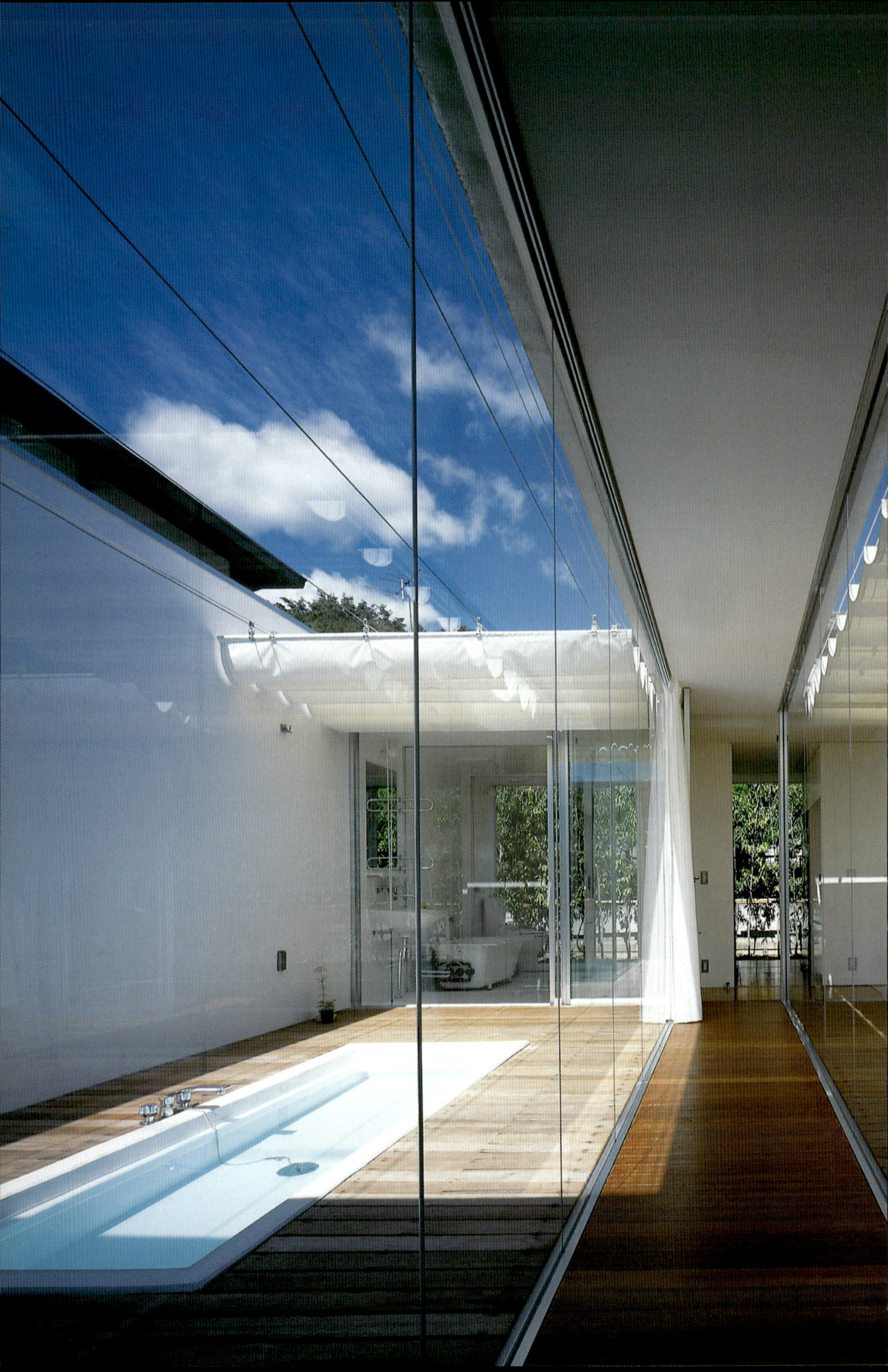

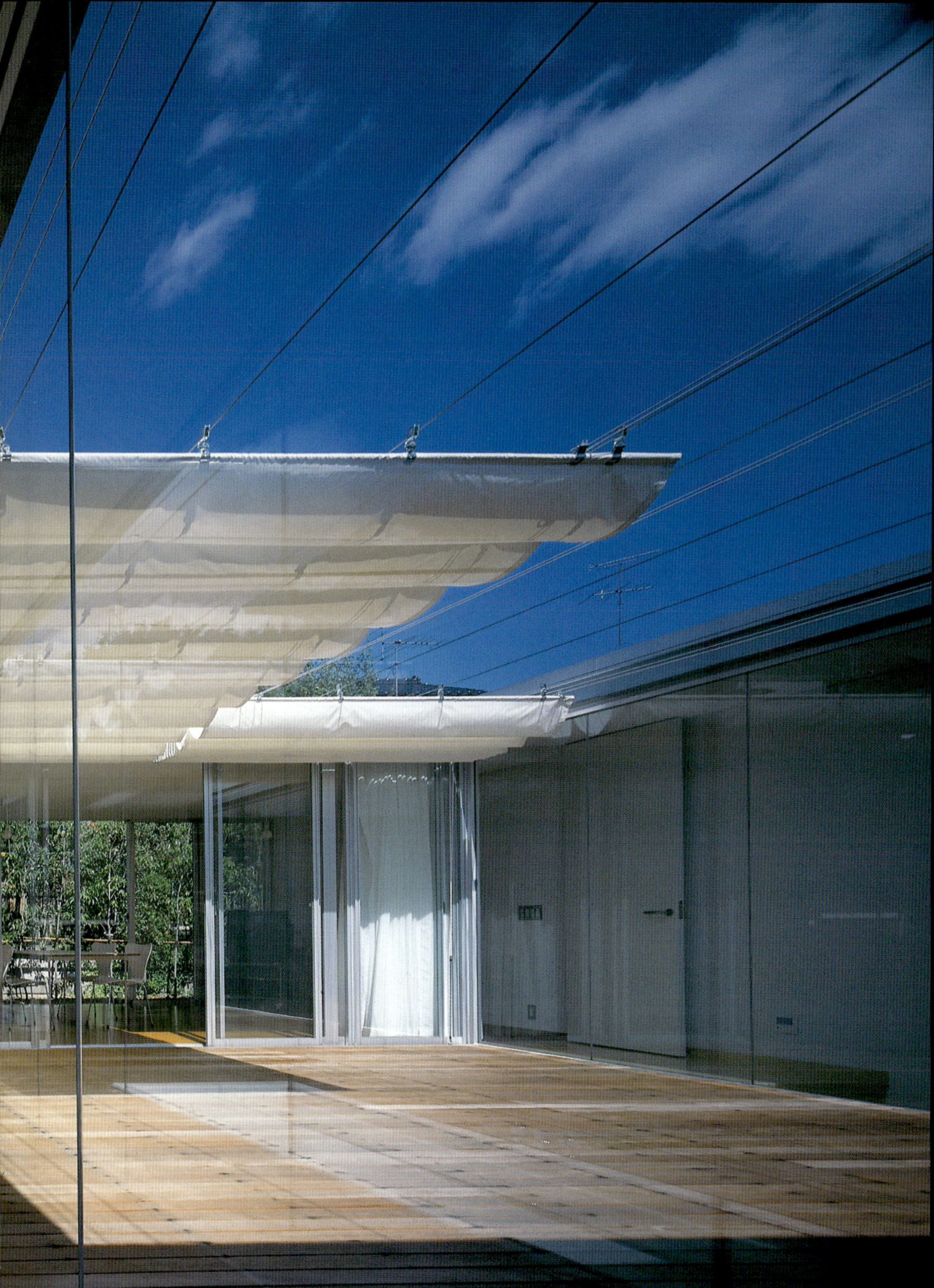

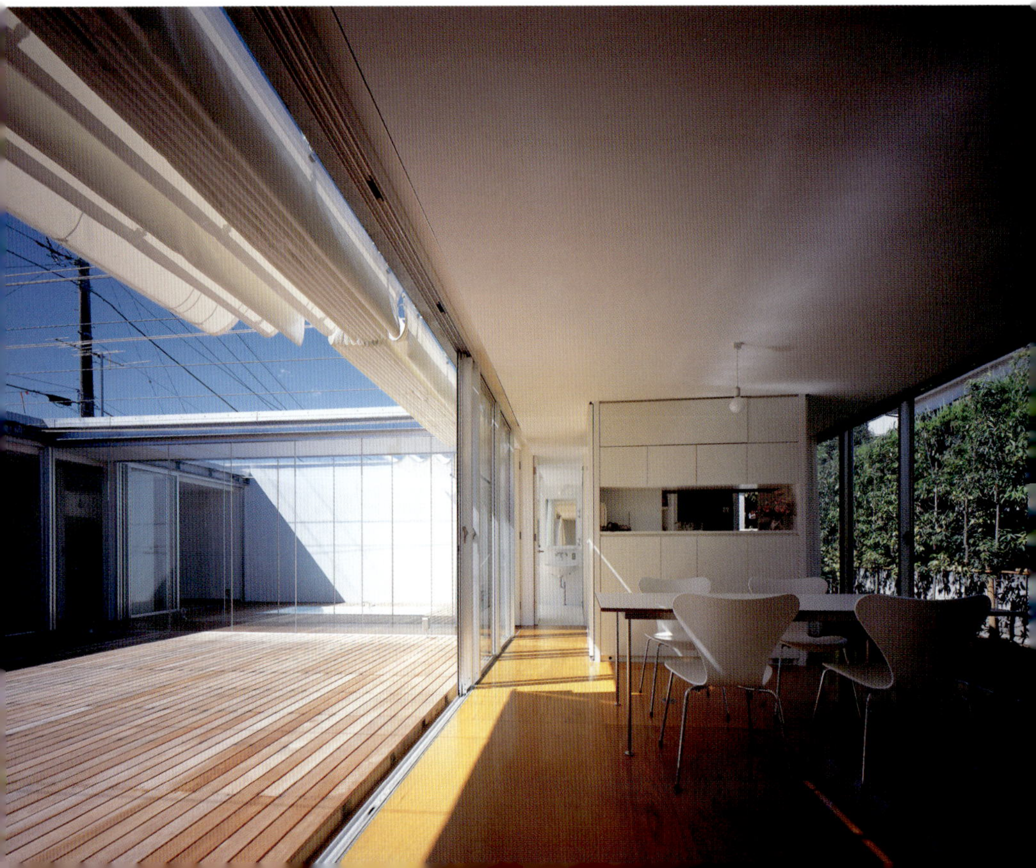

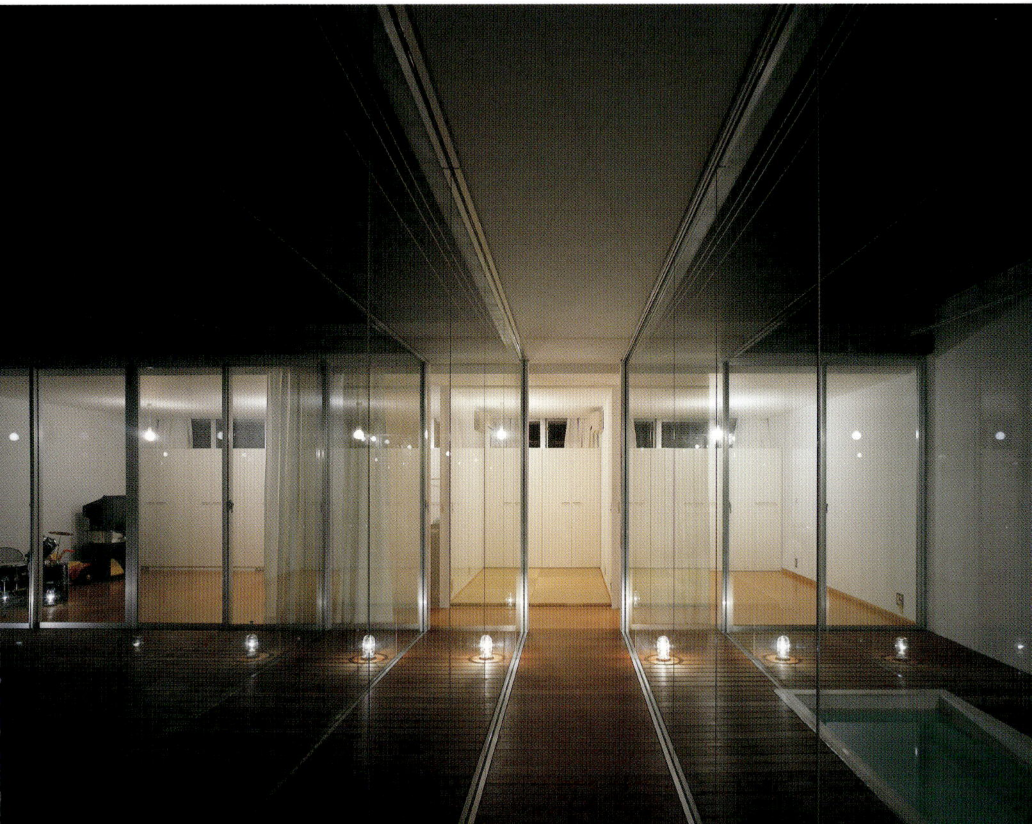

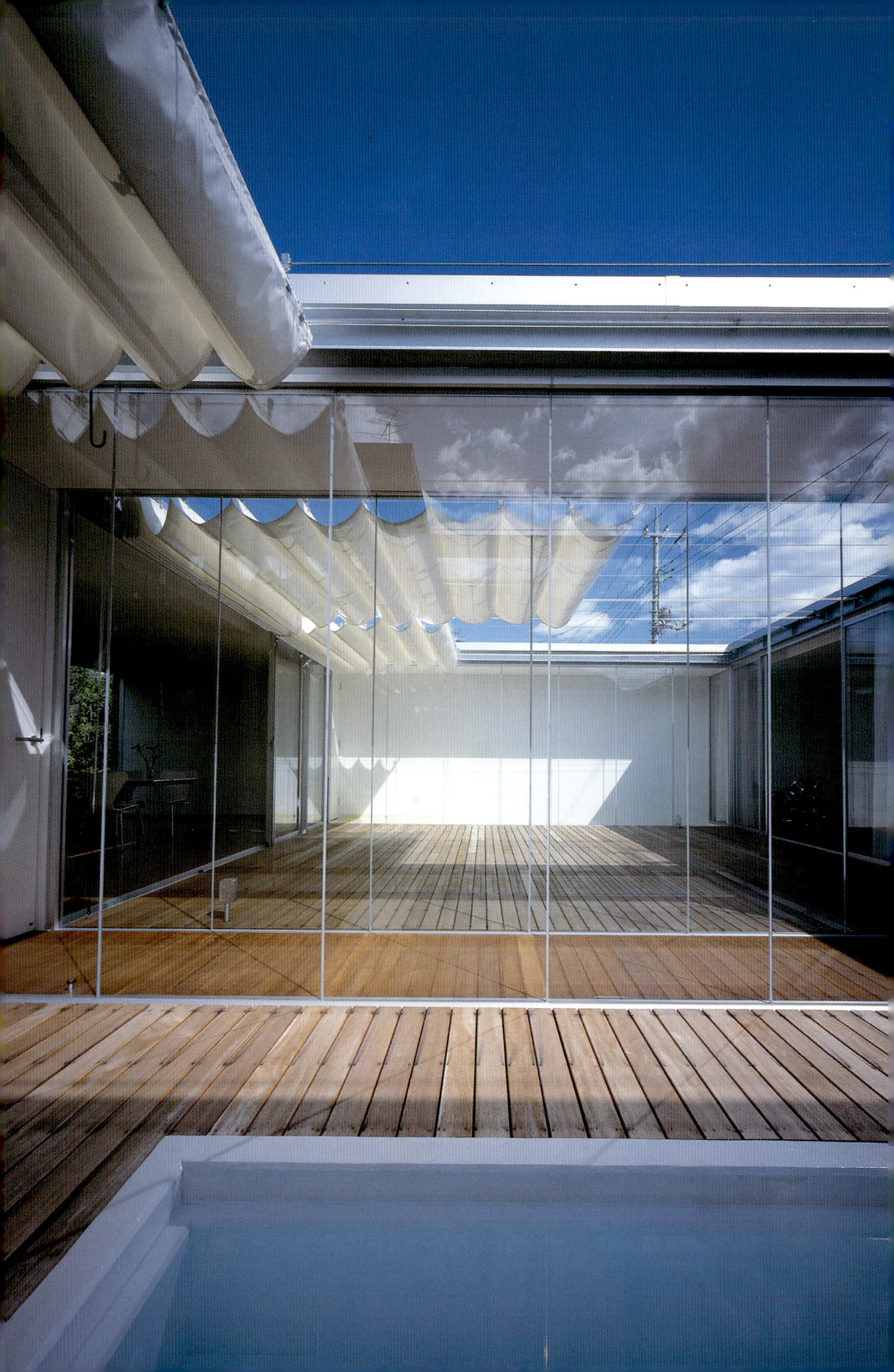

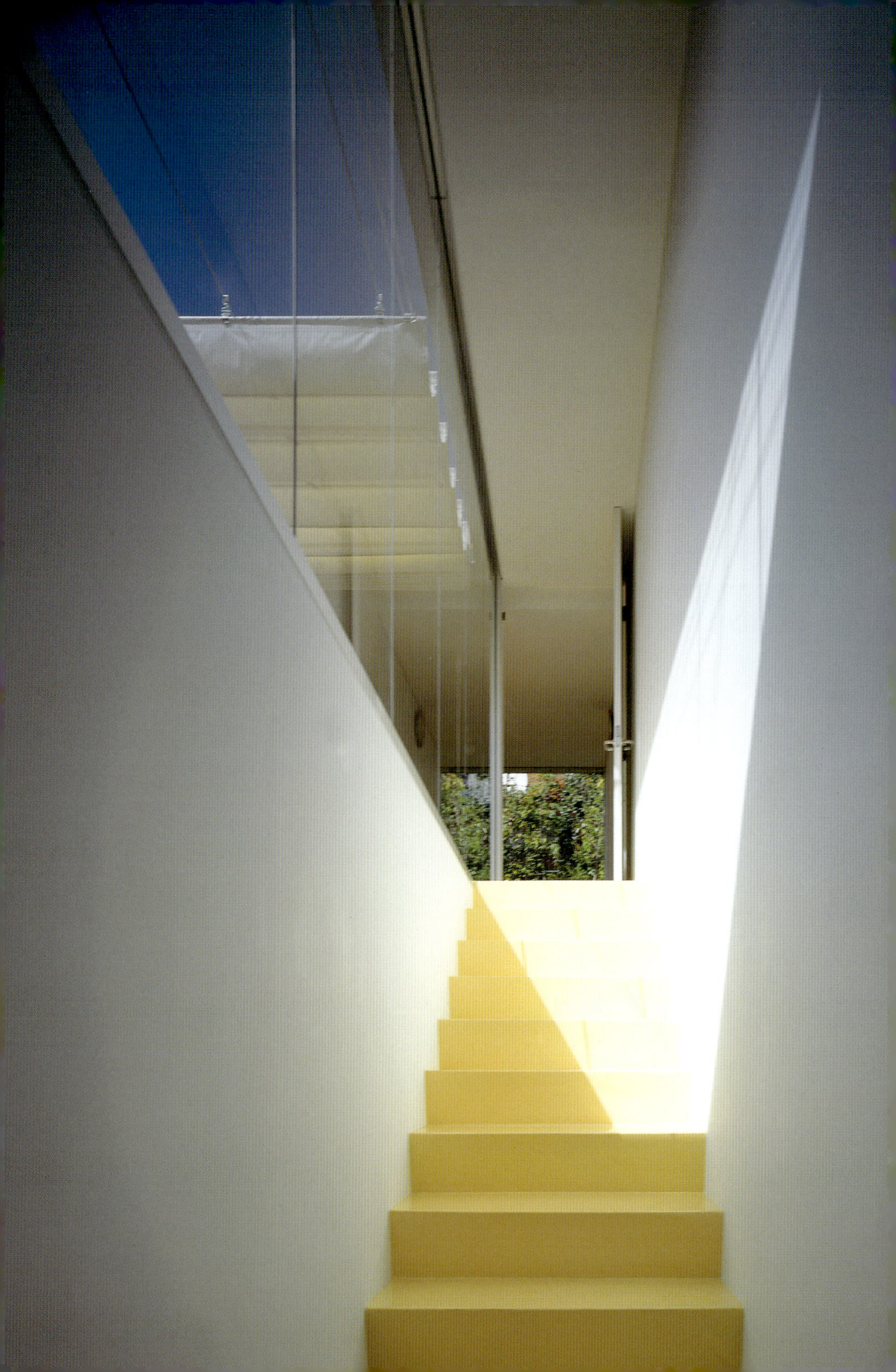

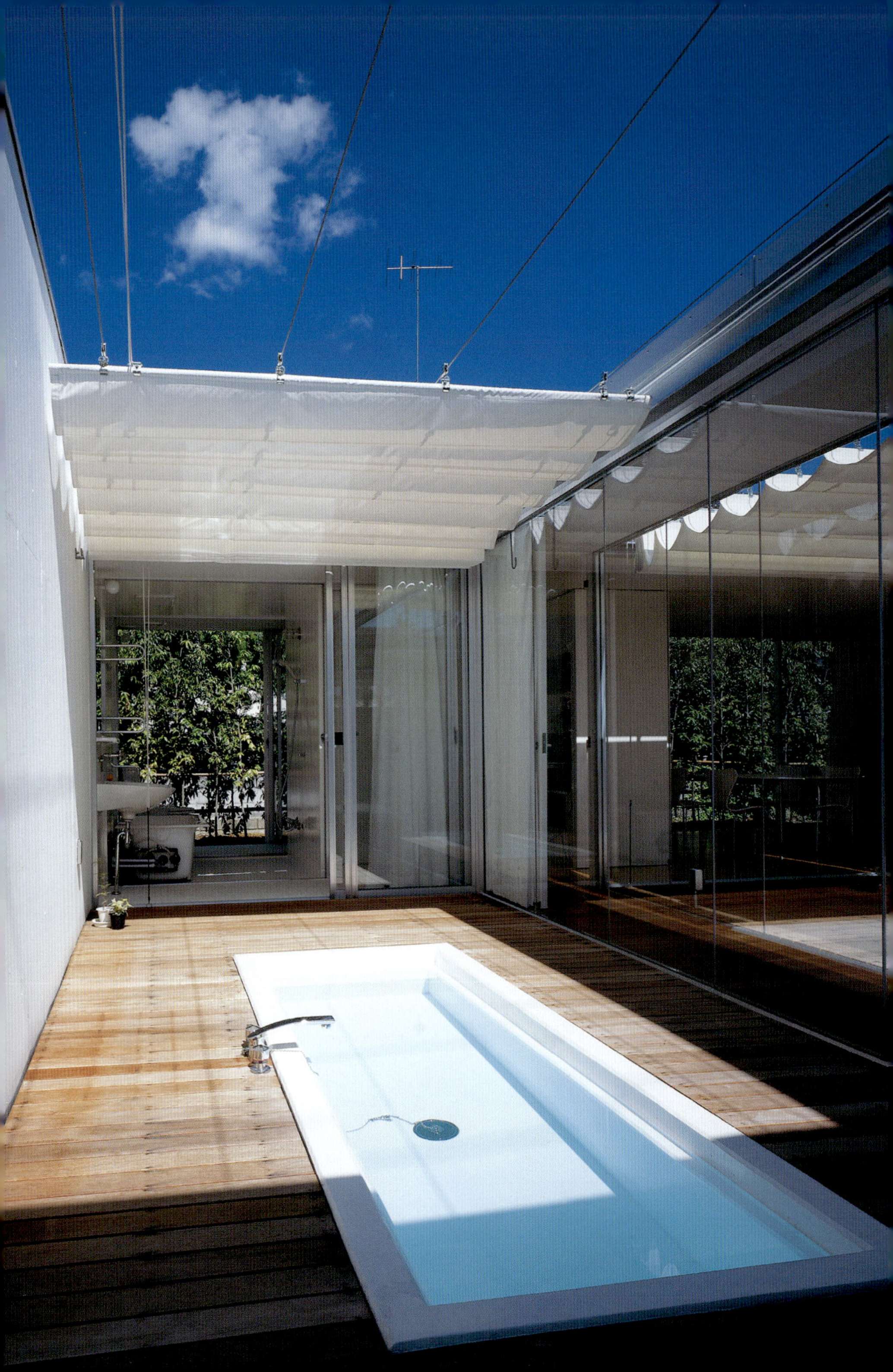

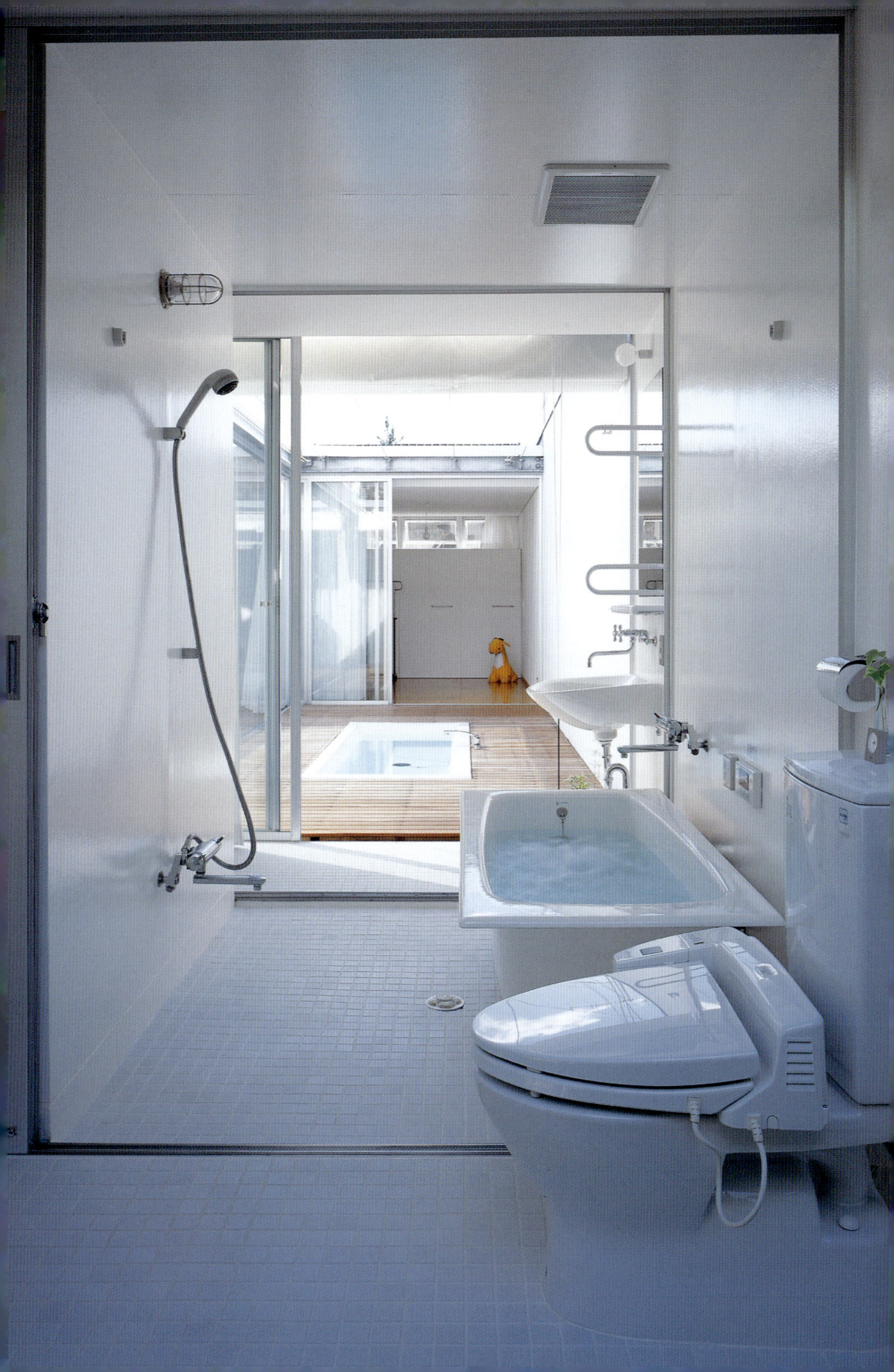

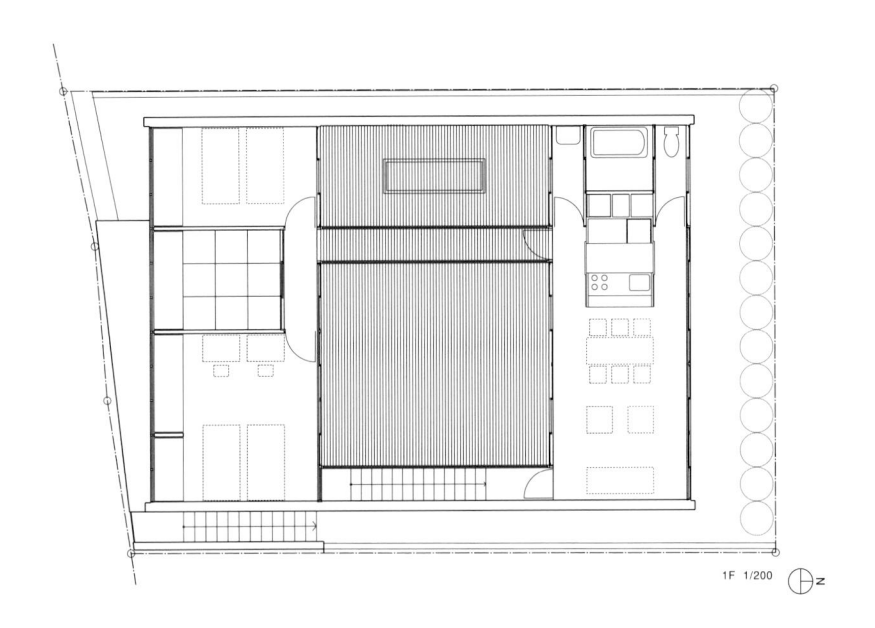

1F 1/200　N

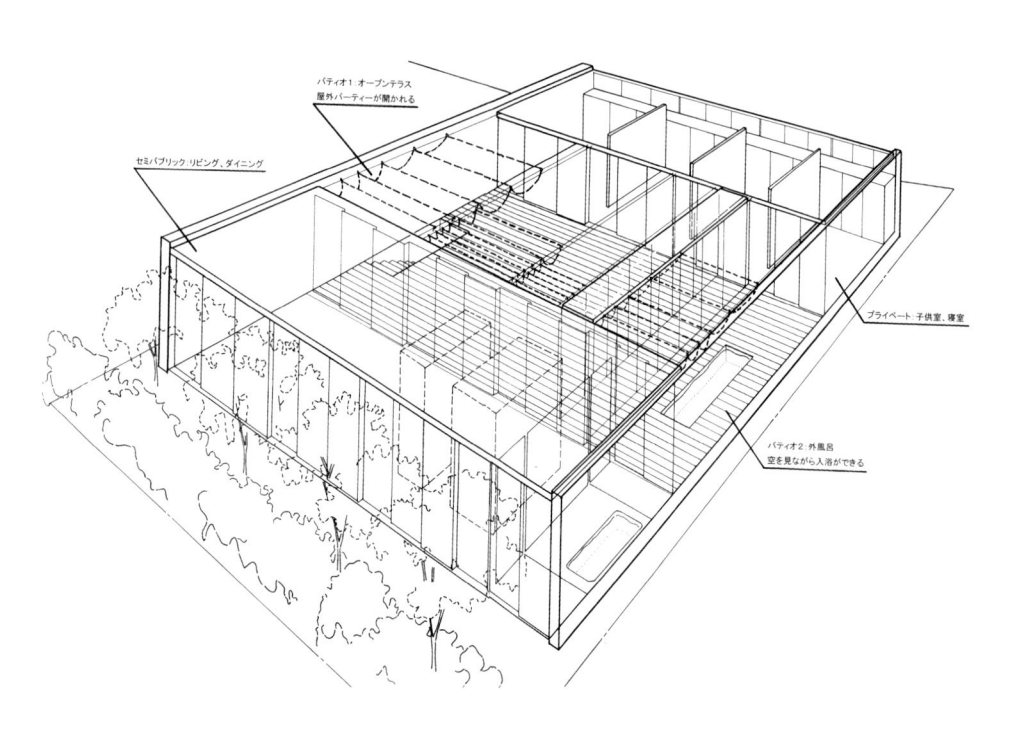

パティオ1：オープンテラス
屋外パーティーが開かれる

セミパブリック：リビング、ダイニング

プライベート：子供室、寝室

パティオ2：外風呂
空を見ながら入浴ができる

| パブリック | プライベート | 中庭 | セミパブリック | 庭 |

オーニング

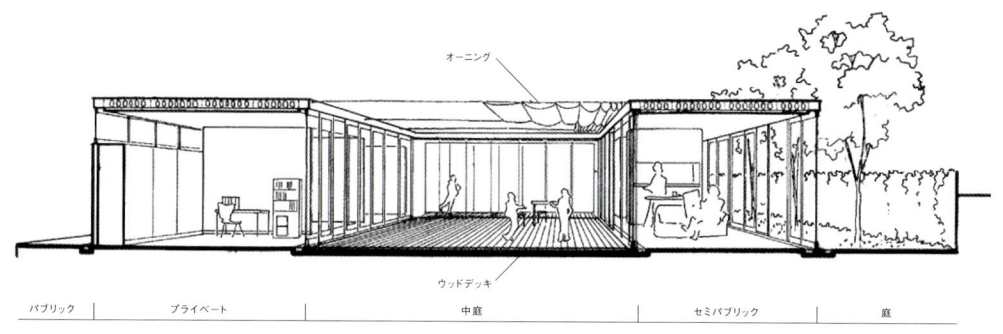

ウッドデッキ

SECTION 1/150

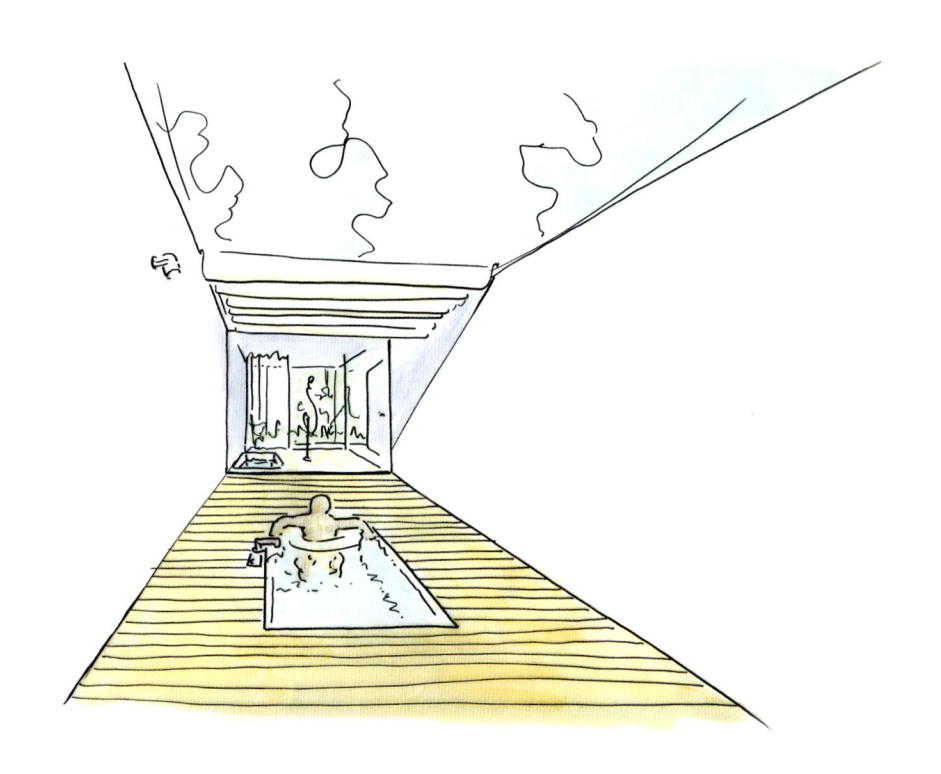

Megaphone House

腰越のメガホンハウス　2000

The Megaphone-shaped house stands on top of a huge rock with a spectacular view over the Pacific Ocean. The 9m x 6m window was fitted with external blinds, curtains, and 6 rail sliding doors to control the light from the sea.

太平洋を望む崖の上に建つメガホン型の家。
水平線だけを切り取る9m×6mの大きな窓。
外部と内部の垂直ブラインドとオーニングが海の日差しを遮る。

07

9 m

6 m

太平洋

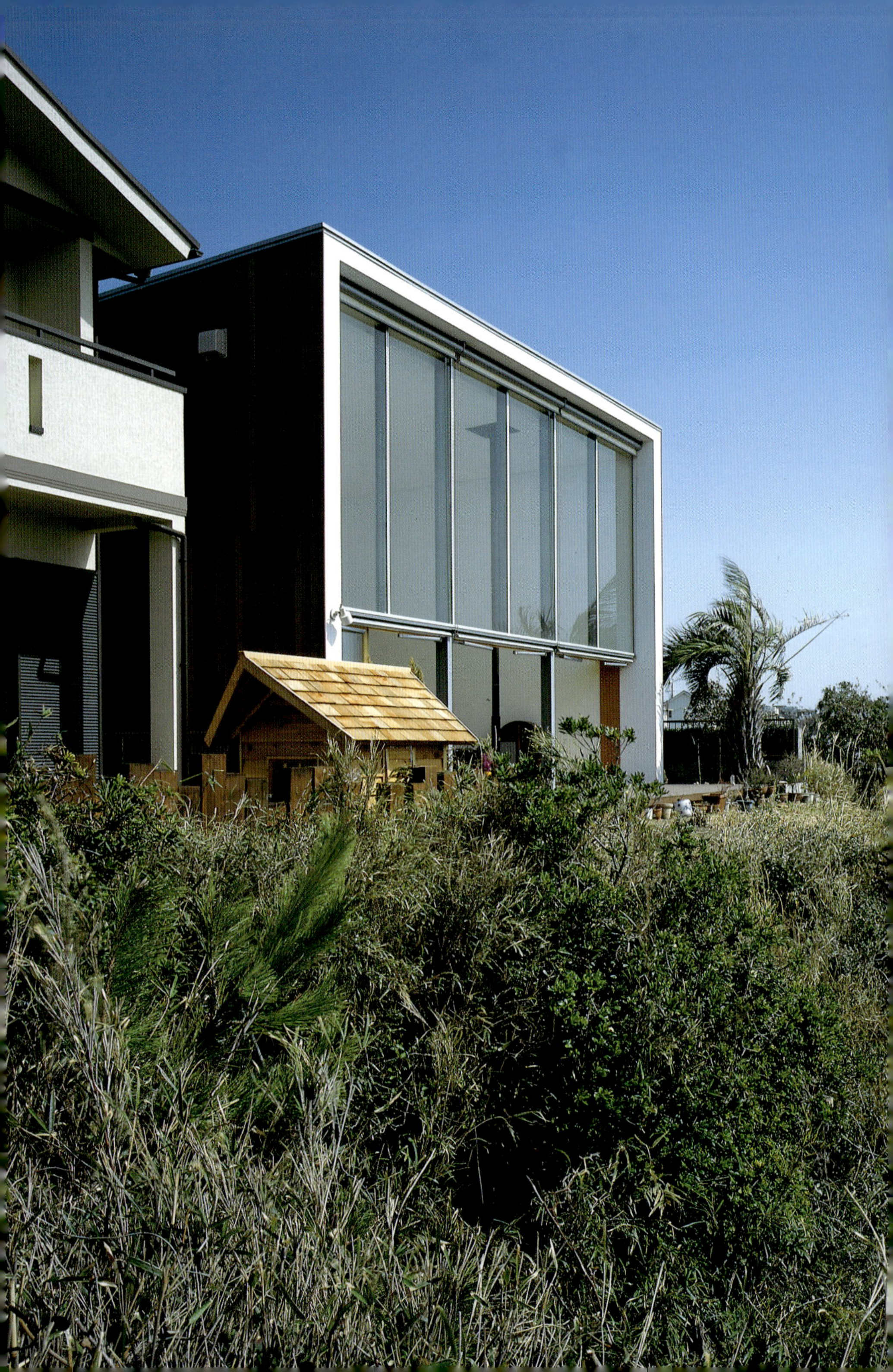

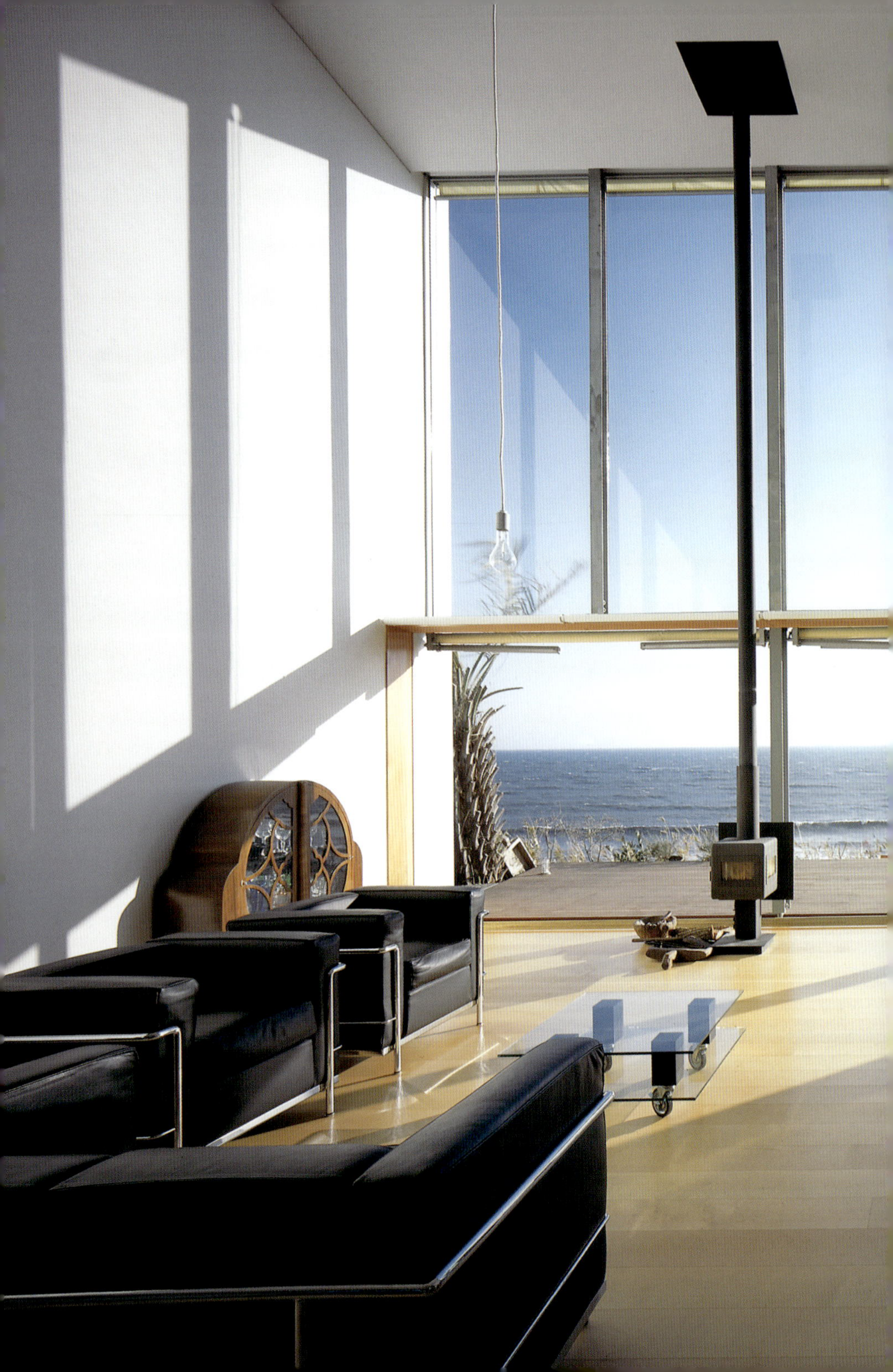

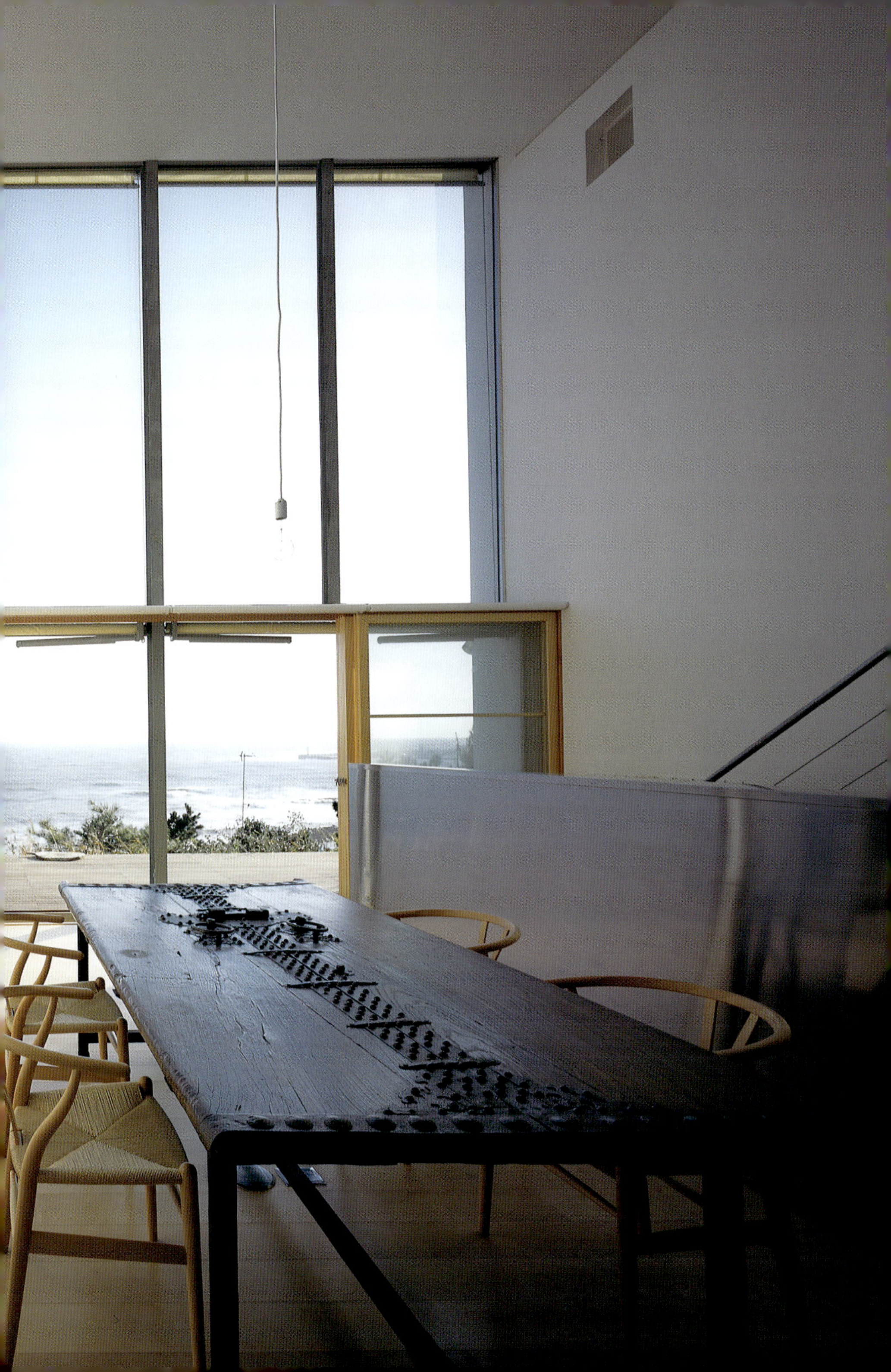

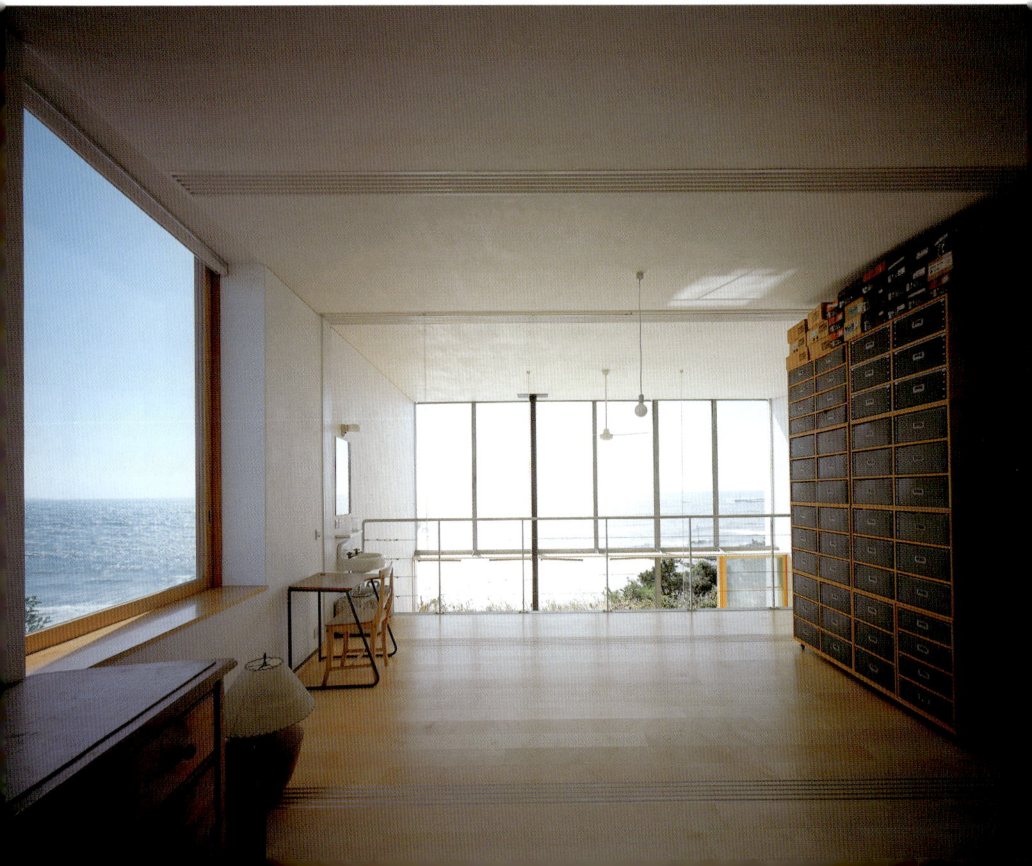

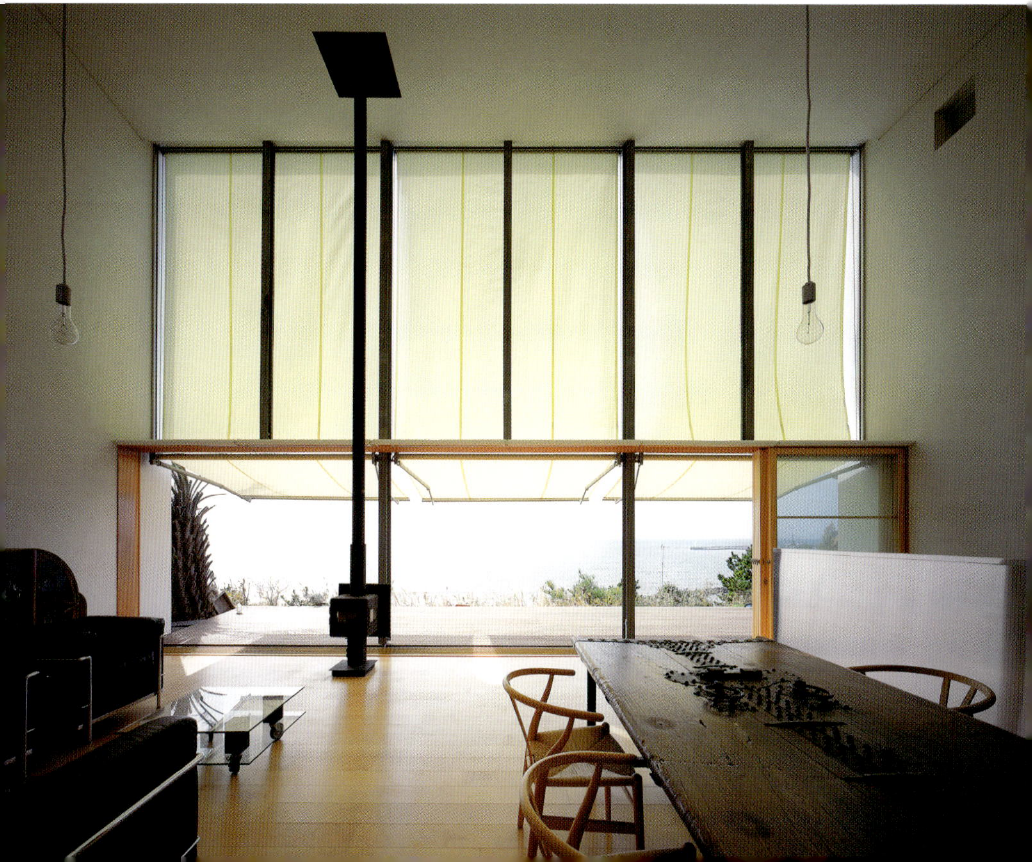

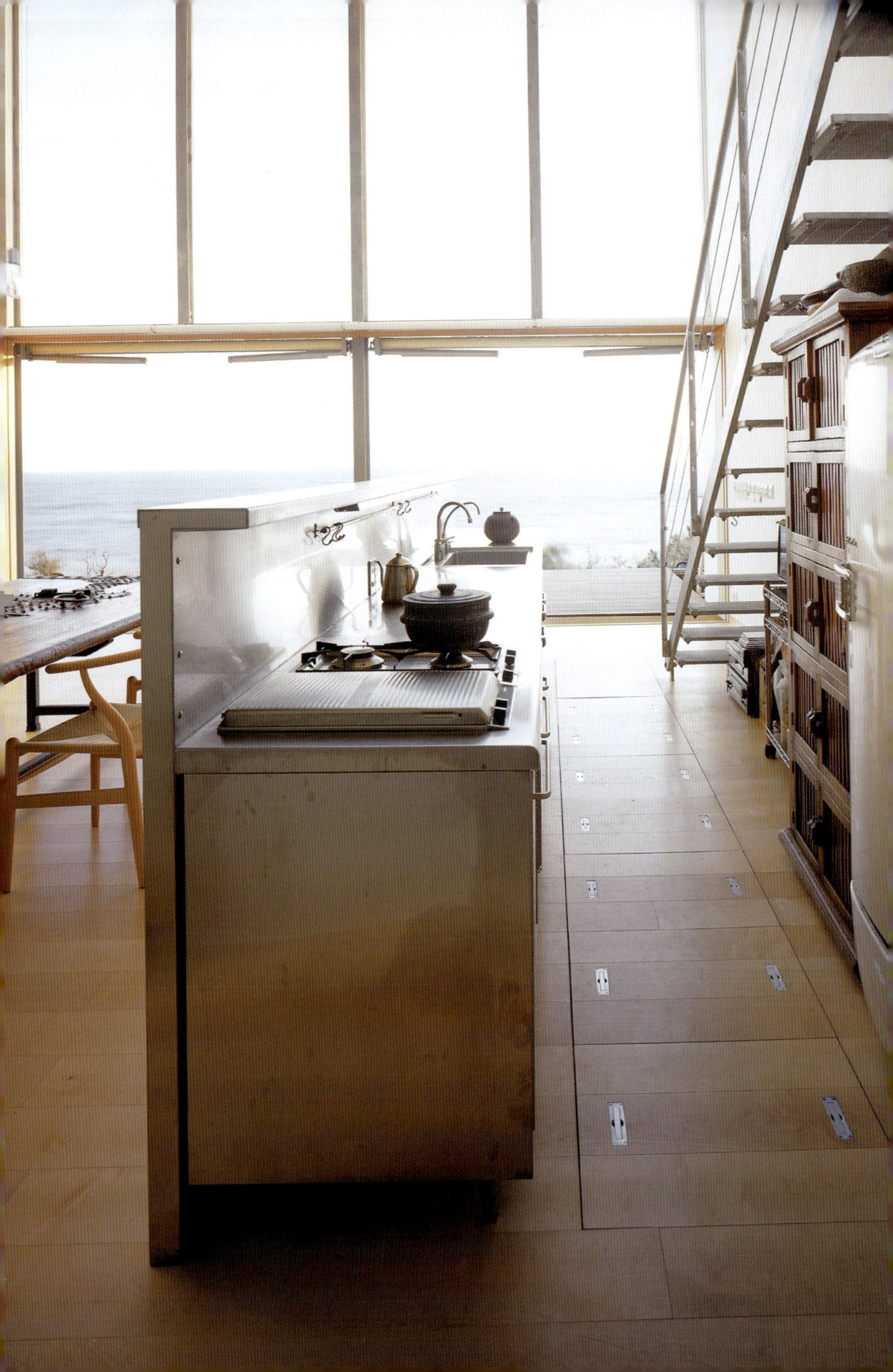

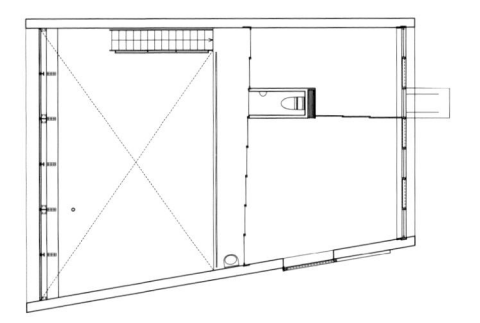

2F 1/250

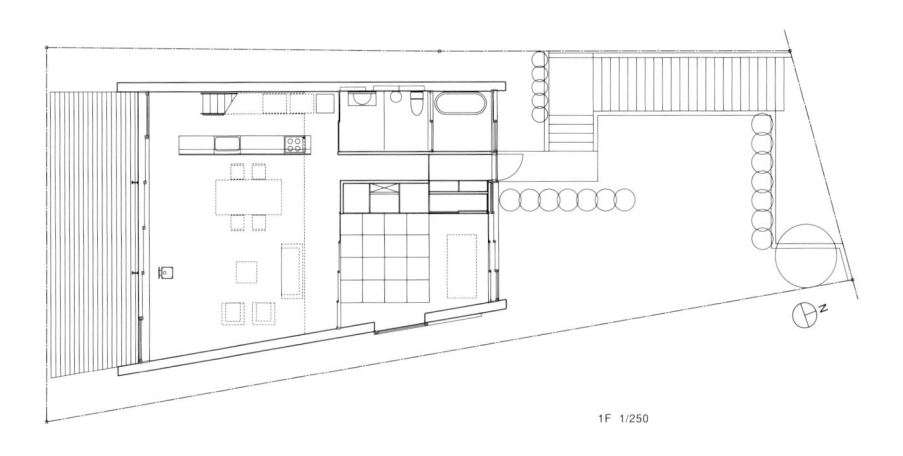

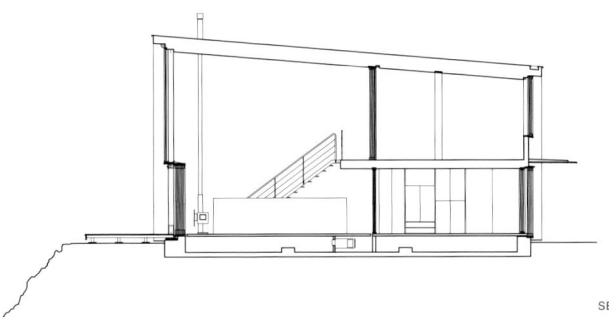

1F 1/250

SECTION 1/250

Roof House

屋根の家　2001

This house boasts chairs, a table, a kitchen and a shower on its rooftop.
Each family member enjoys his own skylight, from which a ladder gives access to the roof.

木デッキでできている屋根の上に、テーブルとイスとキッチンとシャワーがついている家。
屋根へは8つある天窓の好きなところから梯子で上がる。

08

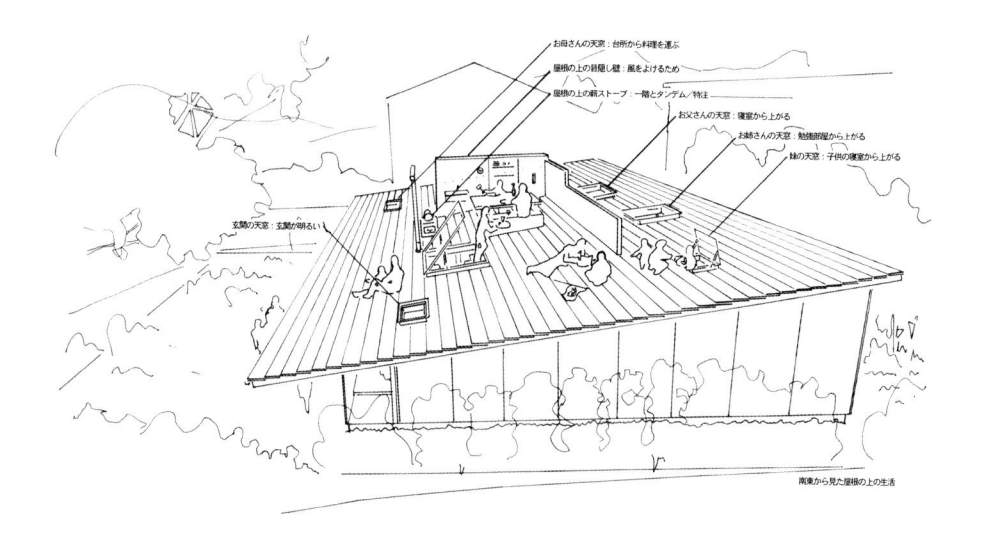

お母さんの天窓：台所から料理を運ぶ
屋根の上の雨隠し壁：風をよけるため
屋根の上の薪ストーブ：一階とタンデム／特注
お父さんの天窓：寝室から上がる
お姉さんの天窓：勉強部屋から上がる
妹の天窓：子供の寝室から上がる
玄関の天窓：玄関が明るい

南東から見た屋根の上の生活

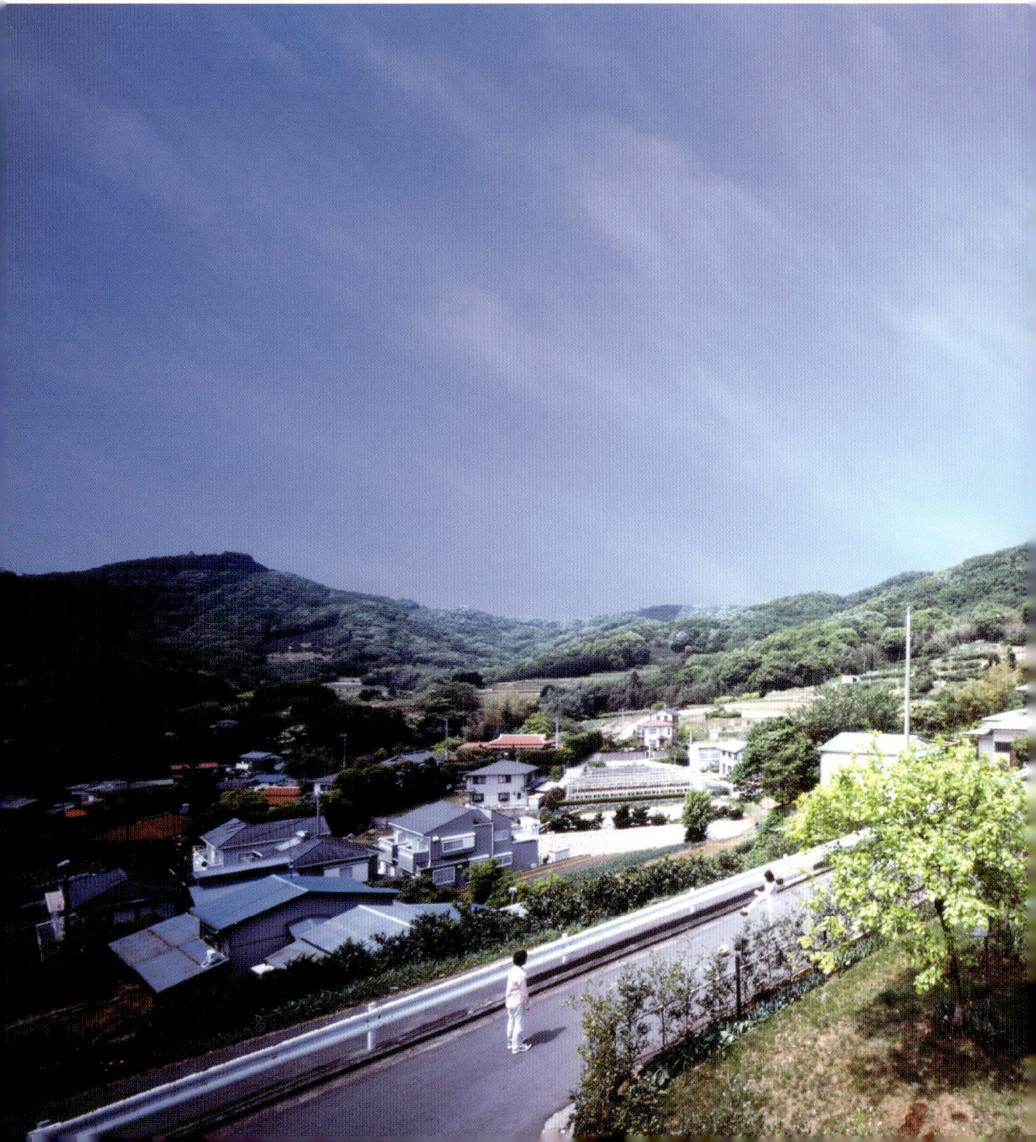

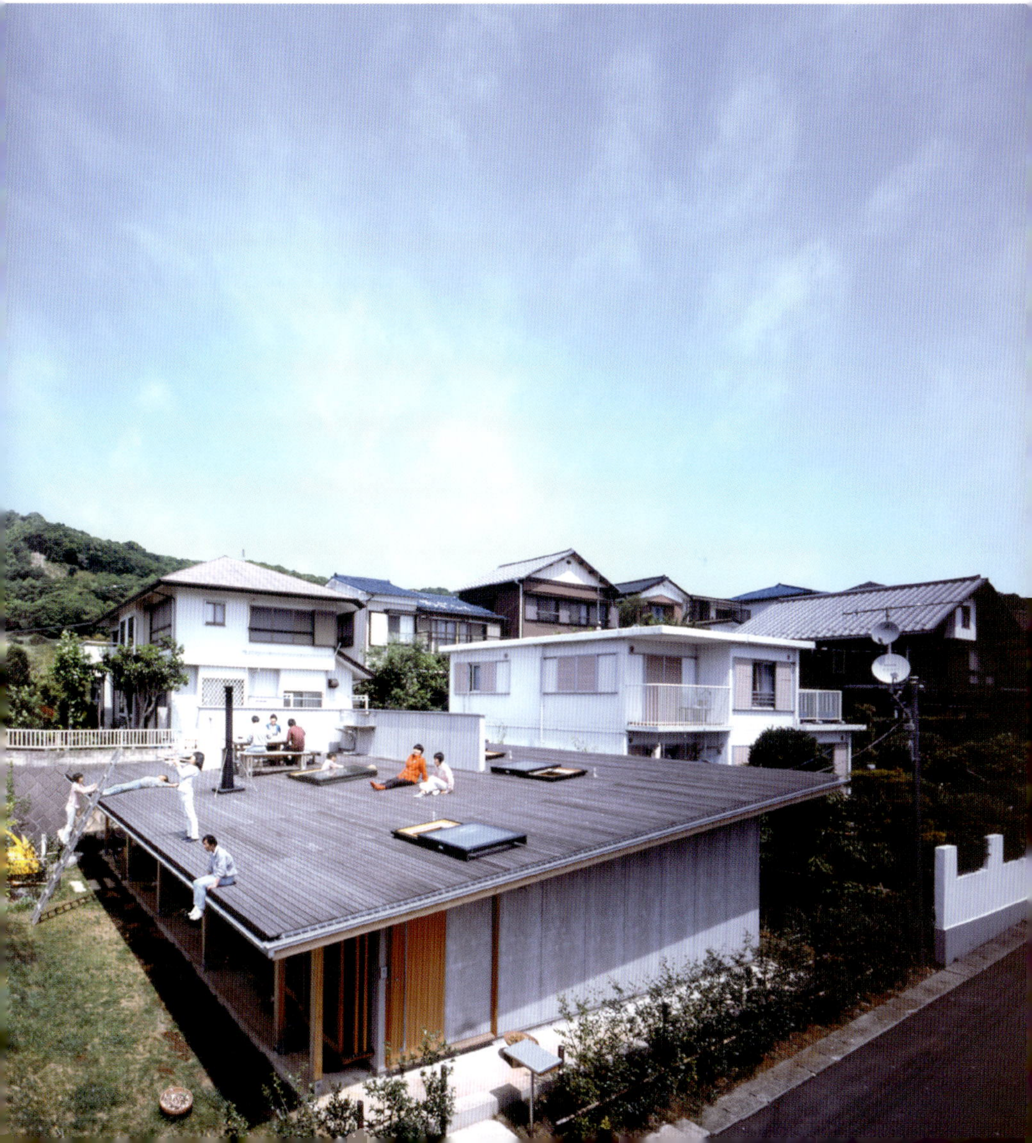

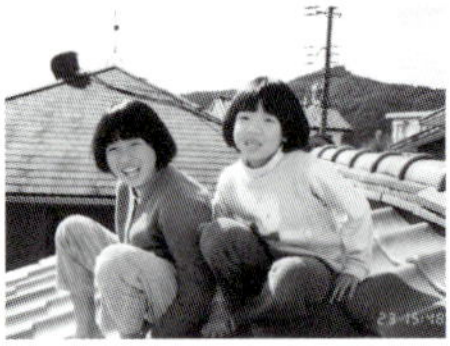

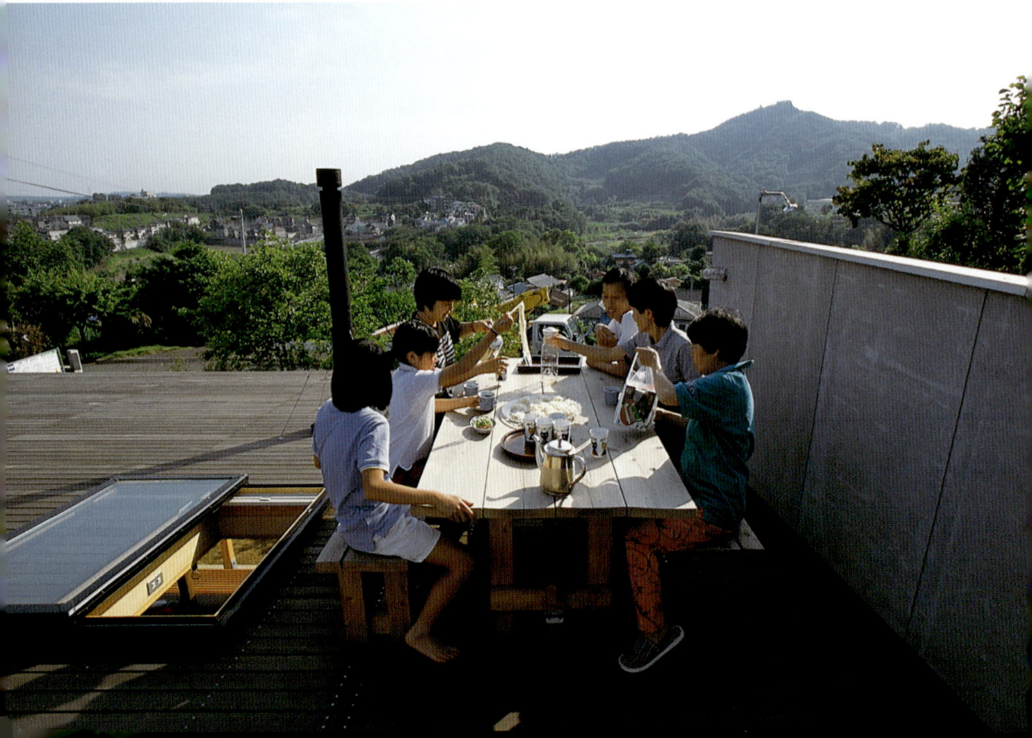

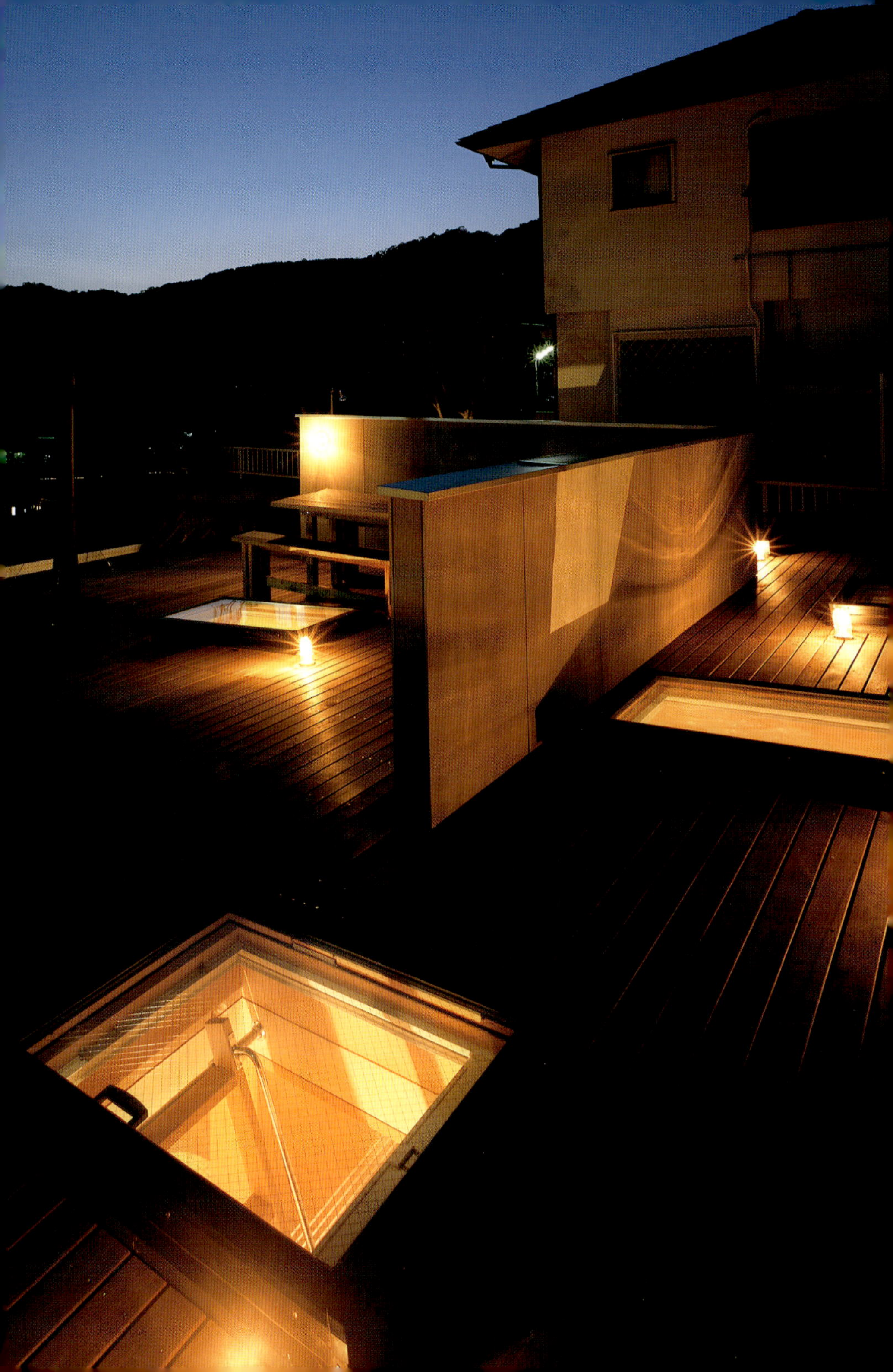

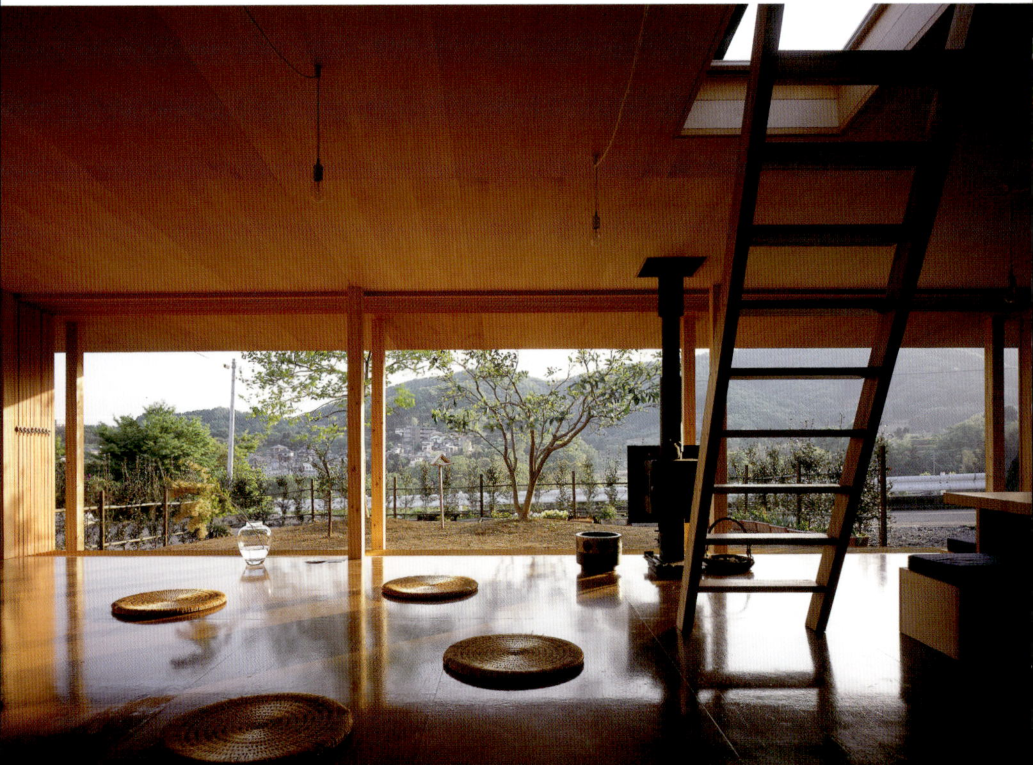

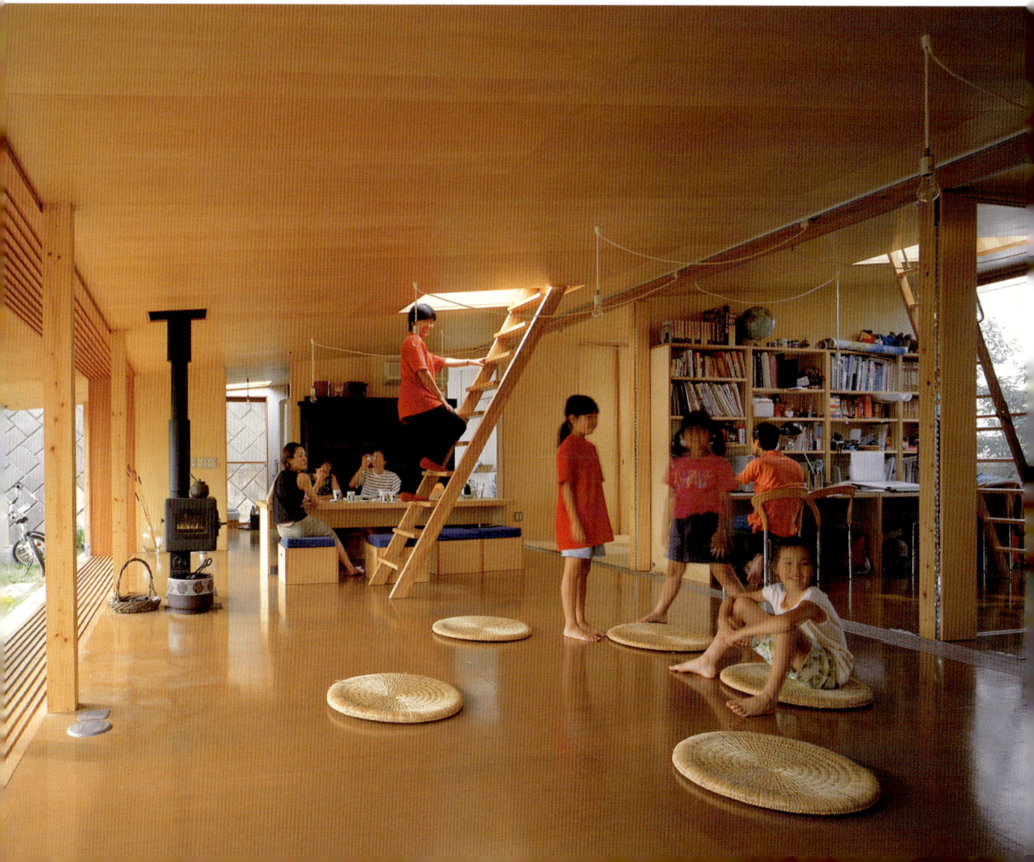

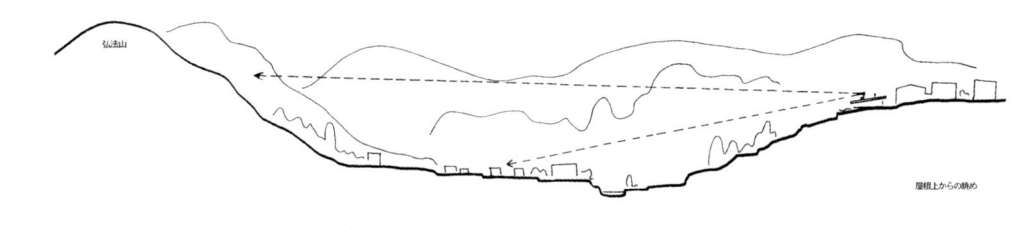

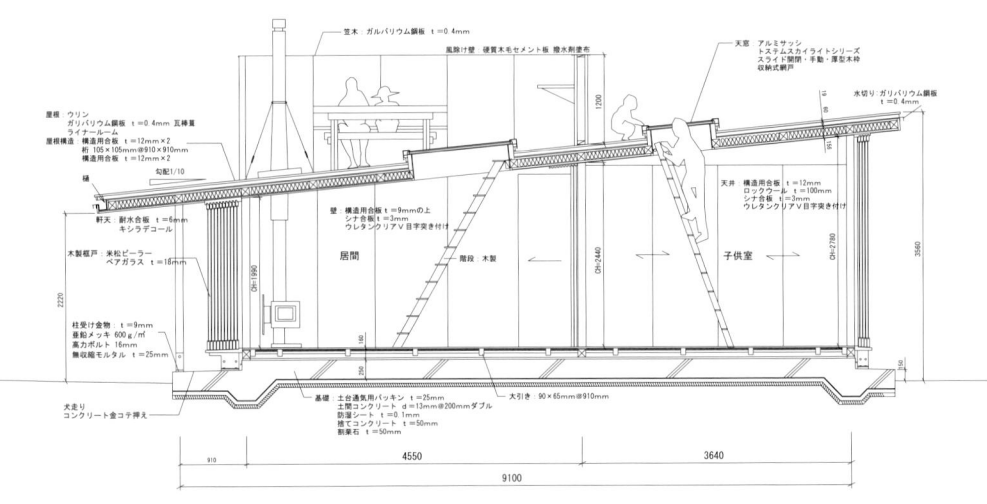

屋根上からの眺め

仏法山

屋根 ウリン	笠木：ガルバリウム鋼板 t=0.4mm	天窓 アルミサッシ

屋根 ウリン
　ガルバリウム鋼板 t=0.4mm 瓦棒葺
屋根構造 構造用合板 t=12mm×2
　桁 105×105mm@910×910mm
　構造用合板 t=12mm×2

笠木：ガルバリウム鋼板 t=0.4mm
風除け壁：硬質木毛セメント板 撥水剤塗布

天窓 アルミサッシ
トステムスカイライトシリーズ
スライド開閉・手動・薄型木枠
収納式網戸

水切り：ガルバリウム鋼板 t=0.4mm

軒天 耐水合板 t=6mm
　キシラデコール

木製框戸 米松ピーラー
　ペアガラス t=18mm

柱受け金物 t=9mm
　溶融亜鉛メッキ 600g/m²
　高力ボルト 16mm
　無収縮モルタル t=25mm

勾配1/10

縁

居間

階段 木製

天井 構造用合板 t=12mm
　ロックウール t=100mm
　シナ合板 t=3mm
　ウレタンクリアV目地突き付け

壁 構造用合板 t=9mmの上
　シナ合板 t=3mm
　ウレタンクリアV目地突き付け

子供室

犬走り
　コンクリート金ゴテ押え

基礎 土台通気用パッキン t=25mm
　土間コンクリート d=13mm@200mmダブル
　防湿シート t=0.1mm
　捨てコンクリート t=50mm
　割栗石 t=50mm

大引き 90×65mm@910mm

CH=1990　CH=2640　CH=2780

2220　3640

910　4550　3640
9100

SECTION 1/100

RF 1/200

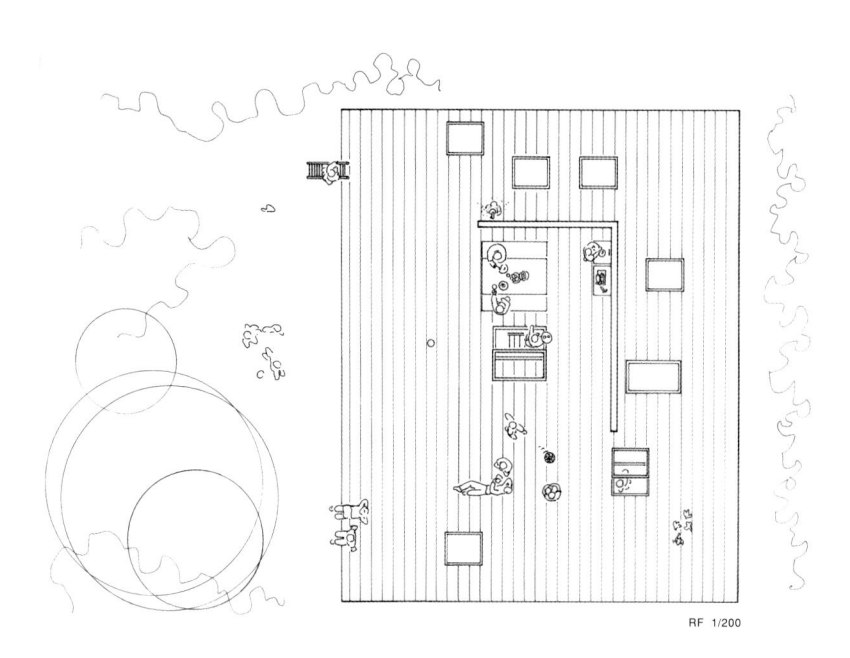

1F 1/200

軒先詳細図1

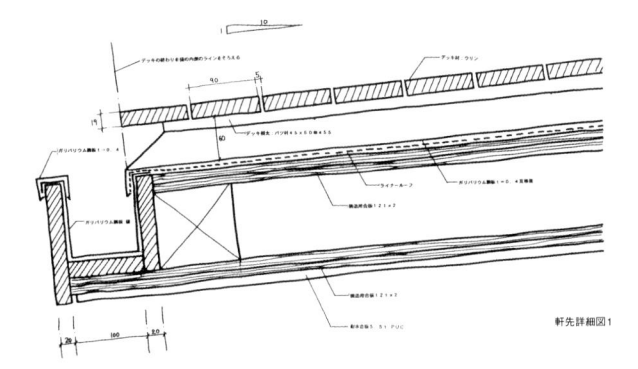

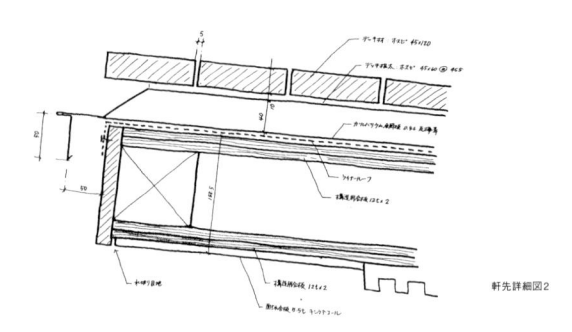

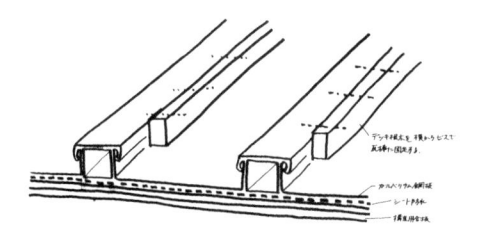

軒先詳細図2

屋根デッキ詳細図1

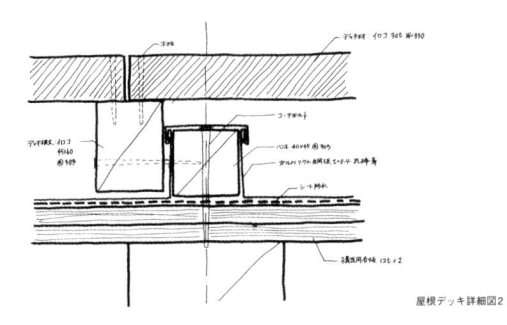

屋根デッキ詳細図2

開口部詳細図

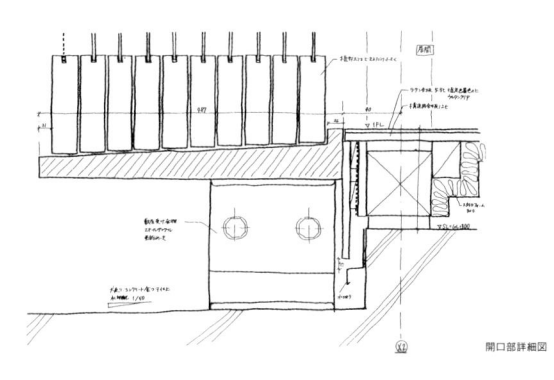

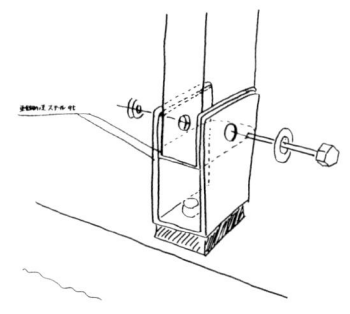

柱（軒下）スチール金物詳細図

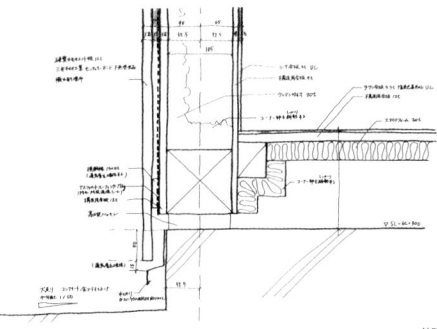

外壁基礎周り詳細図

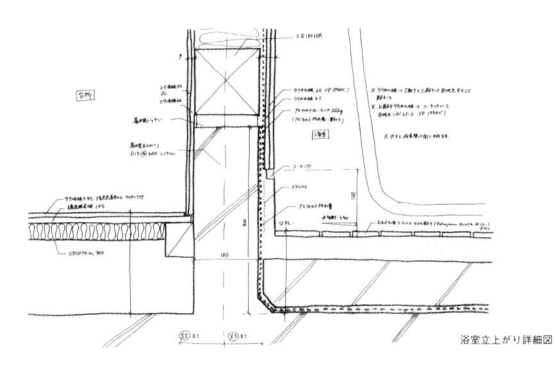

浴室立上がり詳細図

Balcony House

バルコニーの家　2001

Each level was designed as a 3.6m cantilevered balcony.

家全体がバルコニーの家。
風通しが良く視界が広い。
正面は柱がなく空中に浮いている。

09

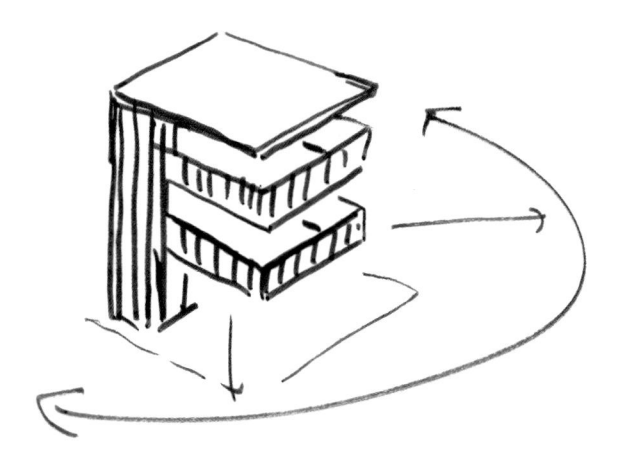

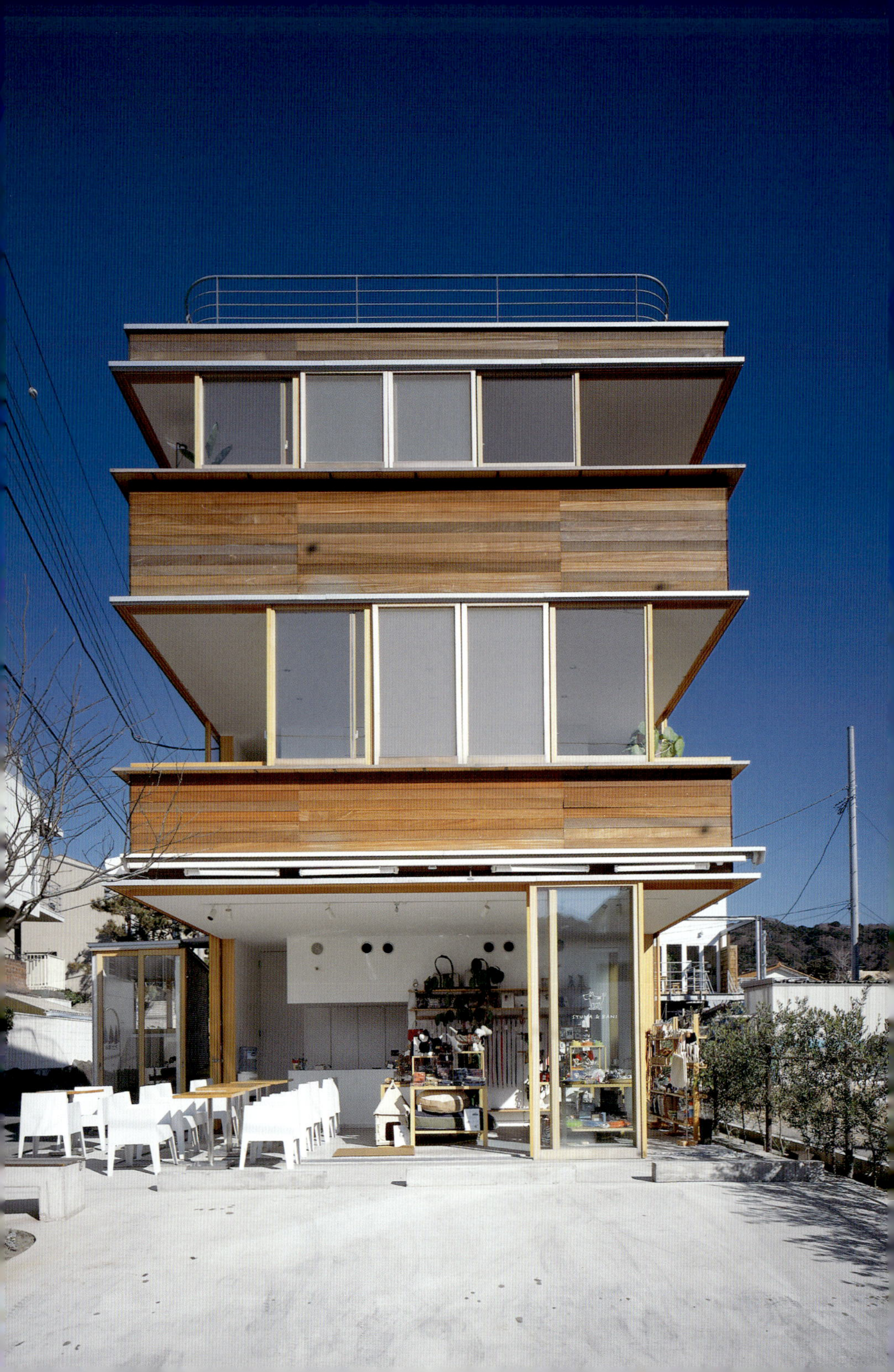

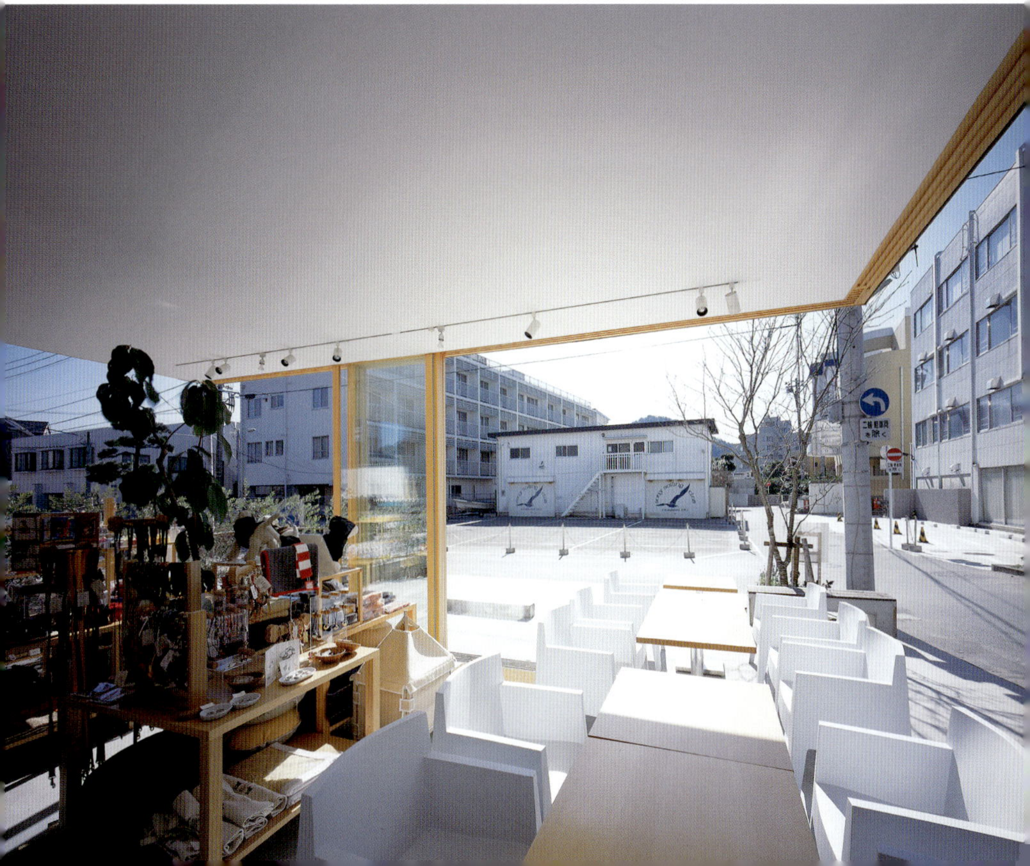

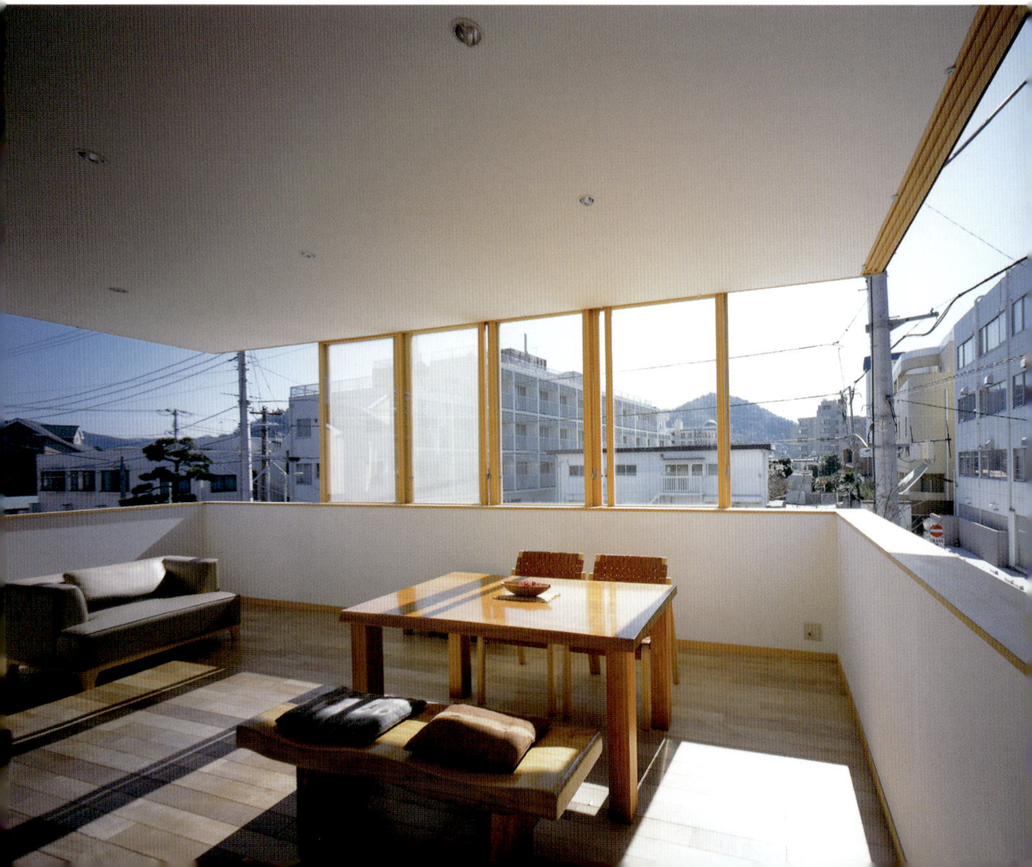

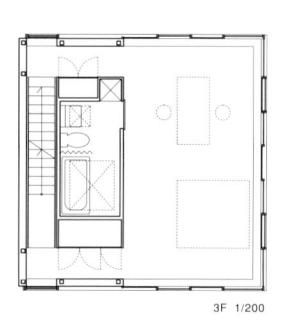

3F 1/200

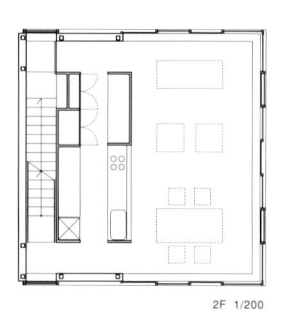

2F 1/200

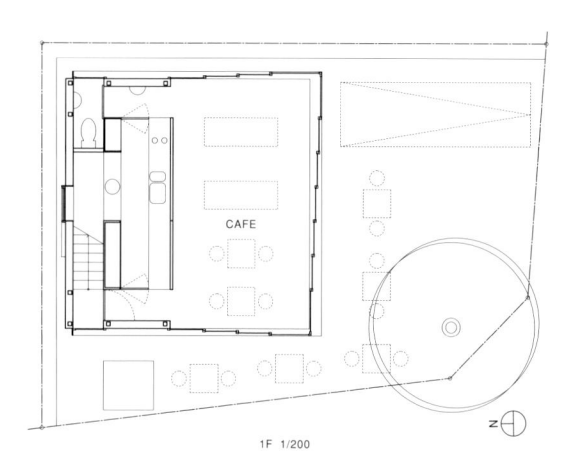

1F 1/200

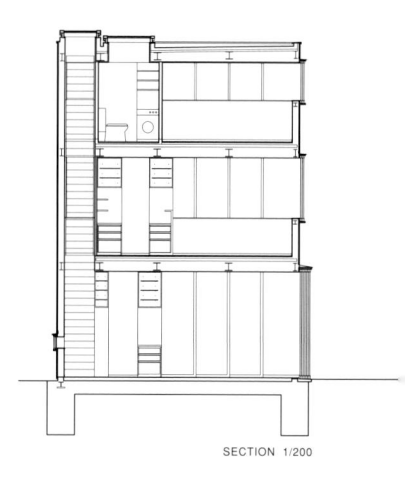

CAFE

N

SECTION 1/200

Wall-less House

壁のない家　2001

The house is supported by a central core and a pair of extremely thin columns. The absence of walls on the ground floor allows the internal space to extend to the garden on 360 degrees.

建ぺい率20％の住宅地に建つ家。
三方にまったく壁がないので、庭や景色全体が部屋のように感じられる。

10

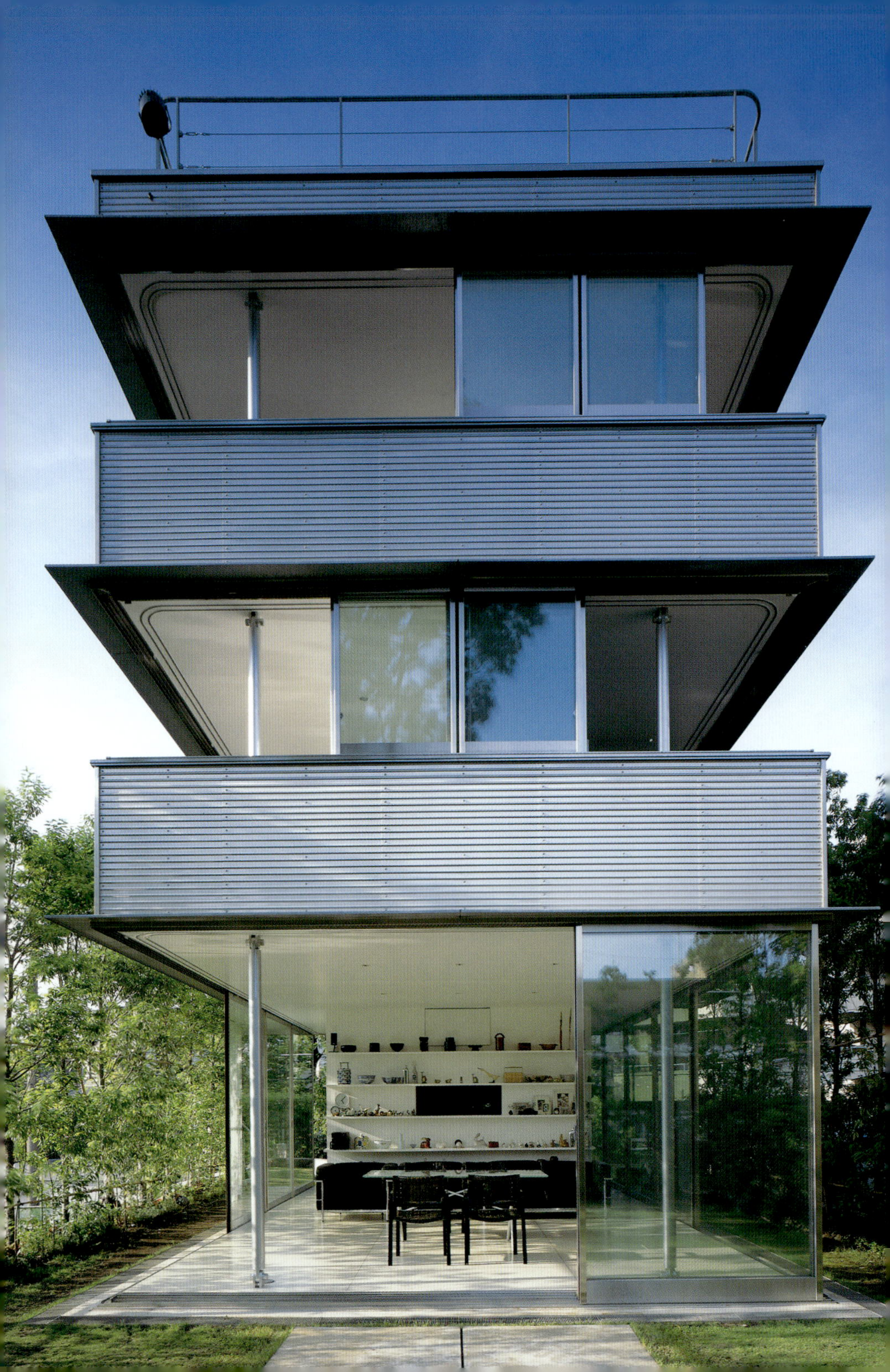

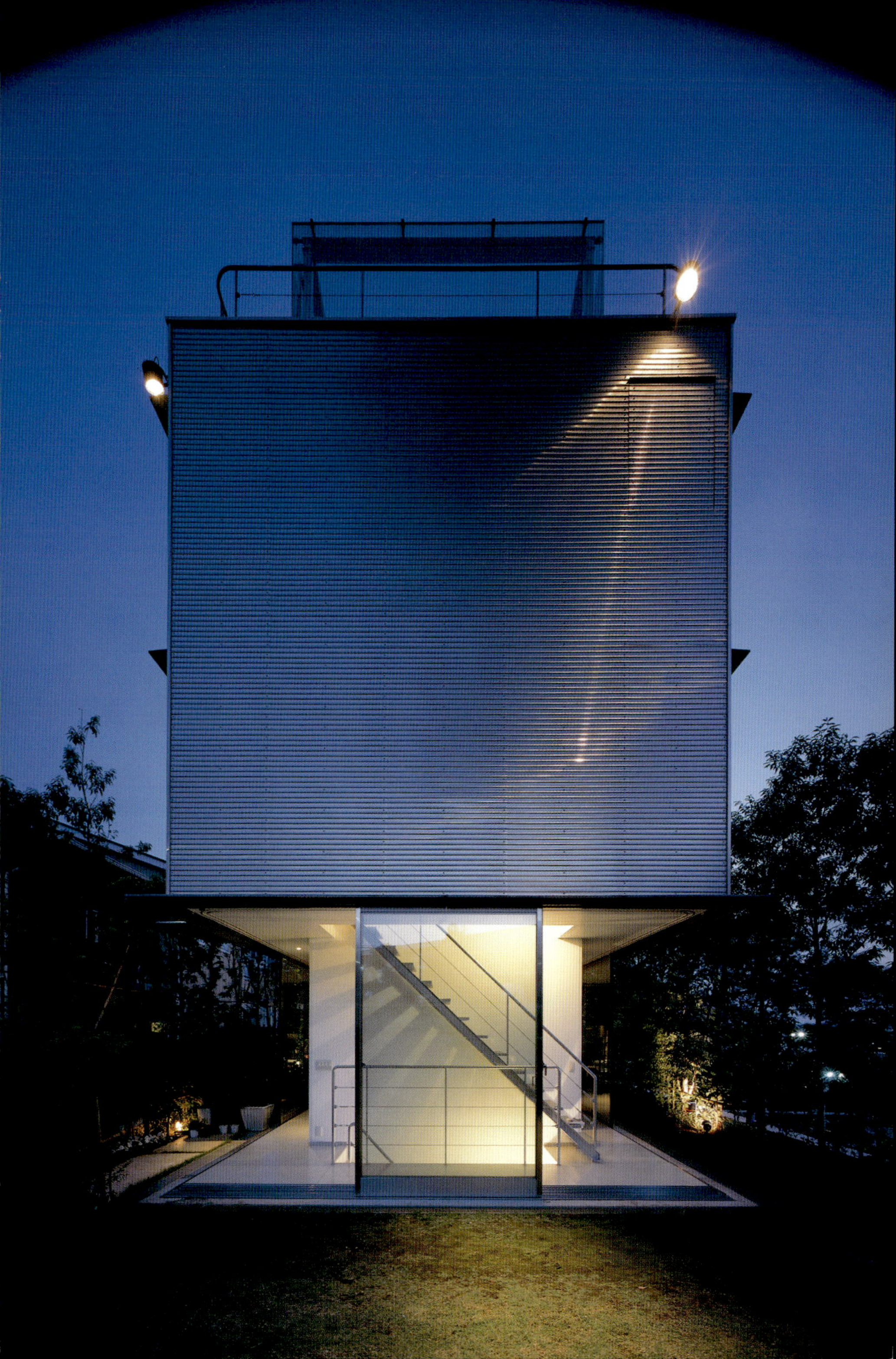

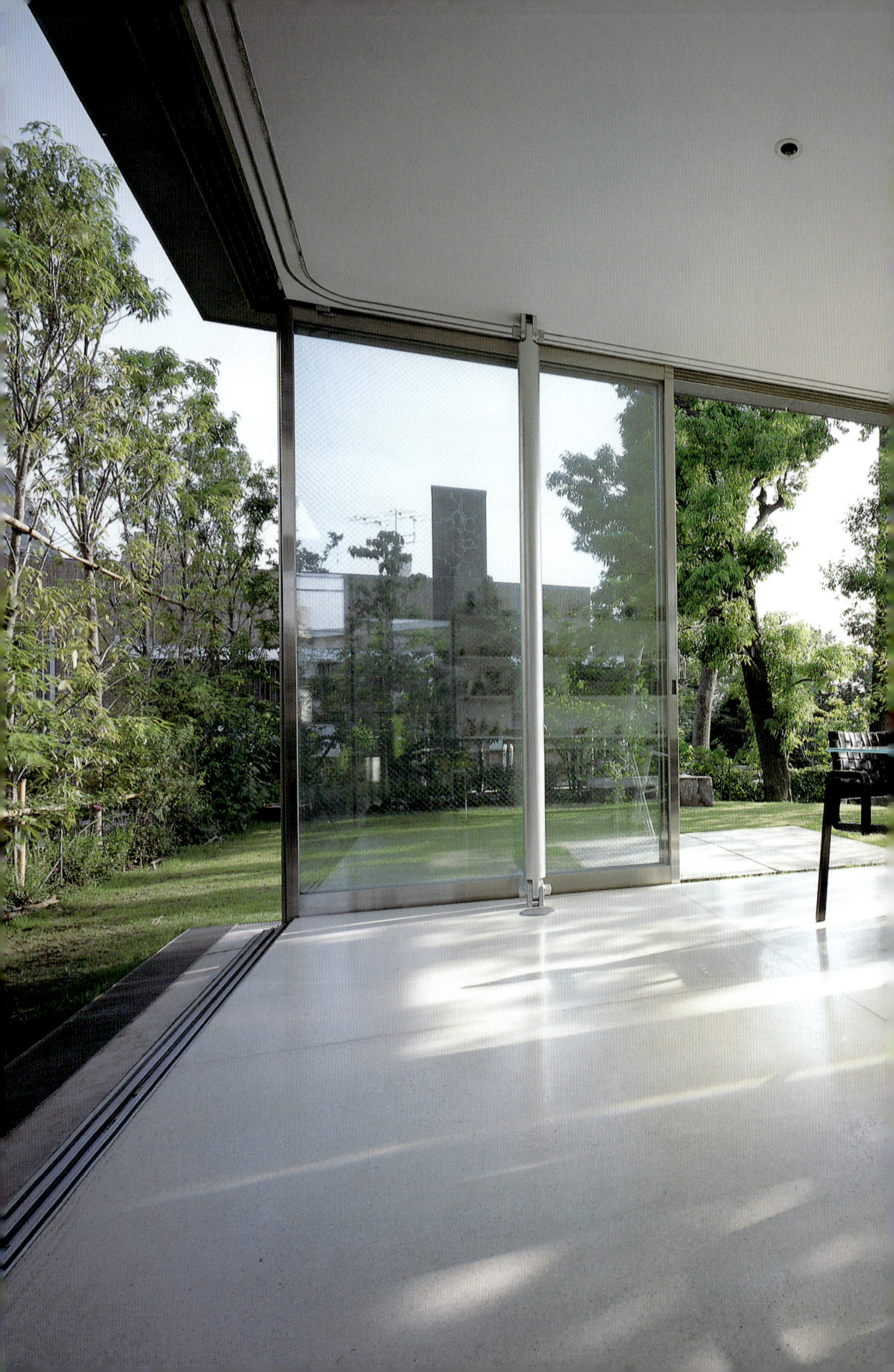

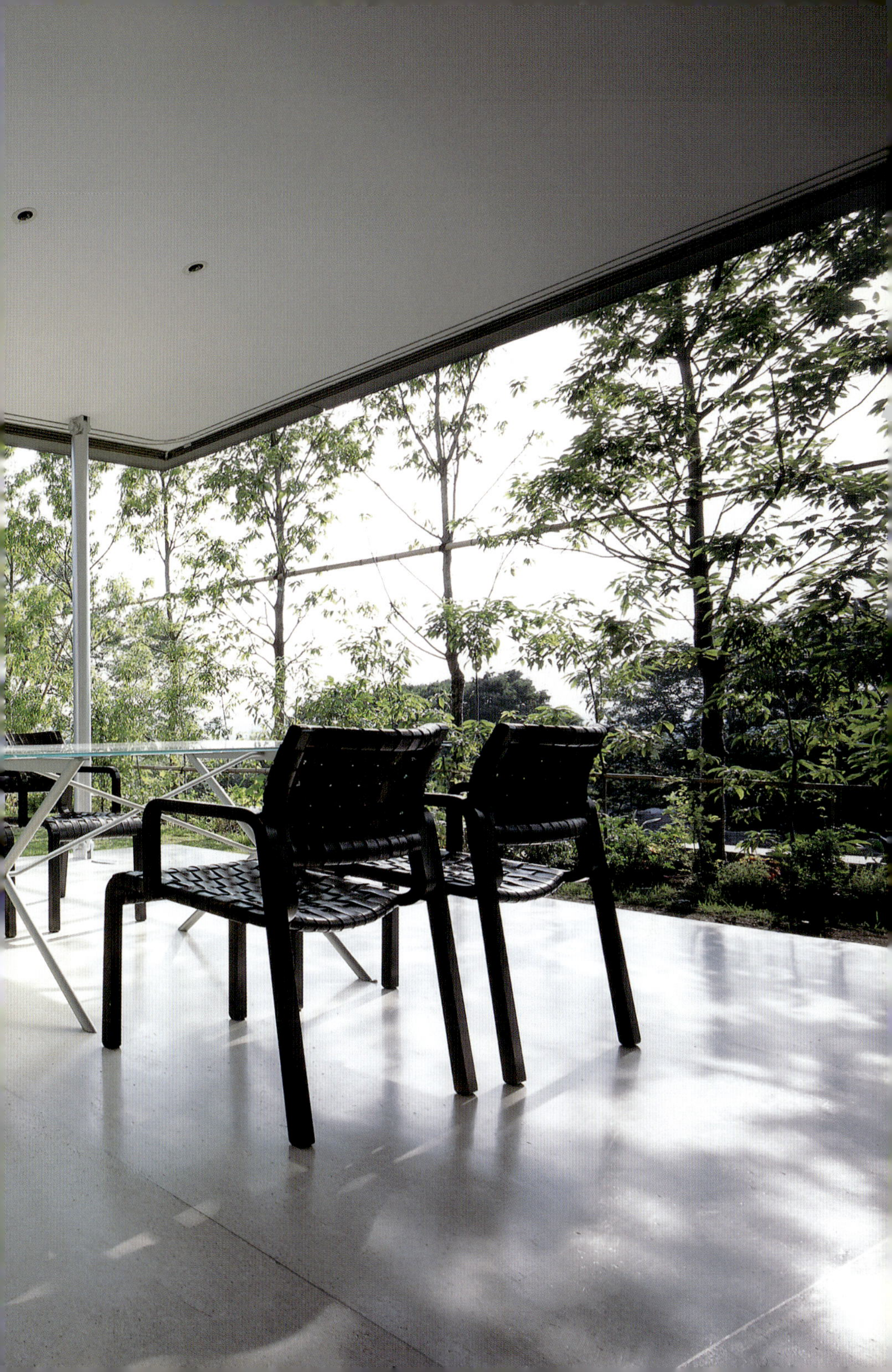

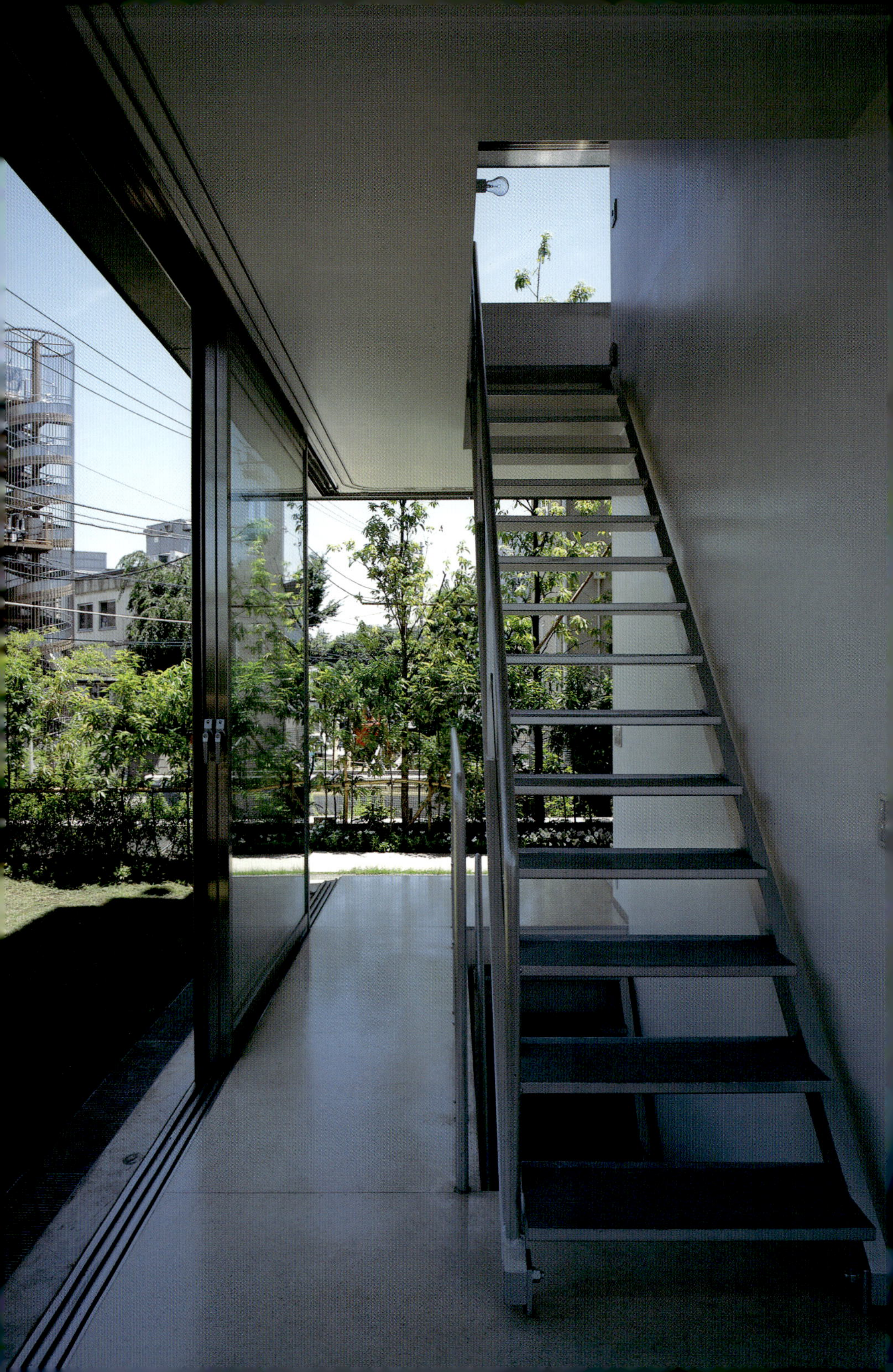

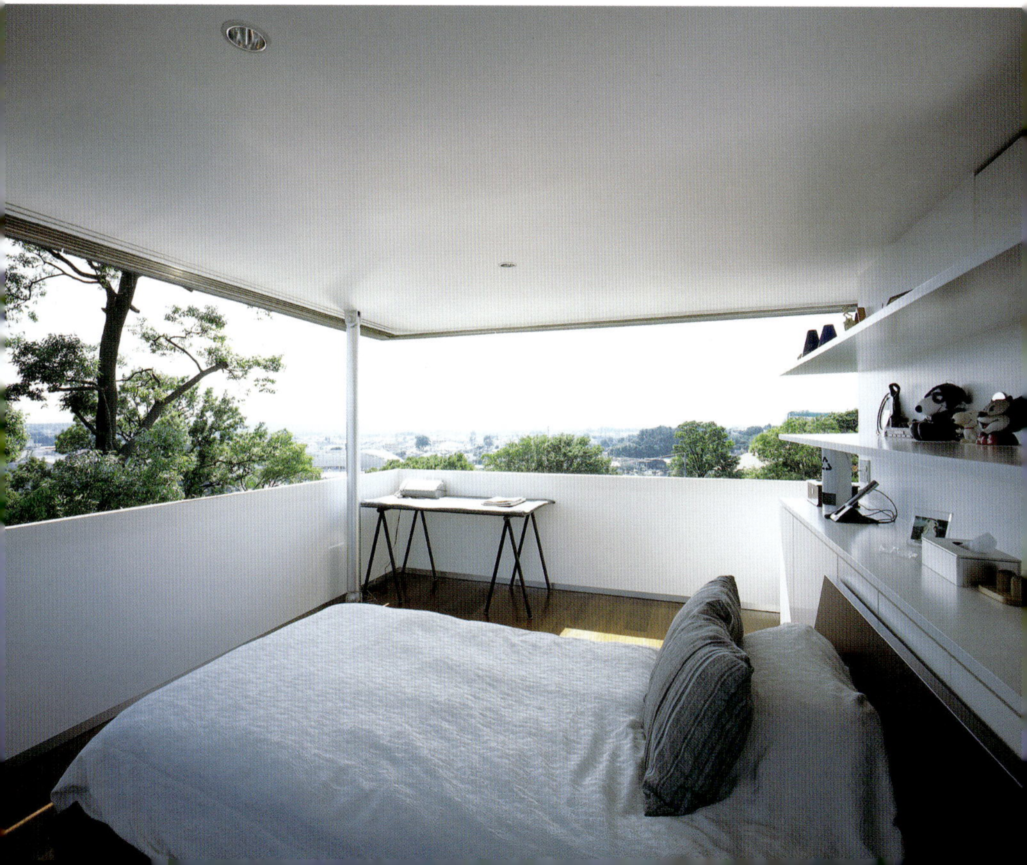

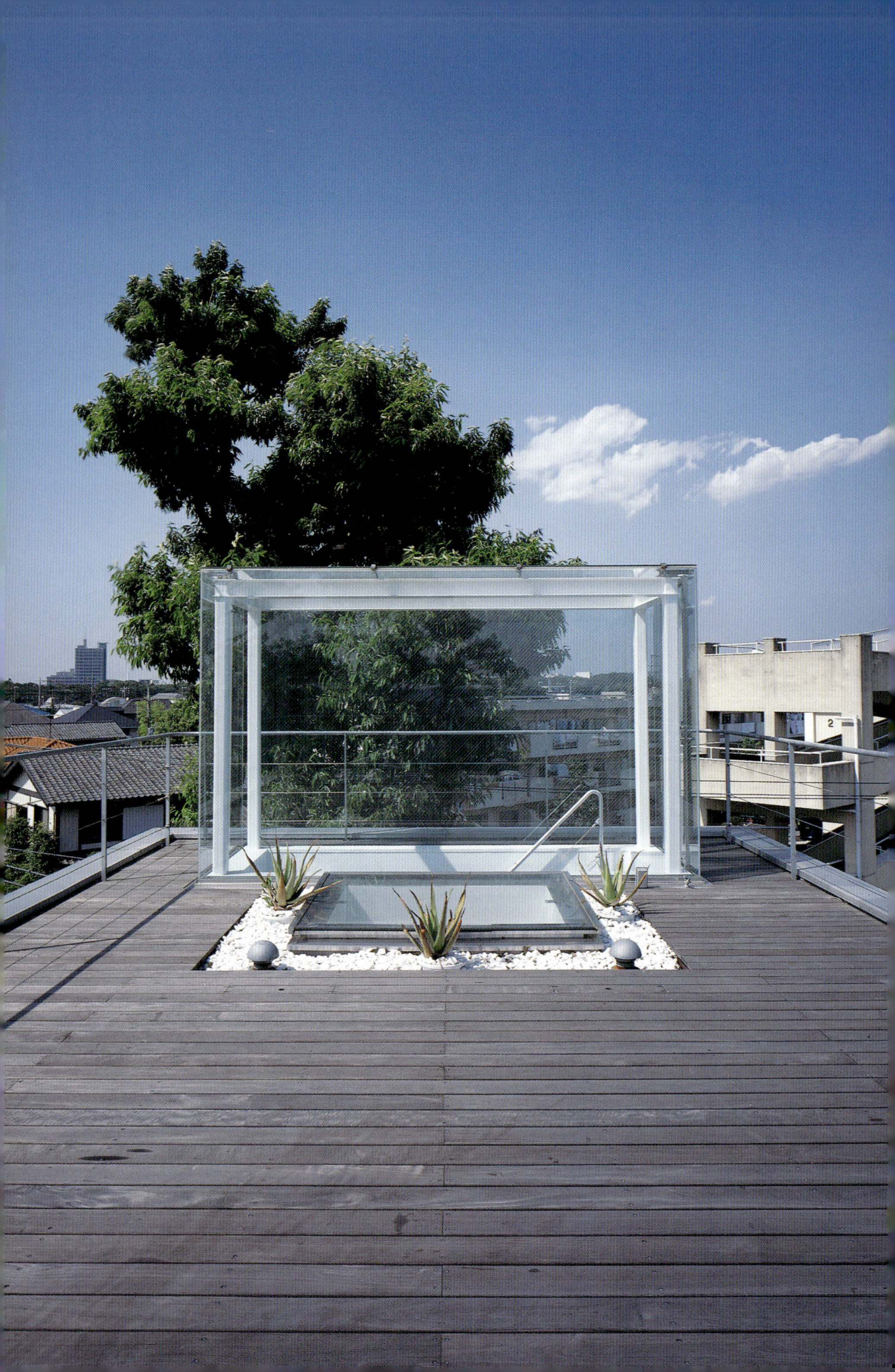

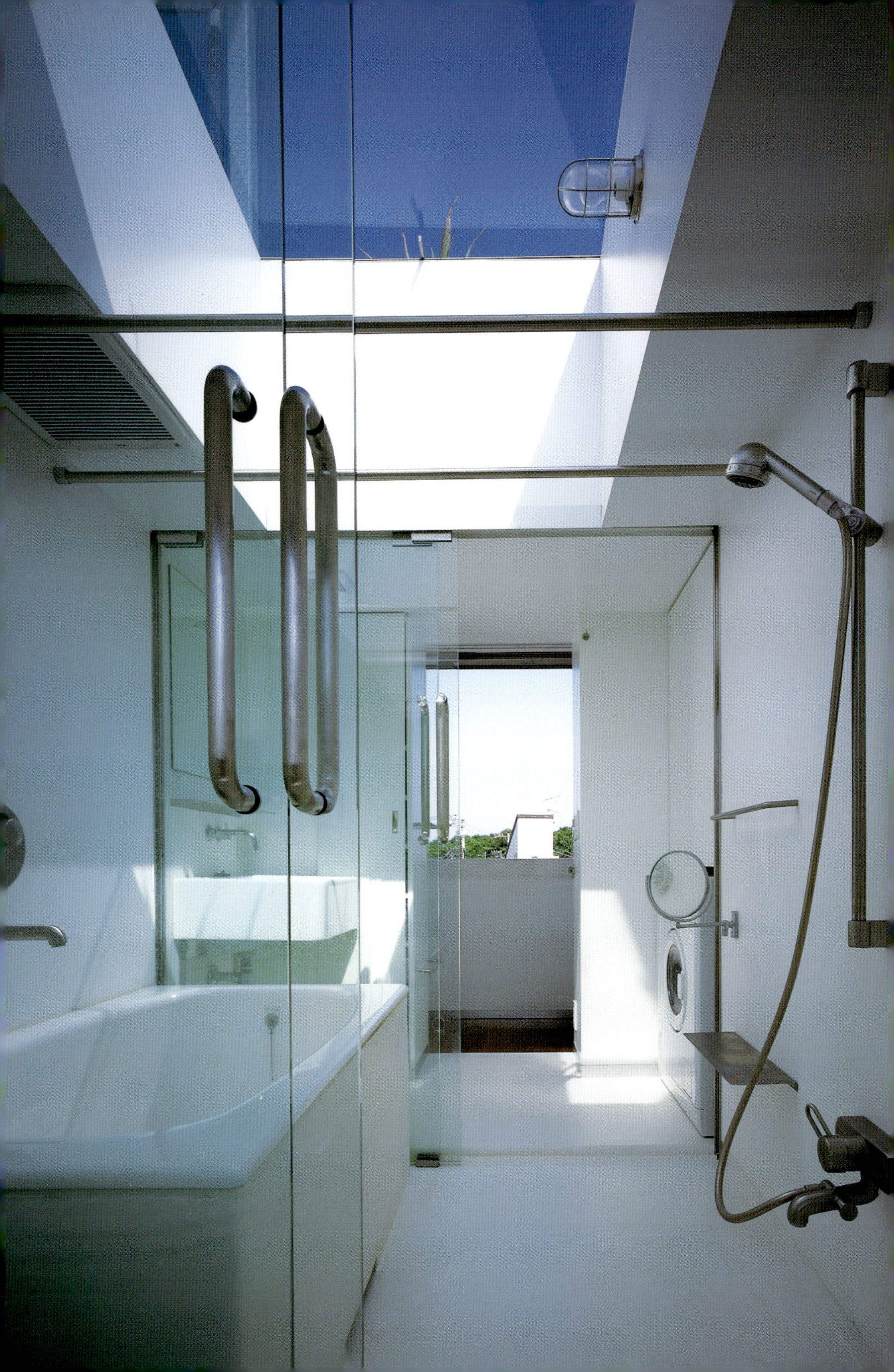

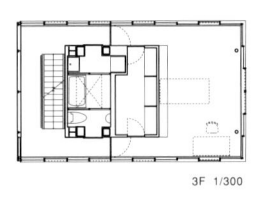

3F 1/300

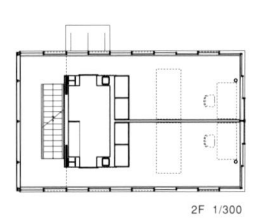

2F 1/300

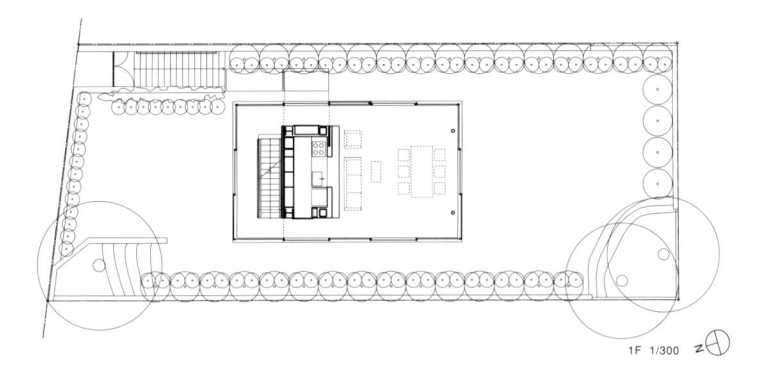

1F 1/300

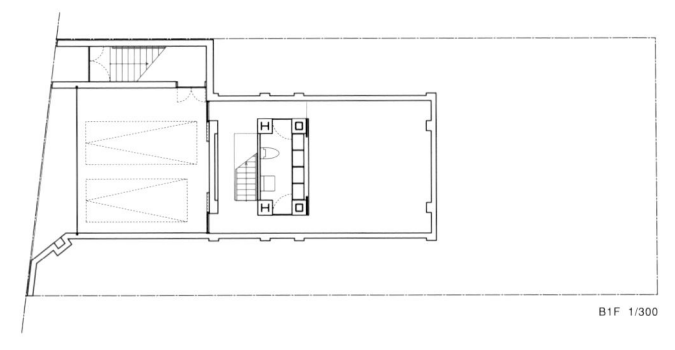

B1F 1/300

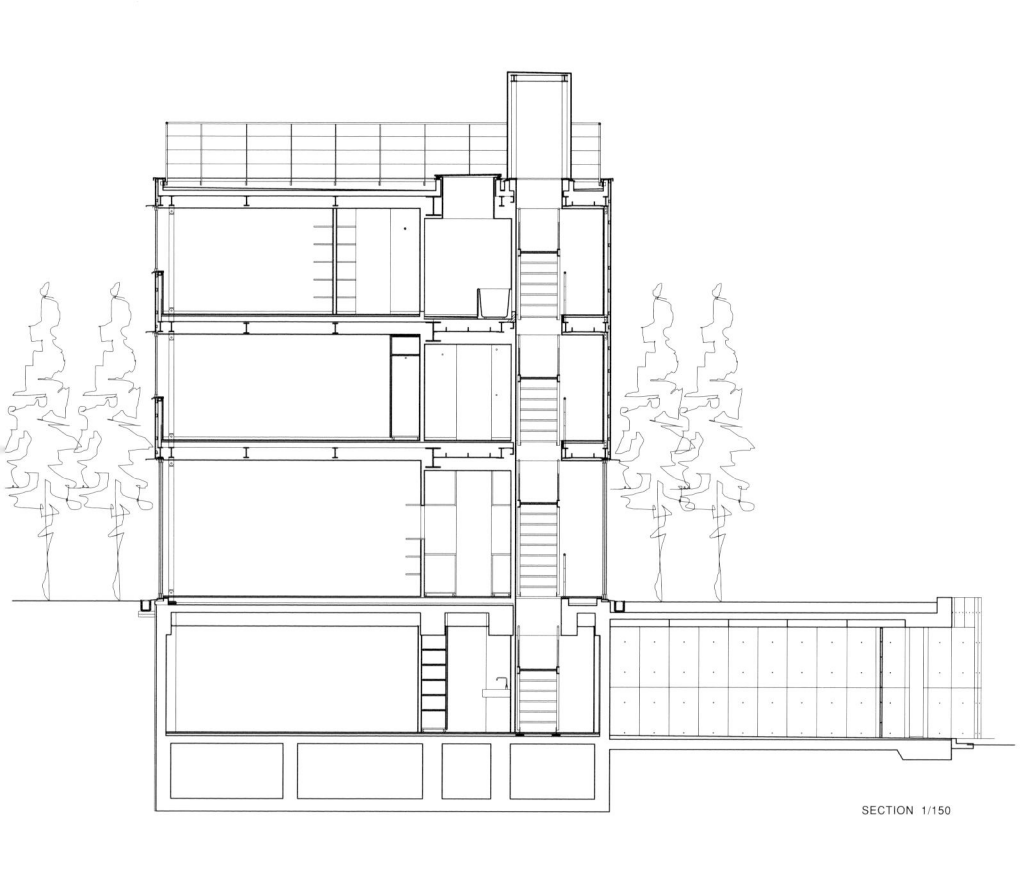

SECTION 1/150

House to Catch the Sky

空を捕まえる家　2001

Once the sliding doors are open, the house becomes a simple box with a huge opening toward the sky. There is no boundary between the inside and the outside.

中庭を囲むガラス戸を戸袋に引き込むと、大きく空に開いた箱になる家。北側斜面に建っているにも関わらず、一日中光が入る。

11

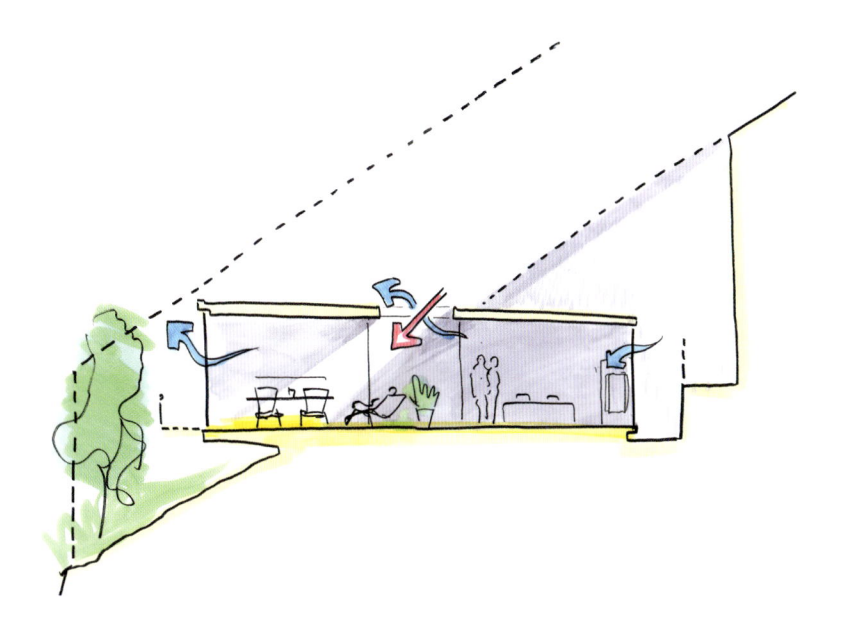

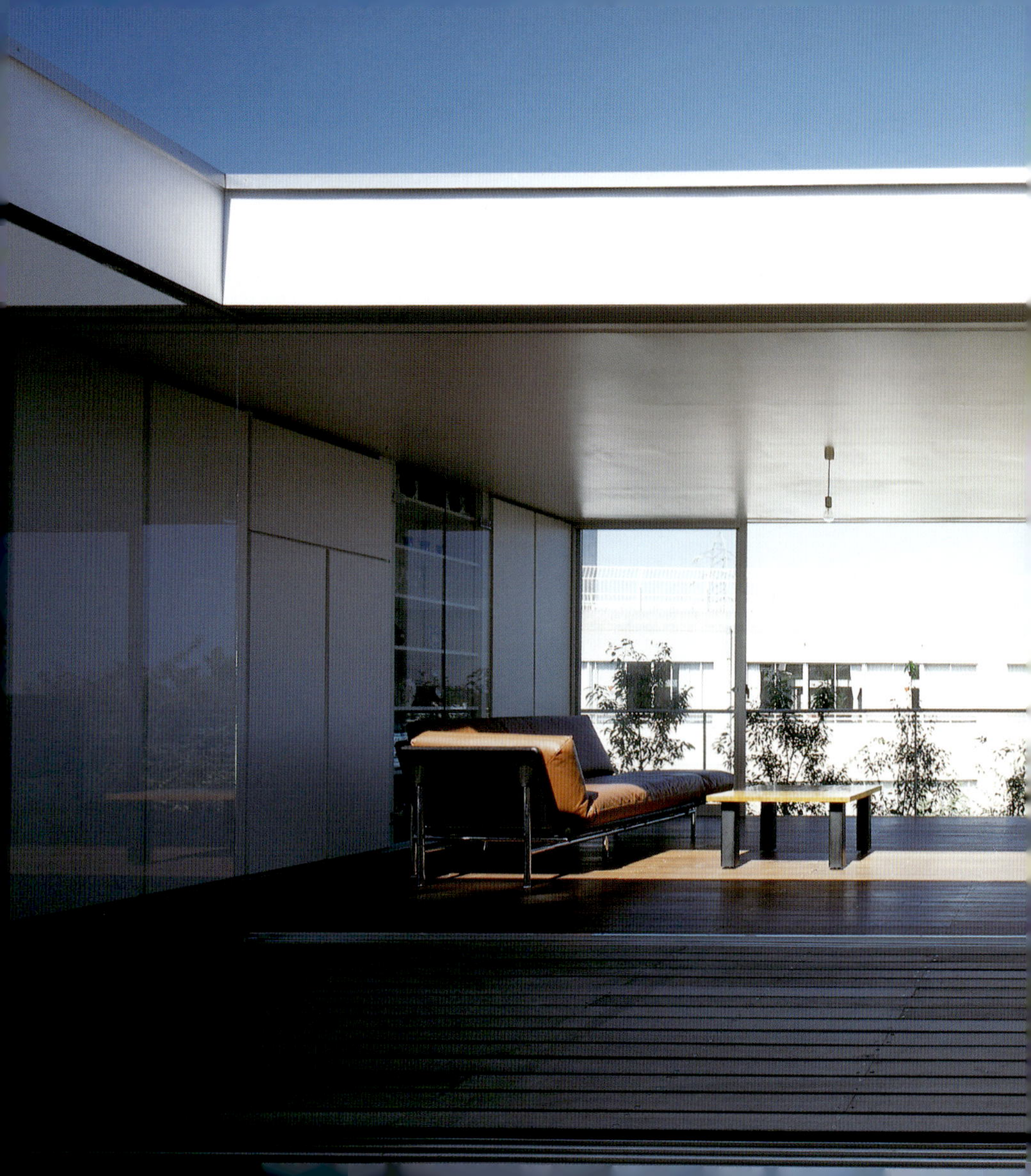

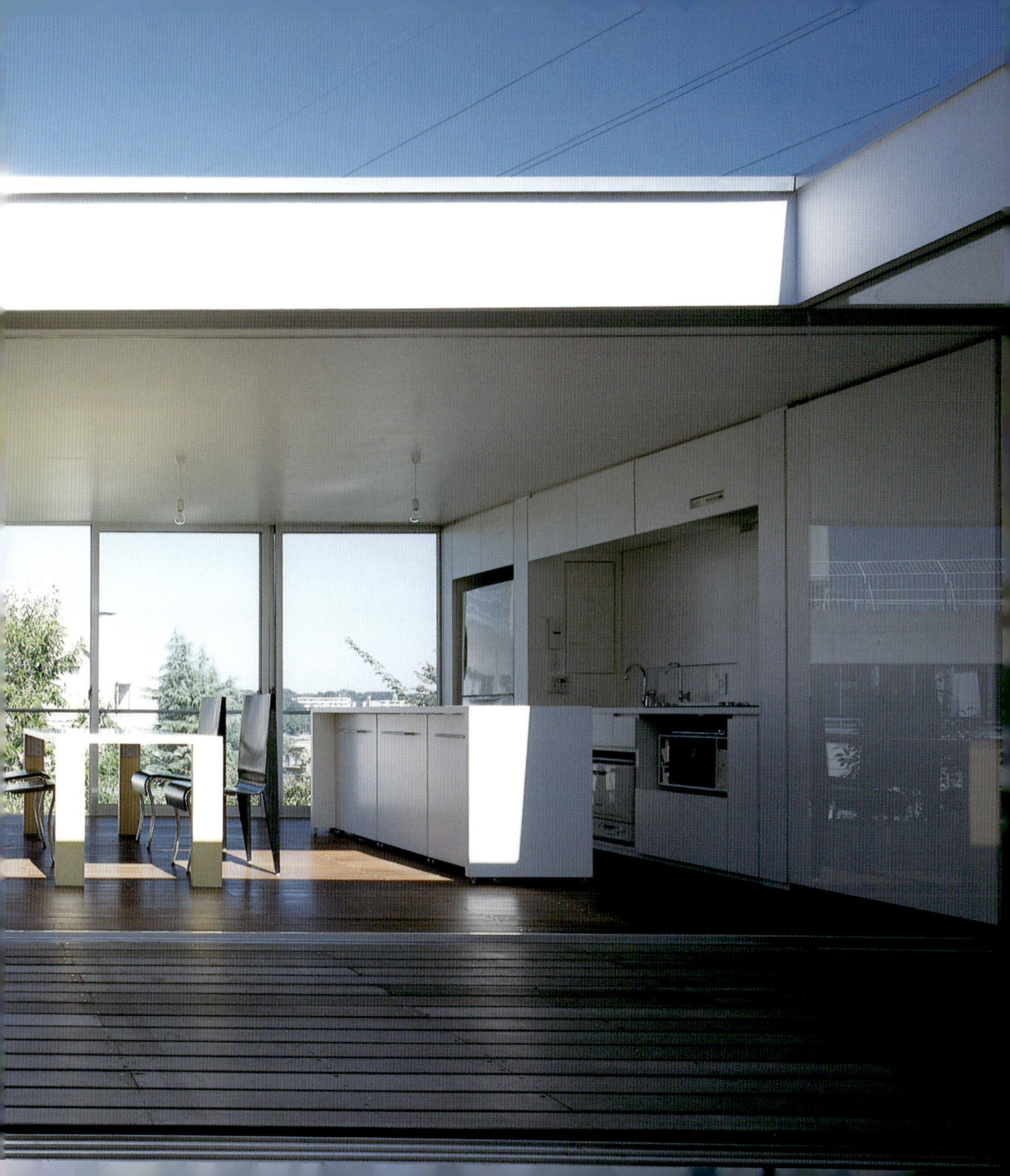

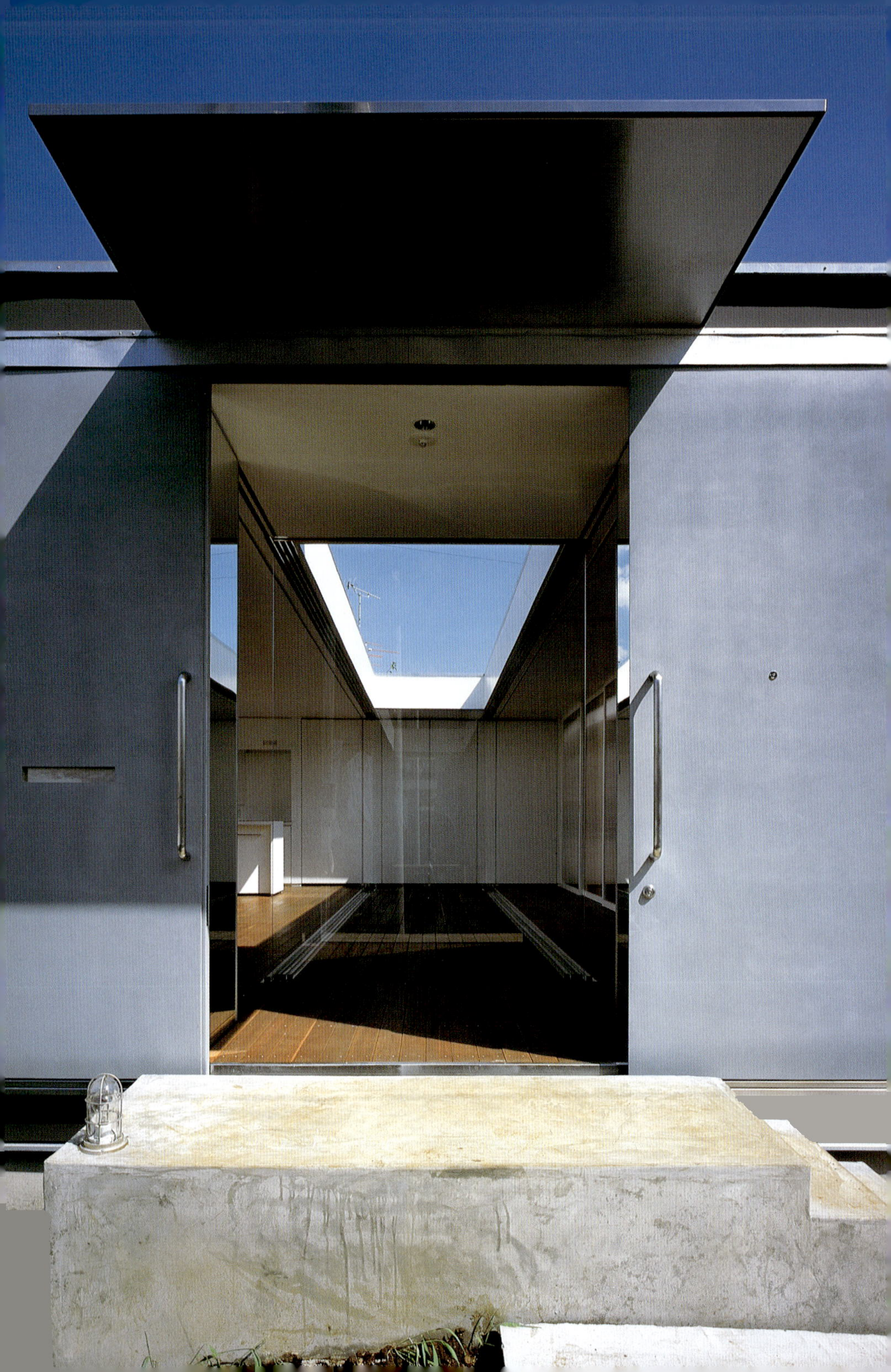

1F 1/150

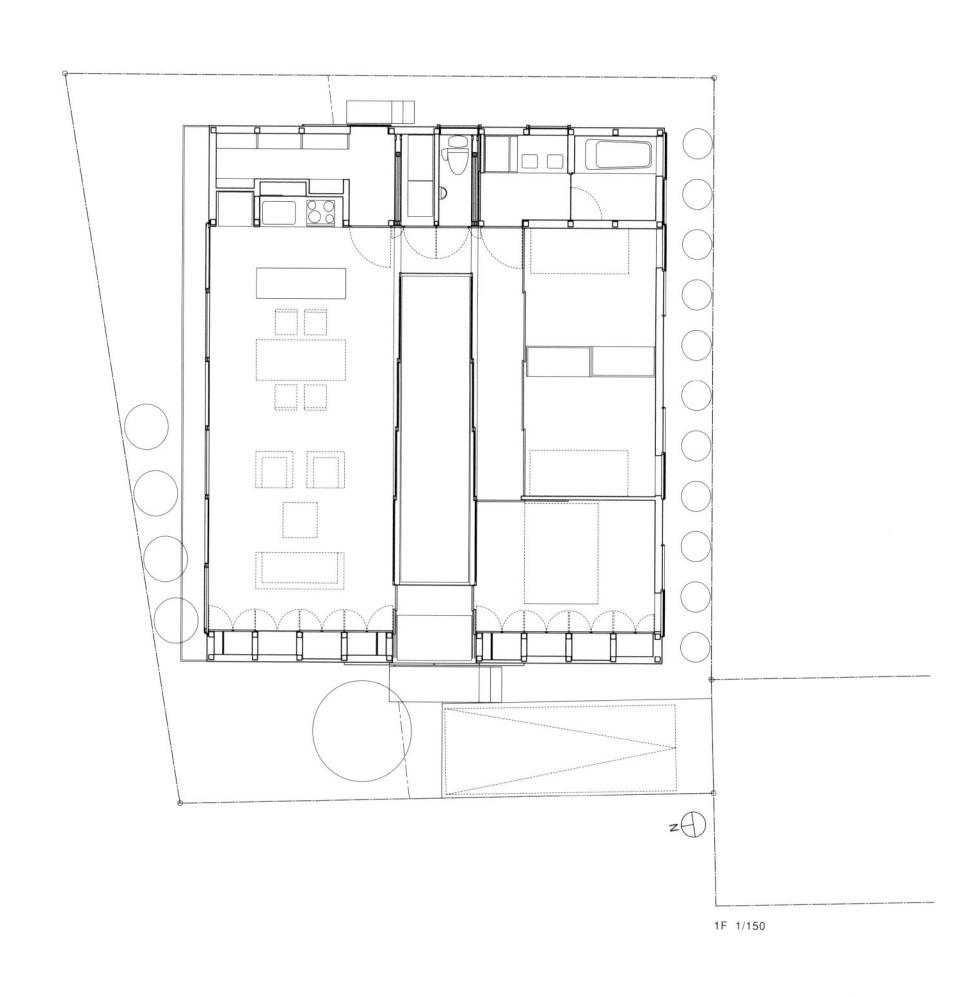

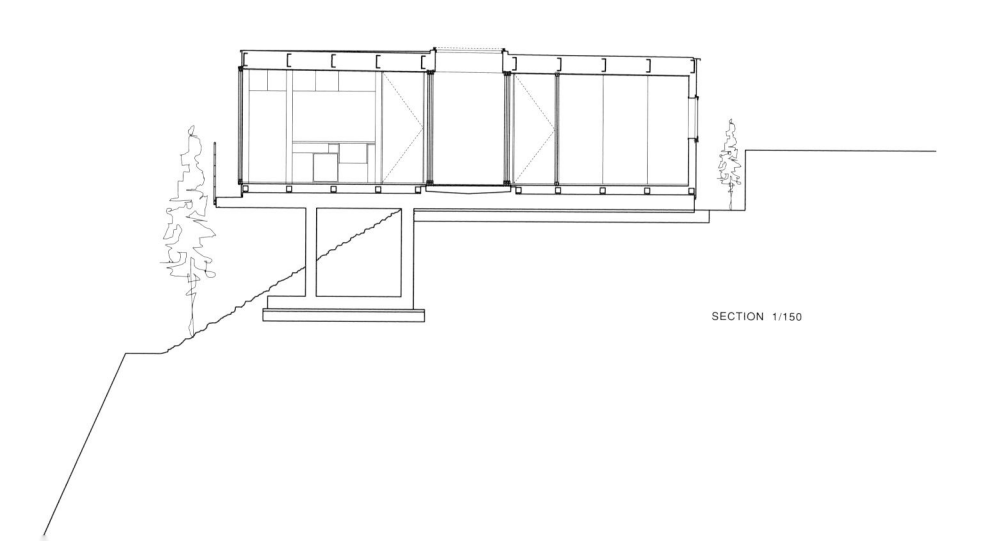

SECTION 1/150

Step House

熱海のステップハウス　2001

The levels follow the curve of the slope.
Each space opens on the Pacific Ocean.

熱海の斜面をそのまま活かした家。
テラスが階段状に繋がった床になっていて、
どこからでも熱海の海が一望できる。

12

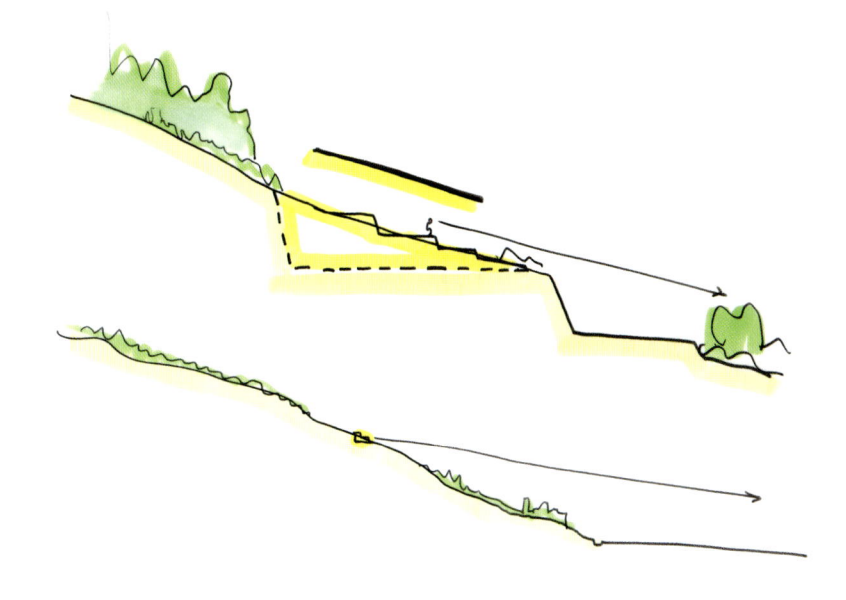

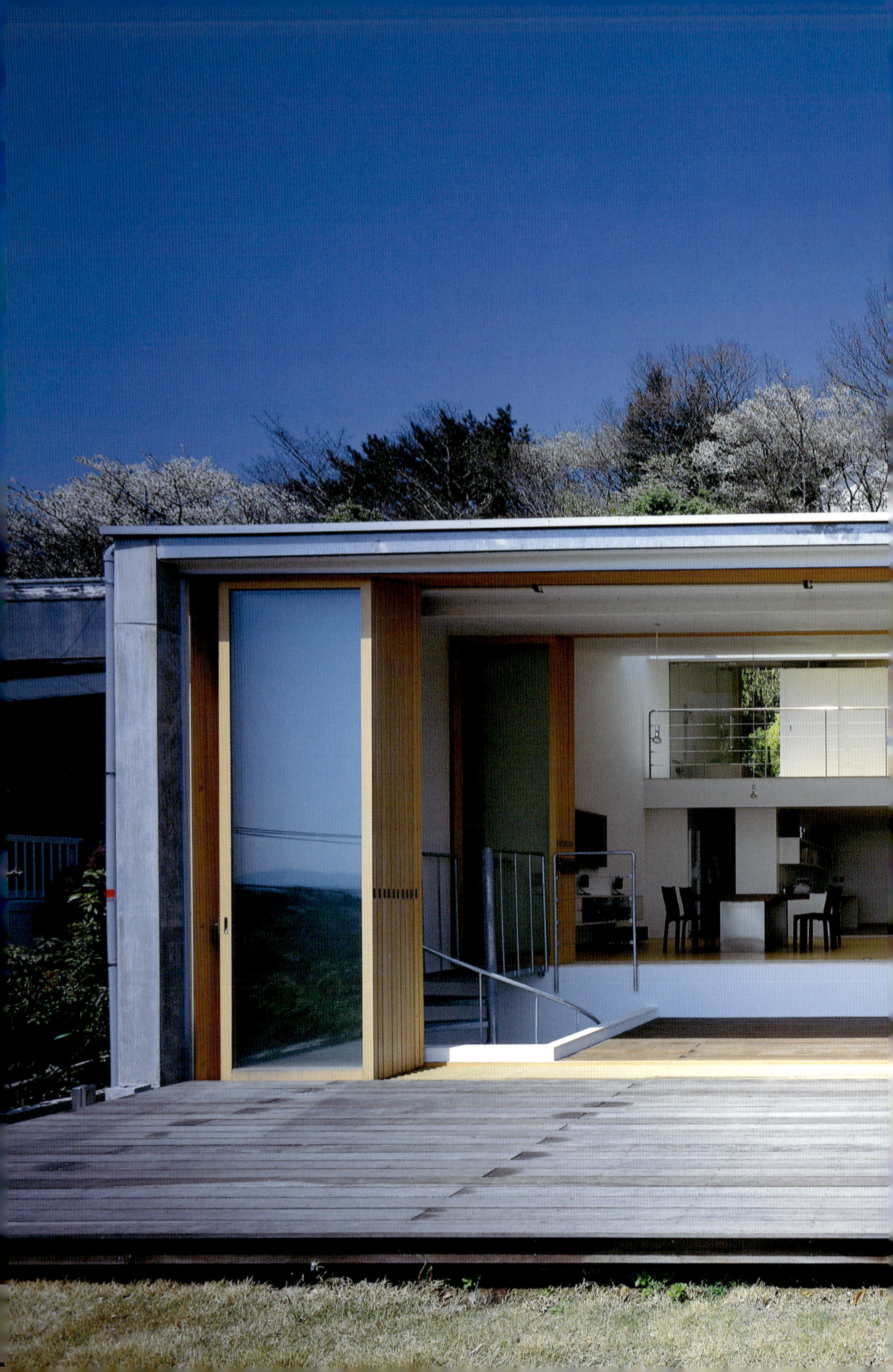

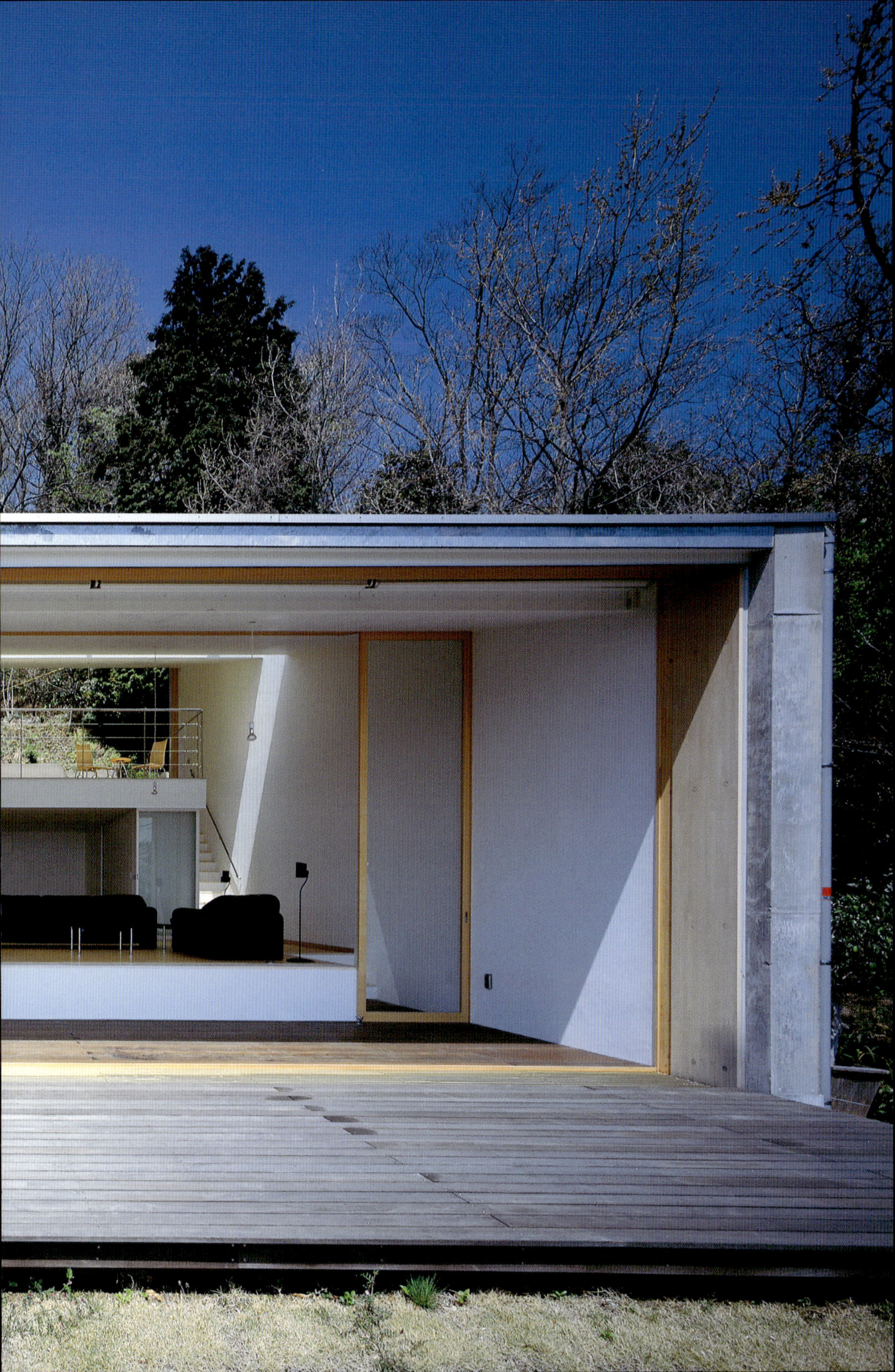

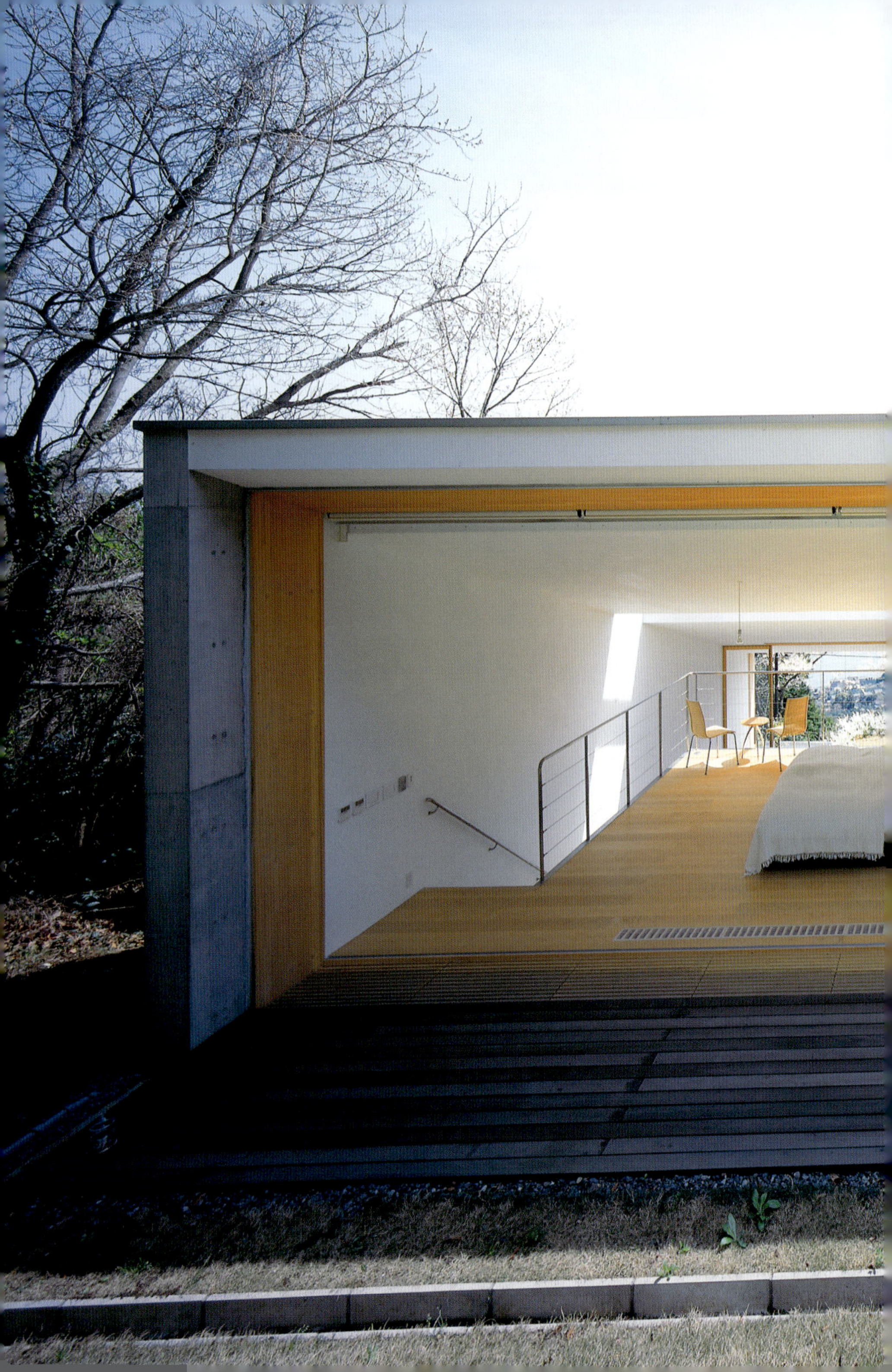

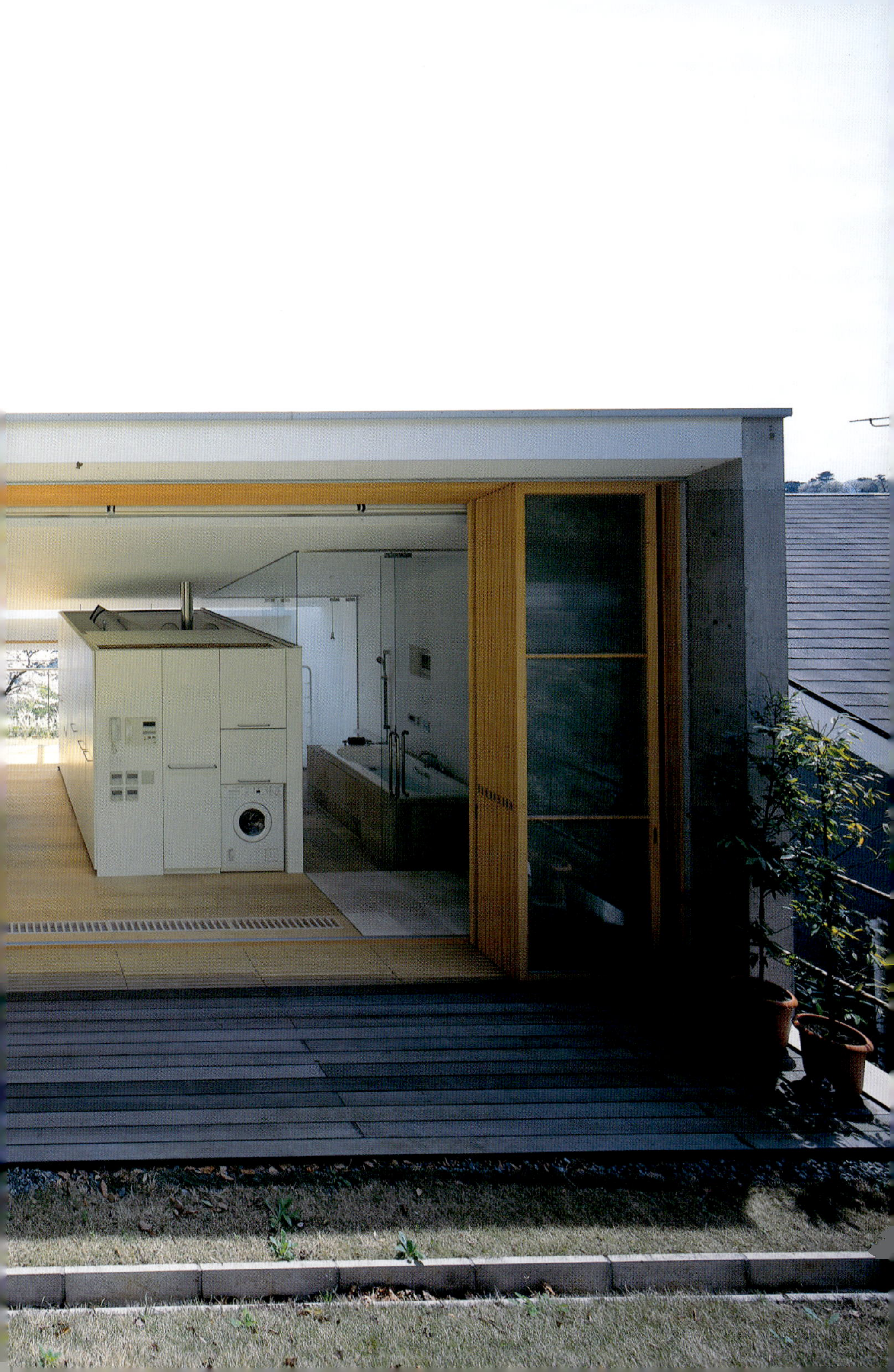

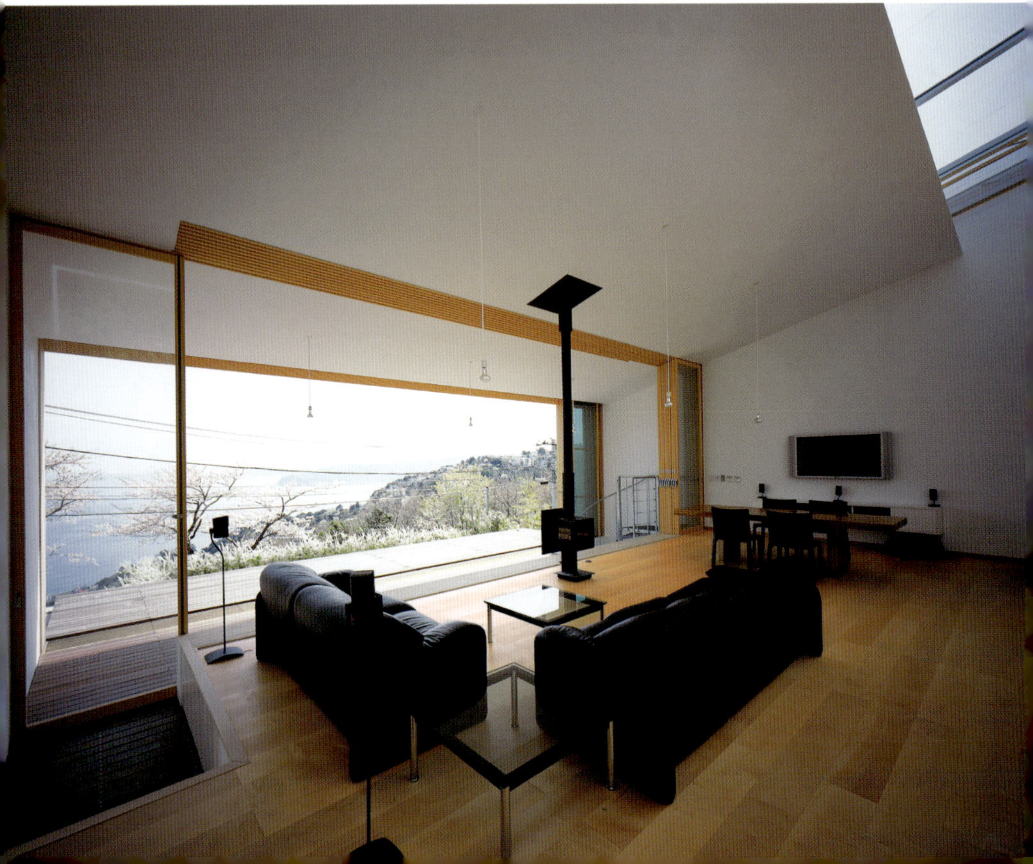

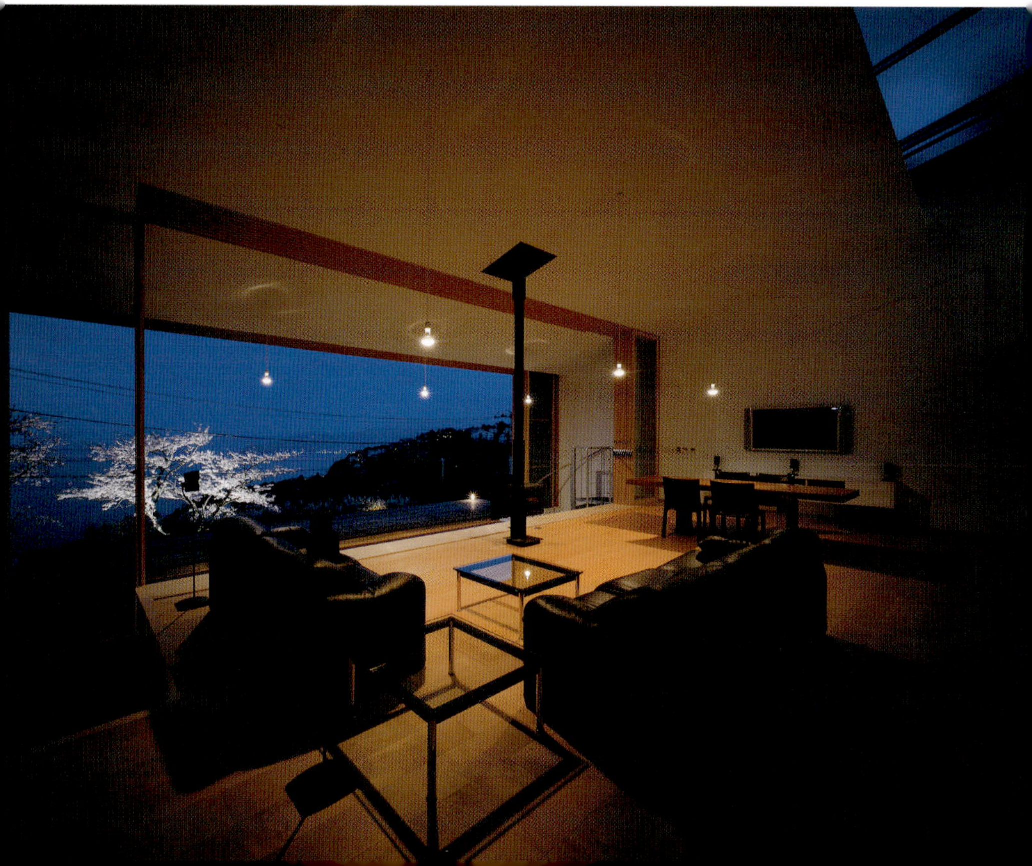

2F 1/300

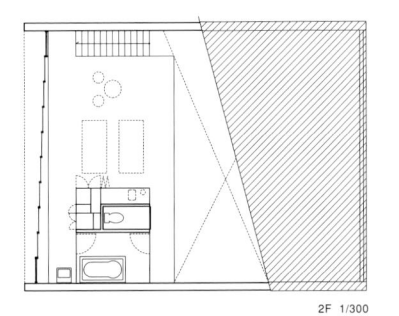

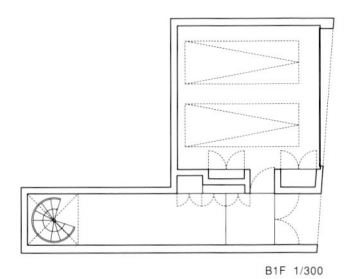

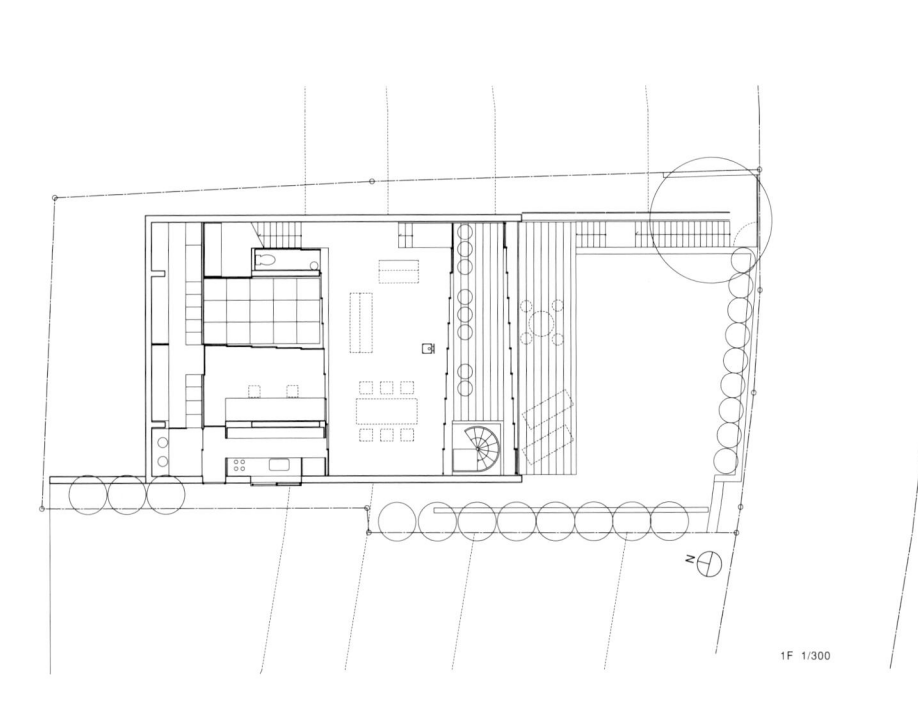

B1F 1/300

1F 1/300

SITE 1/1000

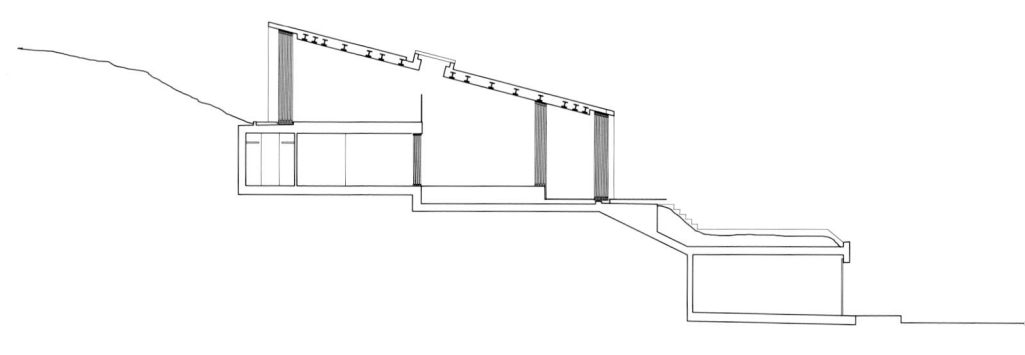

SECTION 1/300

House to Catch the Sky II

空を捕まえる家II　2002

Minimal house surrounded by other buildings on three sides with a 500mm clearance. Privacy is ensured by a unidirectional skylight and by windows equally set at eye-level on all four sides.

三方を隣家に囲まれた最小限の家。
目線の高さに四方向へ開けられた窓と大きな天窓の組み合わせが、開放性とプライバシーを両立させる。

13

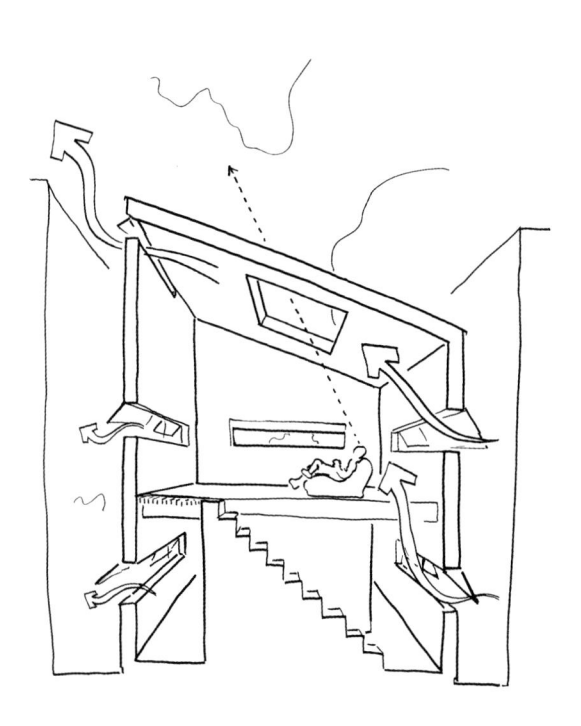

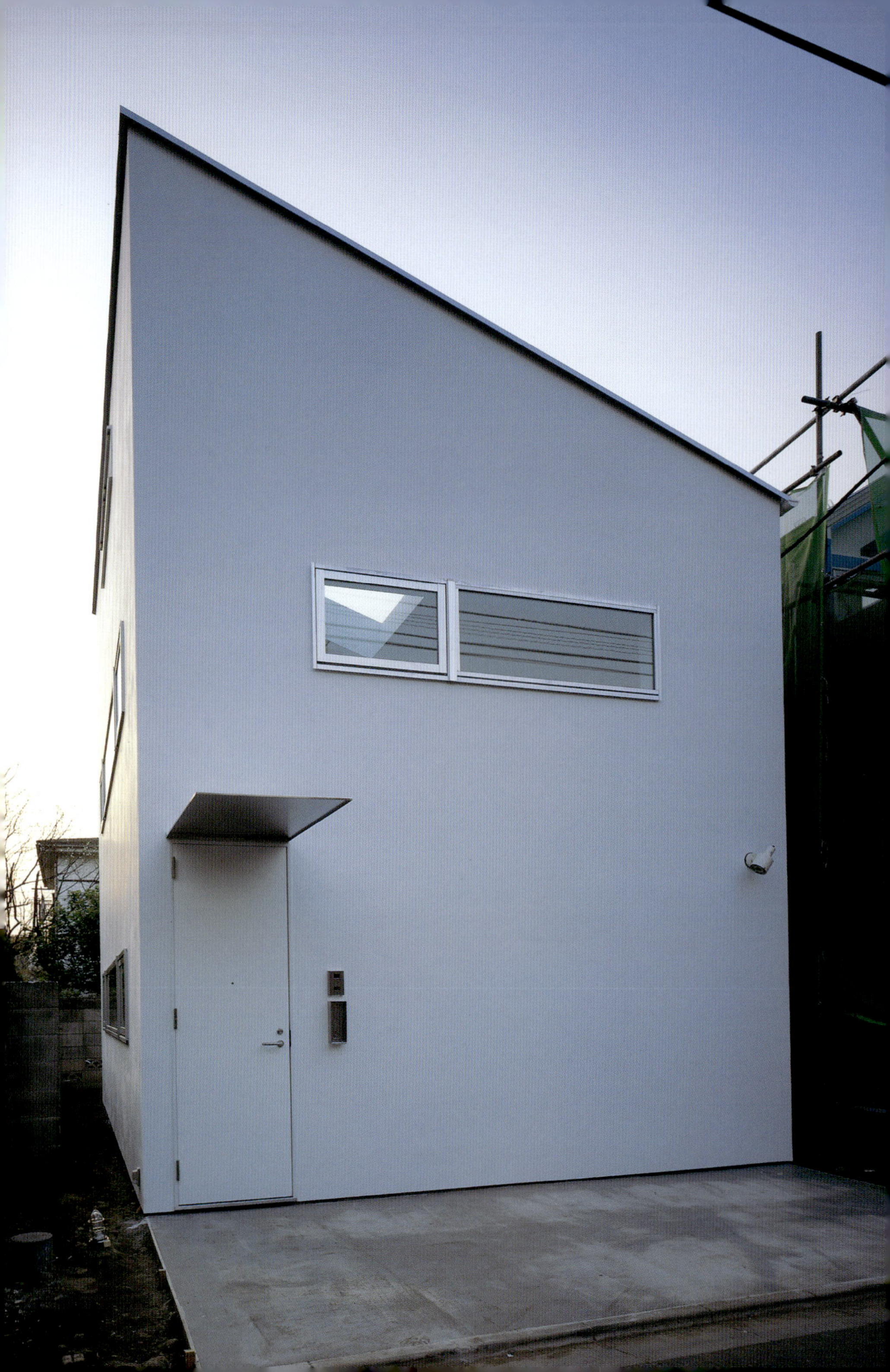

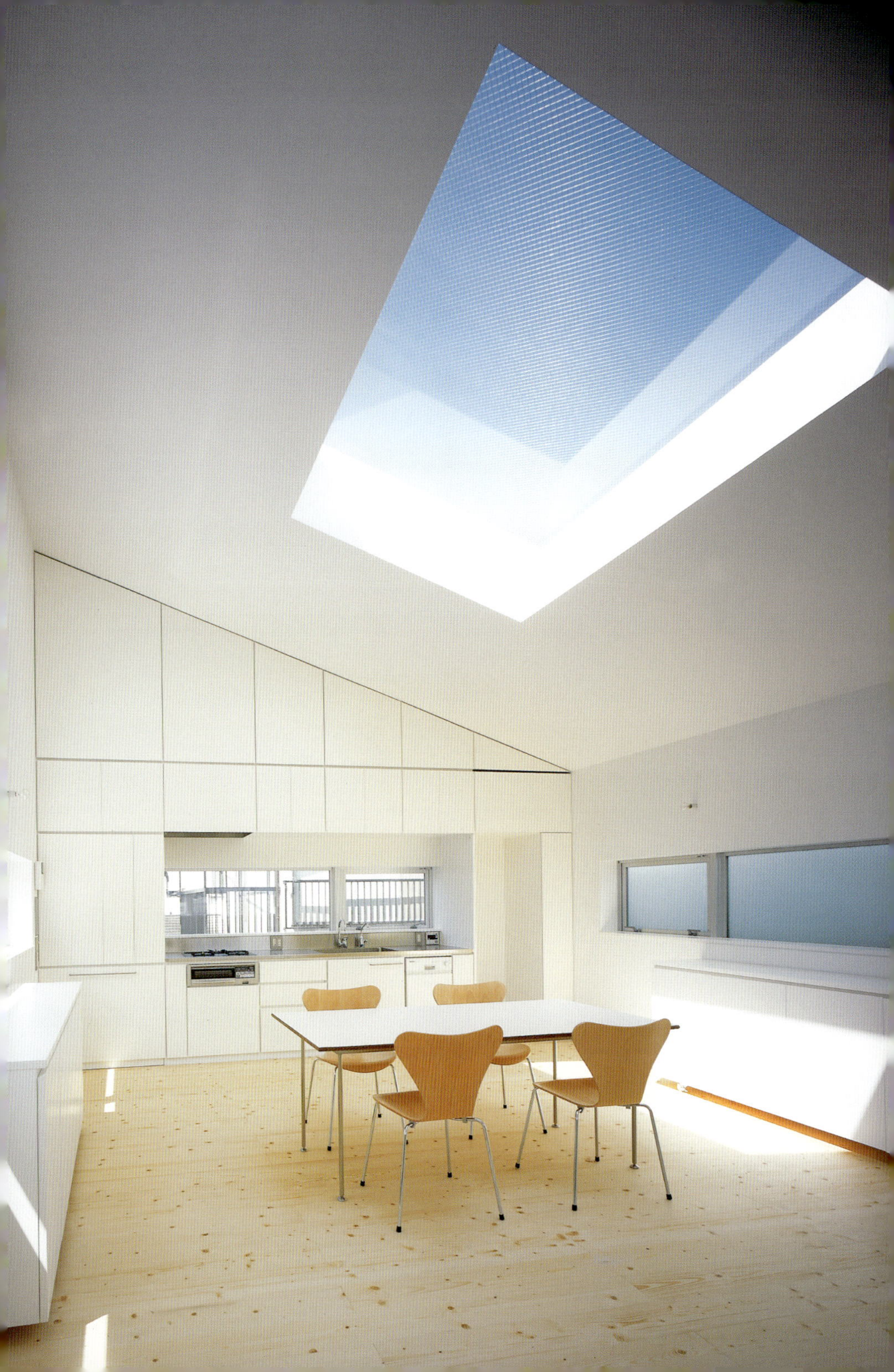

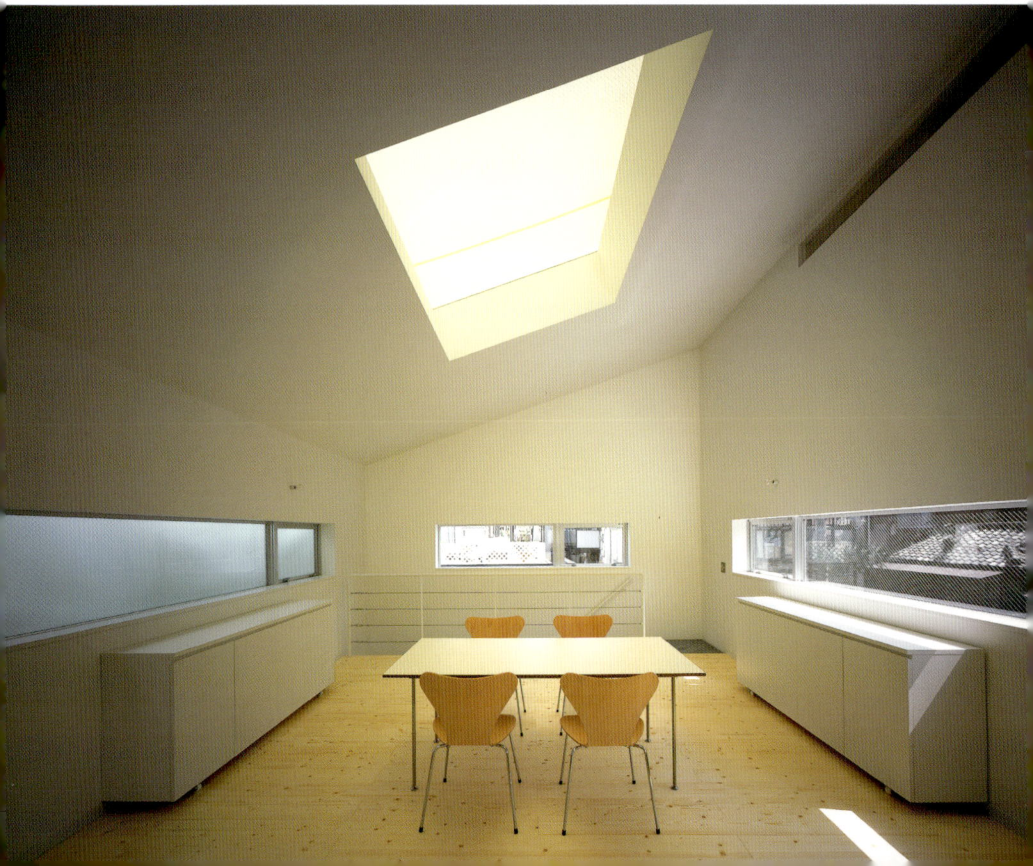

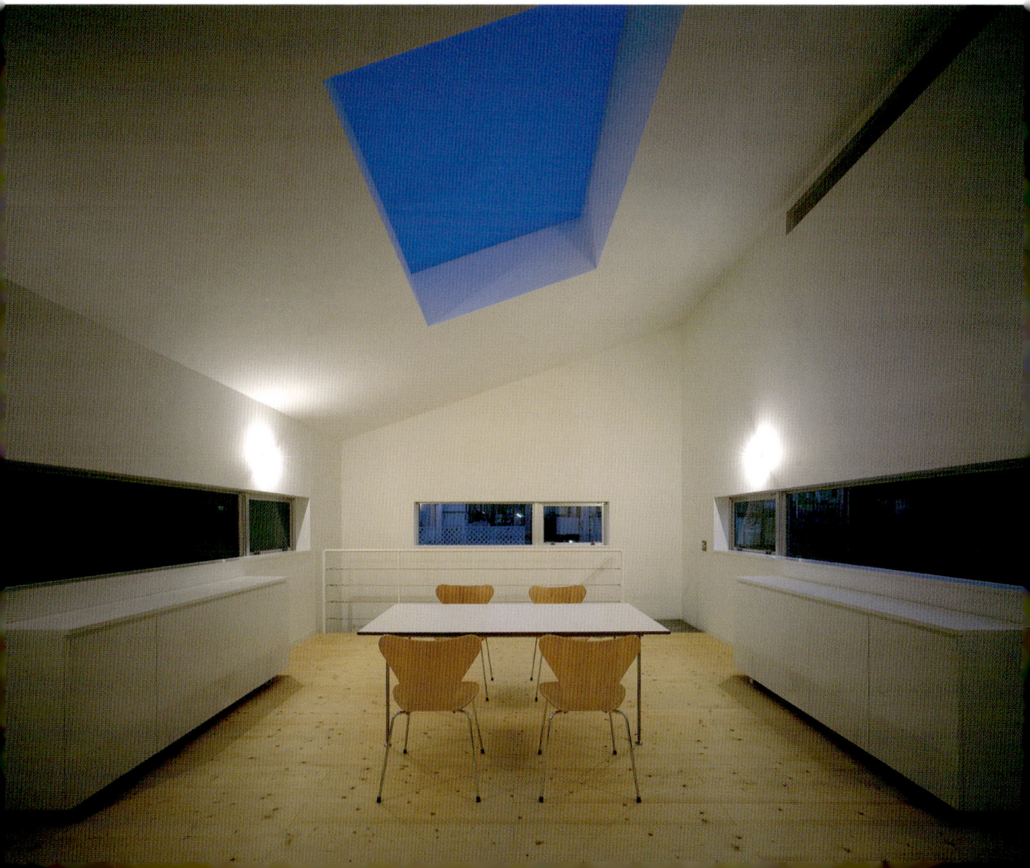

1/1500

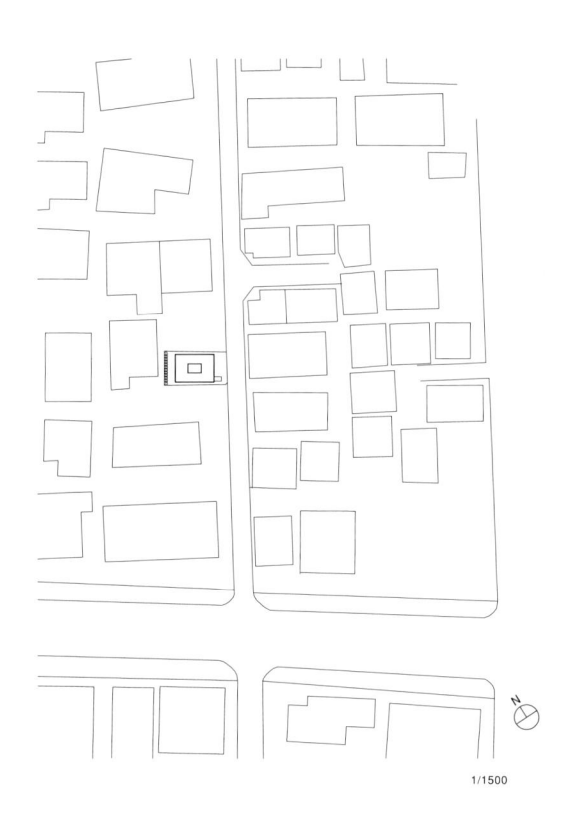

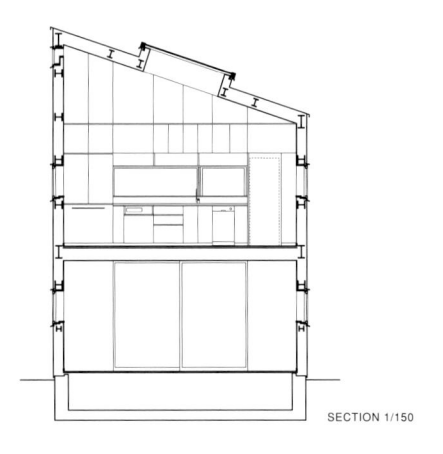

SECTION 1/150

2F 1/150

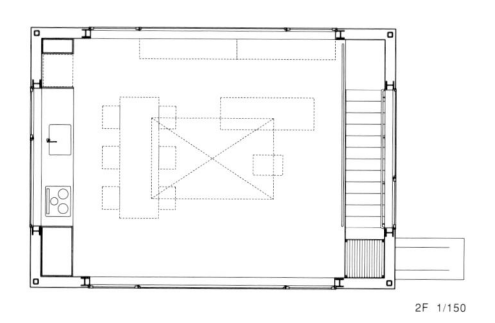

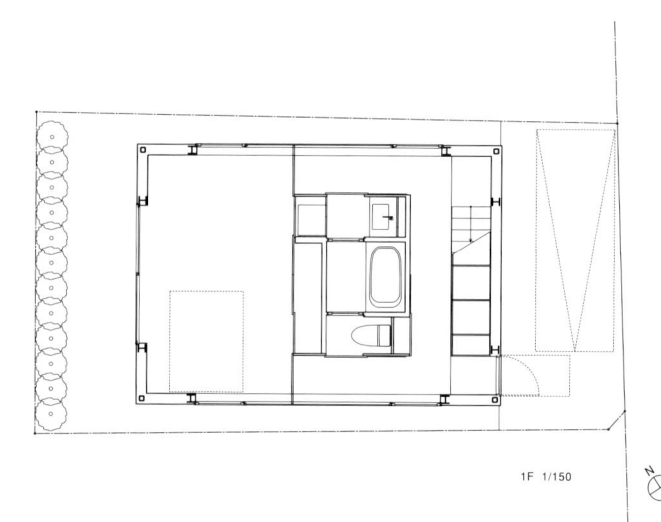

1F 1/150

Anthill House

蟻塚の家　2002

Designed for an animation director, the house's four levels – each in a different color: blue, red, green, and yellow – are connected by staircases curled around the edges of the building.

アニメーション監督の家。
監督のイメージ通り青・赤・緑・黄の原色に塗り分けられた各層を、敷地境界に沿って巻き付く群青色の階段が繋いでいる。

14

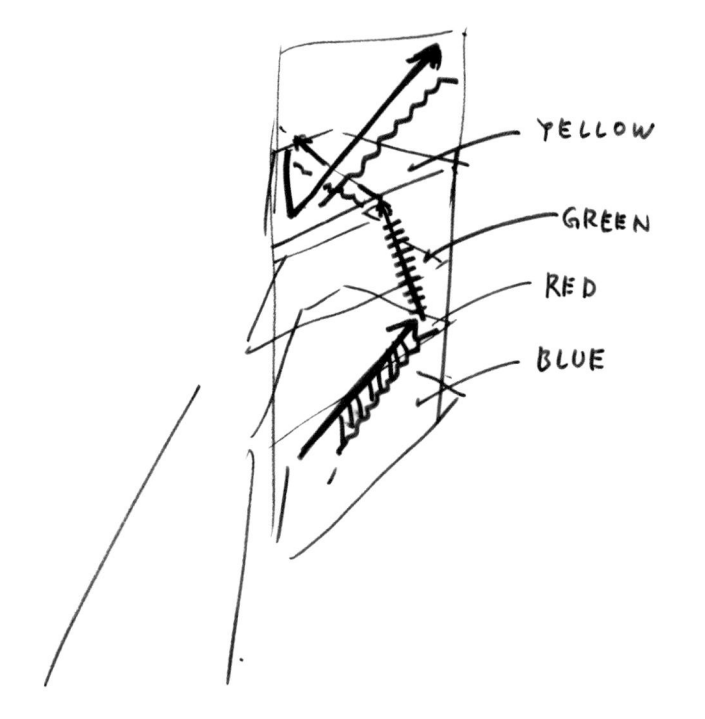

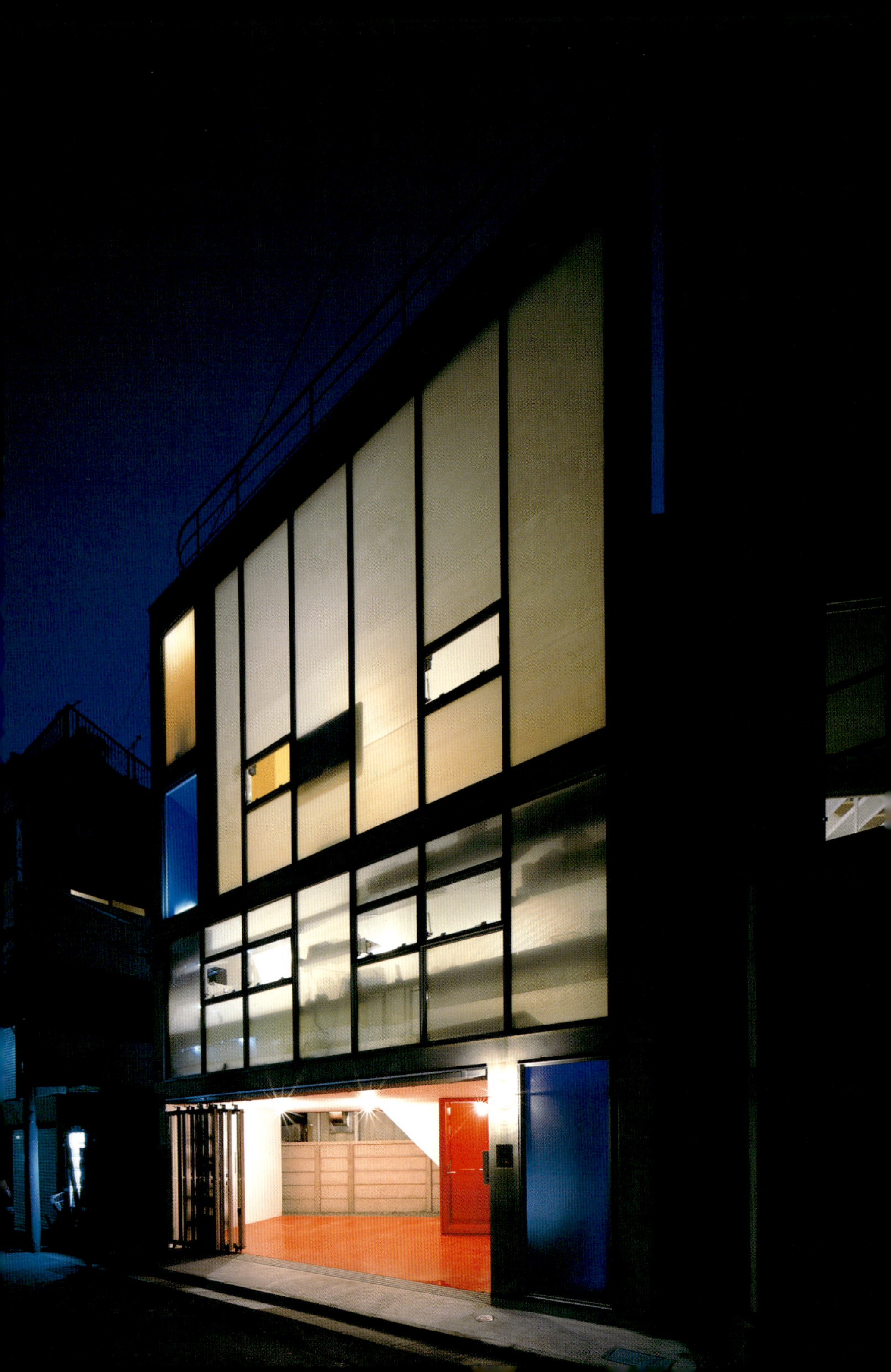

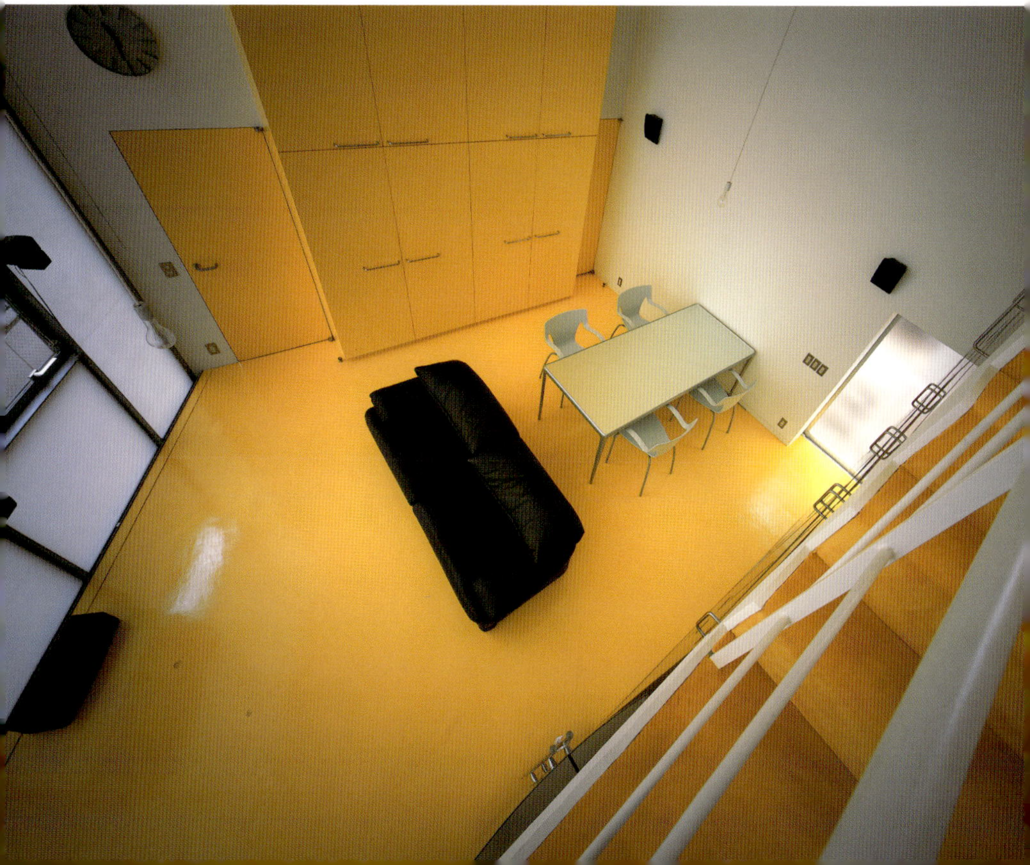

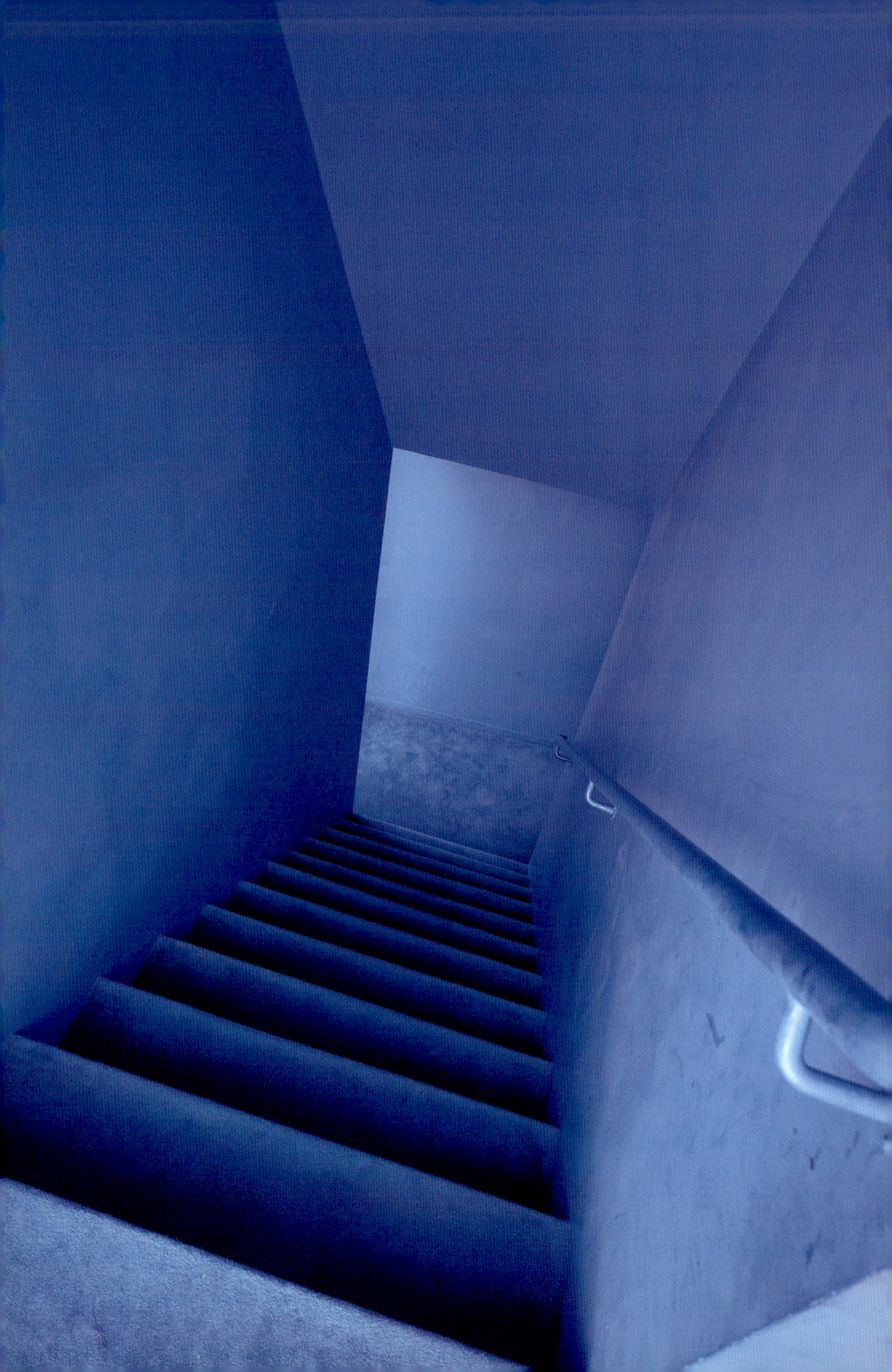

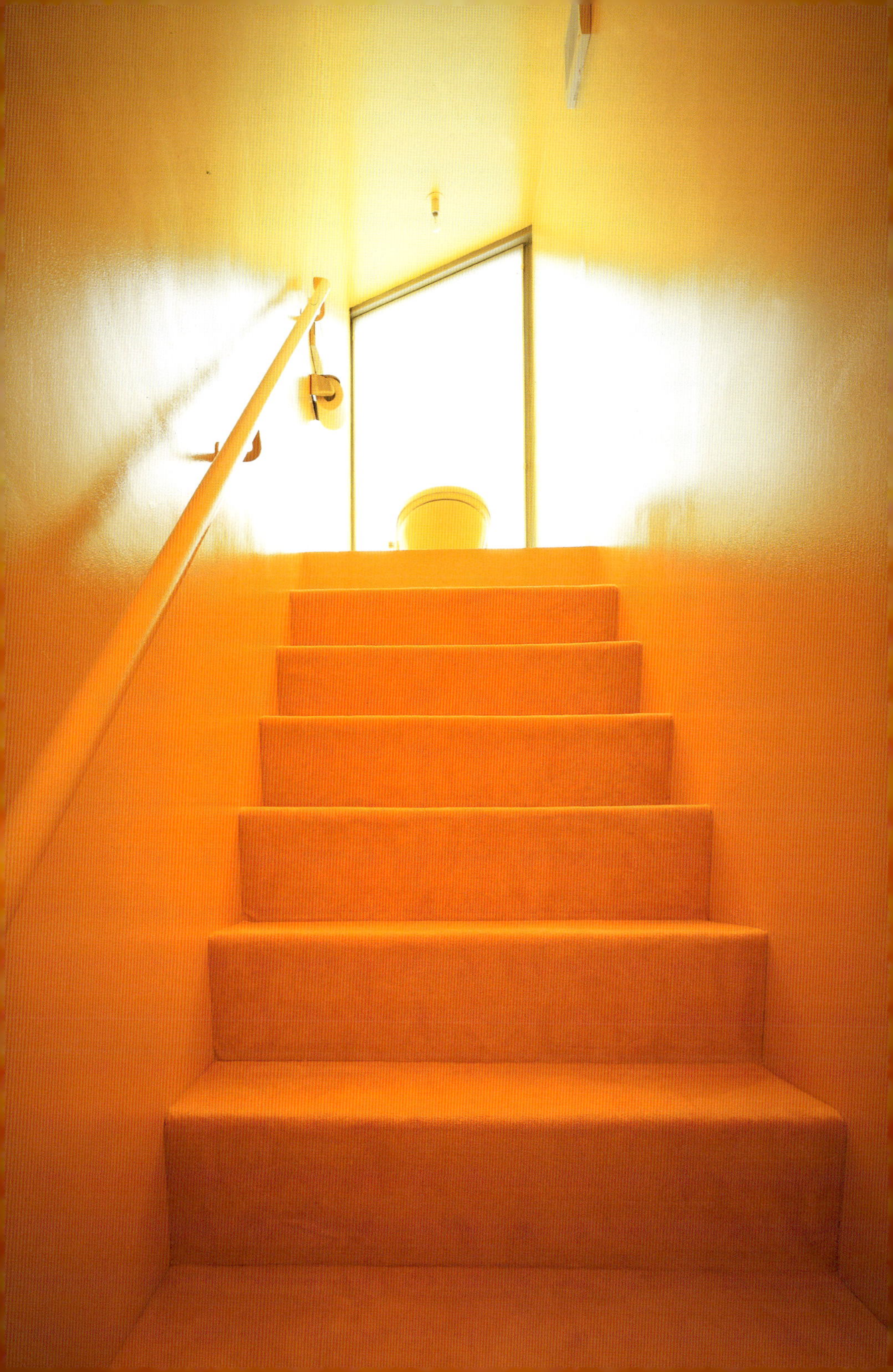

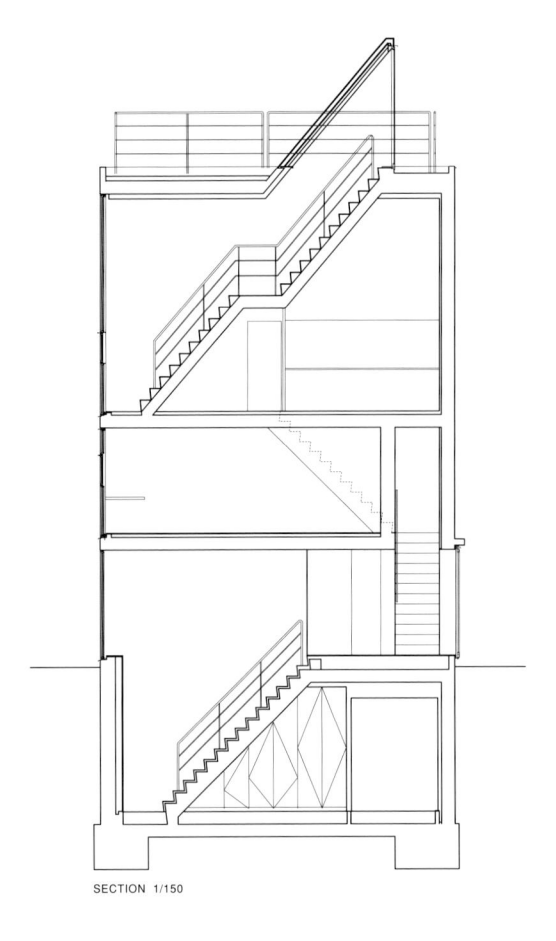

SECTION 1/150

2F 1/200

RF 1/200

1F 1/200

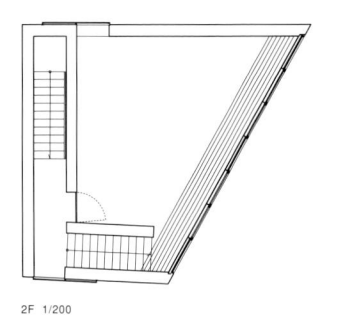

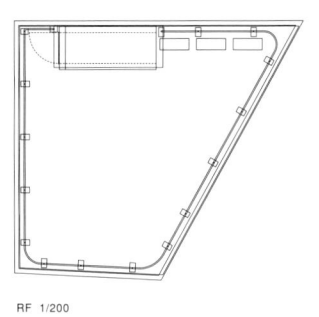

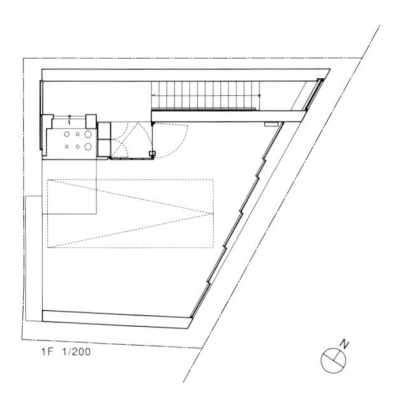

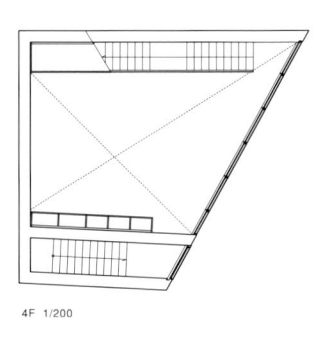

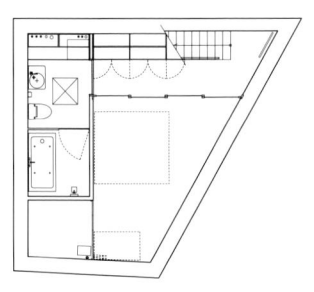

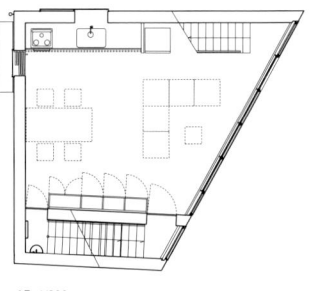

4F 1/200

B1F 1/200

3F 1/200

Thin Roof Sukiya

薄い屋根の数寄屋　2002

The rafters were set perpendicularly to their traditional orientation.
The absence of beams above the *shoji* allows the ceiling to be filled with light.

垂木の方向を在来工法から90度まわした数寄屋。
障子の上に梁がないので、天井いっぱいに光が舐める。

1F 1/300

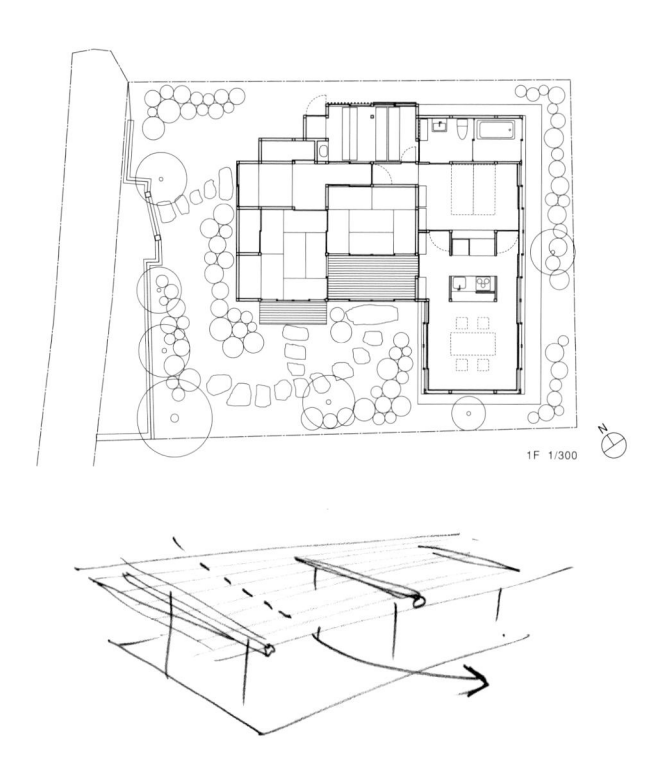

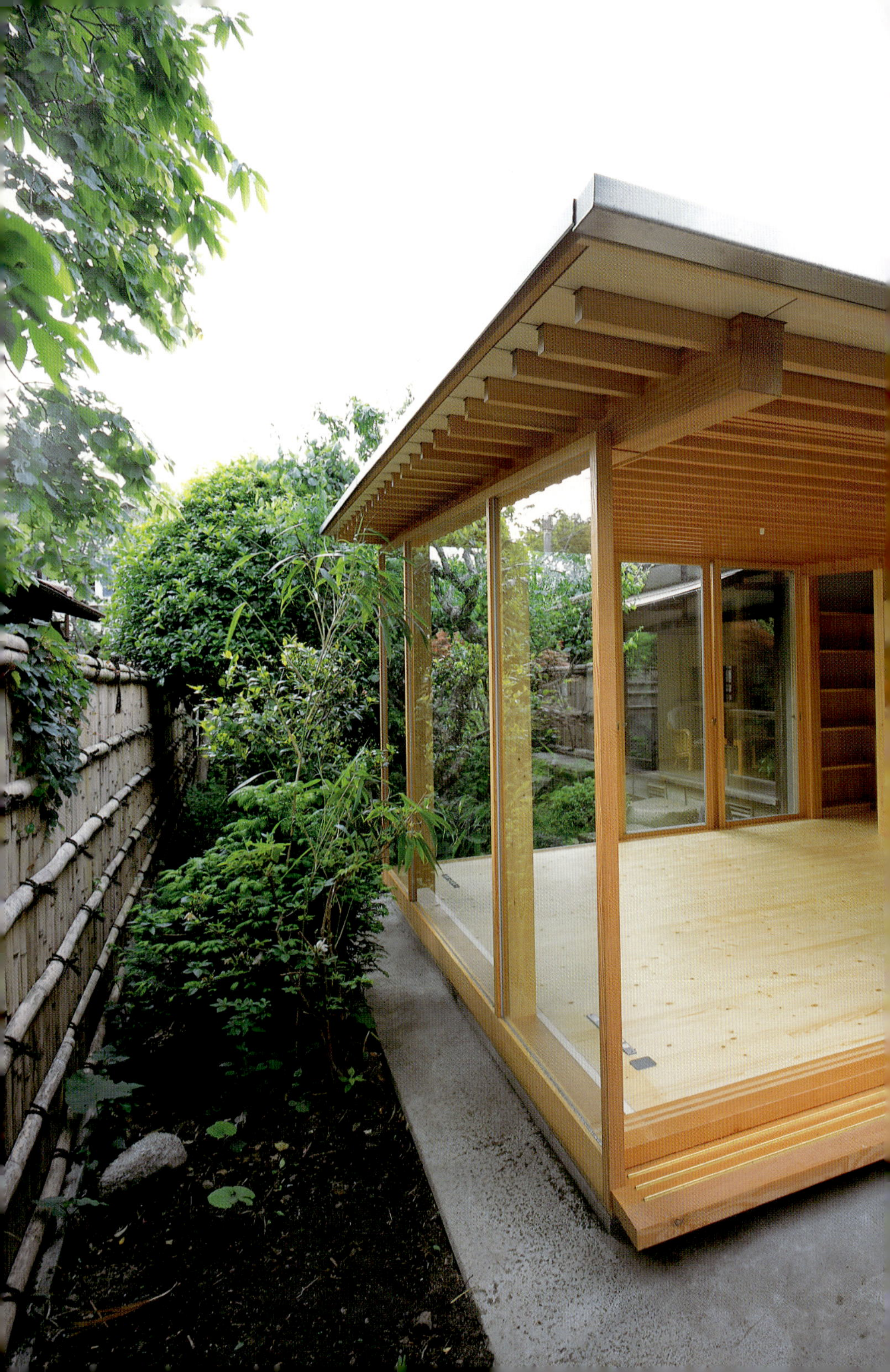

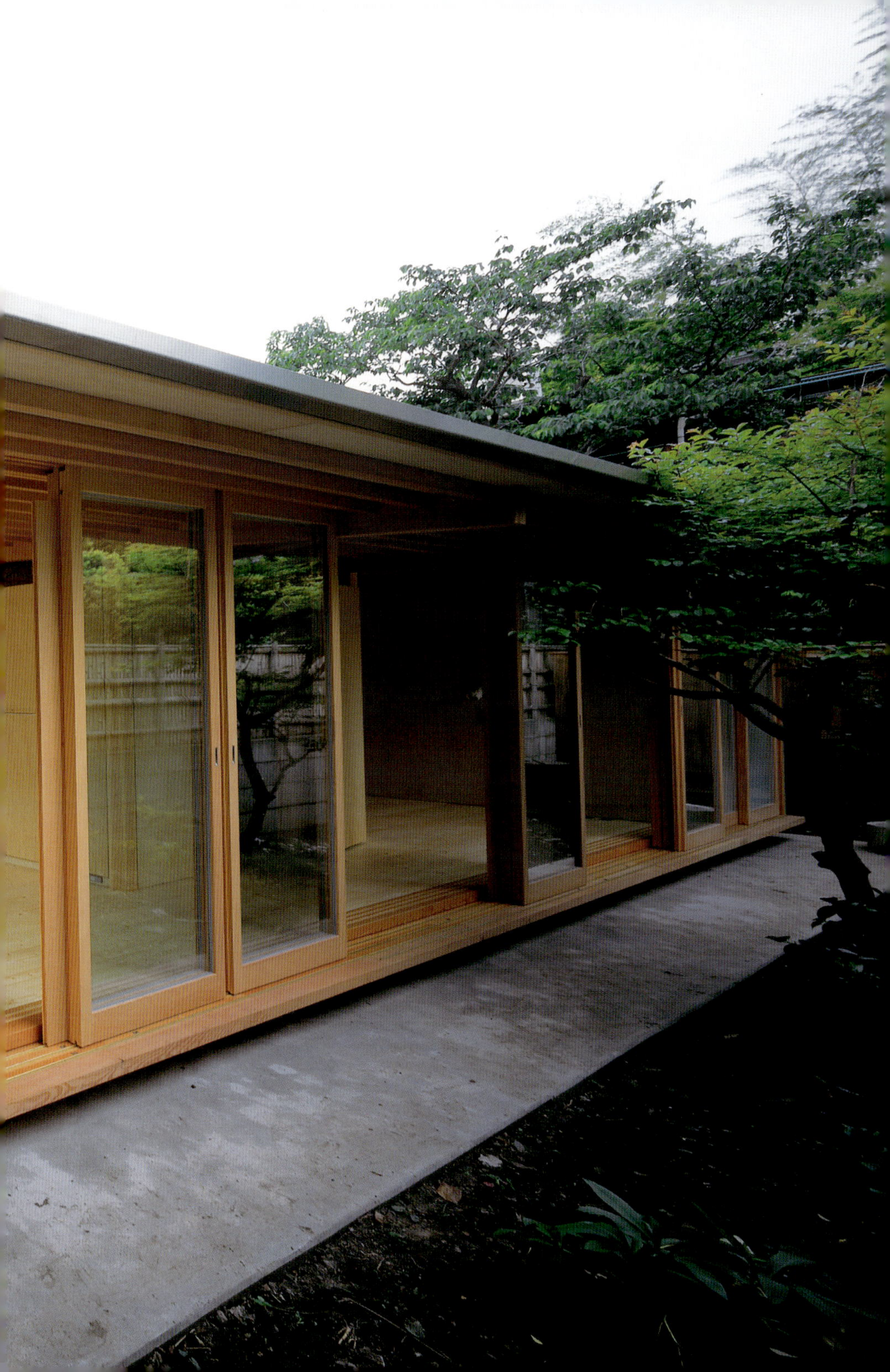

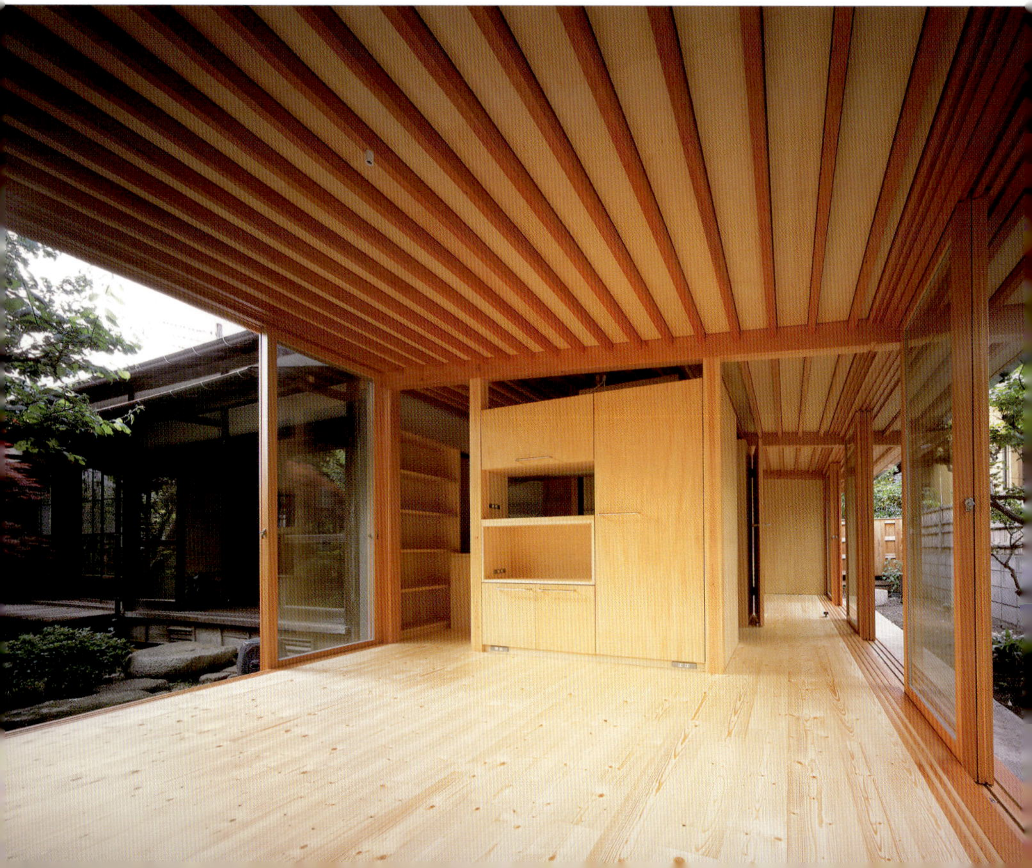

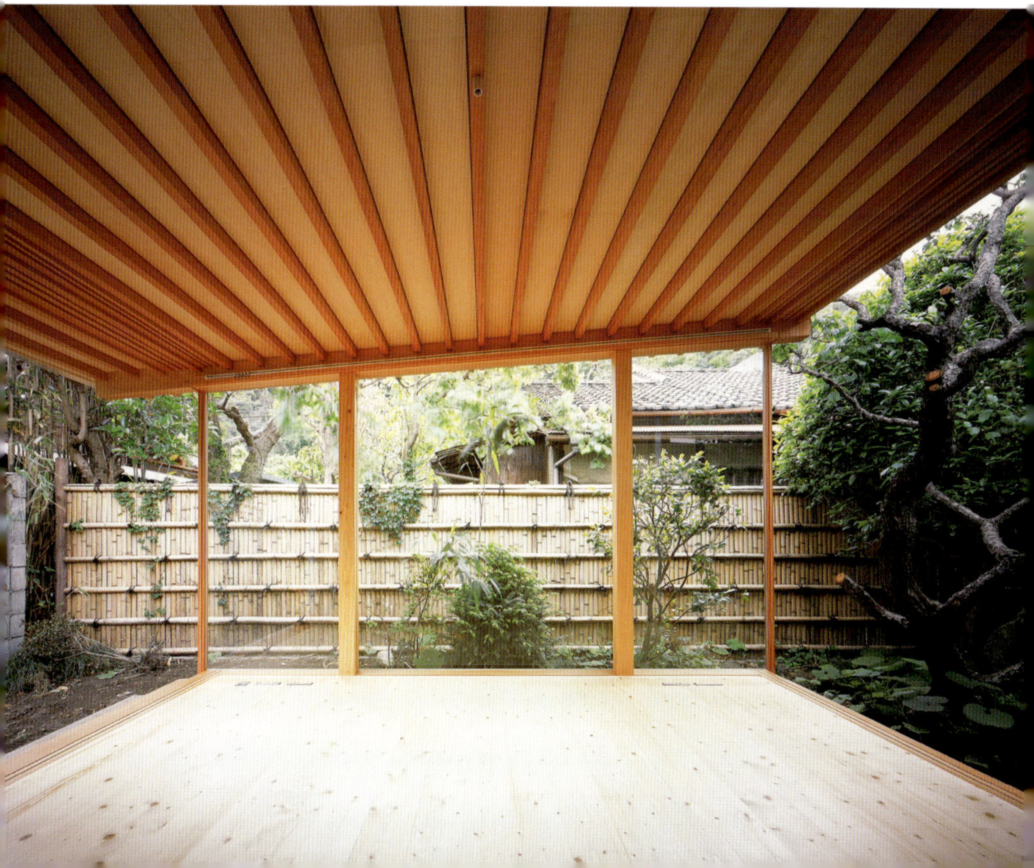

Thin Wall House

薄い壁の家　2002

Located in a dense residential neighborhood, the Thin Wall House was designed to offer a maximum interior volume. The structure is composed of 9mm steel plates and H-100mm x 100mm columns.

敷地の持ちうるボリュームを最大限活用した住宅密集地の家。9mmの鉄板とH-100mm×100mmの柱のみで構成された極薄の壁が敷地の隣地斜線いっぱいに立ち上がる。

16

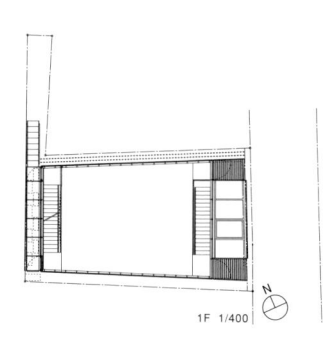

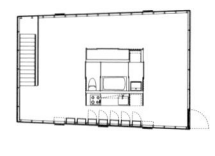

1F 1/400

3F 1/400

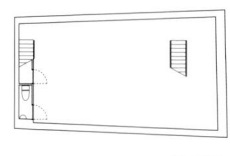

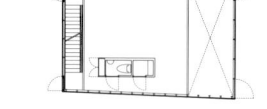

B1 1/400

2F 1/400

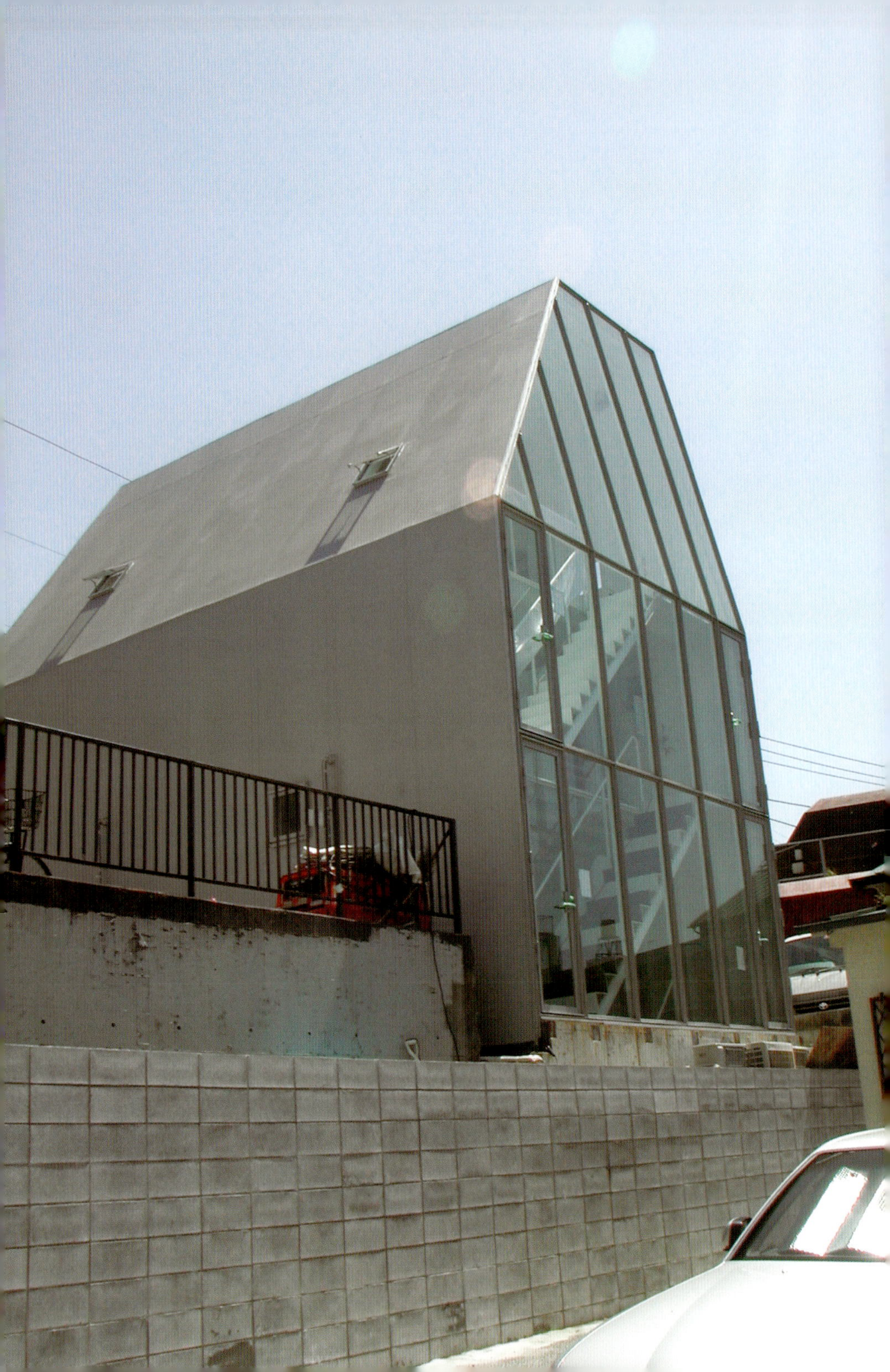

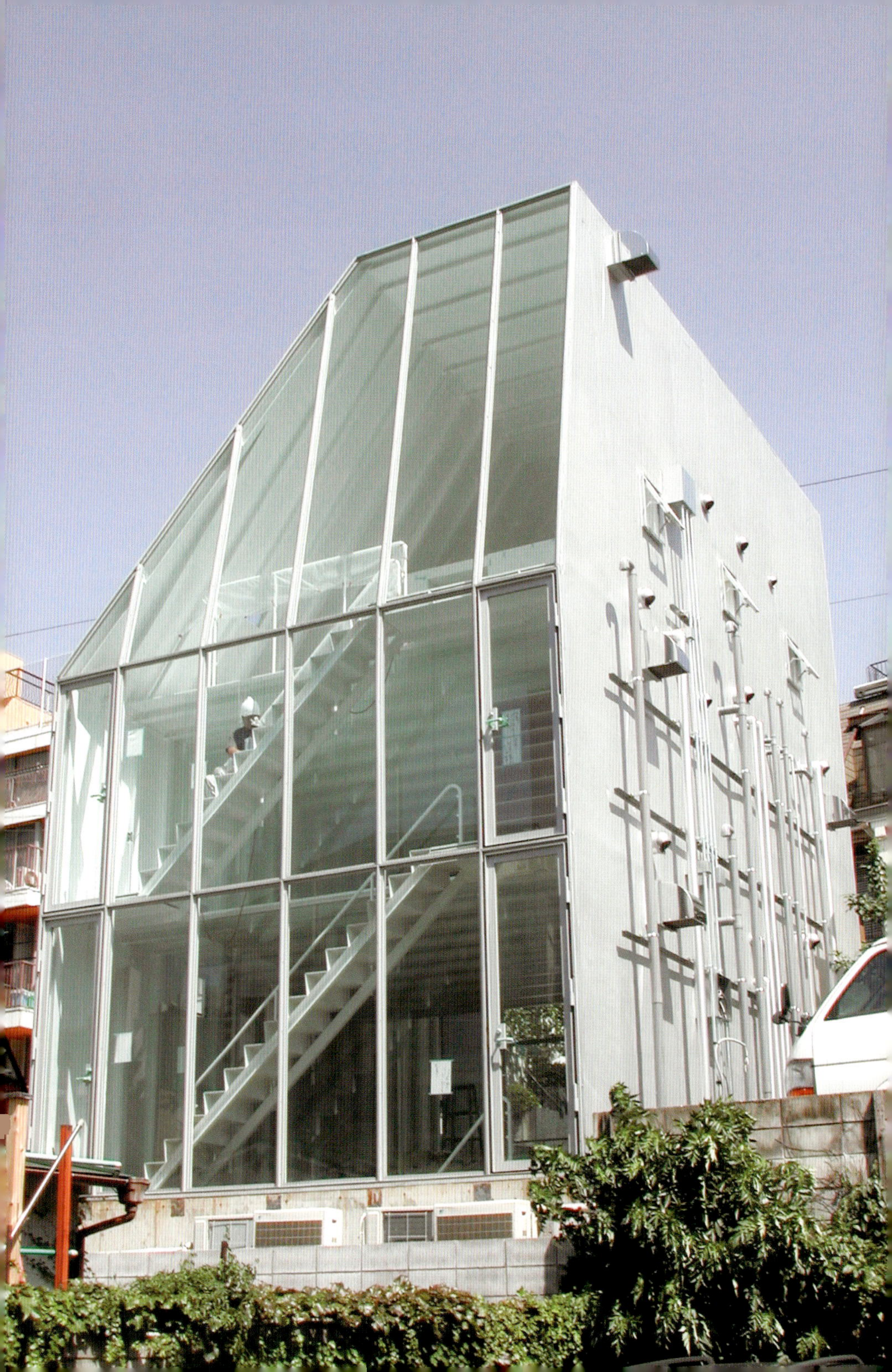

Hounancho "L" condominium

方南町L 2002

The condominium's 5 m-high living rooms are oriented to the south-east. 14 types of living units were interlocked to respond to the complexity of the urban site.

天井高5mをリビングに確保した分譲マンション。
南西二方向に開かれた複雑な条件の敷地に、高低様々なボリュームが14タイプ組み合わされている。

17

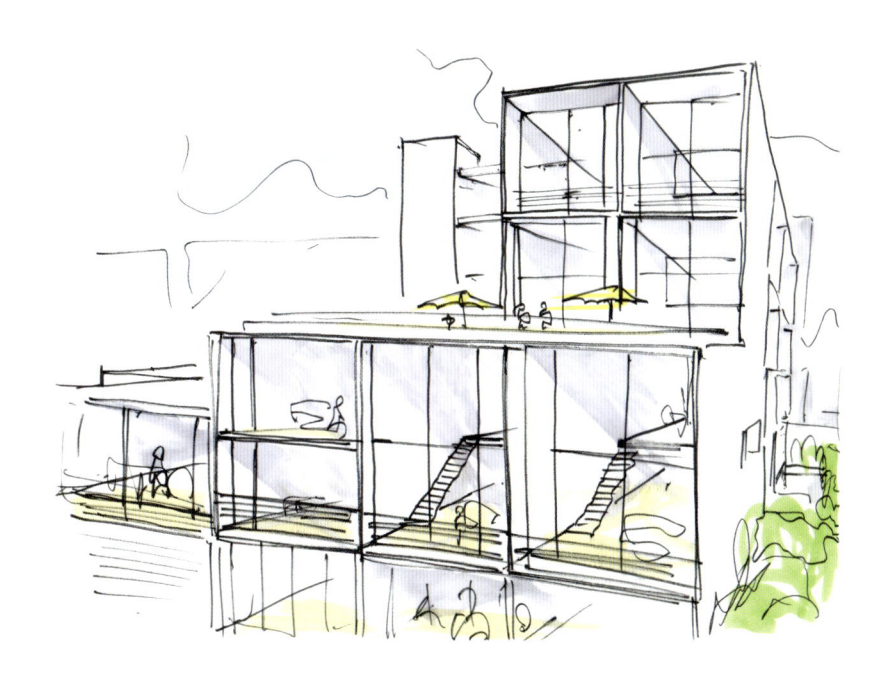

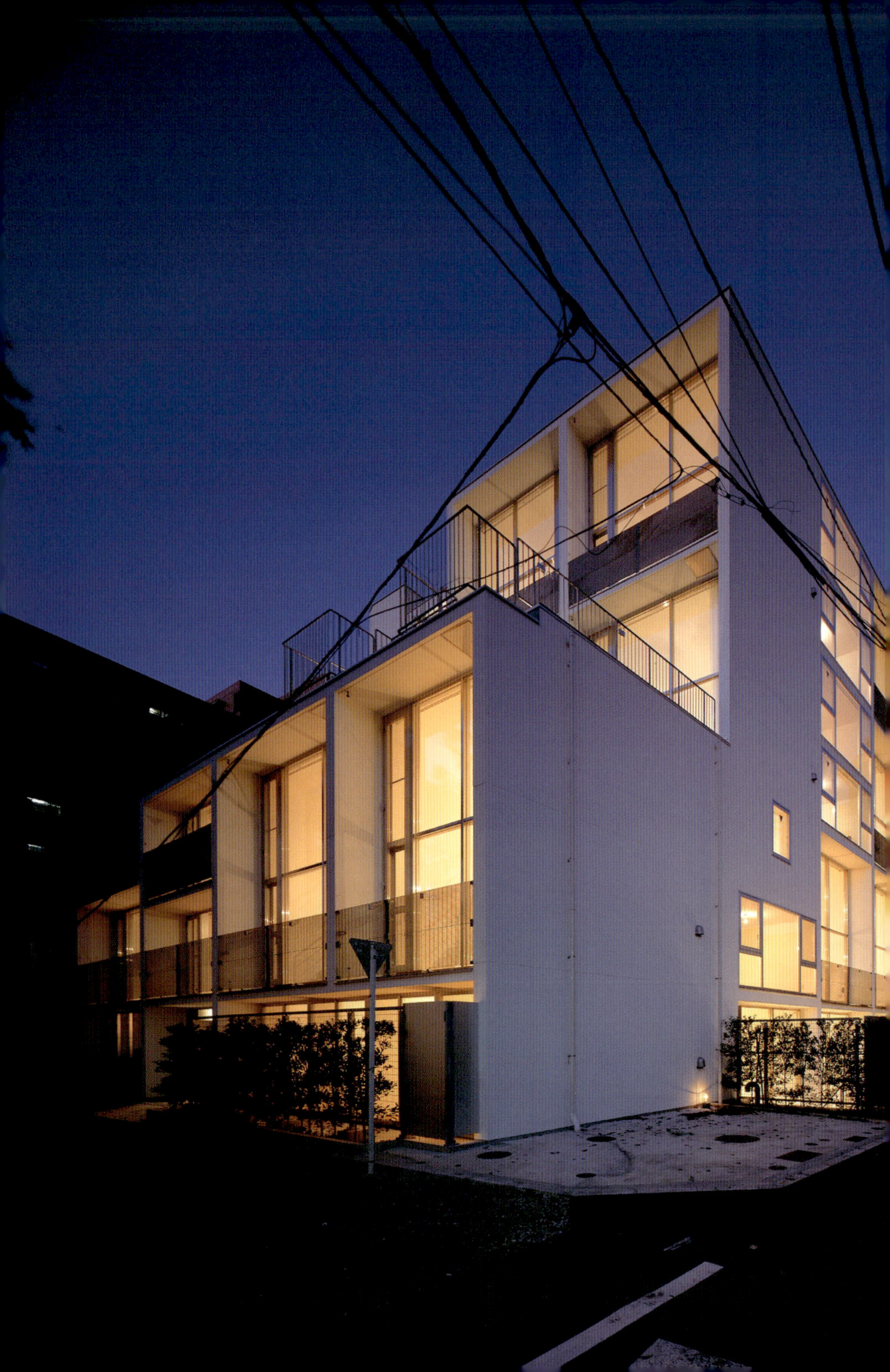

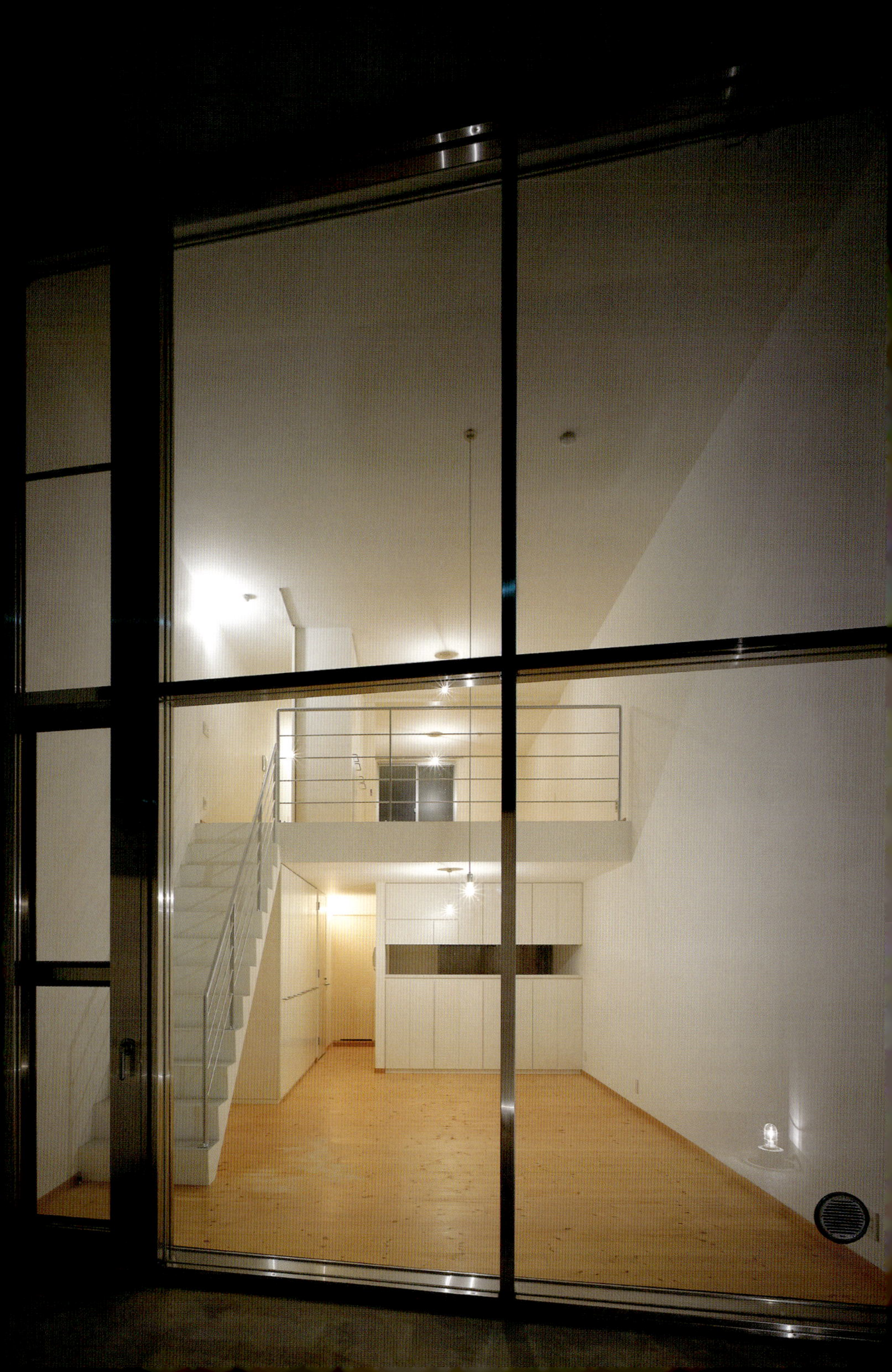

1F 1/500

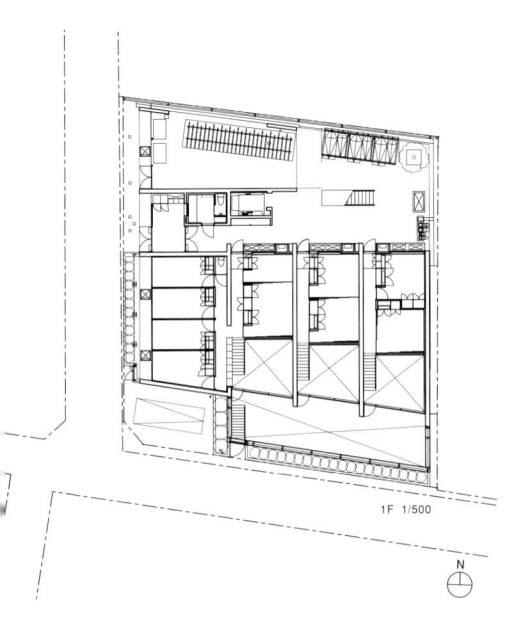

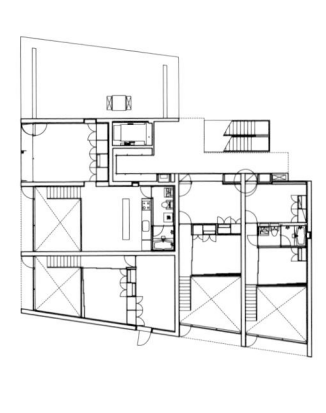

3F 1/500

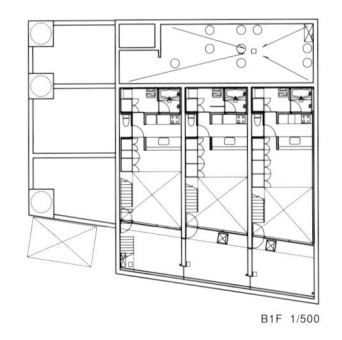

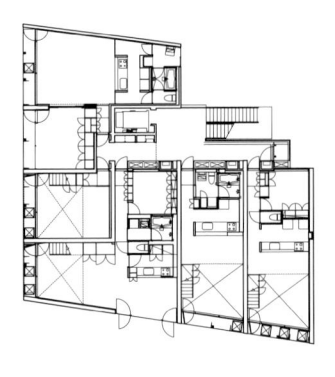

B1F 1/500

2F 1/500

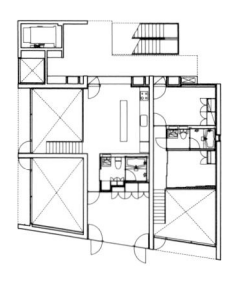

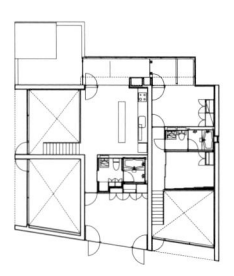

5F 1/500

7F 1/500

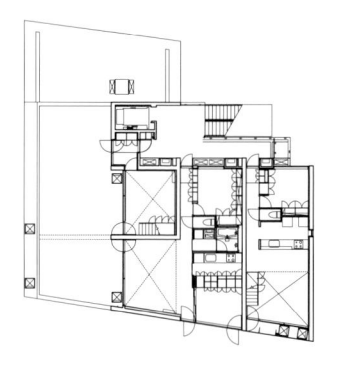

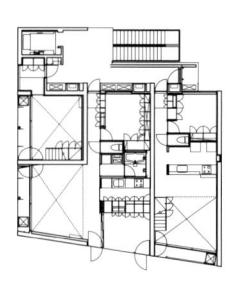

4F 1/500

6F 1/500

Canopy House

軒の家　2002

The interior space extends out into the open, through a wide surrounding balcony which extends 4m on one side. The canopy allows the sliding windows to remain open even when it rains.

軒とデッキが4m空中に突き出した家。
雨に関係なく何時でも戸を開け放つことができる。

18

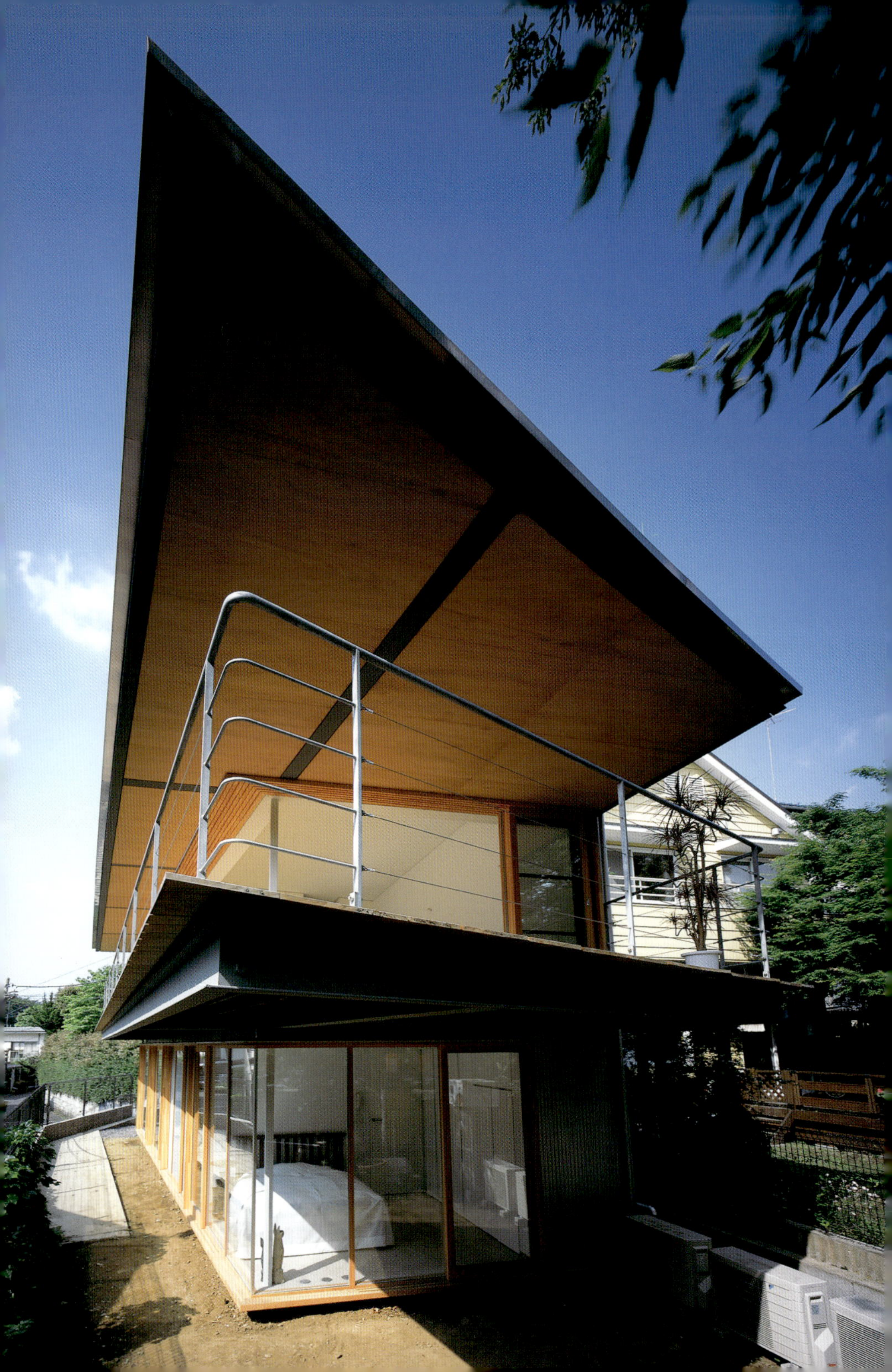

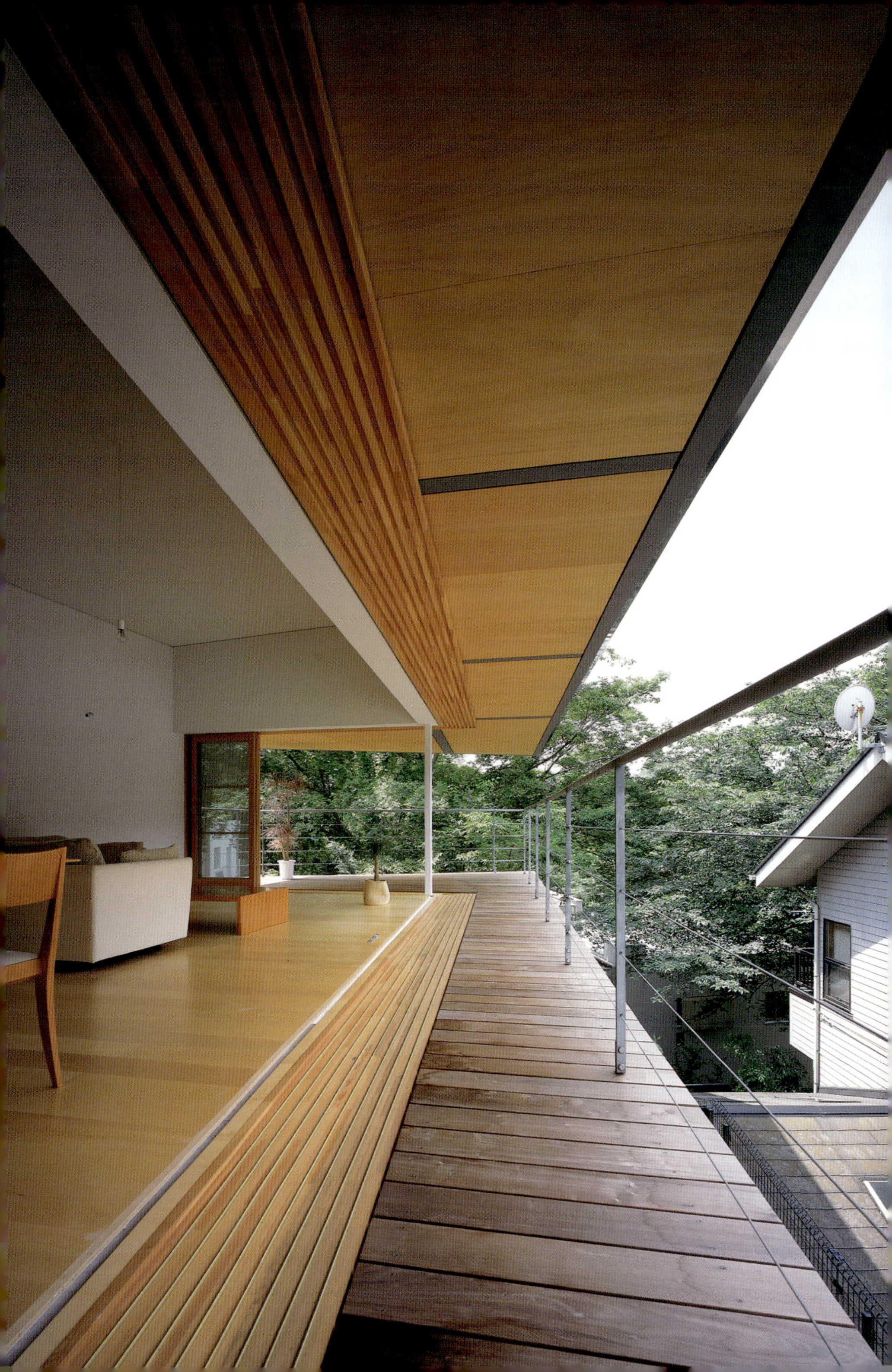

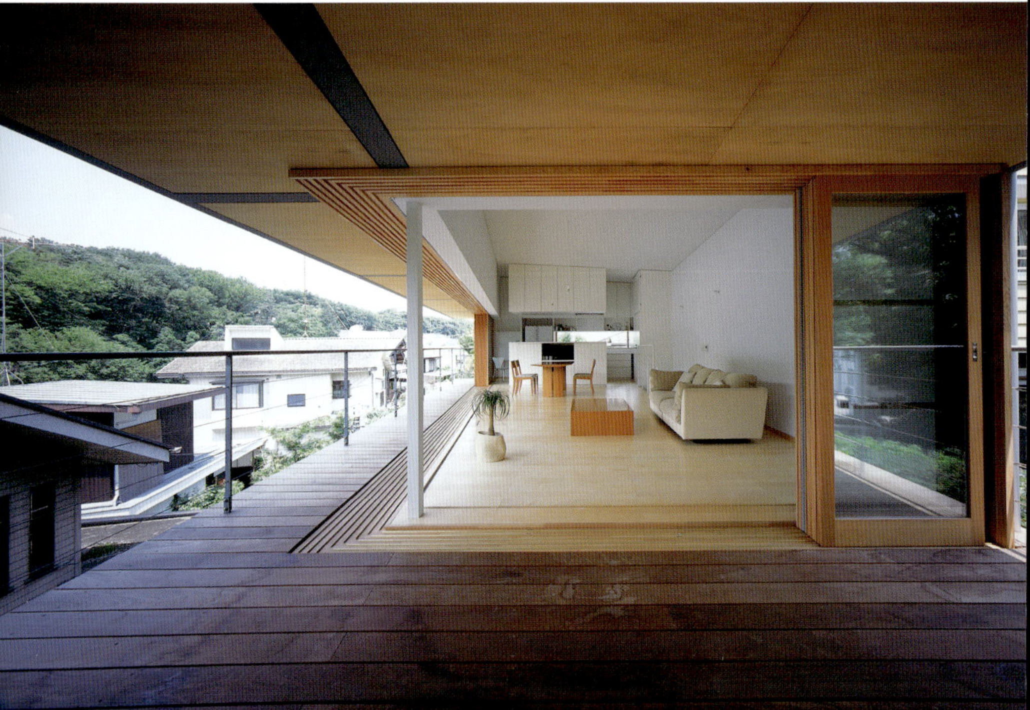

2F 1/200

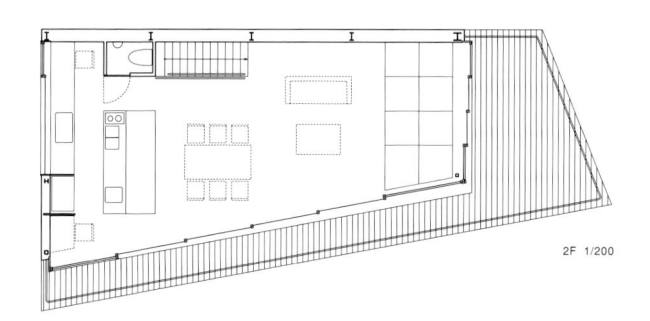

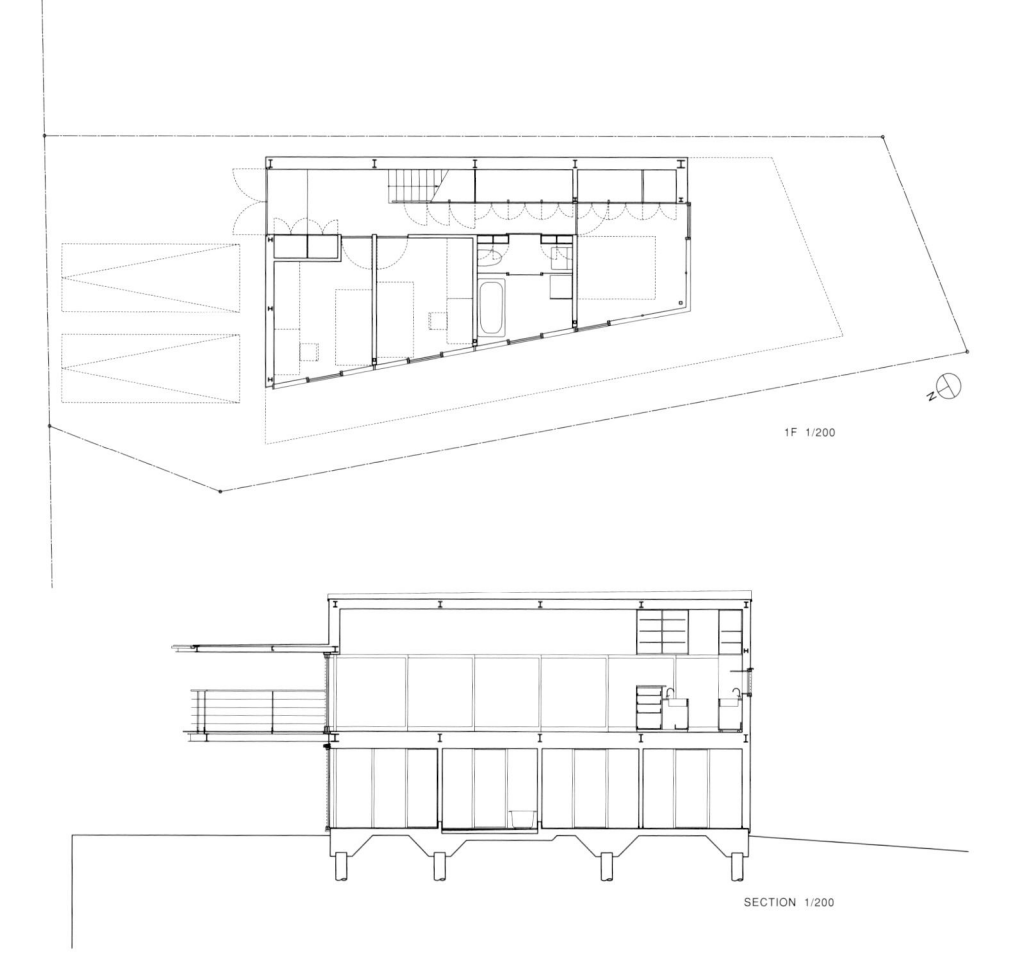

1F 1/200

SECTION 1/200

Saw Roof House

のこぎり屋根の家　2002

The building is stretched over an elongated surface. Its saw-shaped roof captures the southern light through parallel ceiling apertures.

展望が北側に広がる南北に細長い敷地の家。
北側への展望を維持しつつ、屋根面から南の光を採り入れる。

19

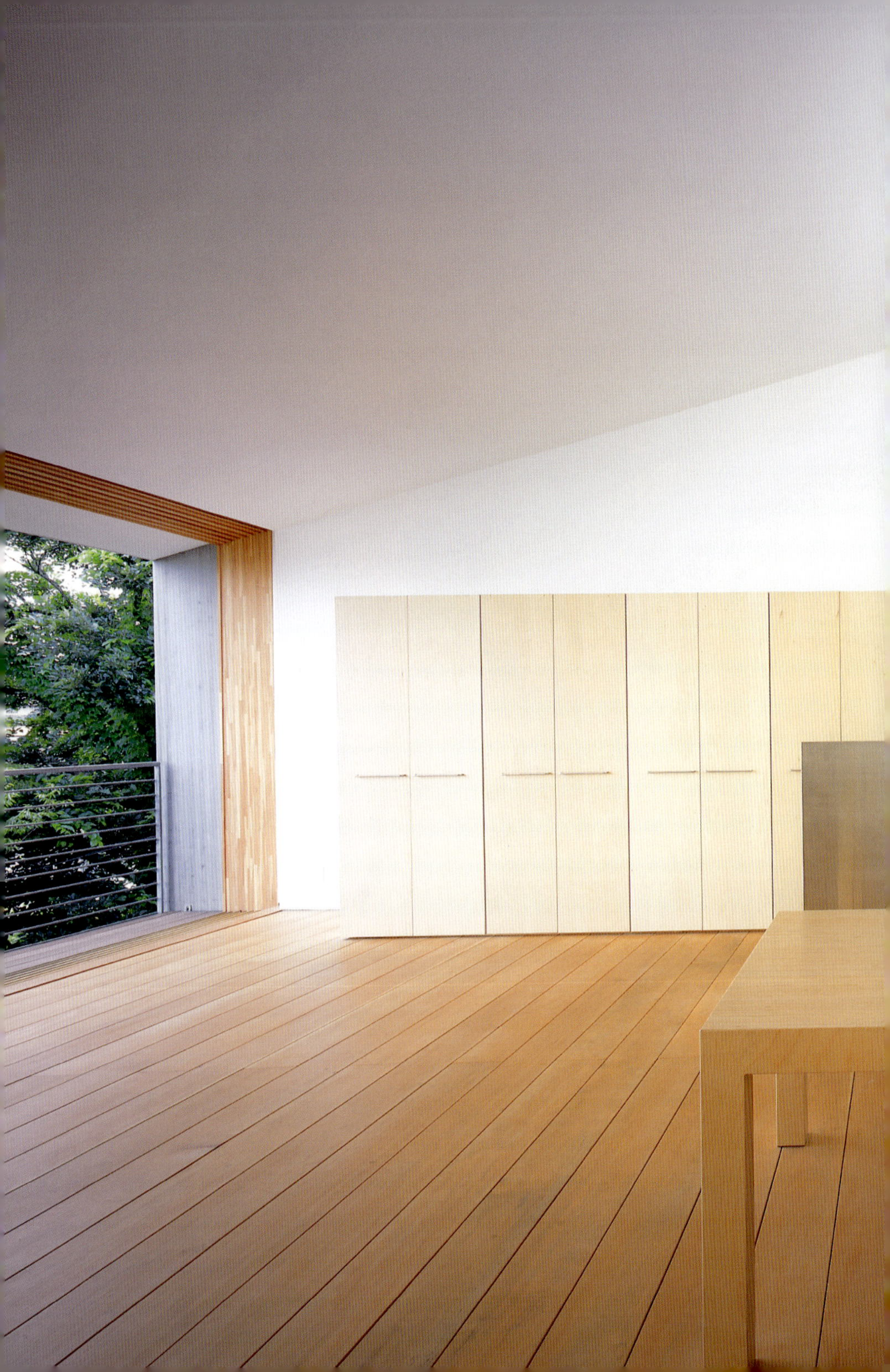

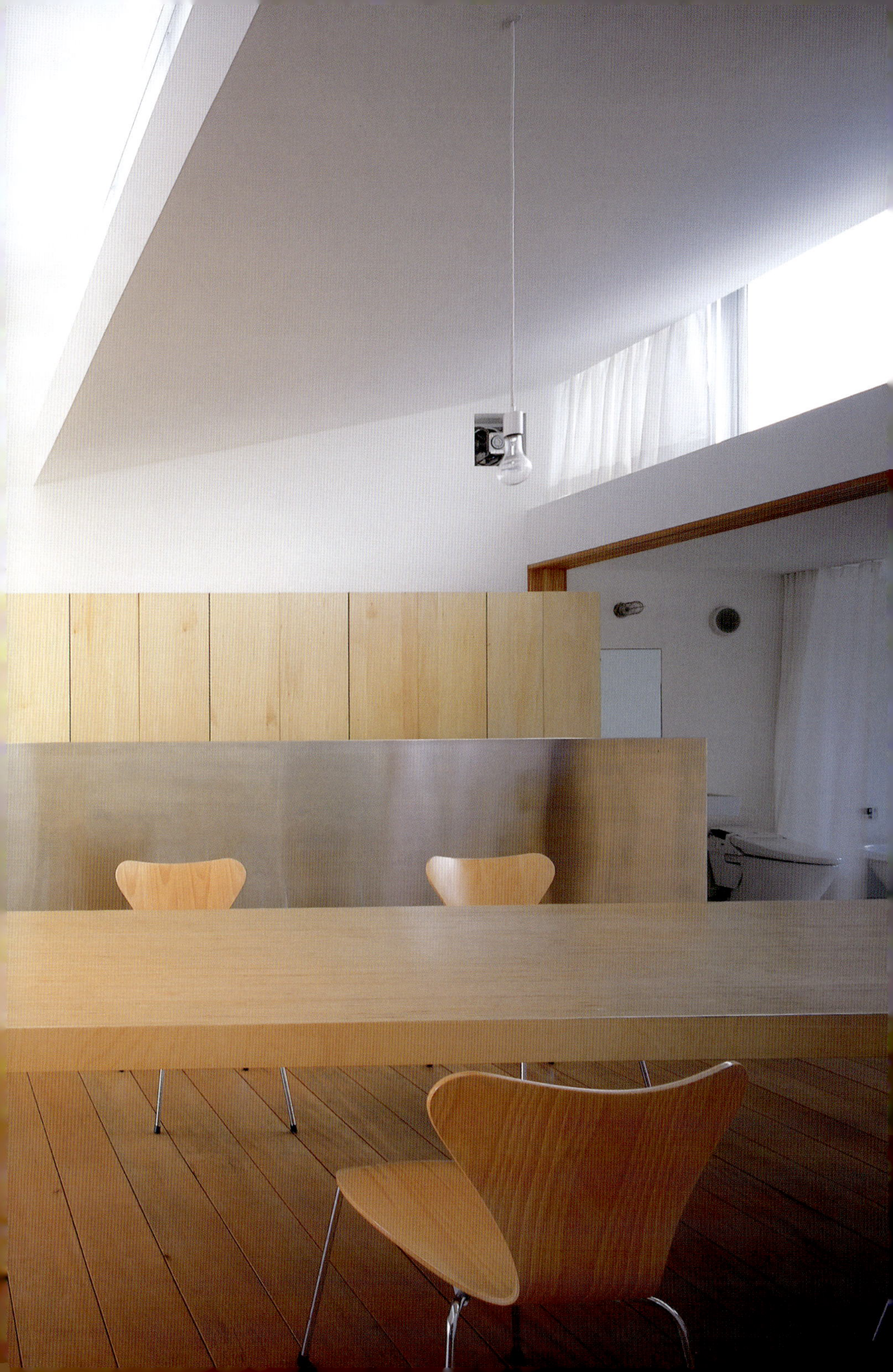

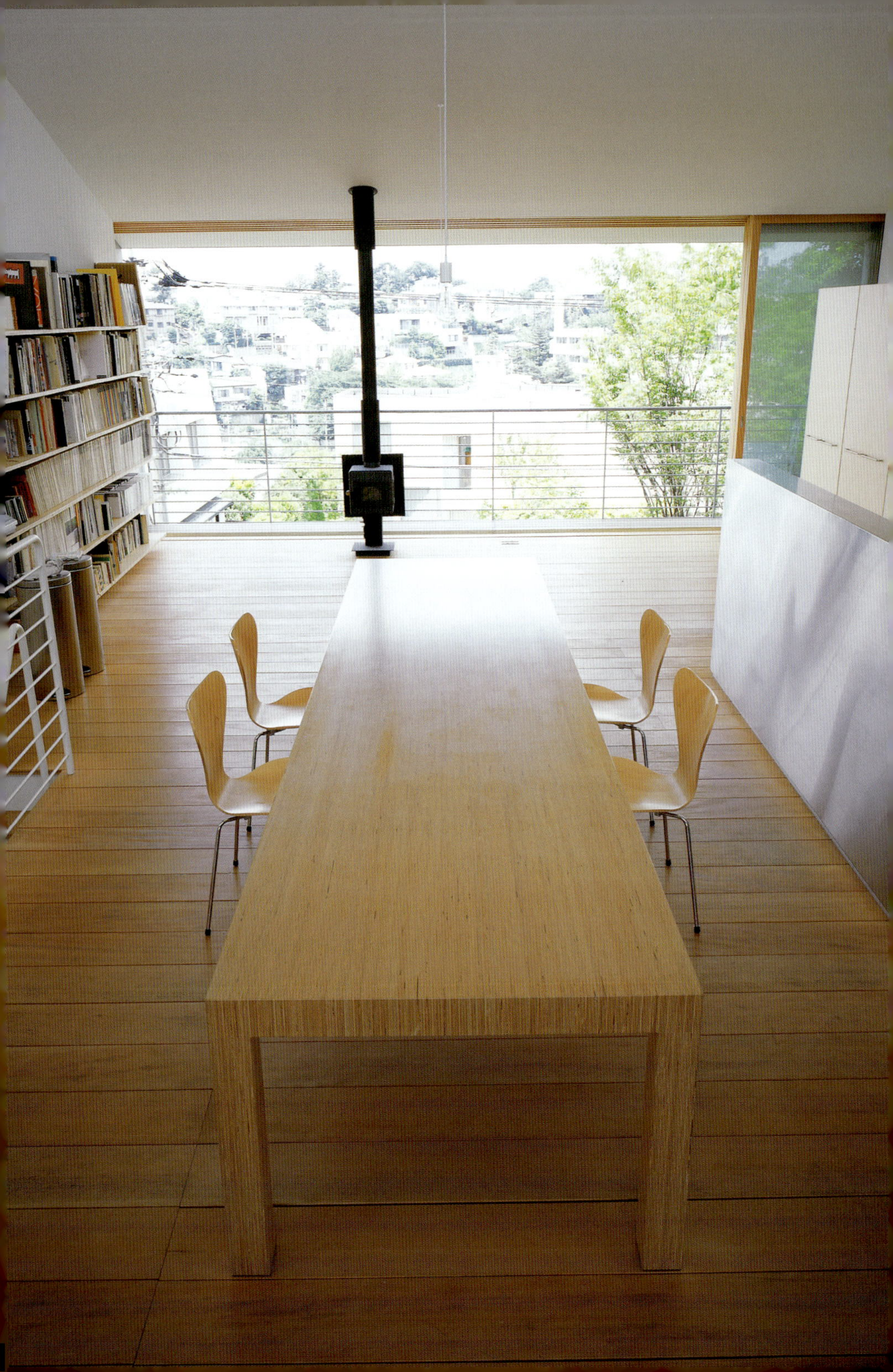

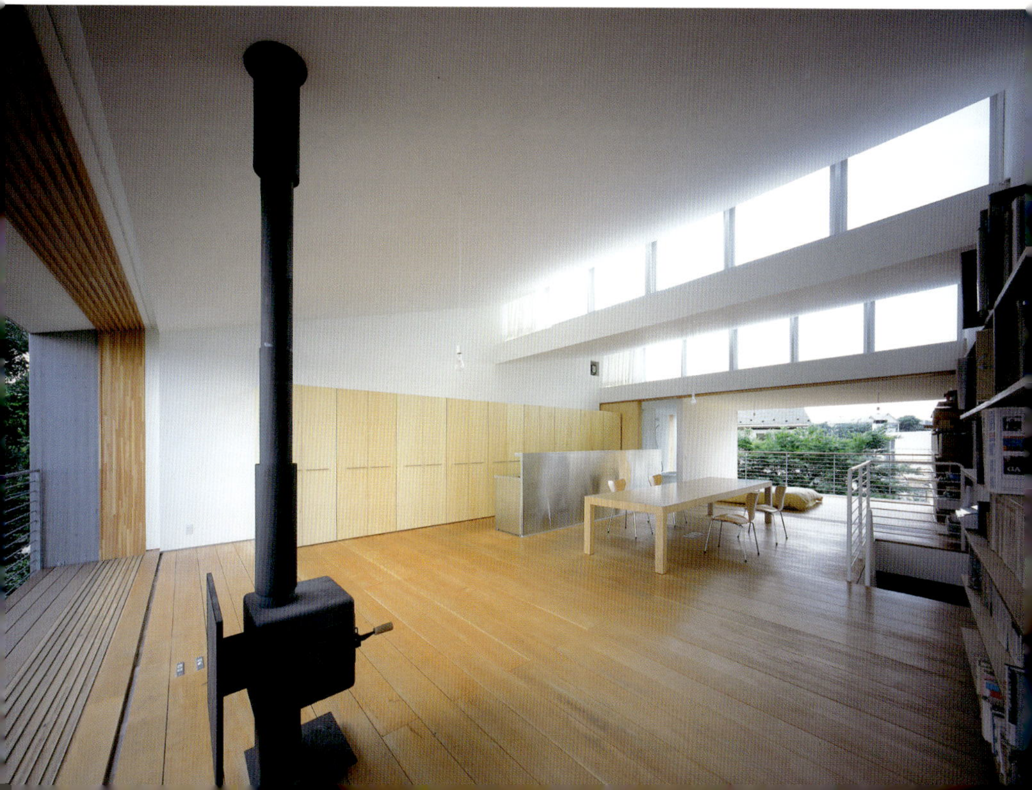

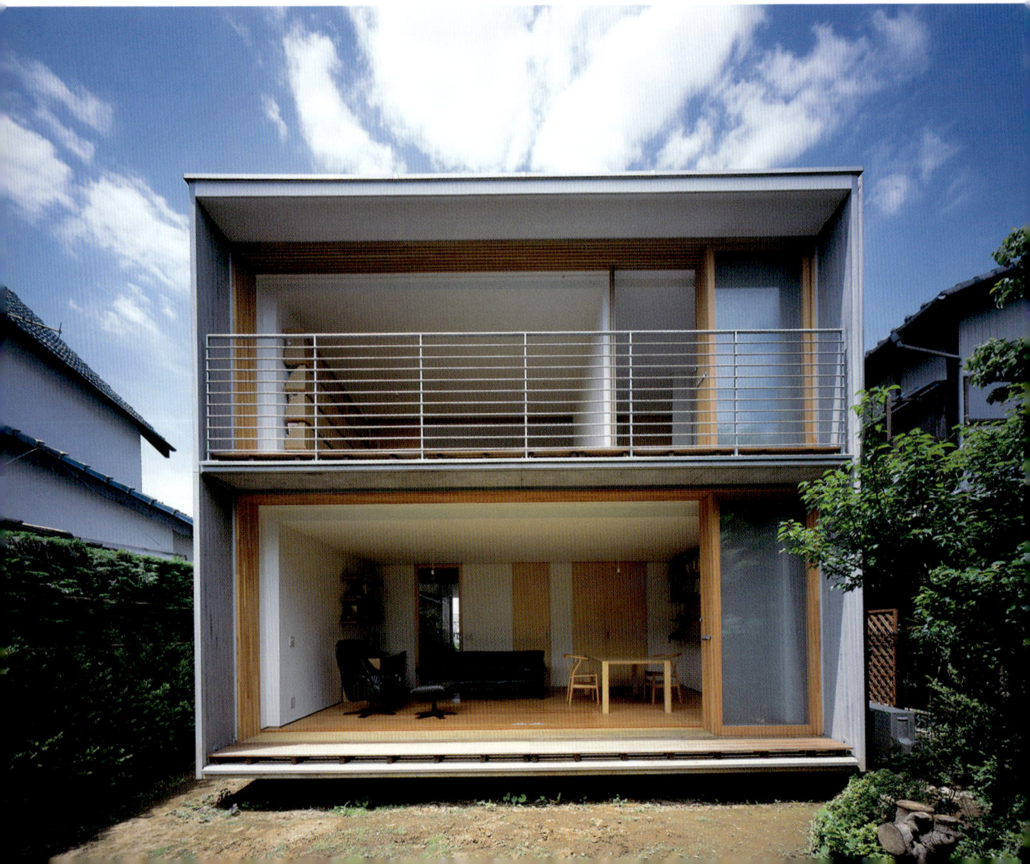

2F 1/250

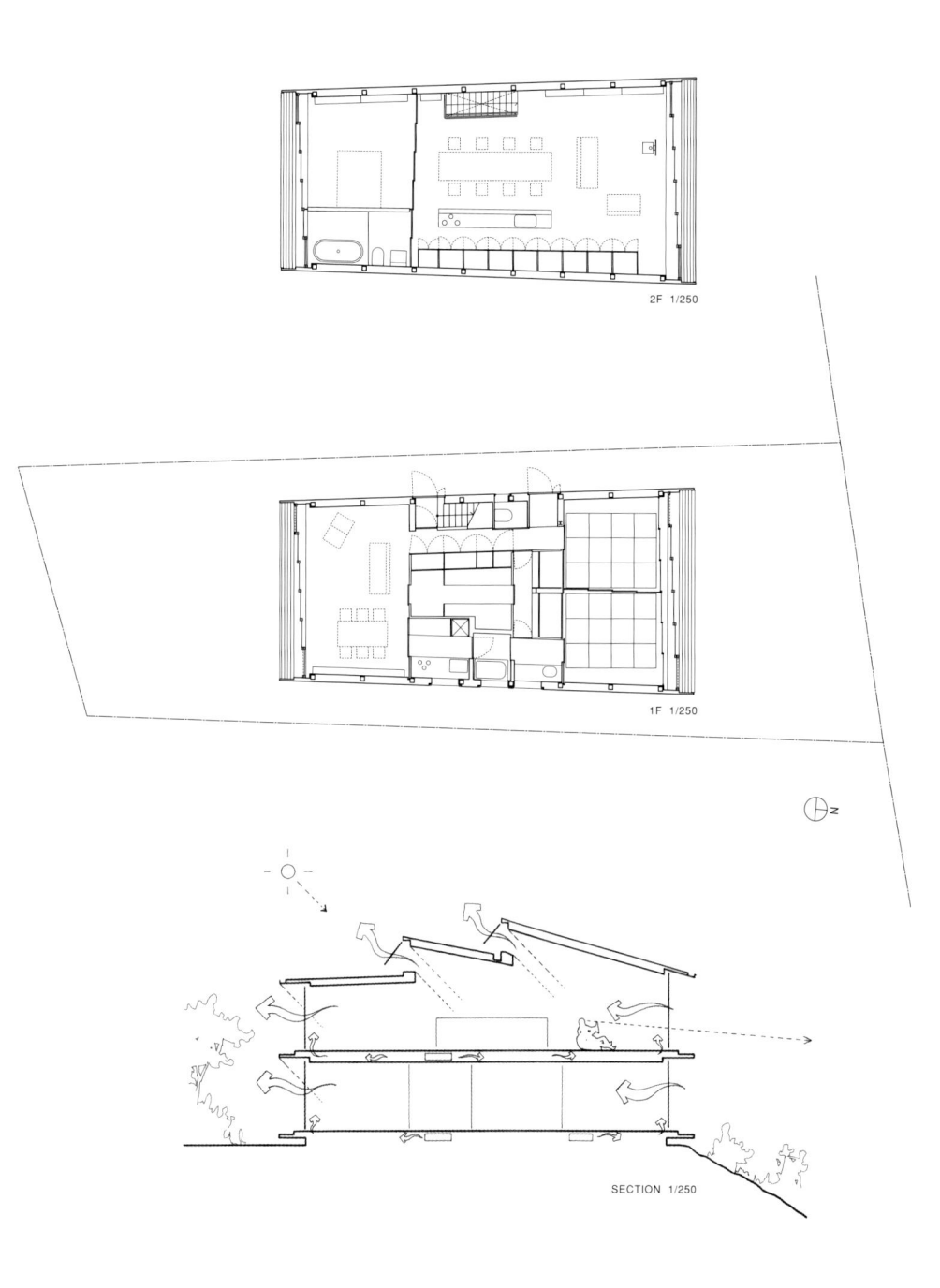

1F 1/250

N

SECTION 1/250

Skylight House

天窓の家　2003

The house faces north, and is surrounded by other residences on three sides. The interior was designed as a single volume, with a generous skylight along the roofline toward the south. The north facade's folding window panels can be opened completely.

三方を隣家に囲まれた北向きの家。
ルーフラインと一体となった大きな天窓のあるワンルーム空間。
北側の窓は折戸になっていて100％開く。

20

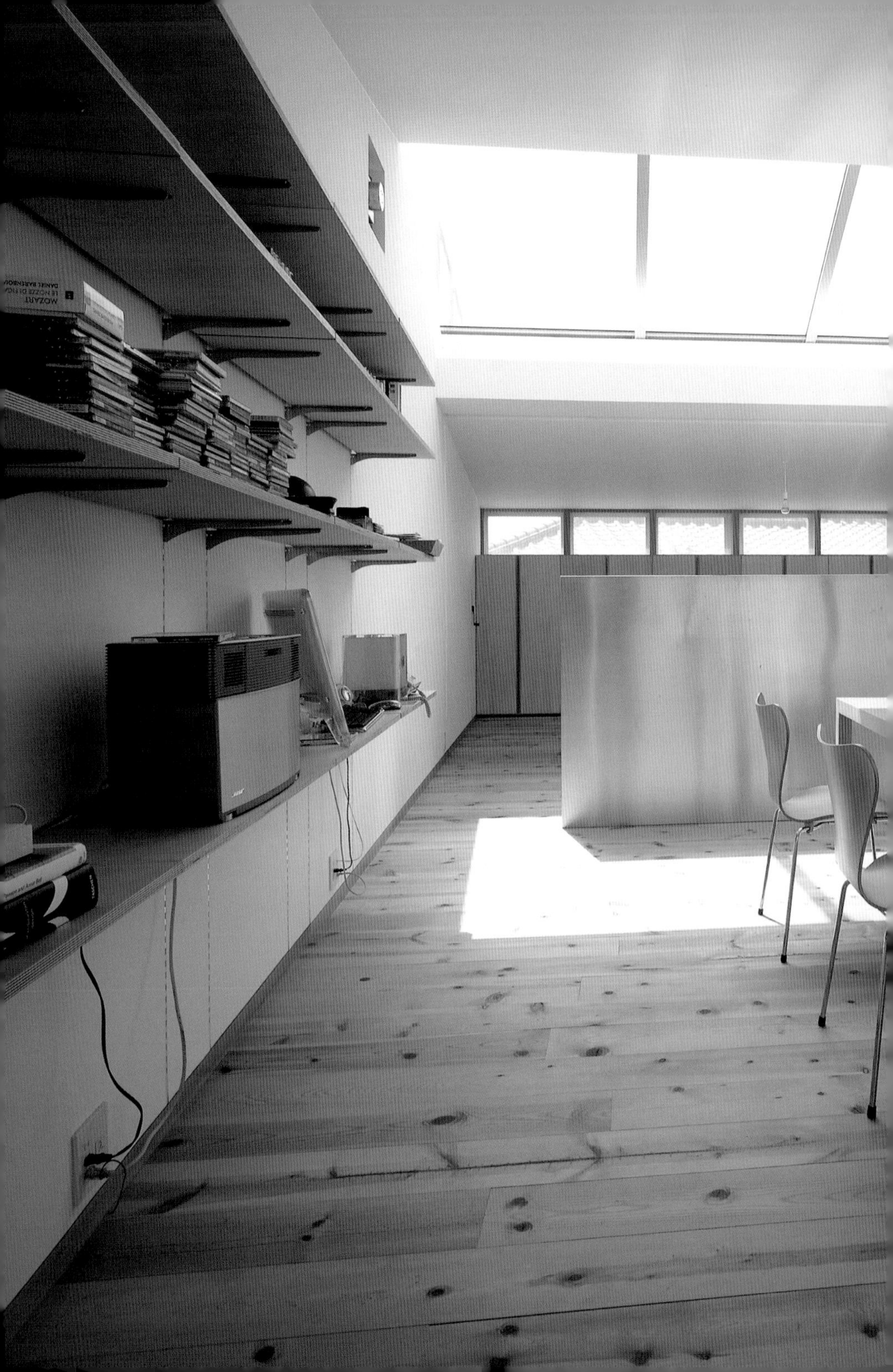

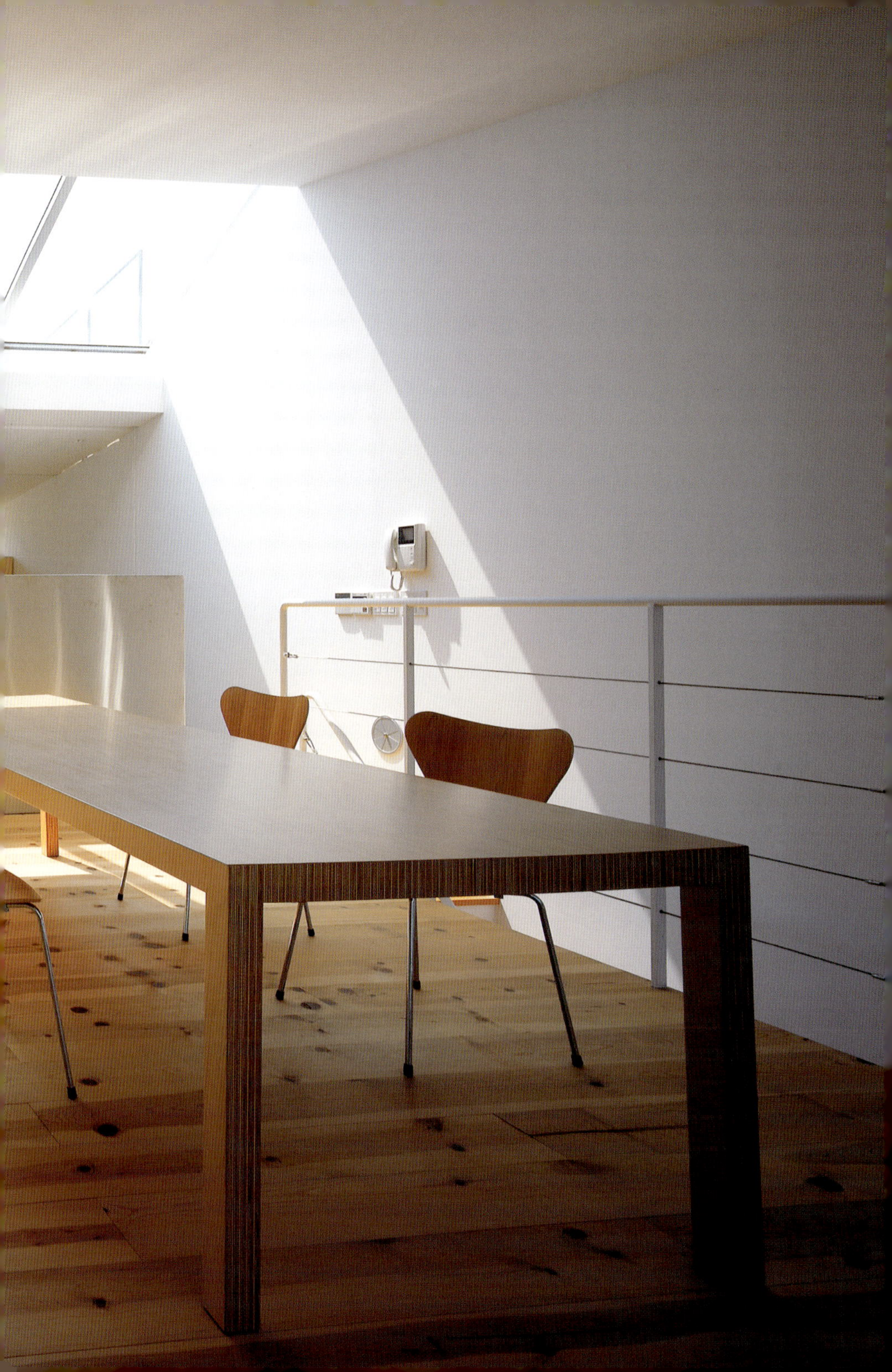

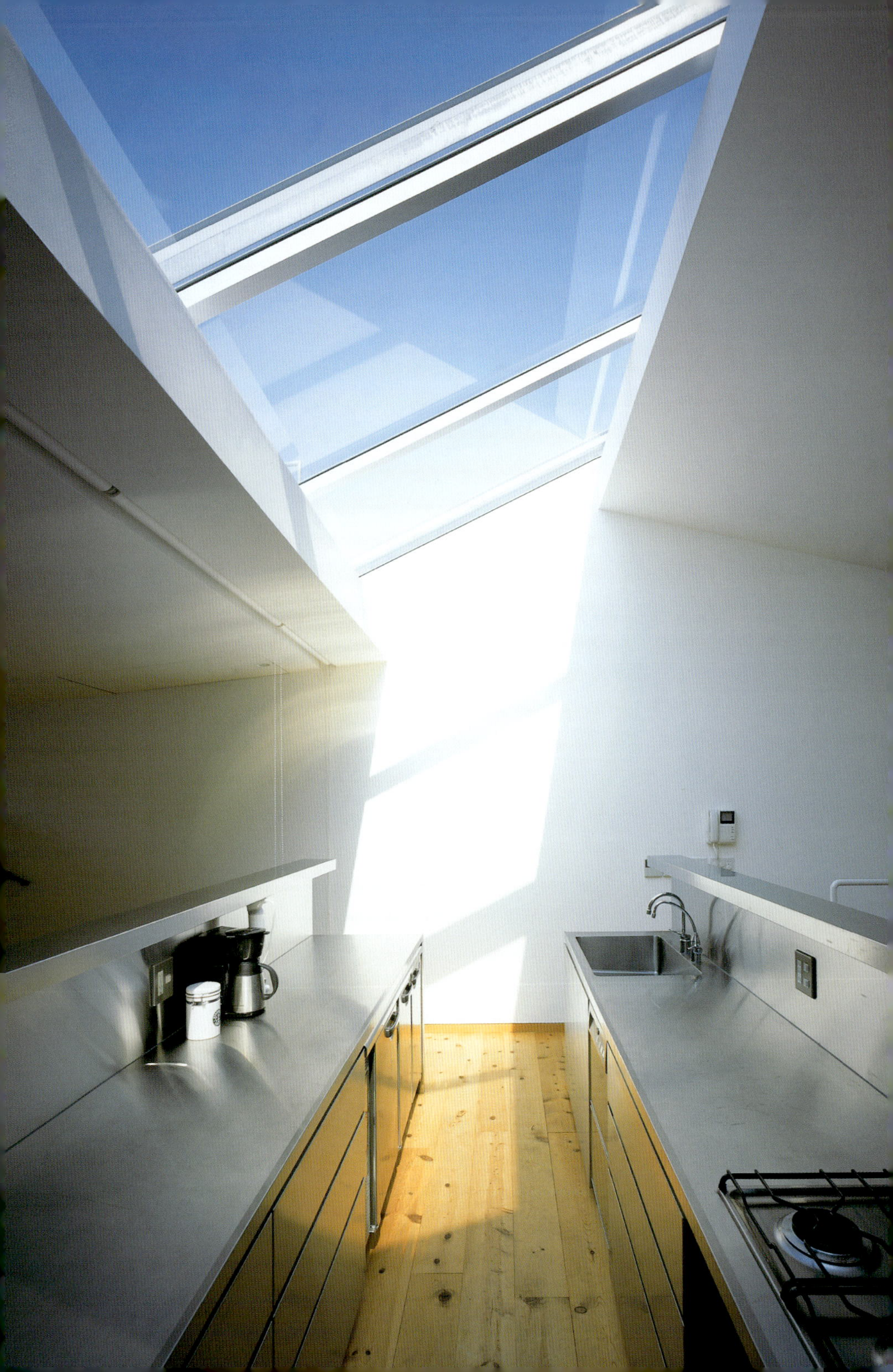

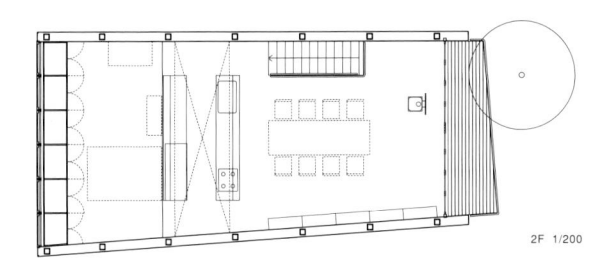

2F 1/200

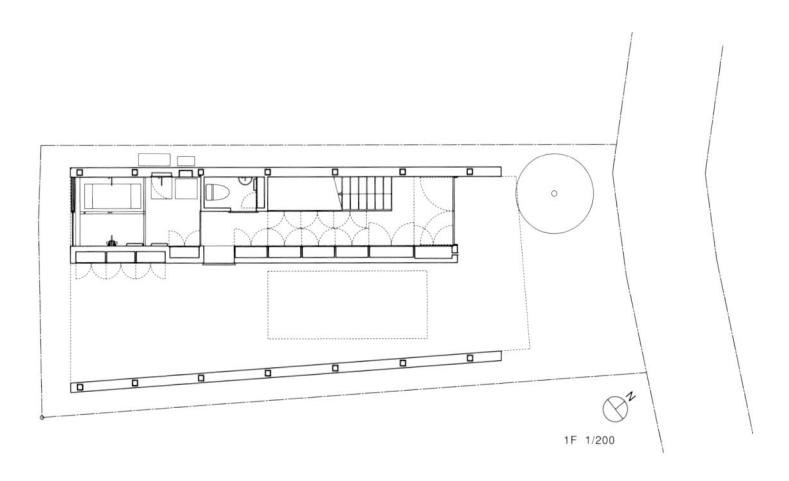

1F 1/200

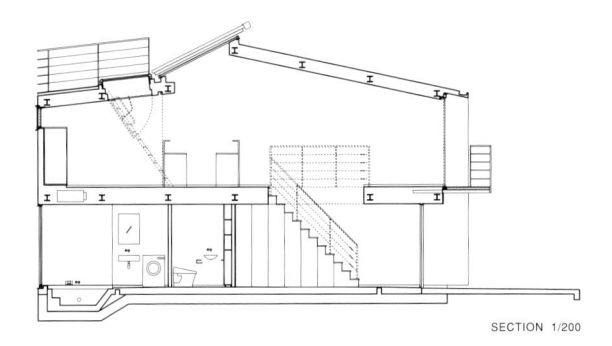

SECTION 1/200

House to Catch the Sky III

空を捕まえる家Ⅲ　2003

The house was designed as a simple rectangular box.
The core lies across the center, under a generous skylight.

四角い単純な箱に、コアを落とし込んで、
その高低差を天窓に利用した家。

21

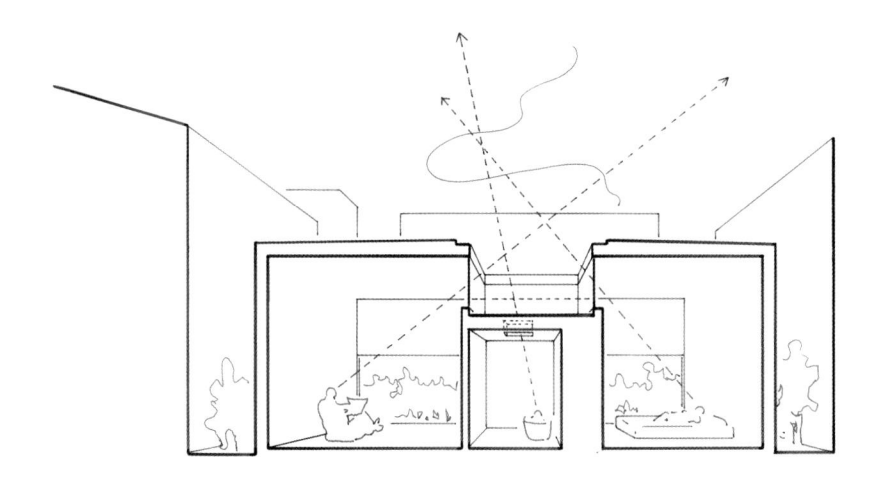

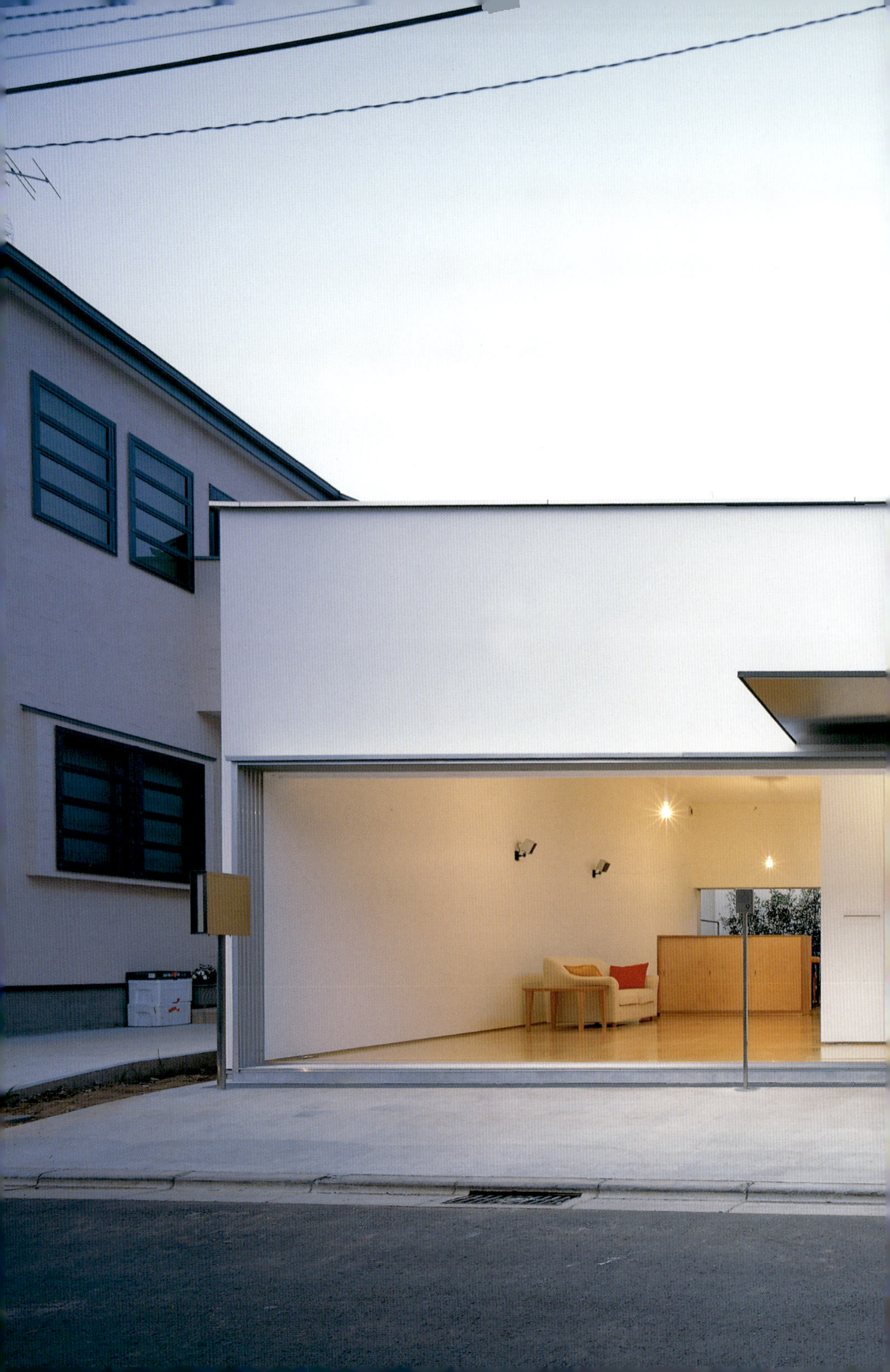

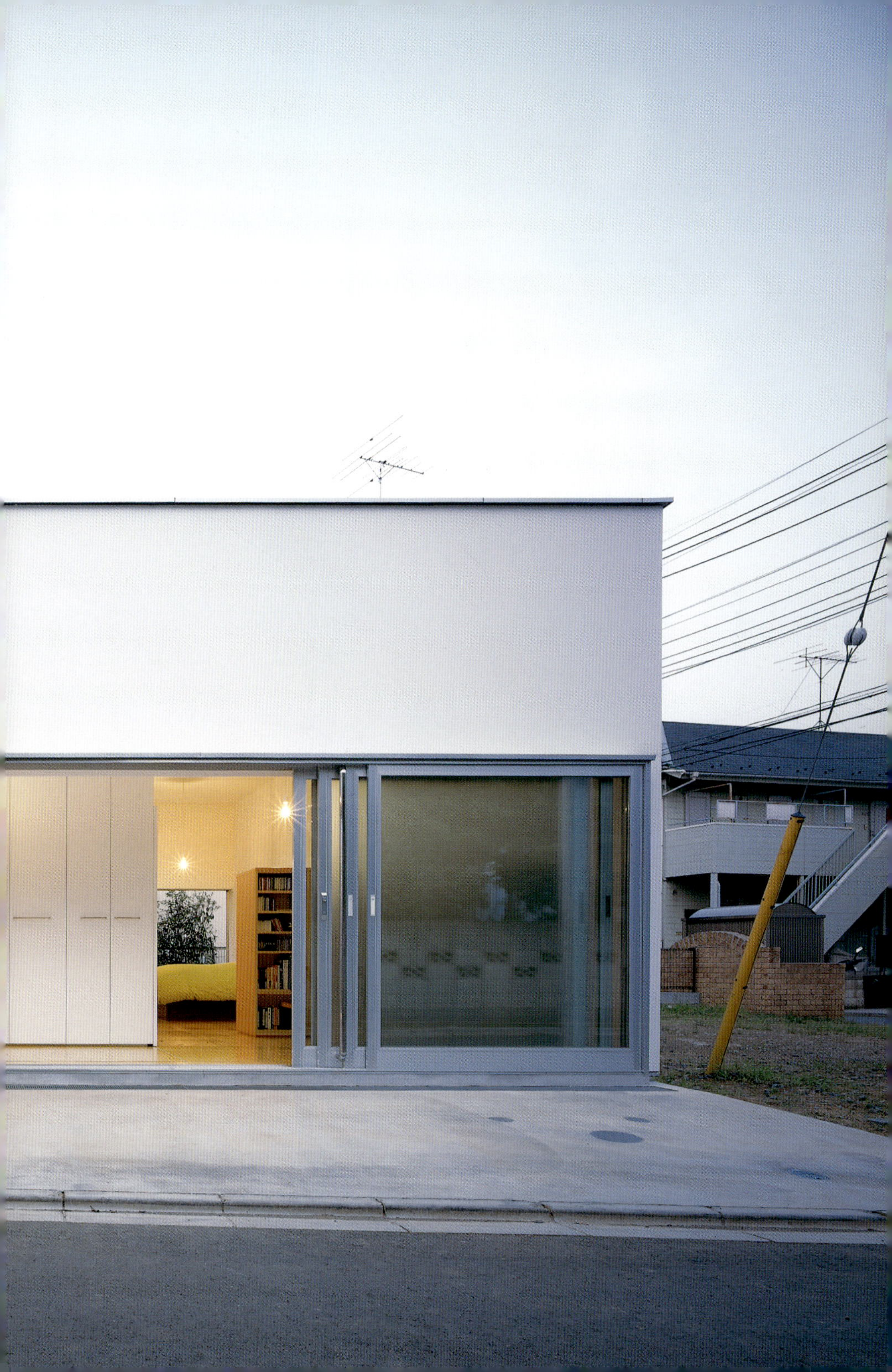

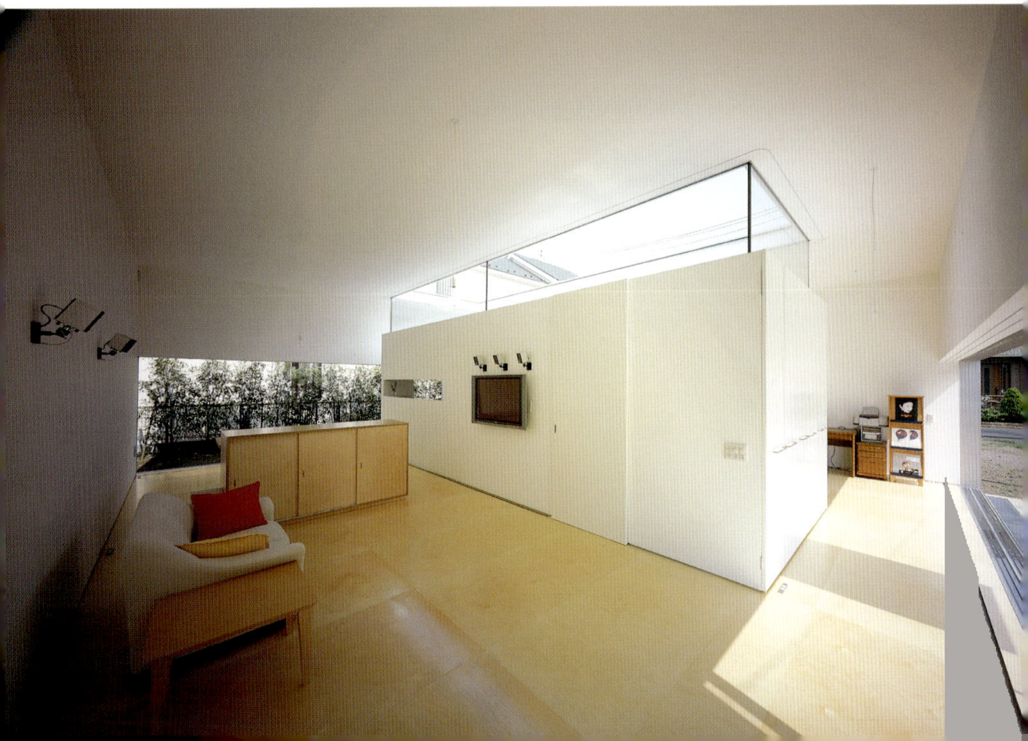

1F 1/150

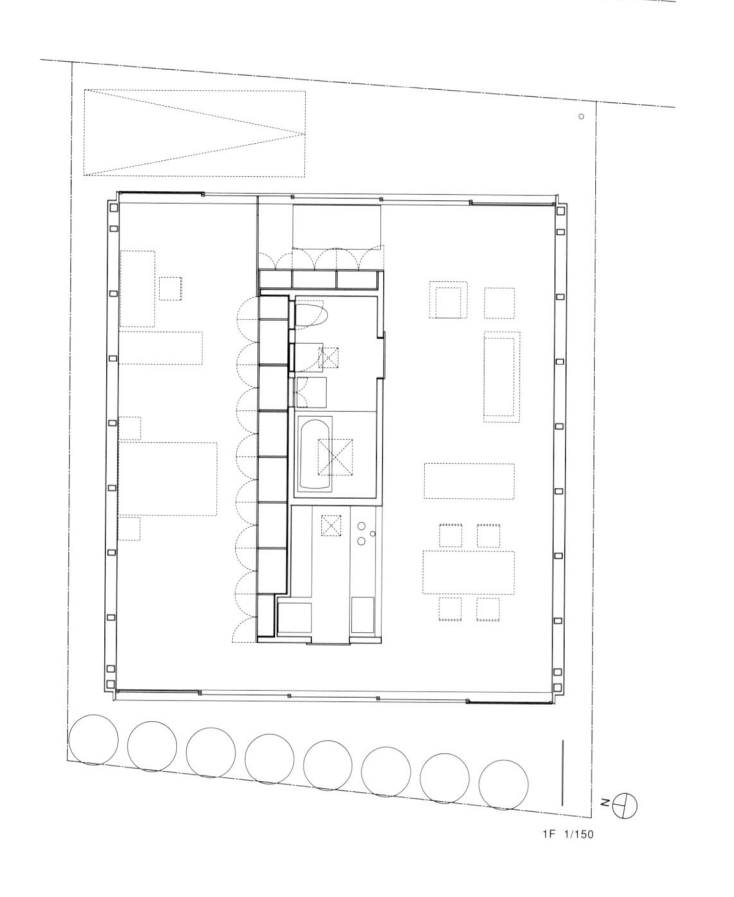

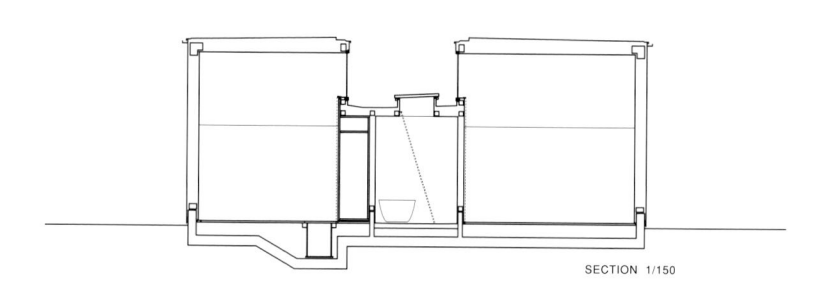

SECTION 1/150

Echigo-Matsunoyama Museum of Natural Science

越後松之山「森の学校」キョロロ　2003

The structure, a 160 m-long Cor-ten steel tube, was designed to resist the pressure brought by accumulated snowfall in the winter (1,500 kg / m^2). Visitors walking through the building can observe large sections of snow through giant acryl windows.

長さ160mのコールテン鋼のチューブ。
深さ5m、1,500Kg/m^{2}の雪荷重に耐える。
大きなアクリル窓を通して、雪の断面を観察できる。

22

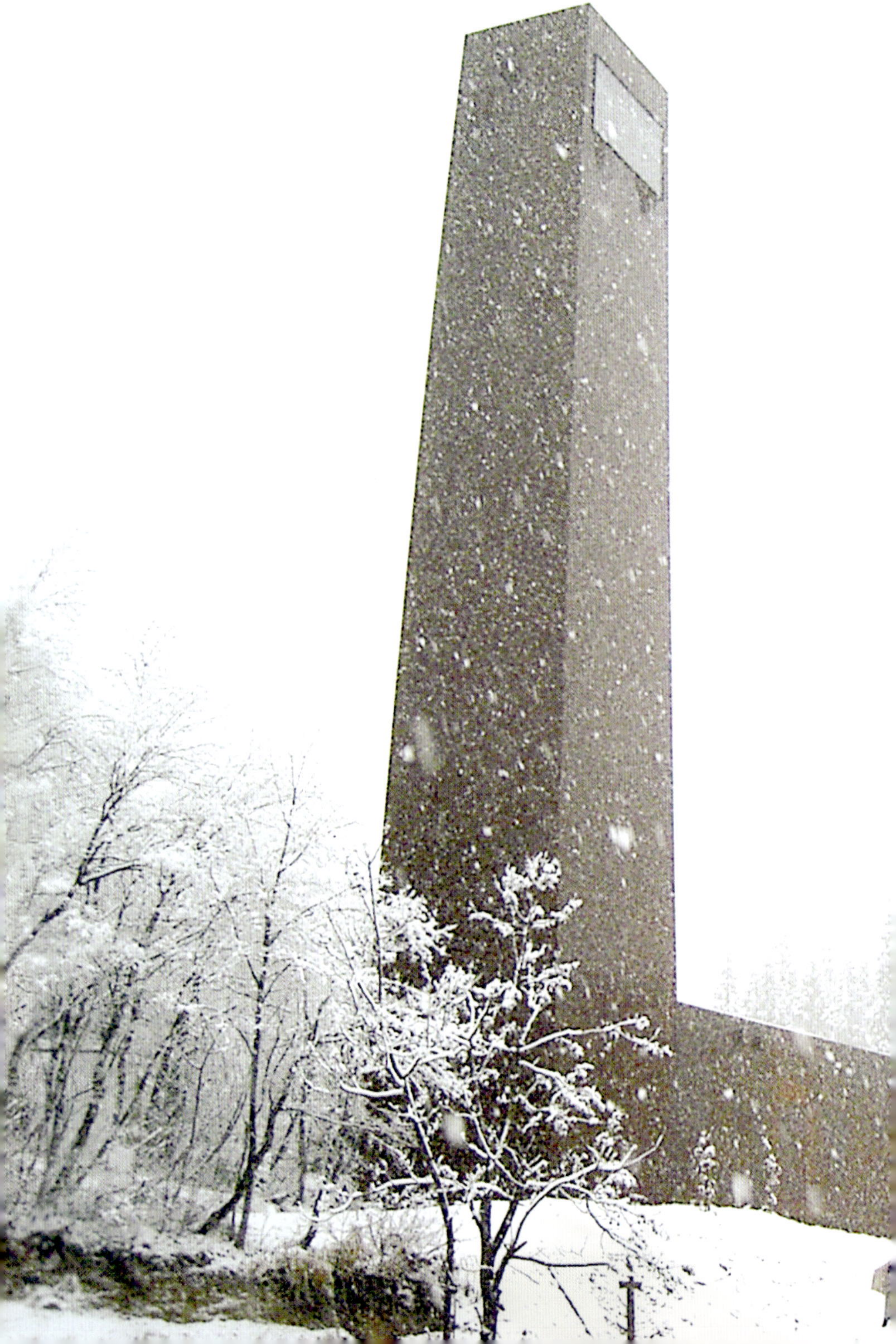

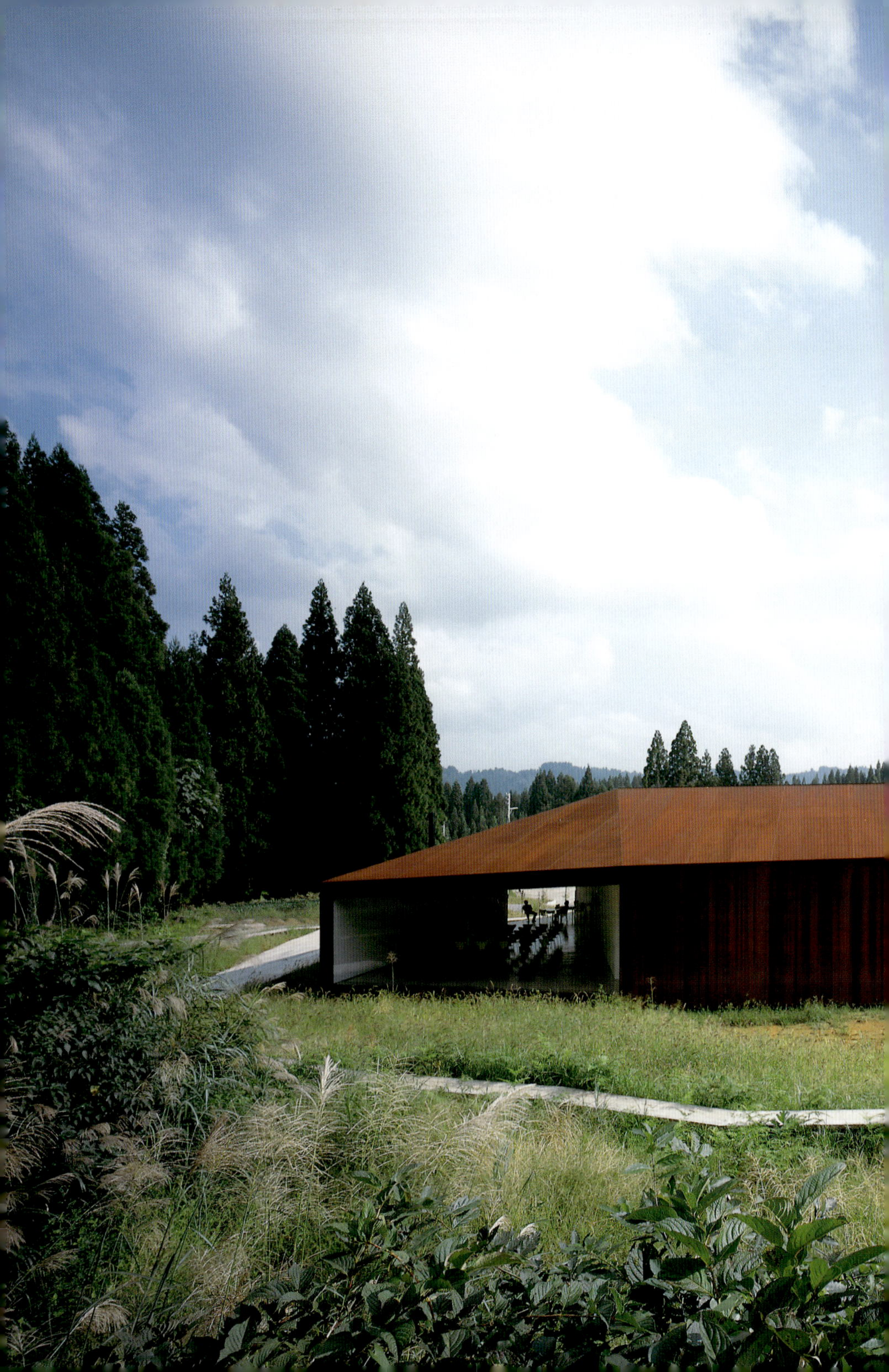

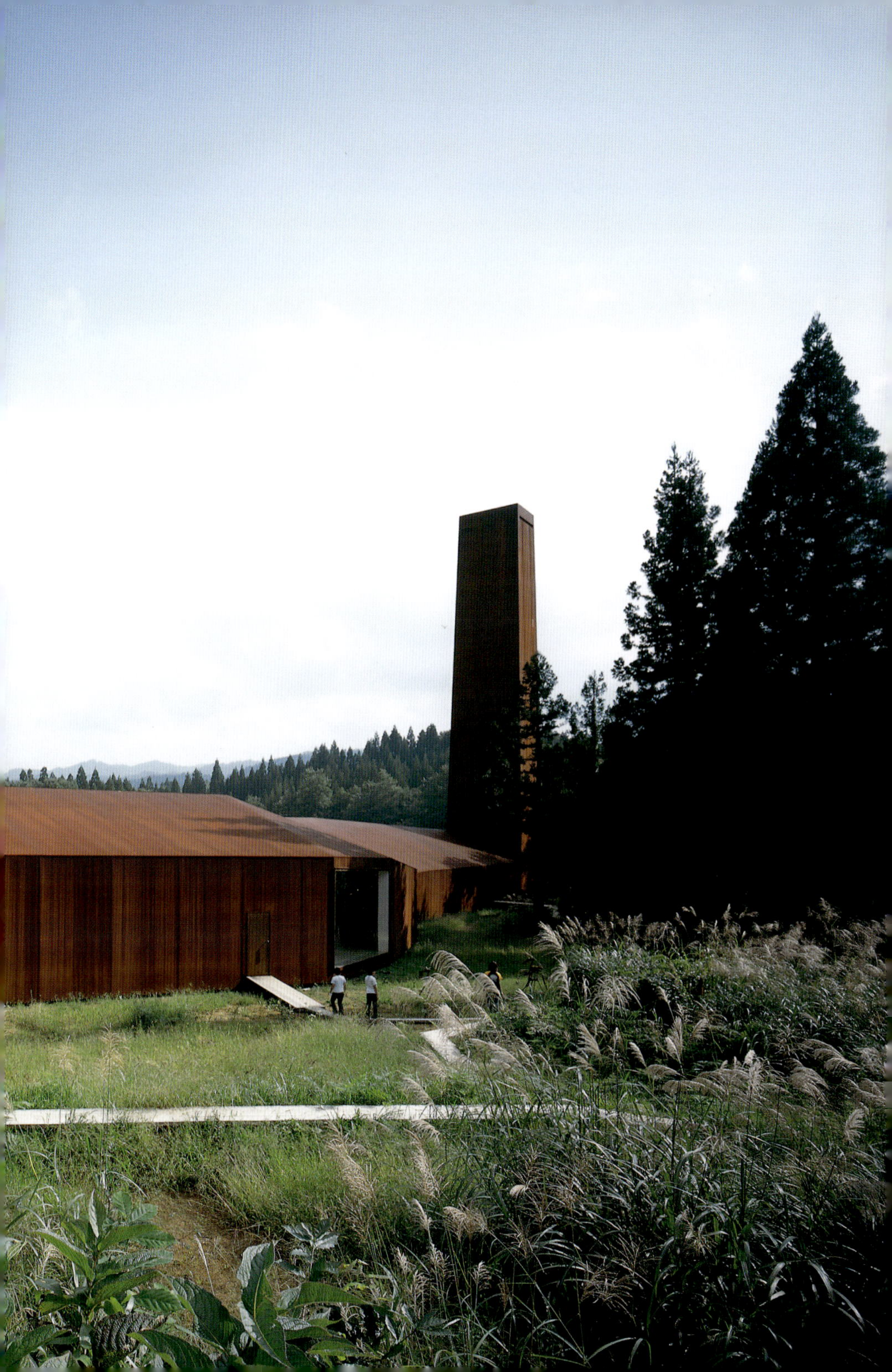

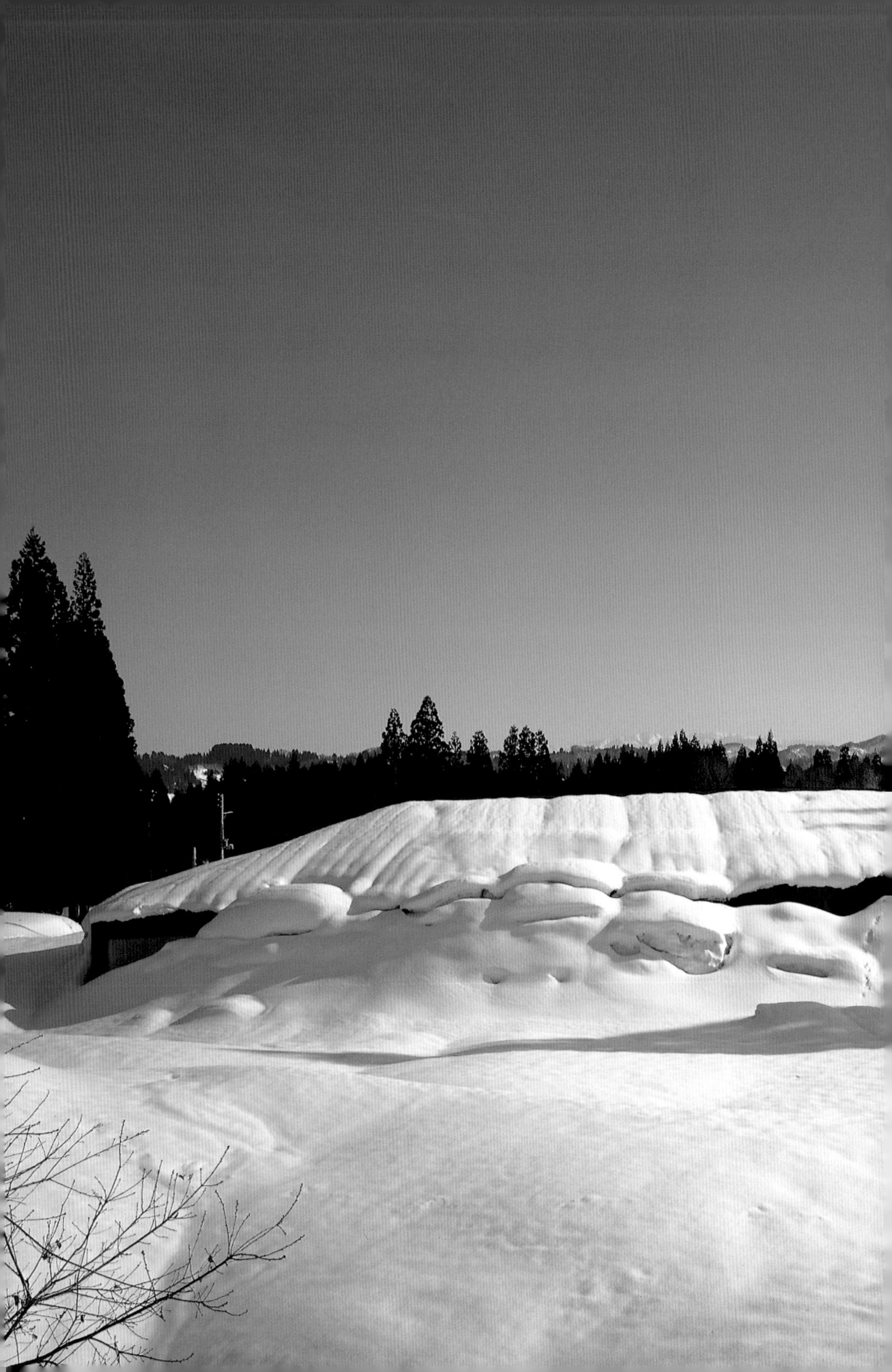

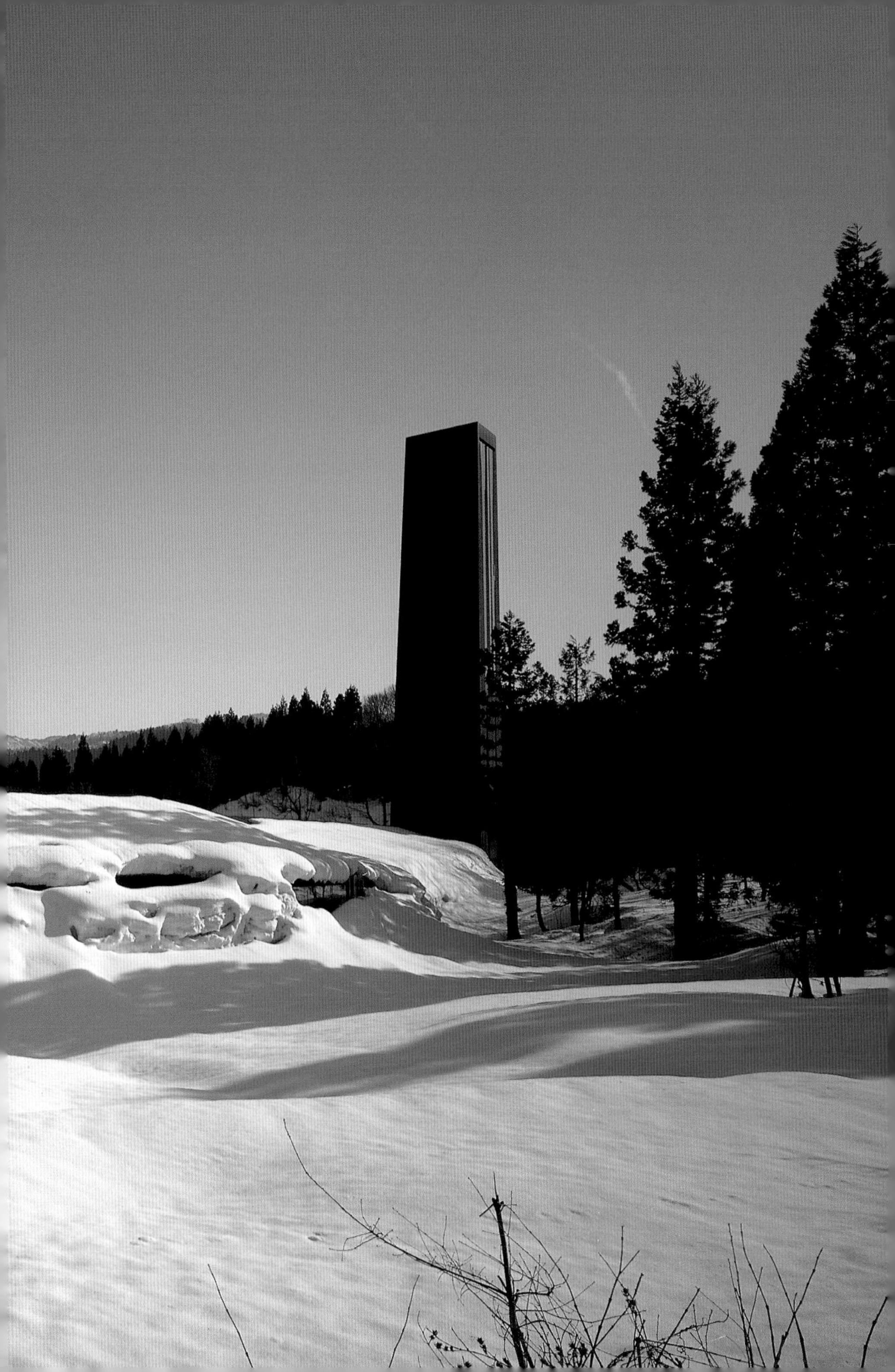

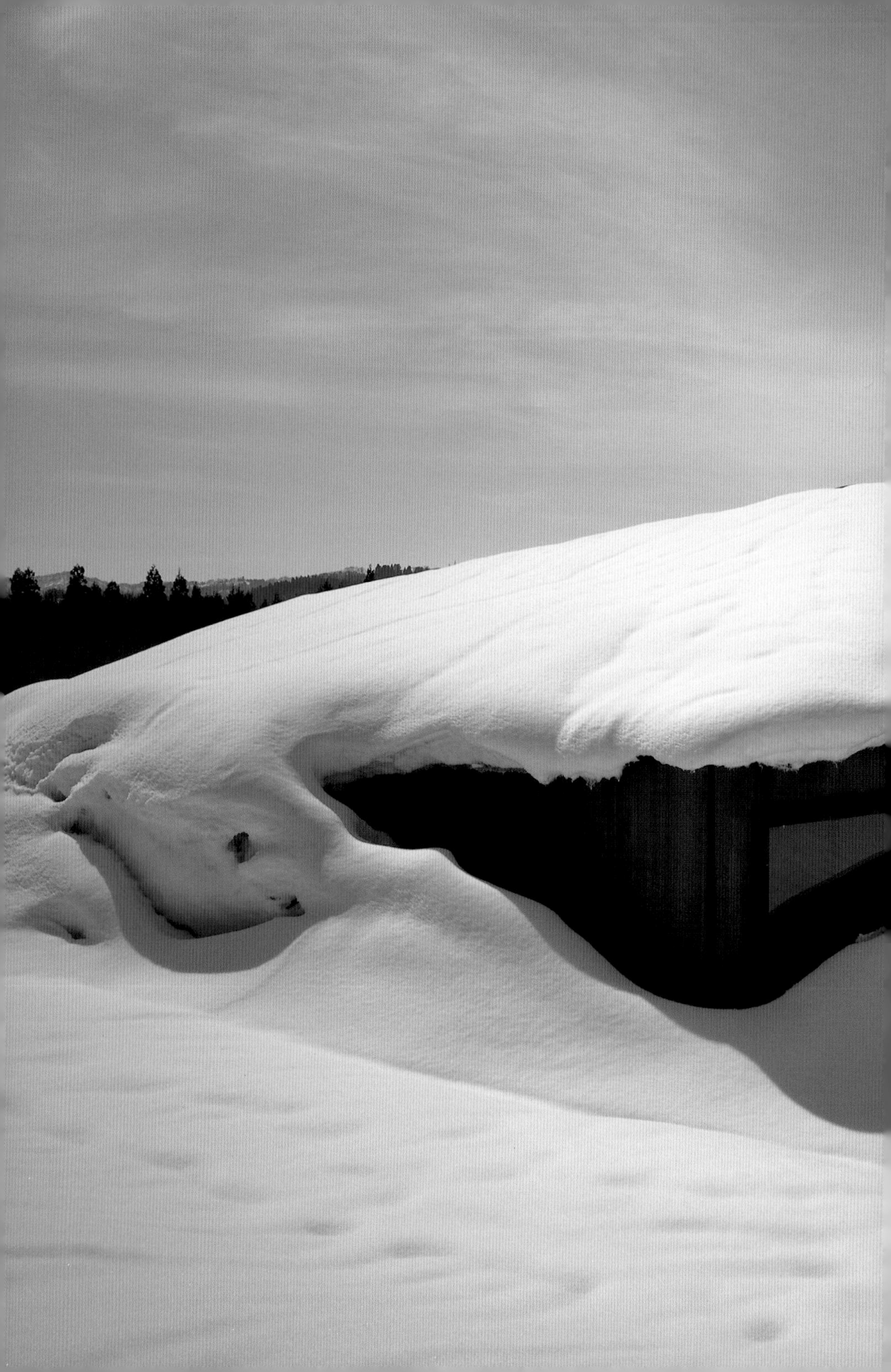

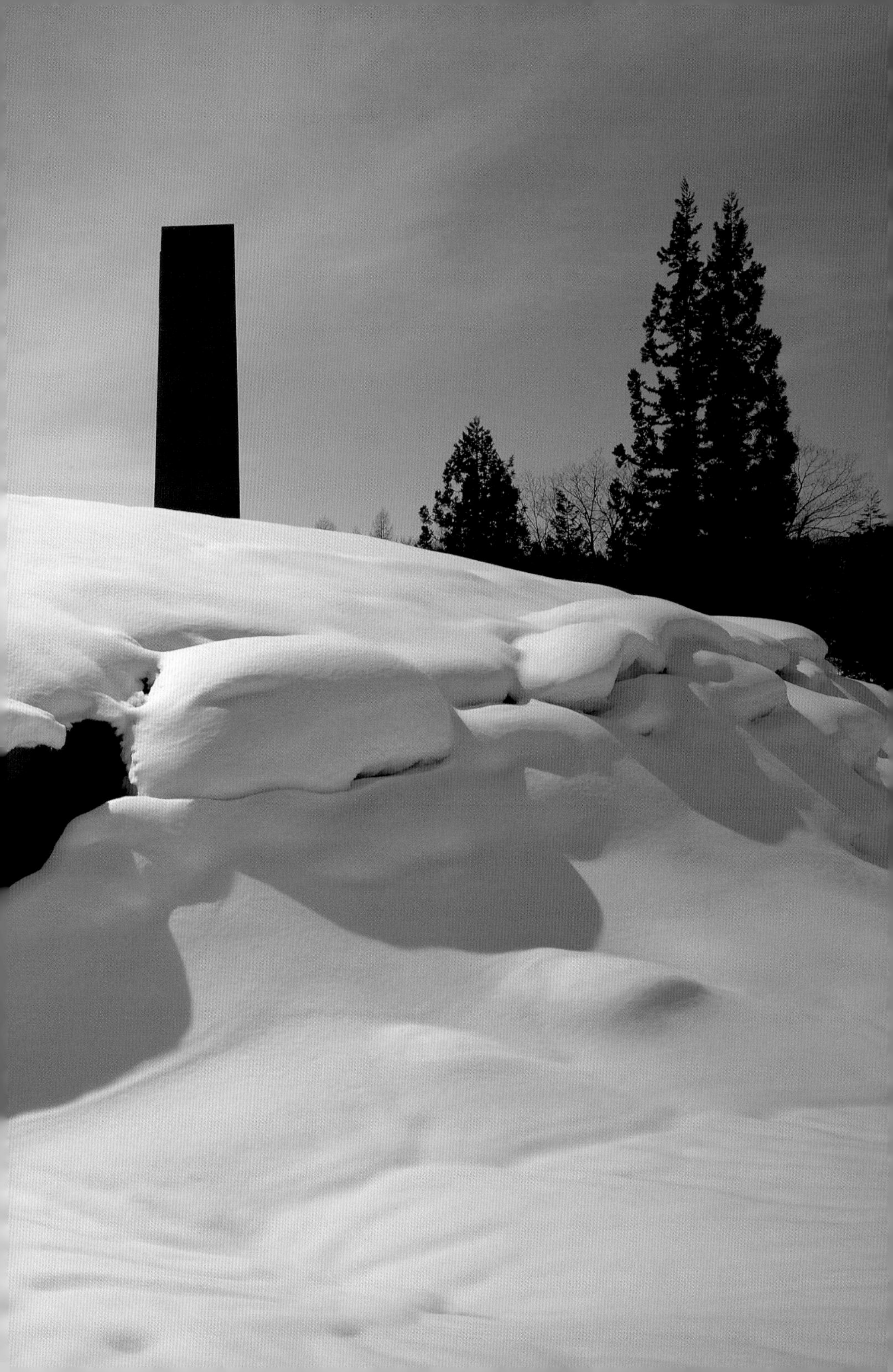

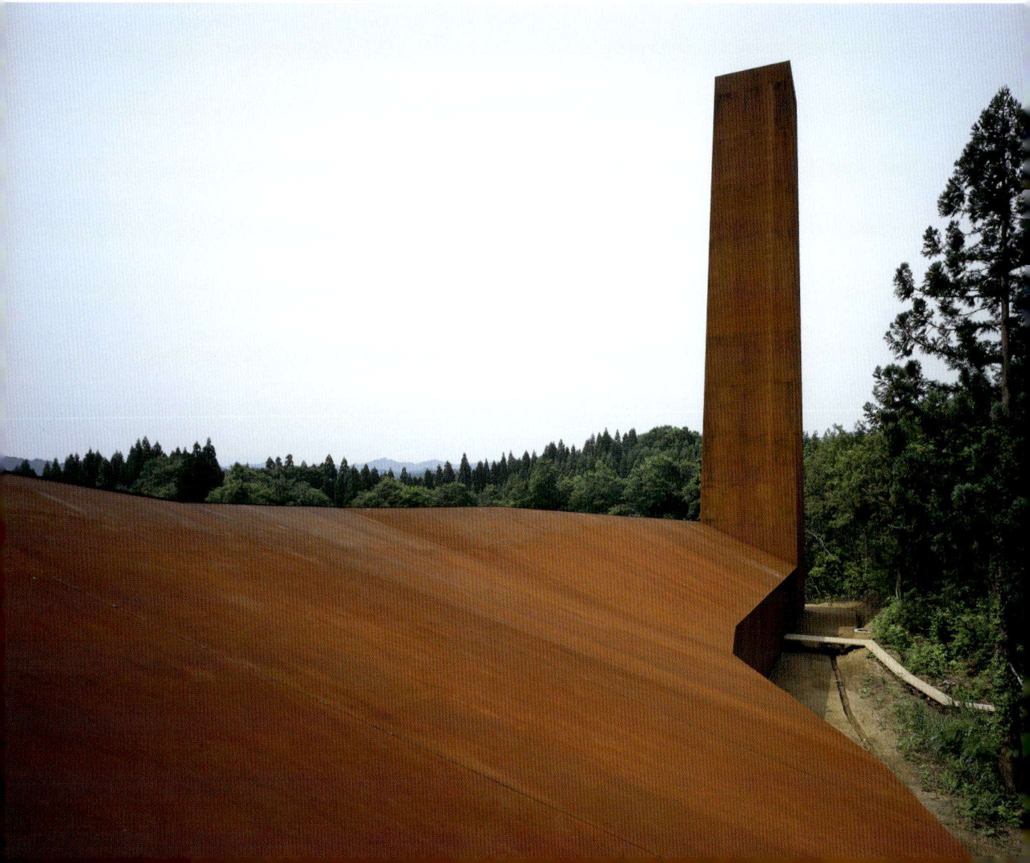

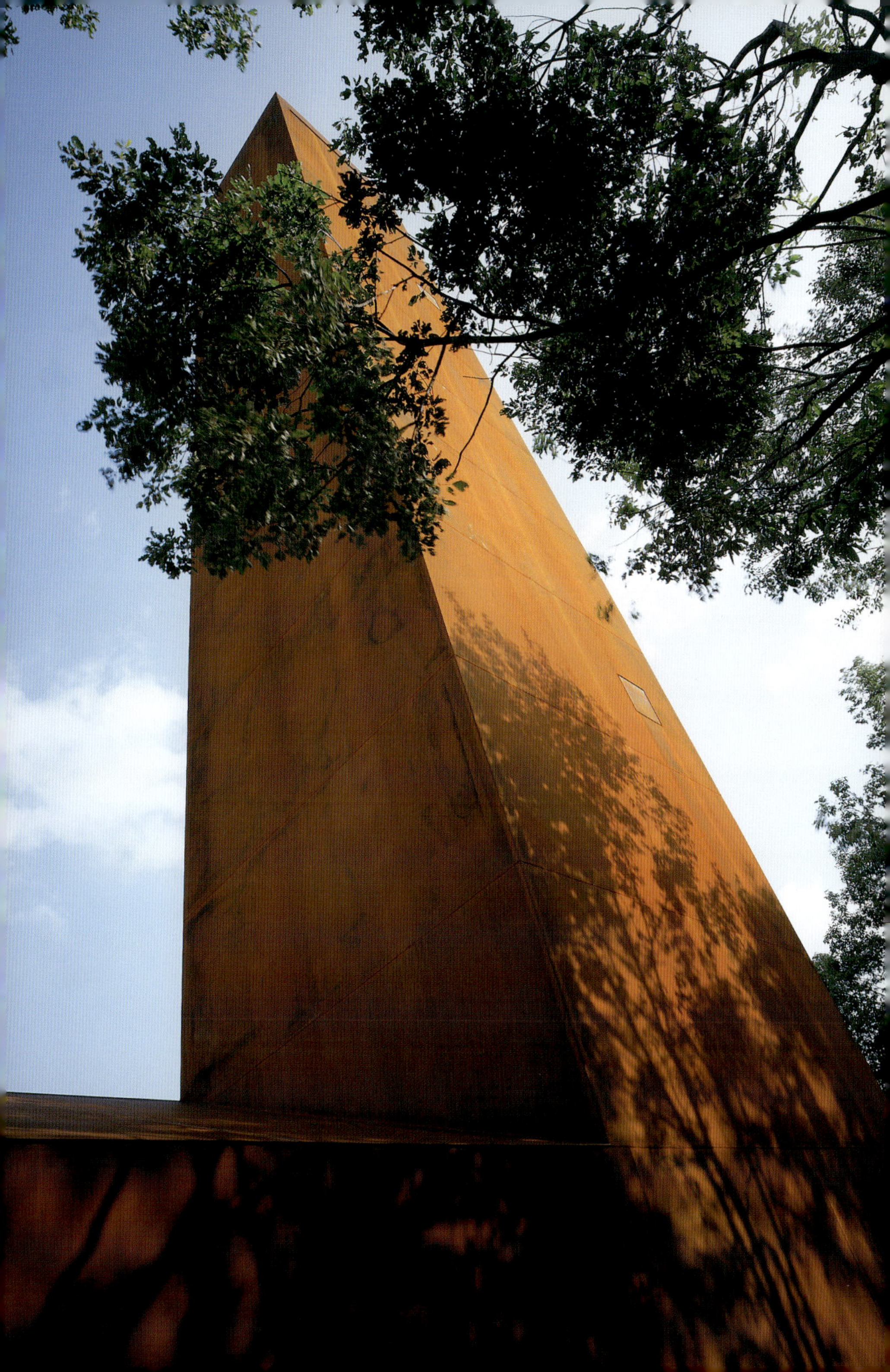

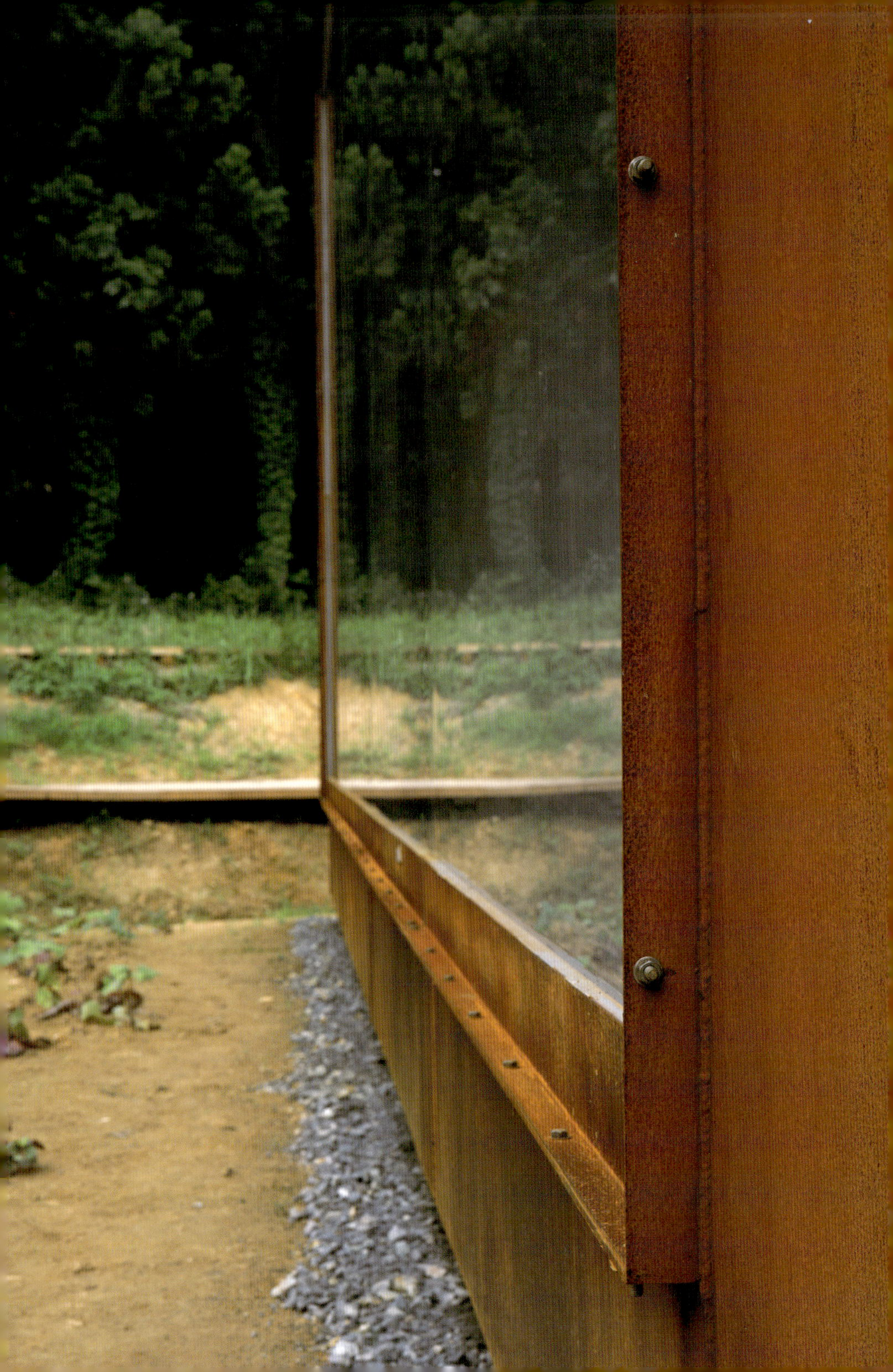

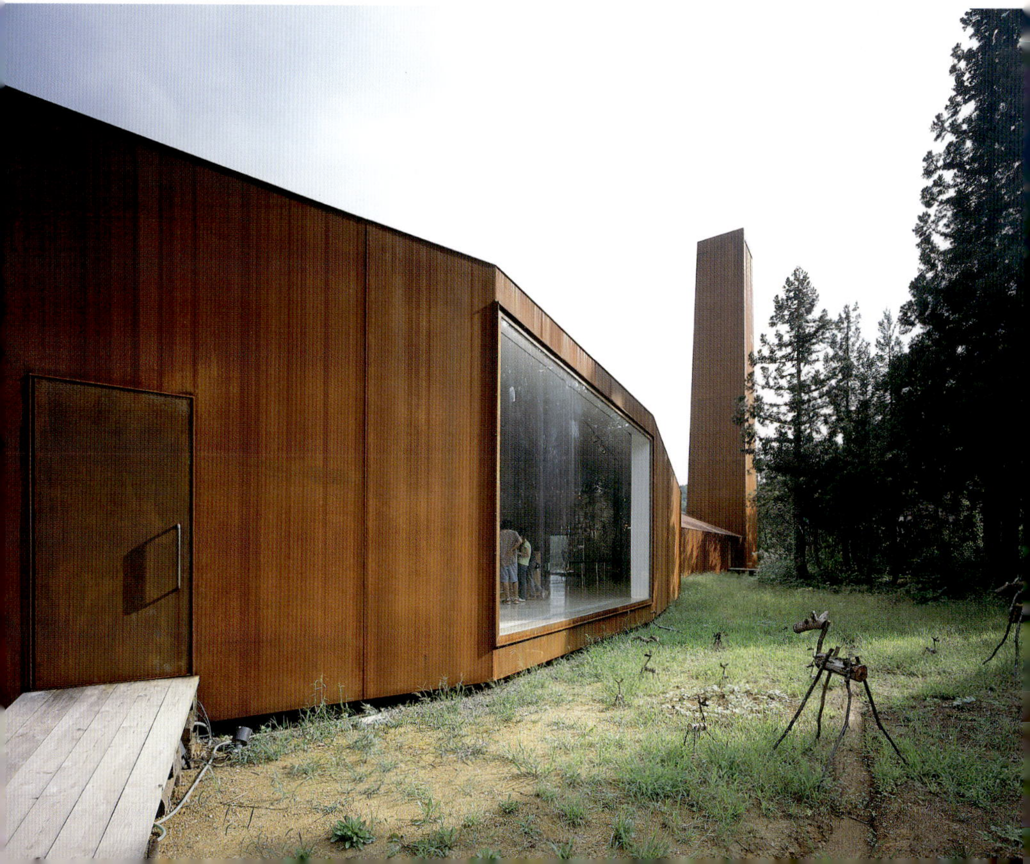

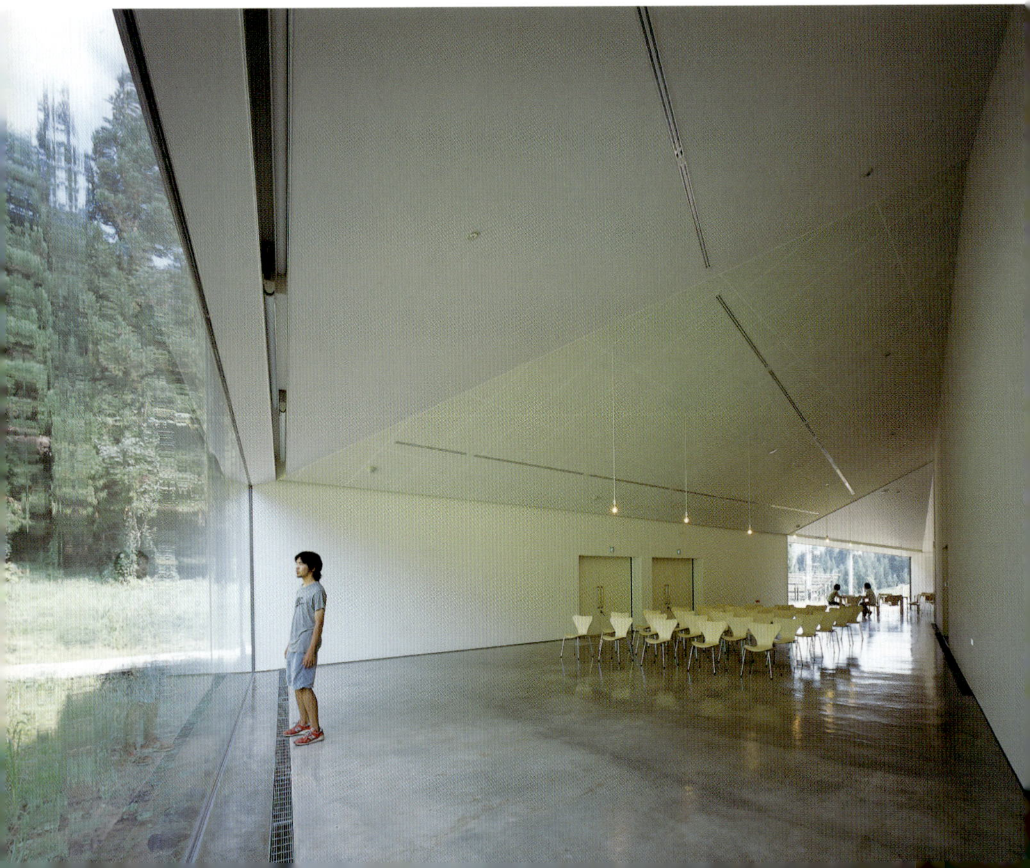

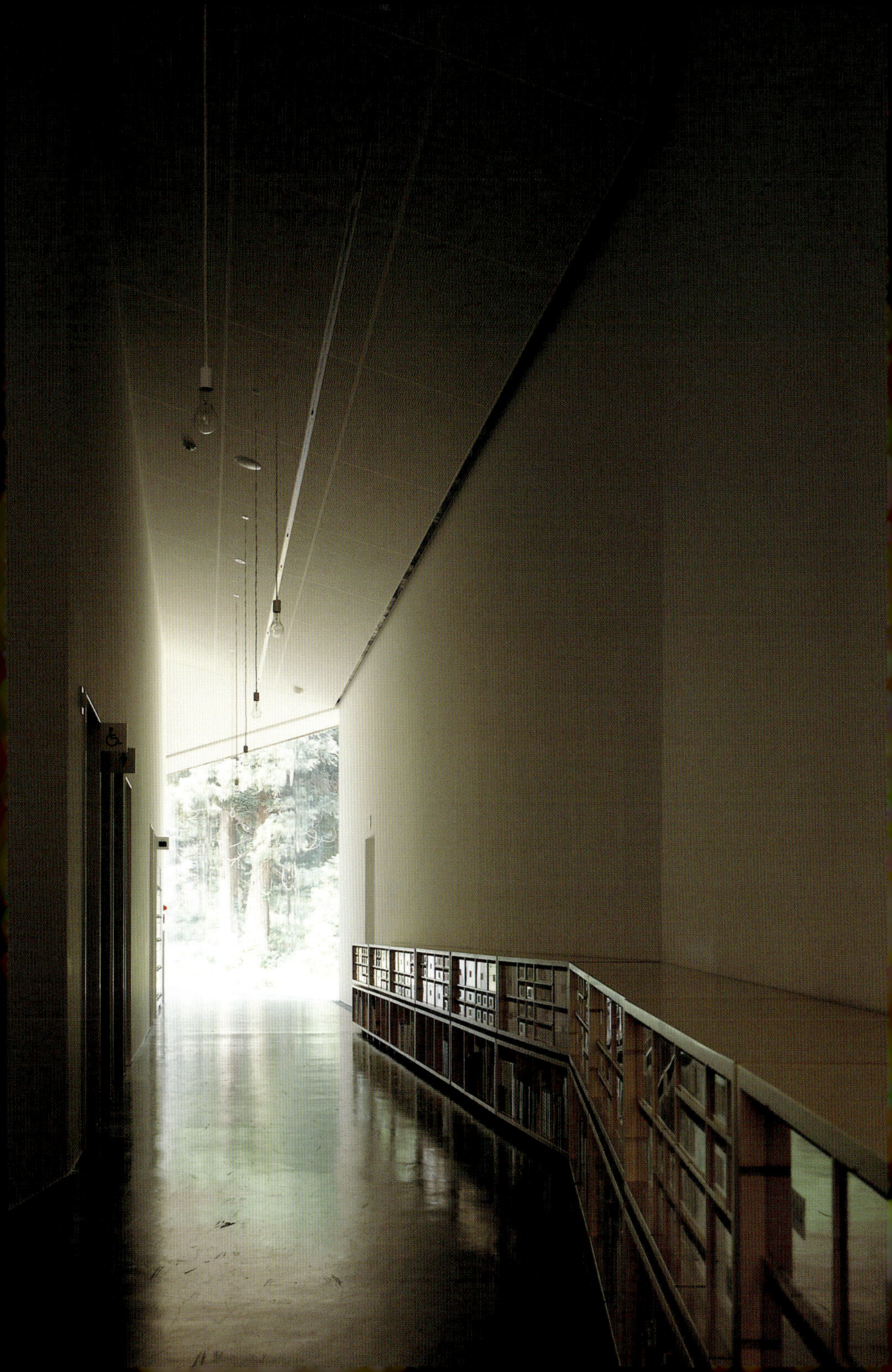

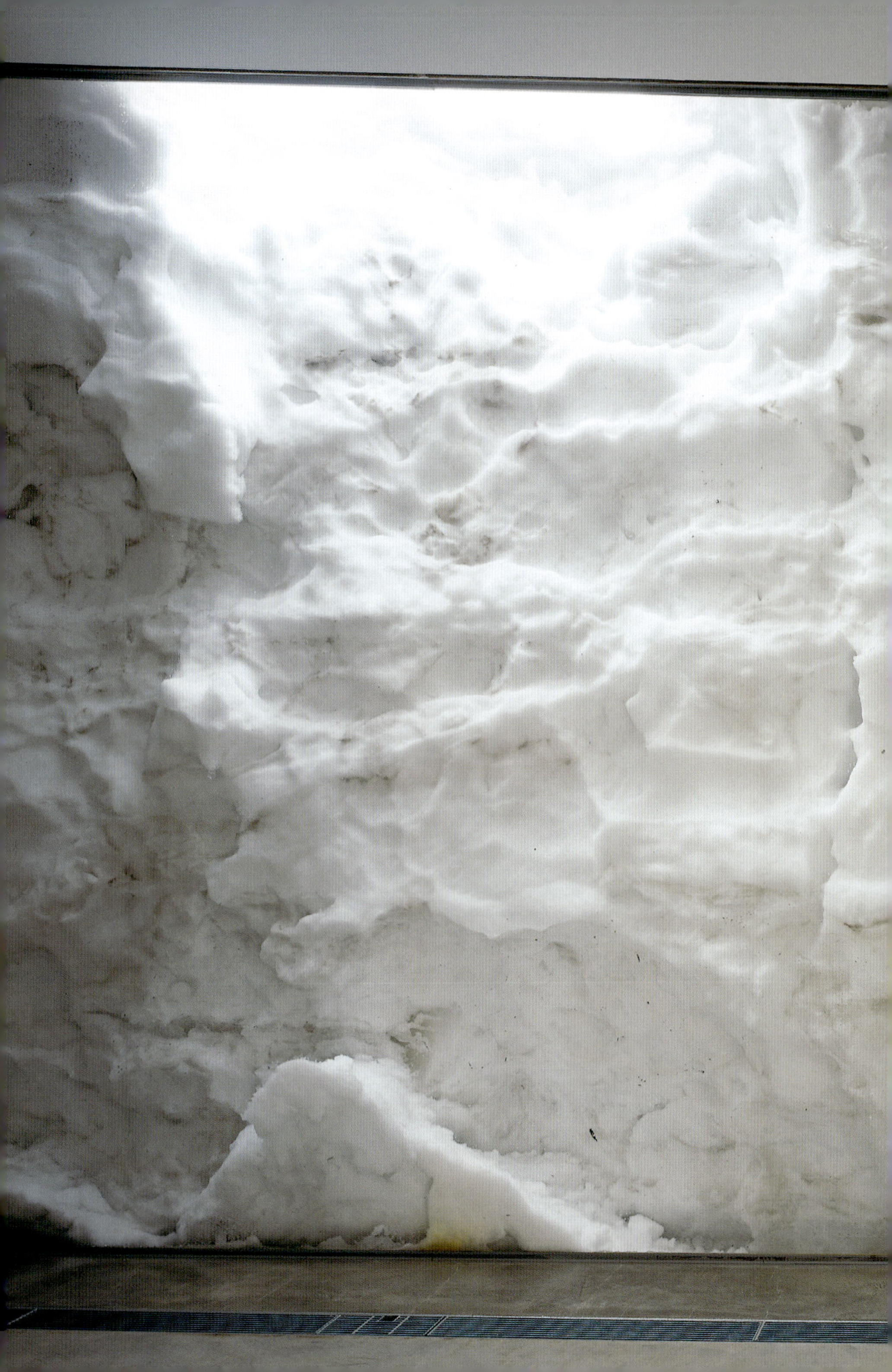

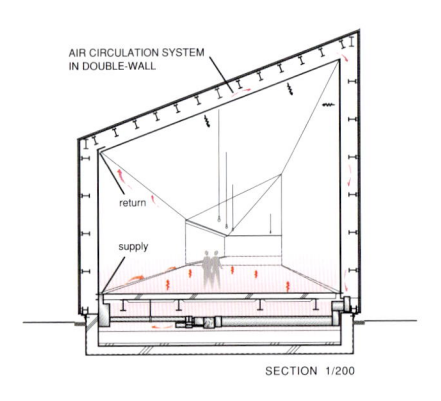

AIR CIRCULATION SYSTEM
IN DOUBLE-WALL

return
supply

SECTION 1/200

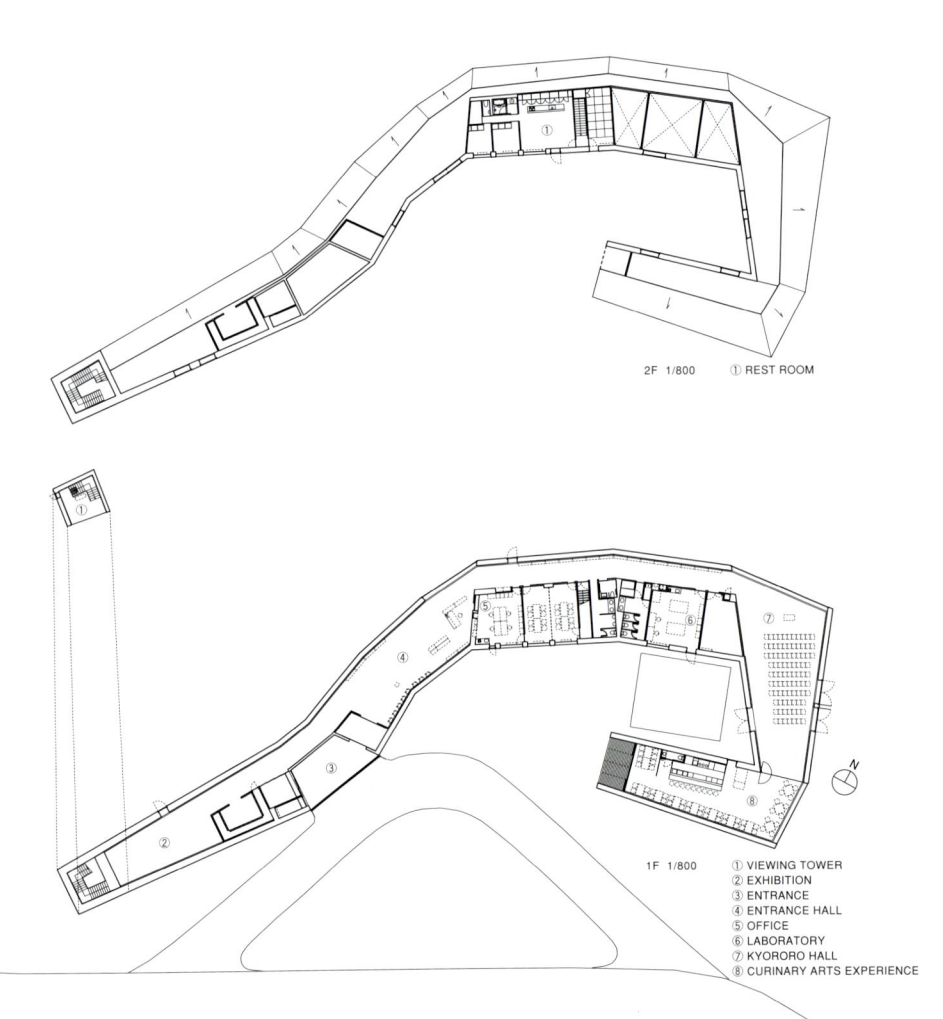

2F 1/800   ① REST ROOM

1F 1/800
① VIEWING TOWER
② EXHIBITION
③ ENTRANCE
④ ENTRANCE HALL
⑤ OFFICE
⑥ LABORATORY
⑦ KYORORO HALL
⑧ CURINARY ARTS EXPERIENCE

DETAIL 1/20

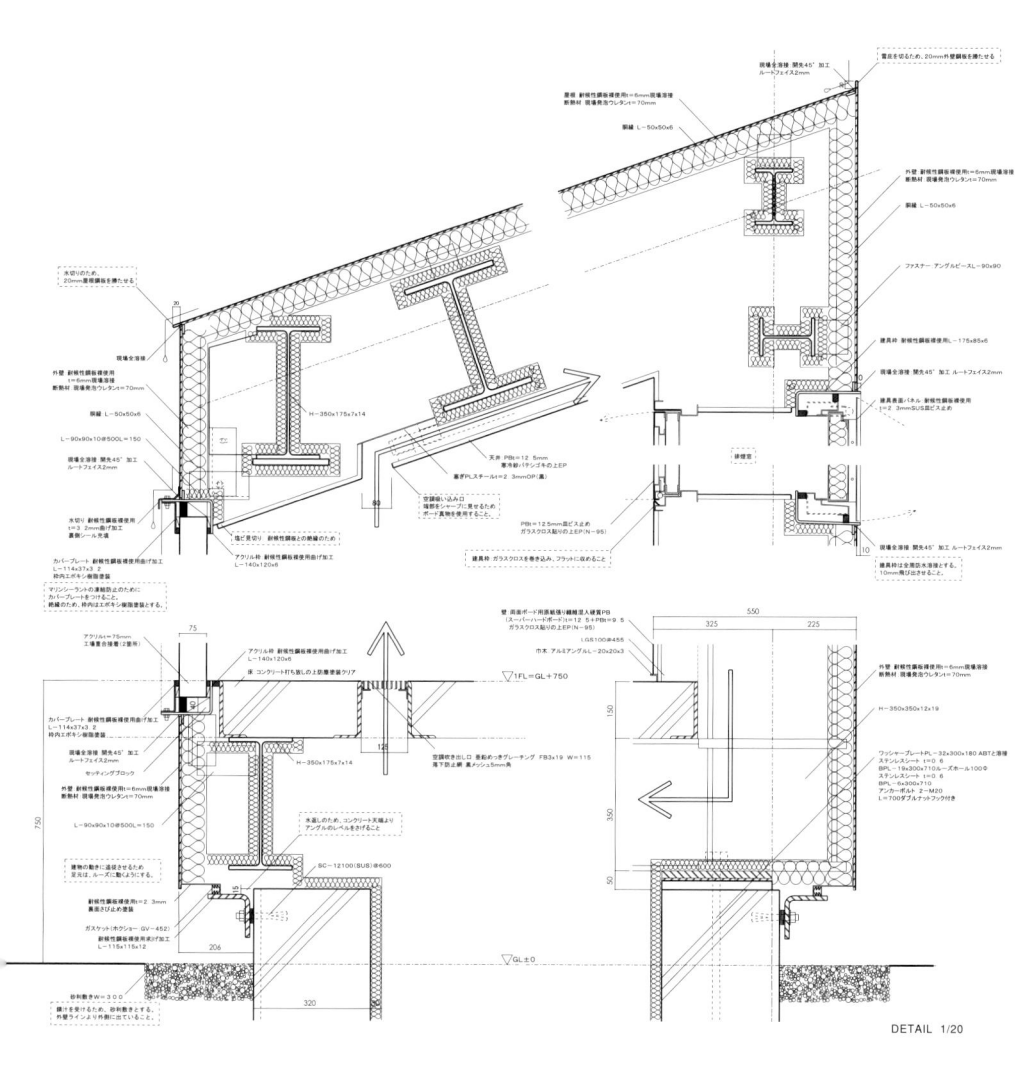

Toyota L&F Hiroshima

トヨタL&F広島本社　2003

The 45m-wide gate-like structure relies on a pillar/beam rigid frame. It was designed to house both offices and a forklift maintenance facility in a column-less space. The facade can be fully opened by sliding three 8.5m-tall doors.

45m×34m、天井高8.5mの無柱空間の整備場兼本社屋。高さ8.5mの3連大扉が全開する。

23

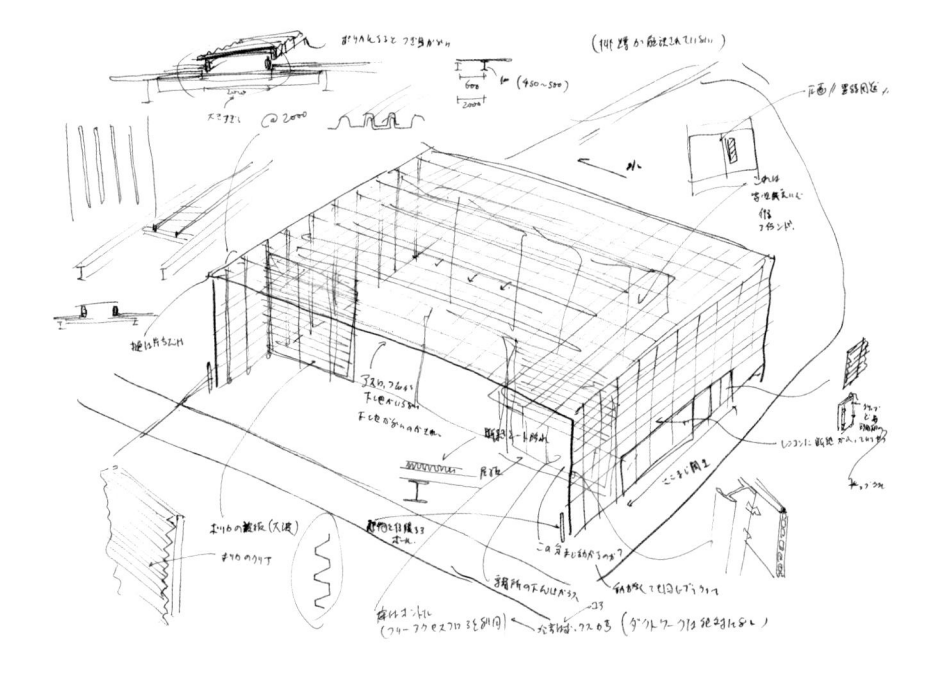

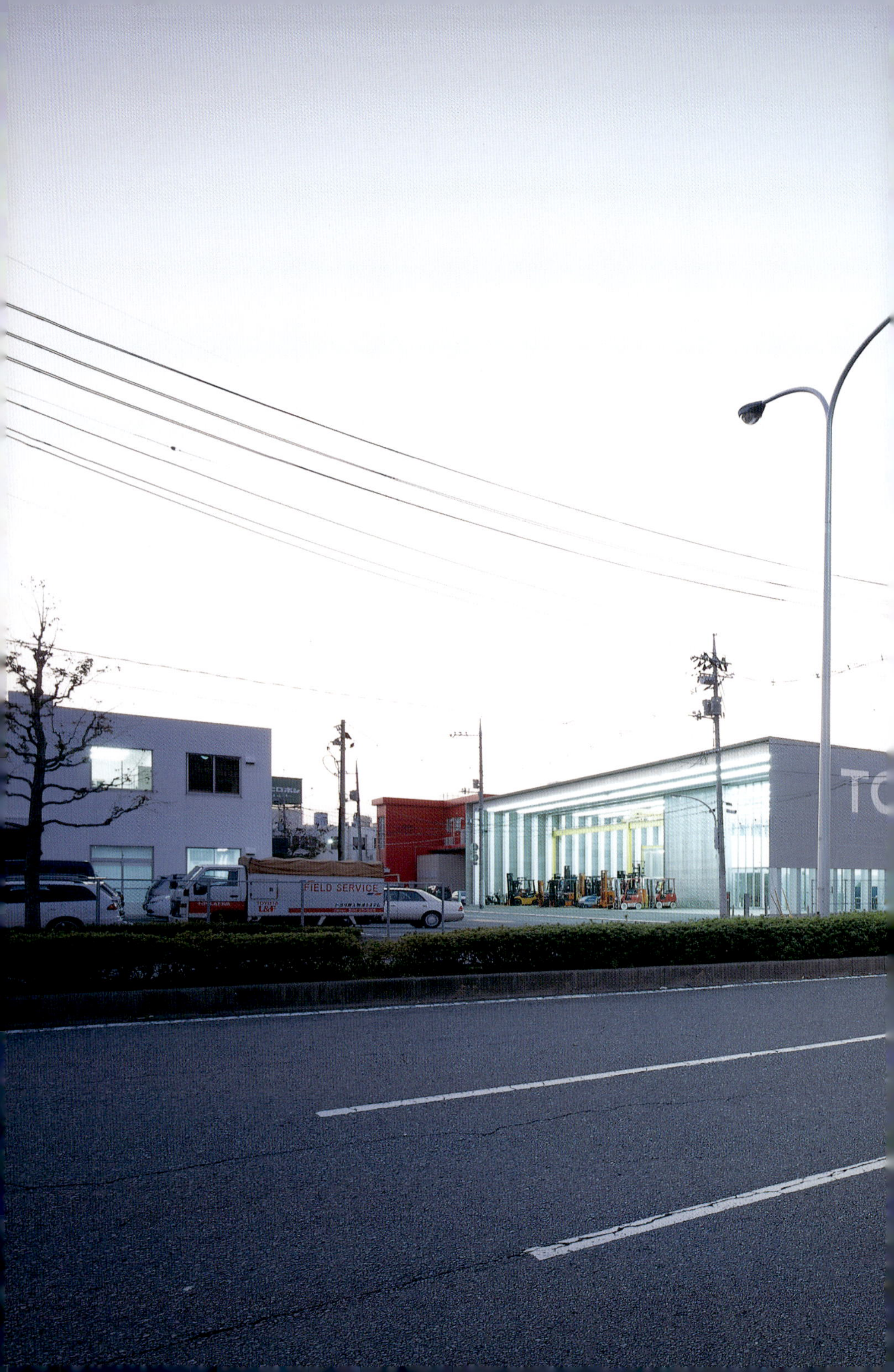
FIELD SERVICE

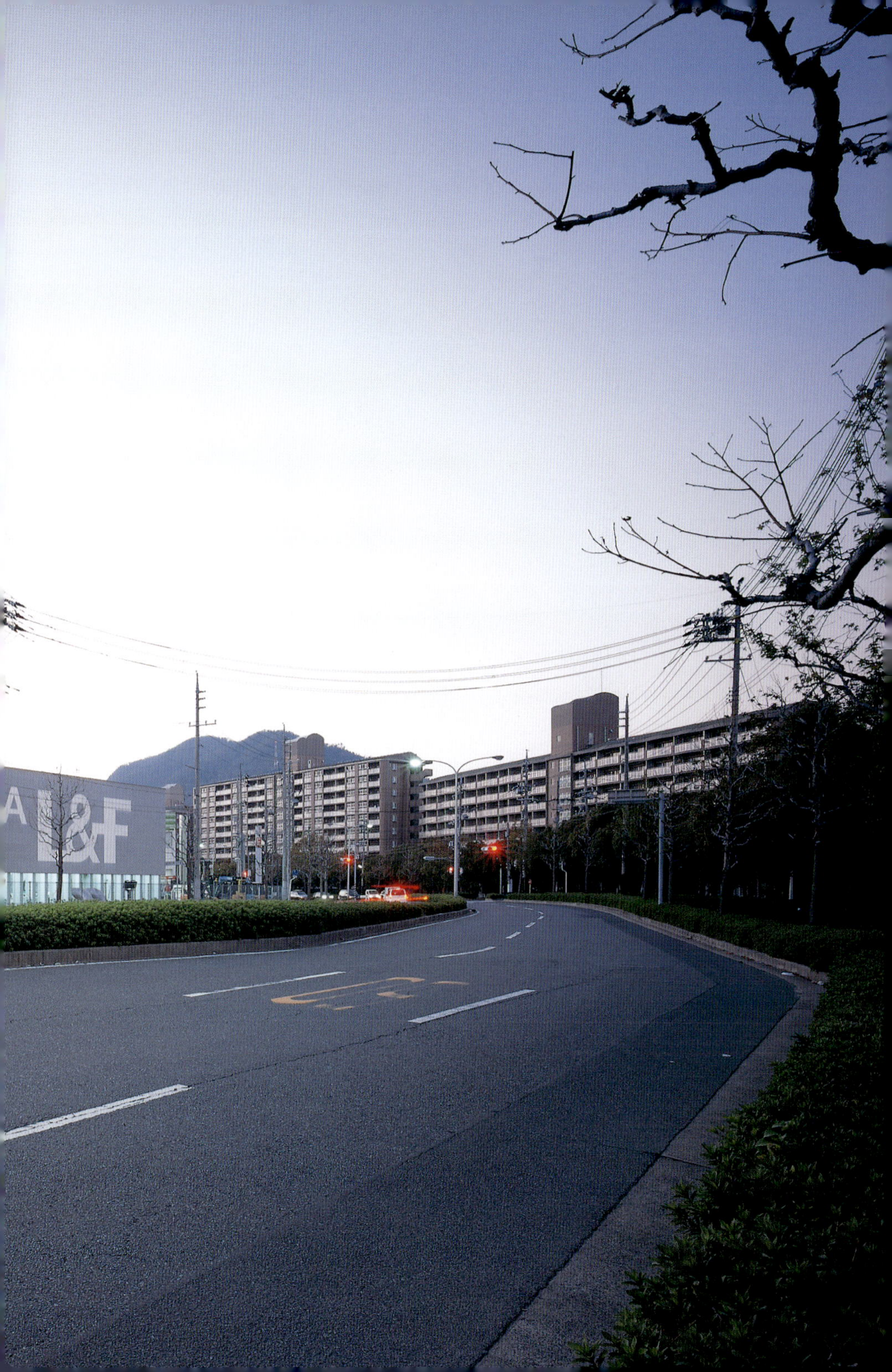

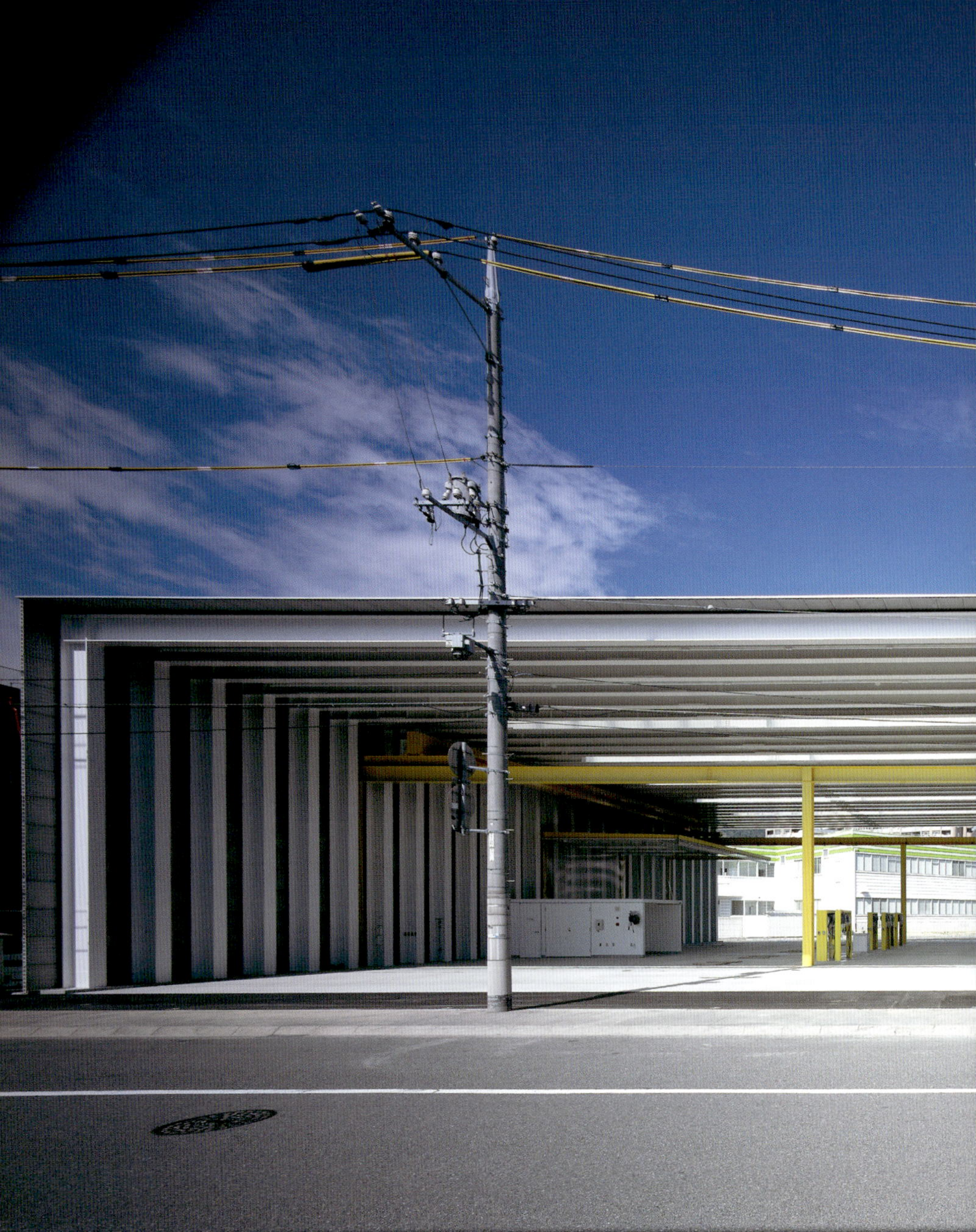

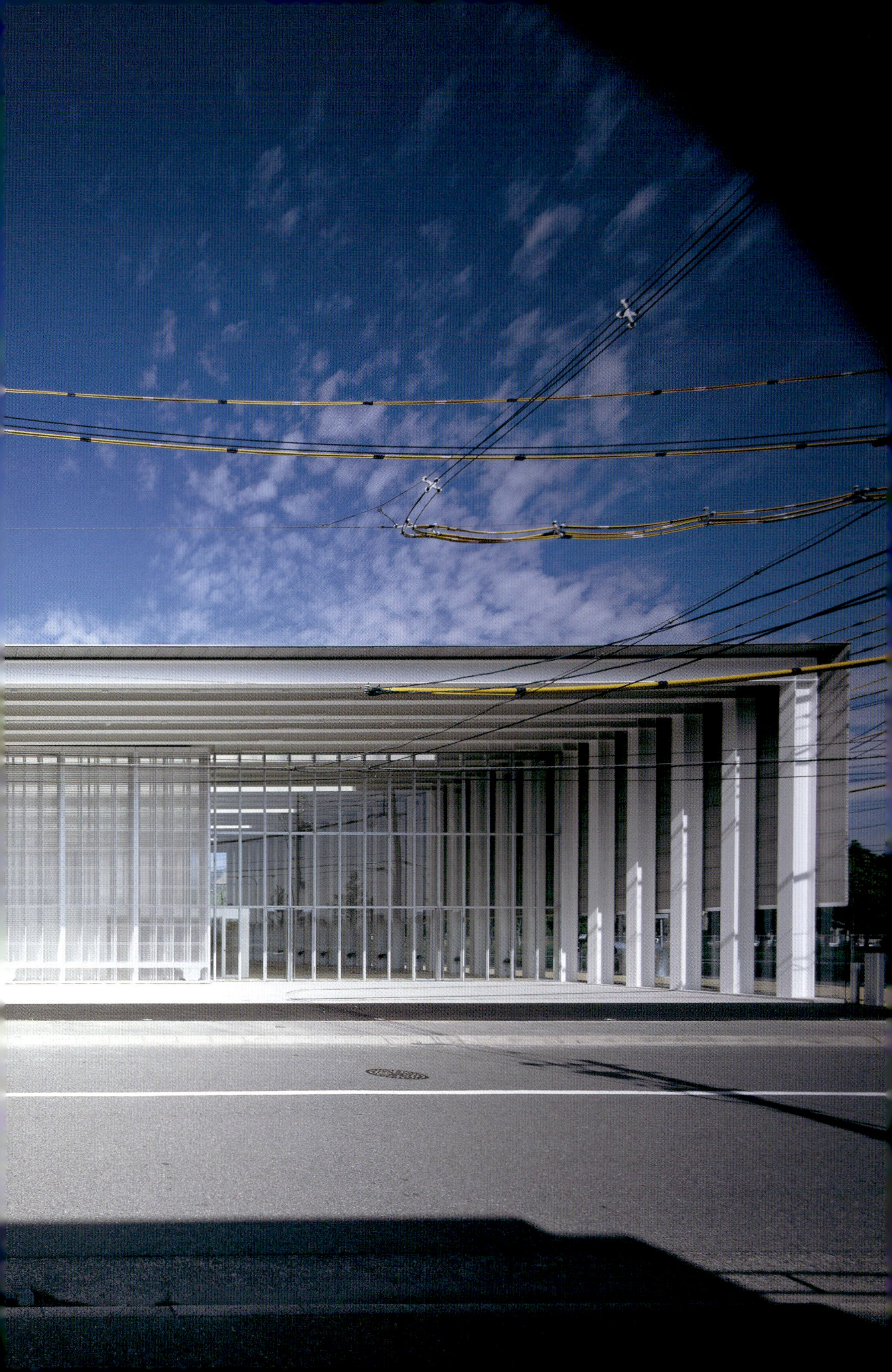

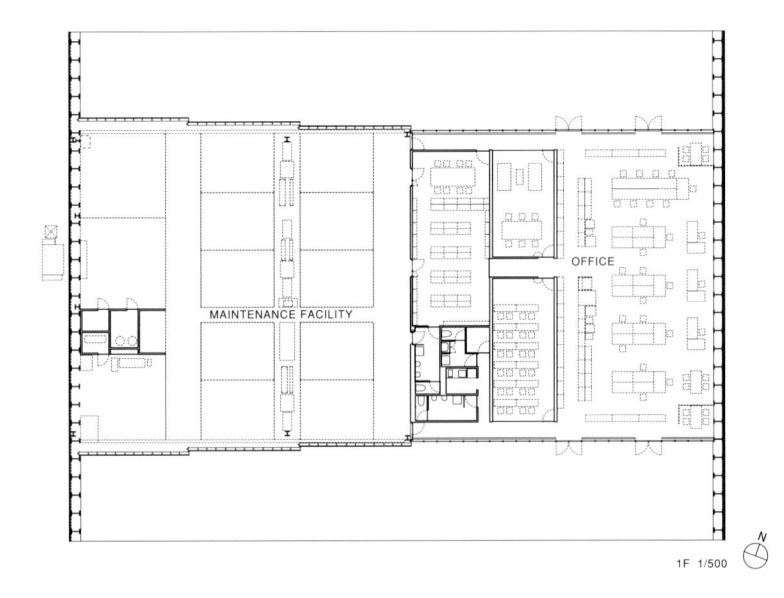

MAINTENANCE FACILITY

OFFICE

1F 1/500

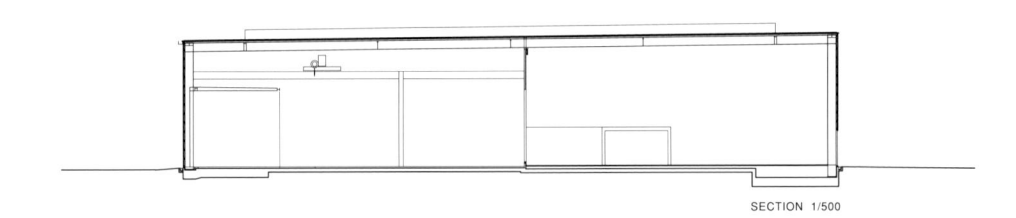

SECTION 1/500

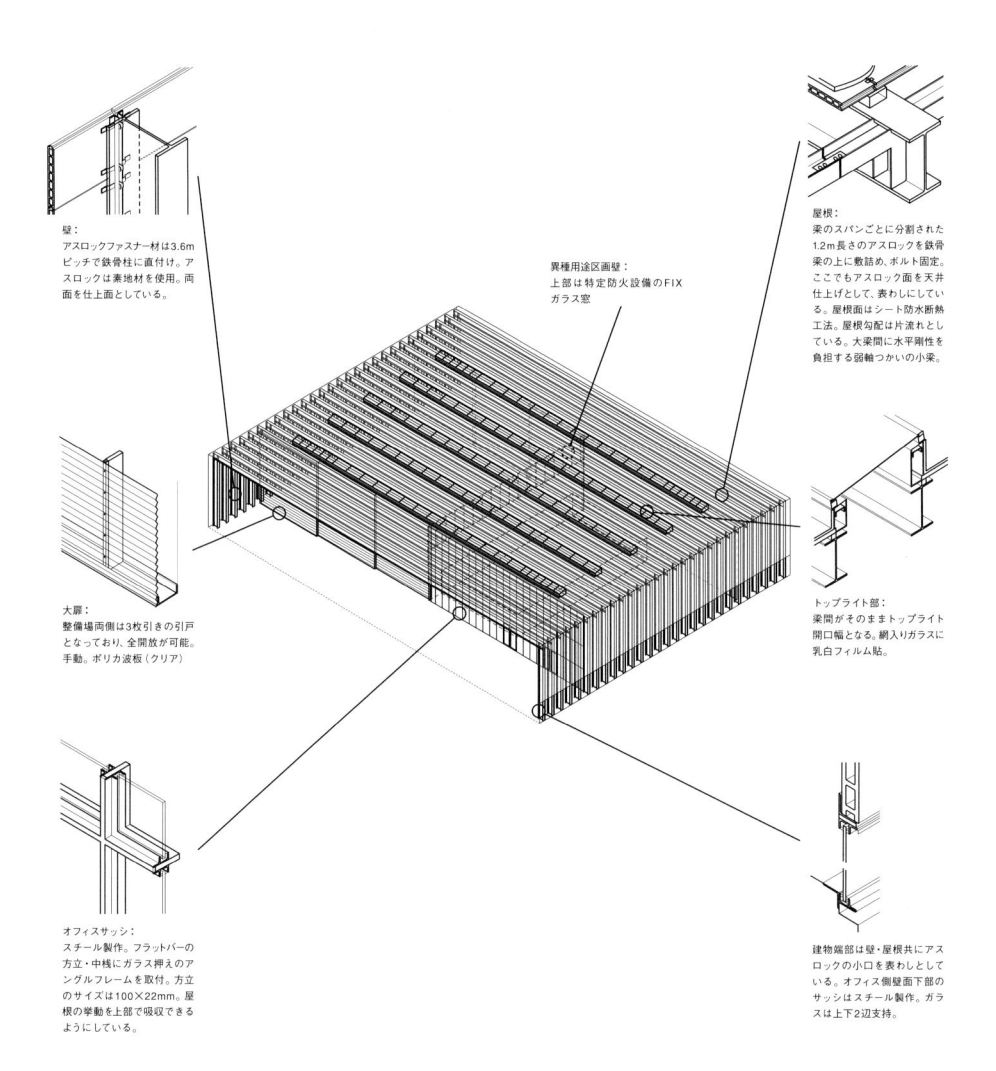

壁:
アスロックファスナー材は3.6mピッチで鉄骨柱に直付け。アスロックは裏地材を使用。両面を仕上面としている。

異種用途区画壁:
上部は特定防火設備のFIXガラス窓

屋根:
梁のスパンごとに分割された1.2m長さのアスロックを鉄骨梁の上に敷詰め、ボルト固定。ここでもアスロック面を天井仕上げとして、表わしにしている。屋根面はシート防水断熱工法。屋根勾配は片流れとしている。大梁間に水平剛性を負担する弱軸つかいの小梁。

大扉:
整備場両側は3枚引きの引戸となっており、全開放が可能。手動。ポリカ波板（クリア）

トップライト部:
梁間がそのままトップライト開口幅となる。網入りガラスに乳白フィルム貼。

オフィスサッシ:
スチール製作。フラットバーの方立・中桟にガラス押えのアングルフレームを取付。方立のサイズは100×22mm。屋根の挙動を上部で吸収できるようにしている。

建物端部は壁・屋根共にアスロックの小口を表わしとしている。オフィス側壁面下部のサッシはスチール製作。ガラスは上下2辺支持。

Engawa House

縁側の家　2003

The elongated house faces the owner's parents house across a courtyard. The 16 m-long portion of the rectangle facing the yard can be turned into a porch by opening all its sliding window panels.

中庭をはさんで母屋と向き合う細長い家。
16mの大開口を開けると家全体が縁側となる。

24

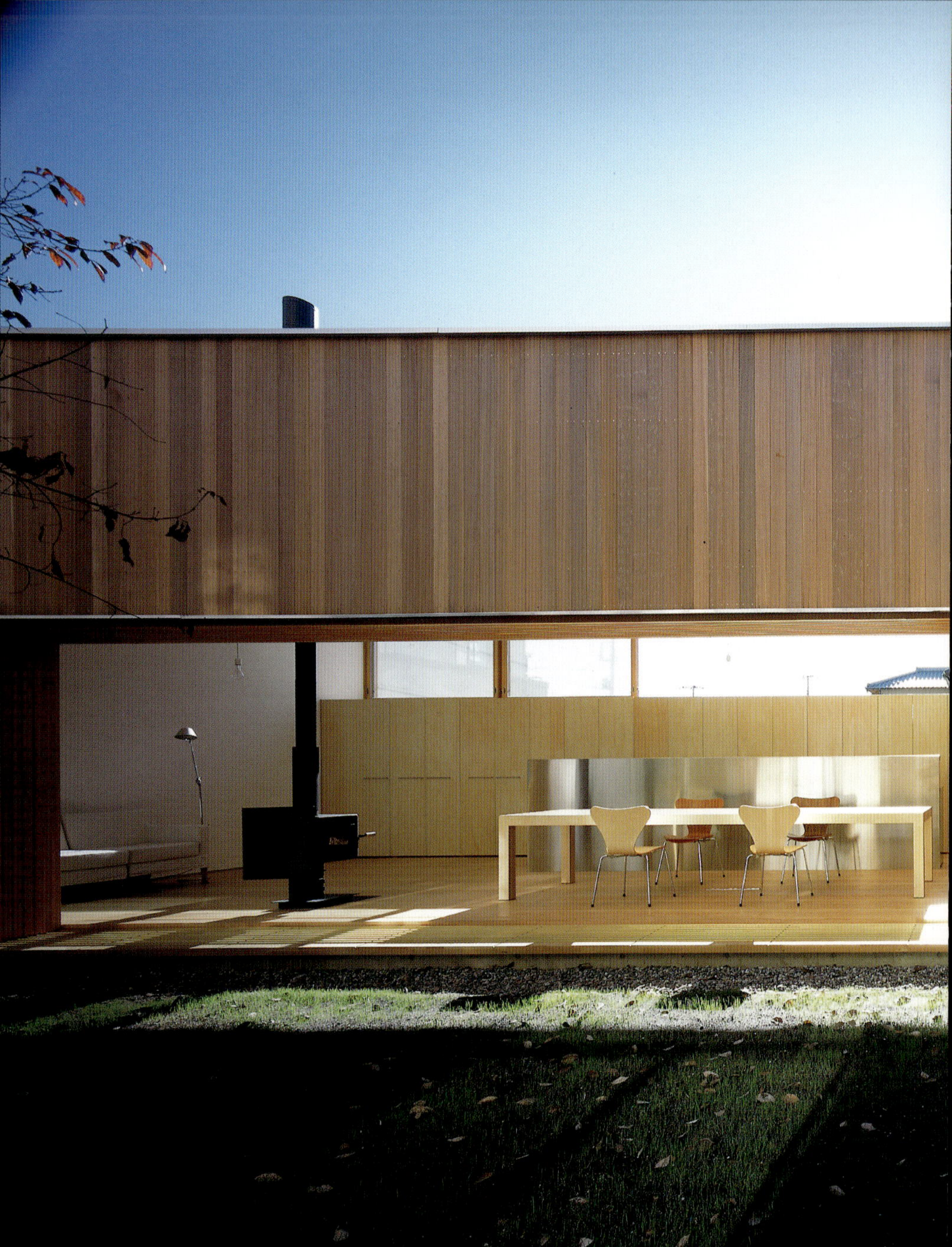

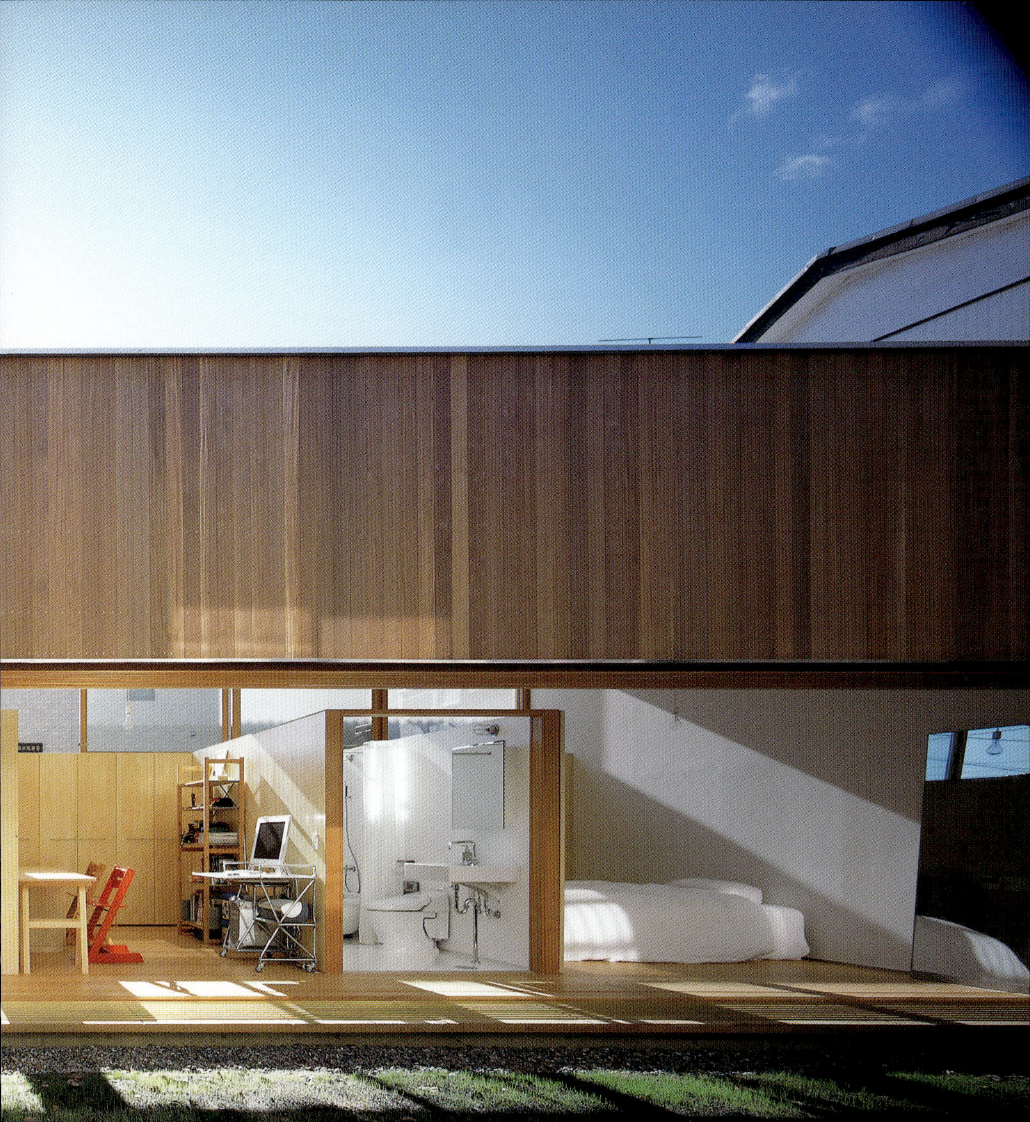

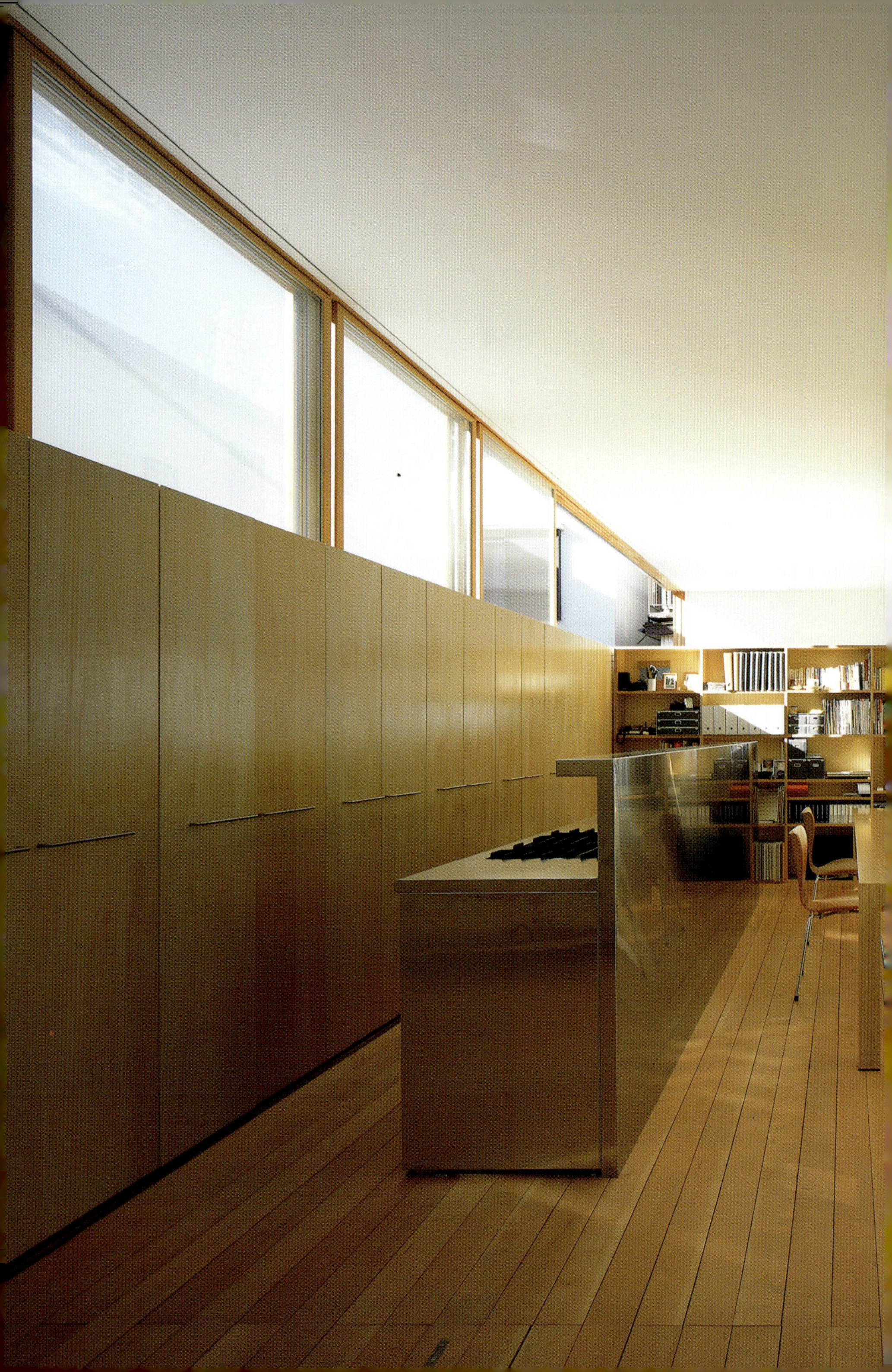

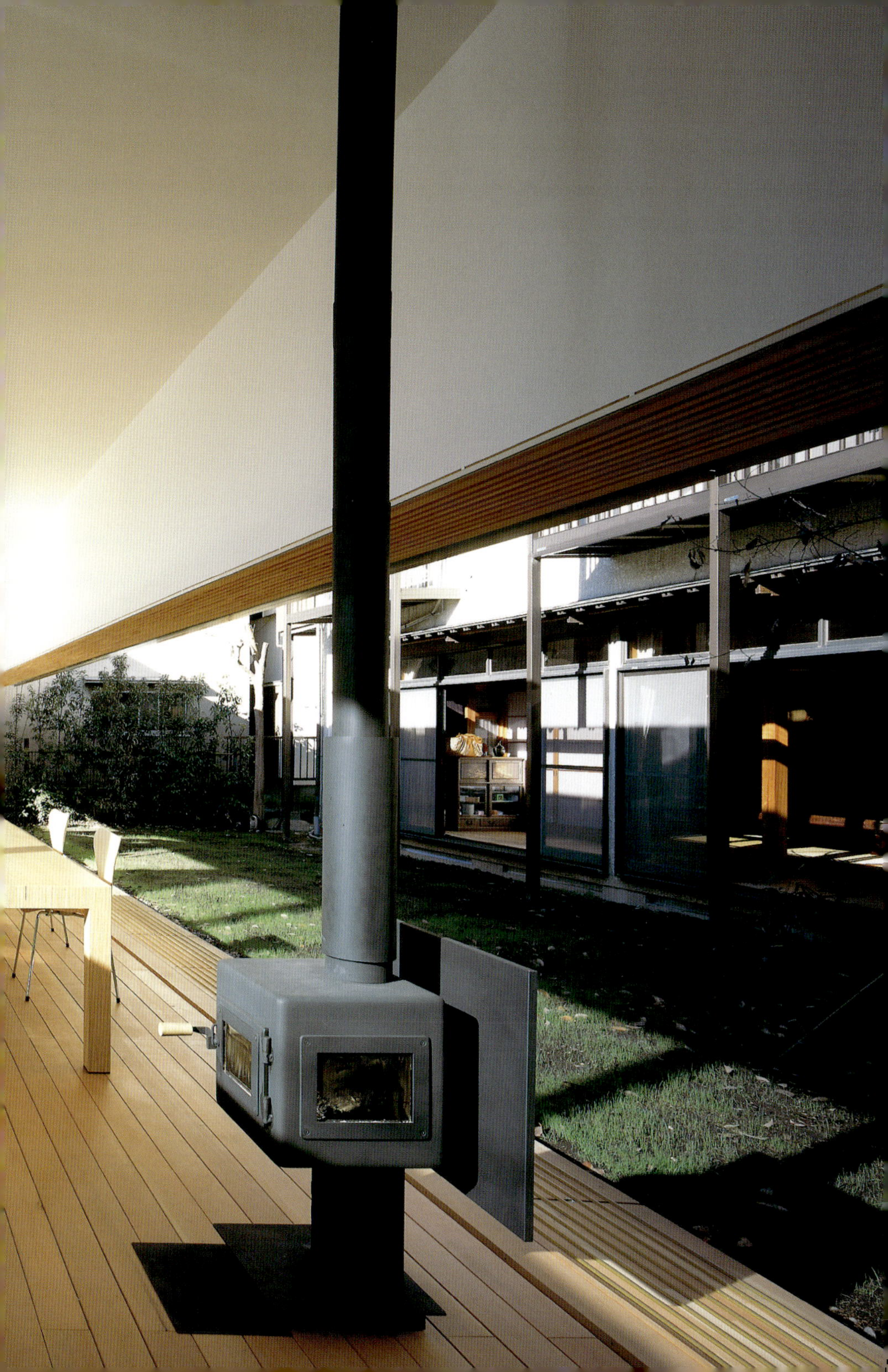

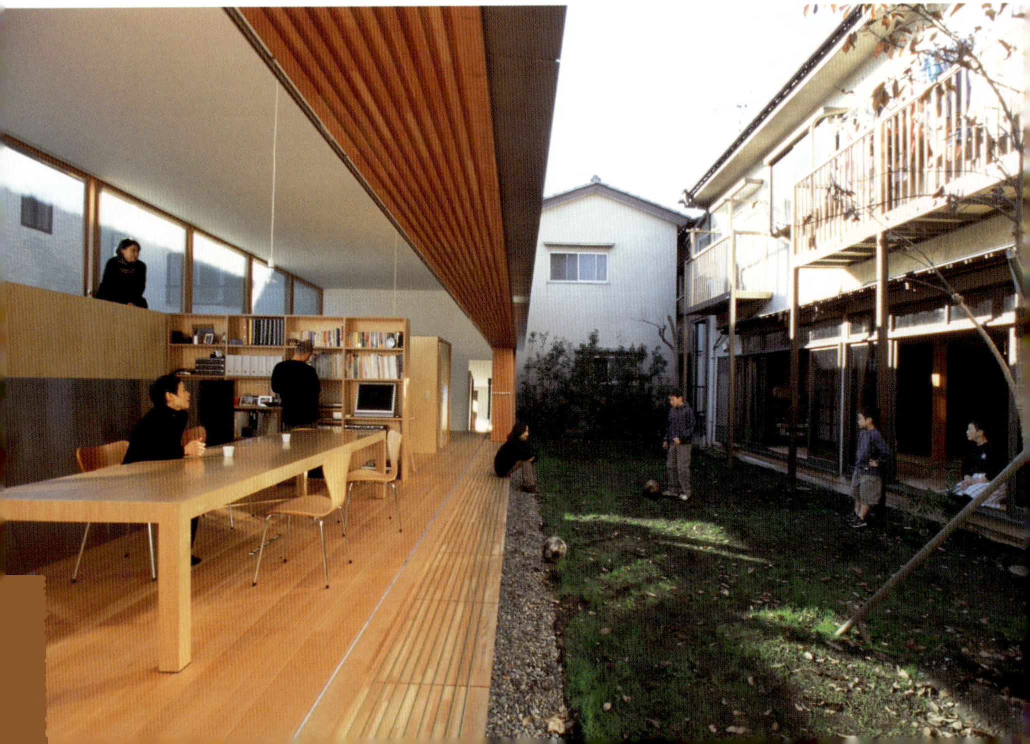

お母さんの家

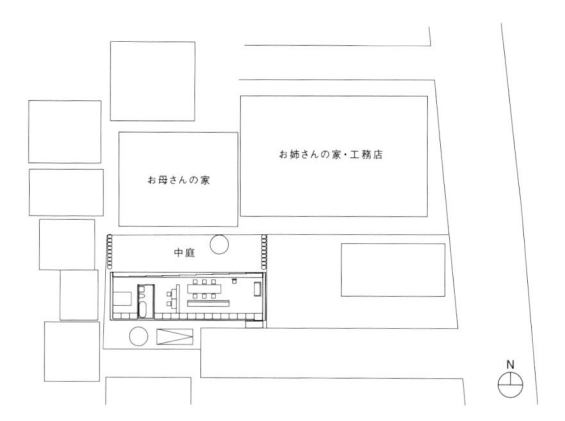

お姉さんの家・工務店

中庭

SITE 1/800

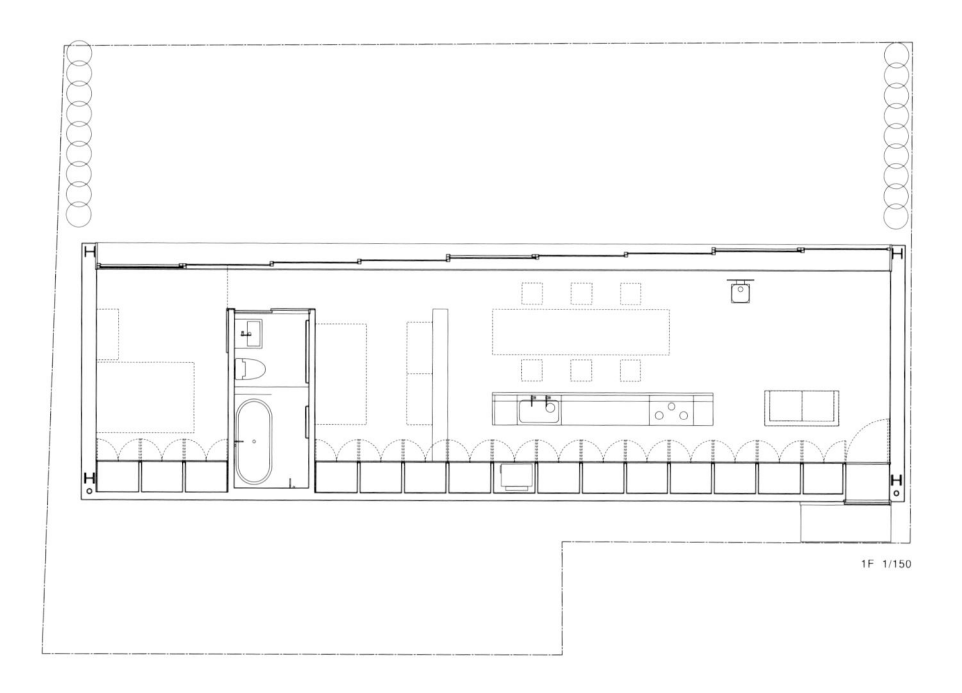

1F 1/150

House to Catch the Sky IV

空を捕まえる家Ⅳ　2003

The site is surrounded by other houses on four sides. Privacy is ensured by the depth of the courtyard.

旗ざお状敷地に位置する四方を家に囲まれた家。
深いコートヤードのプロポーションがプライバシーを保つ。

25

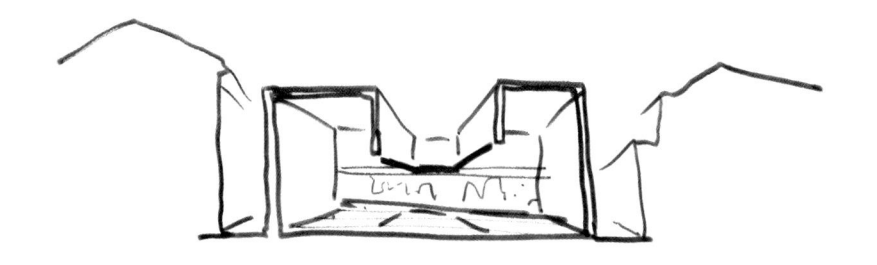

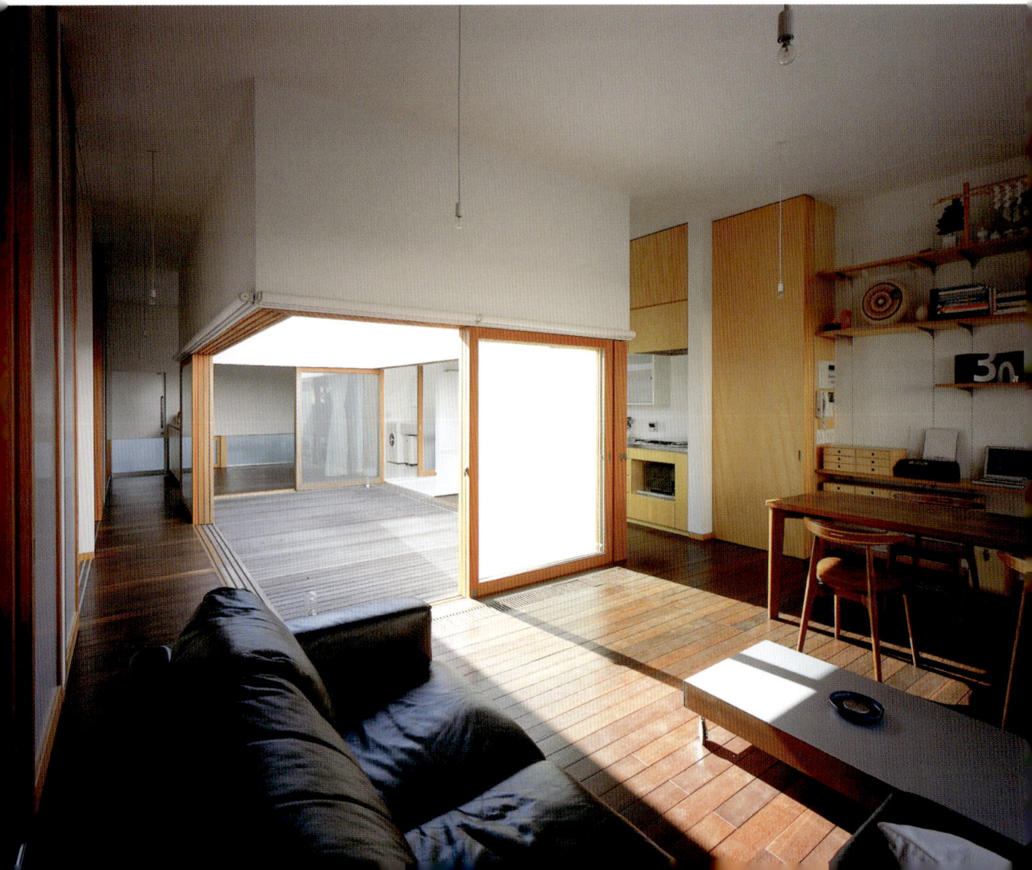

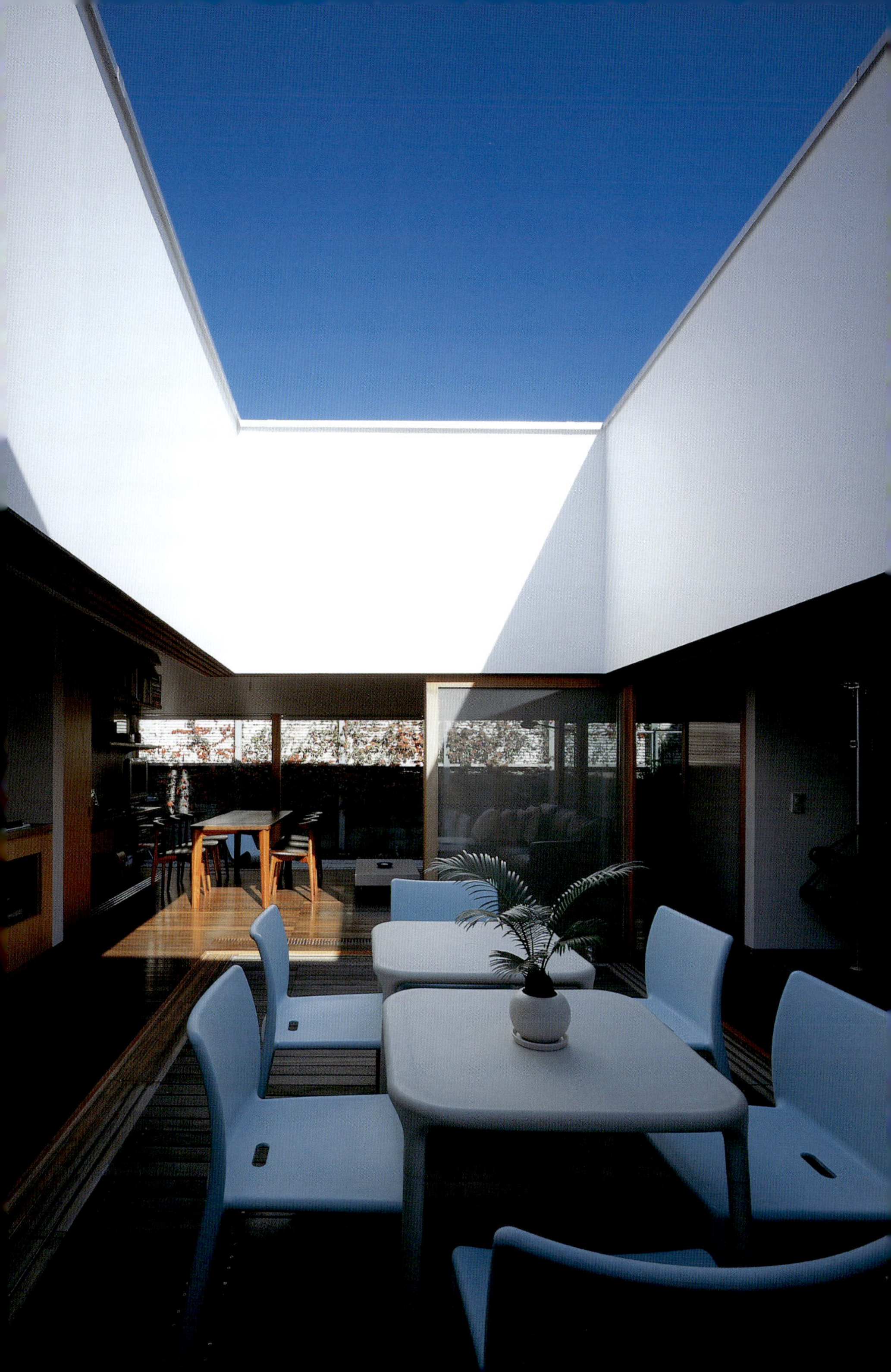

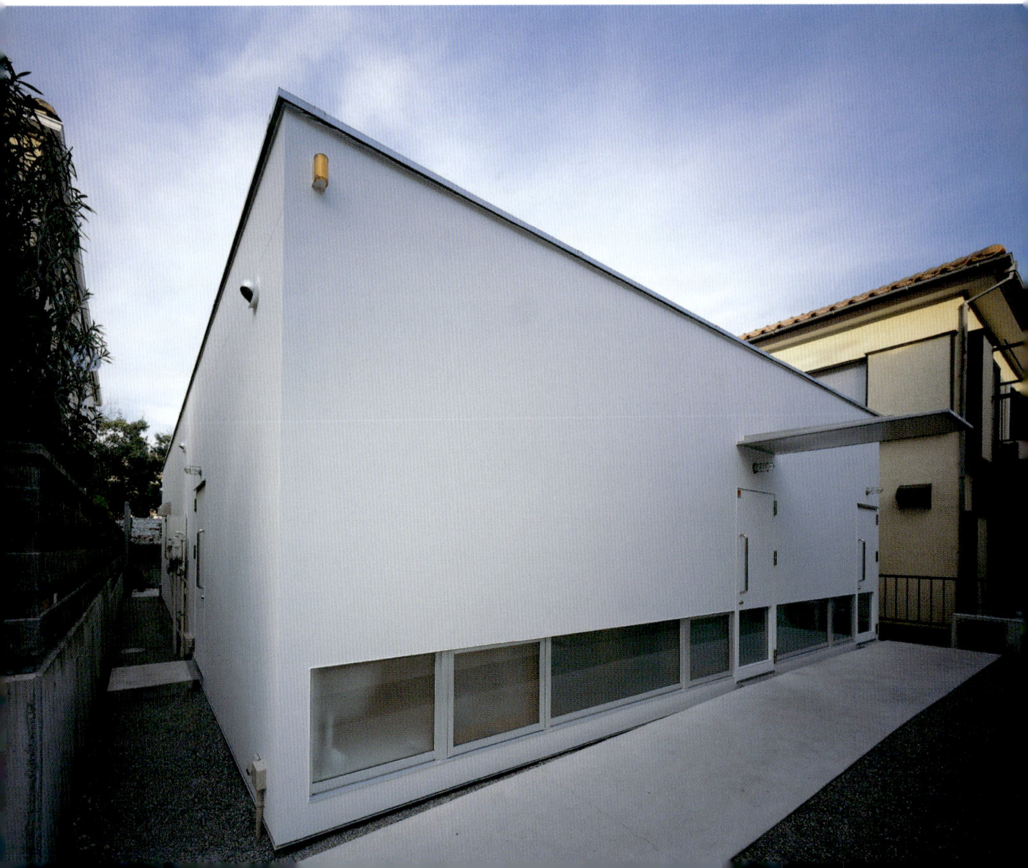

1F 1/250

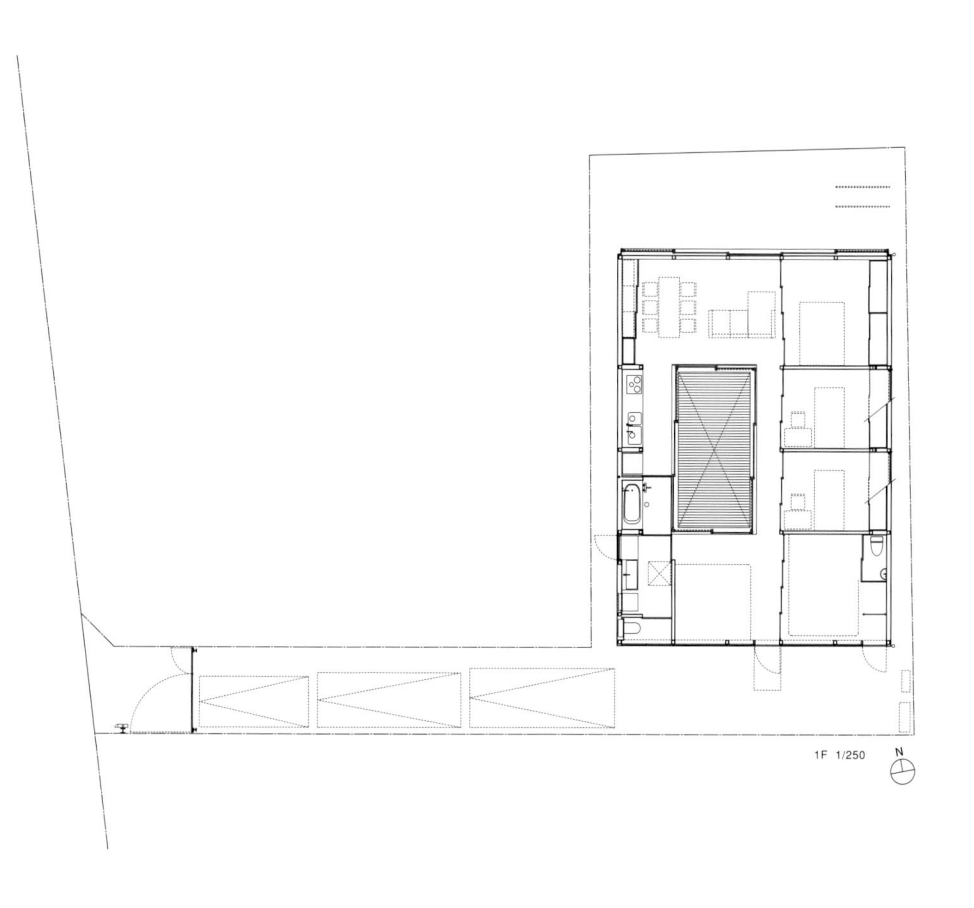

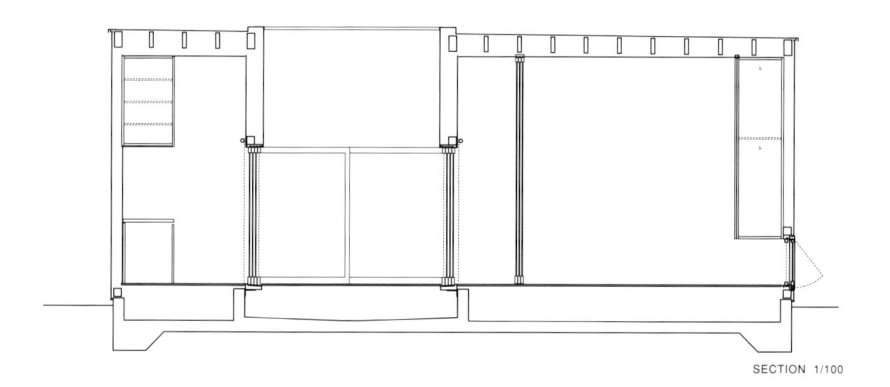

SECTION 1/100

Floating House

フローティングハウス　2003

The reliance on a single wall to support the upper floor allows the house to be completely open on three sides.

三方向に開いた住居。
一方面の壁だけで支えられている。

26

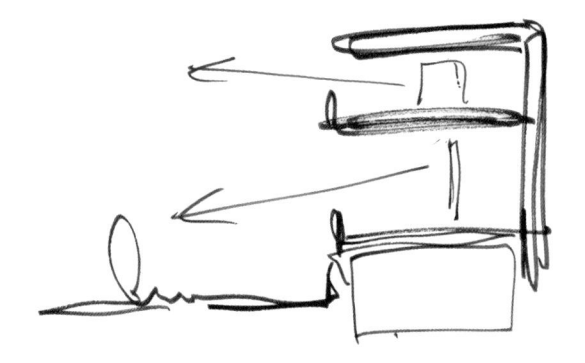

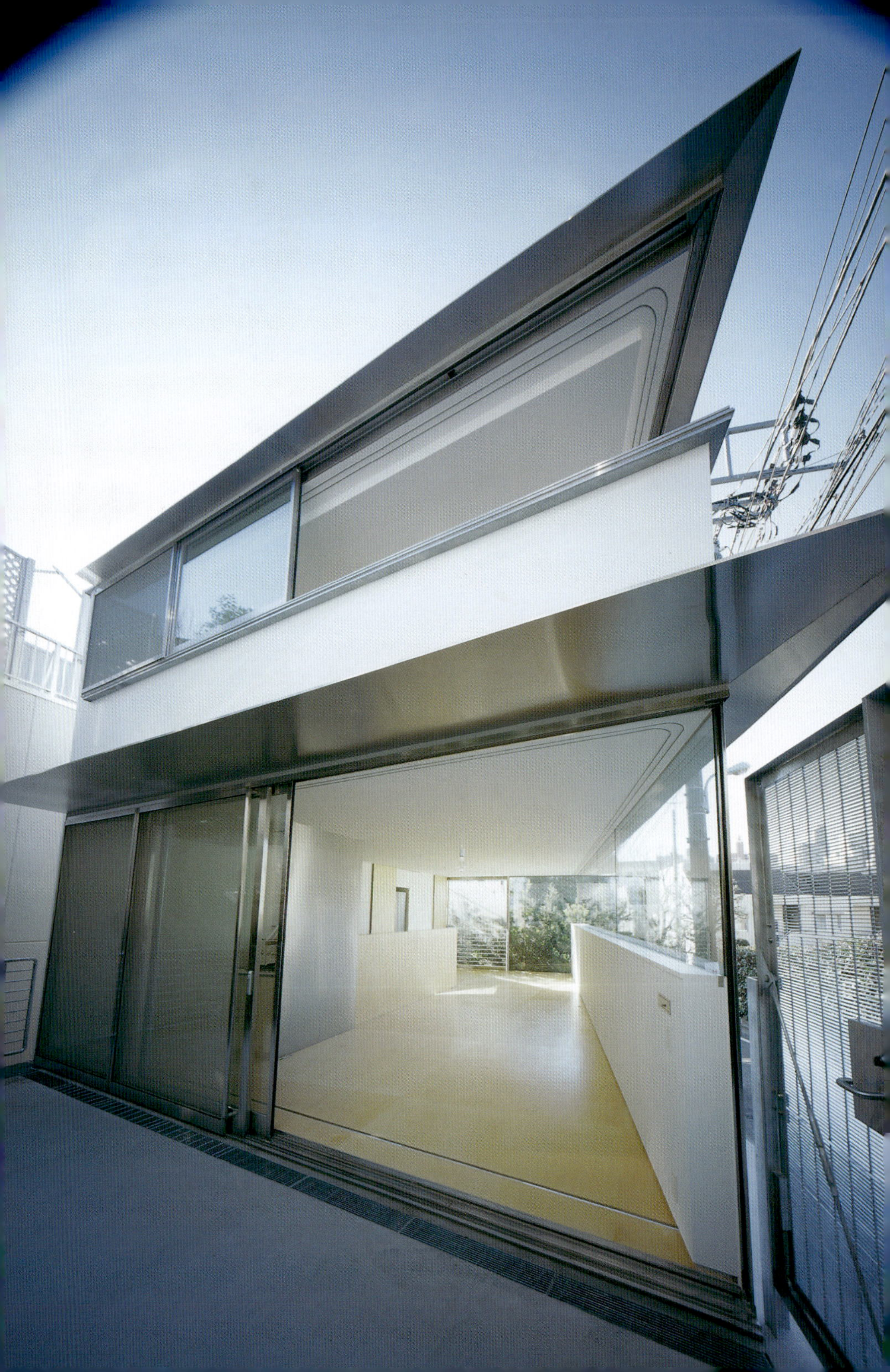

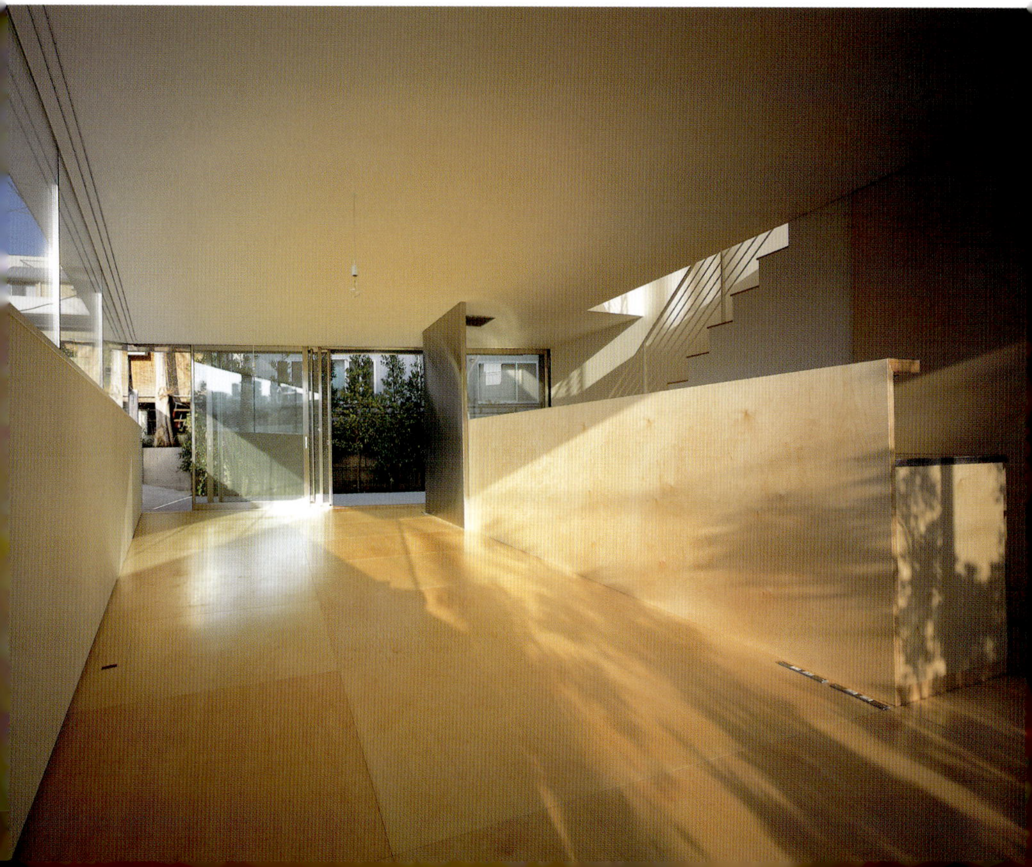

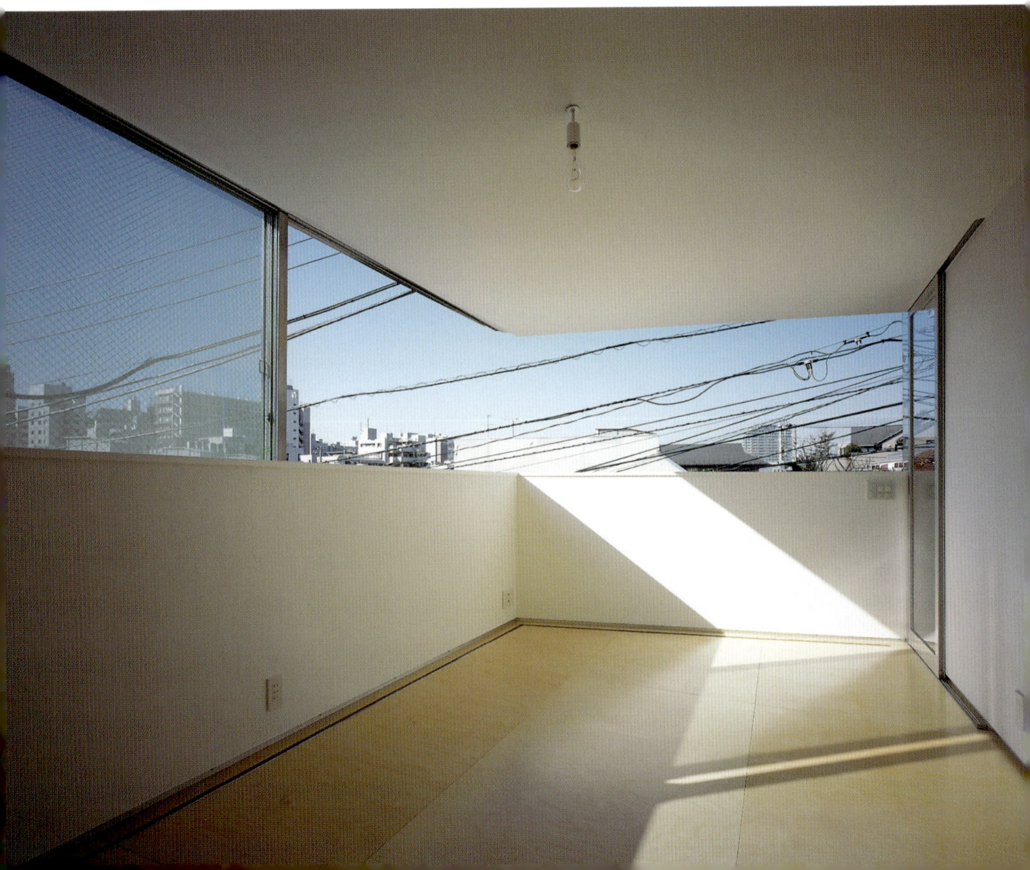

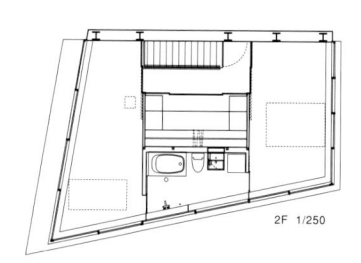

2F 1/250

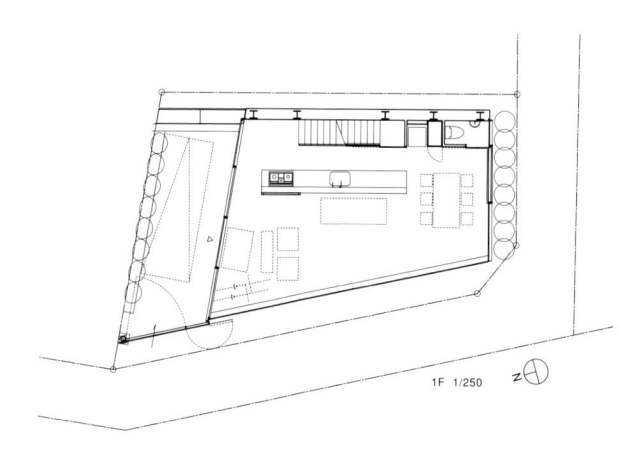

1F 1/250

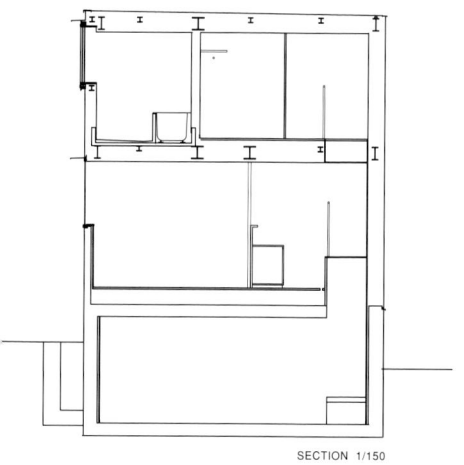

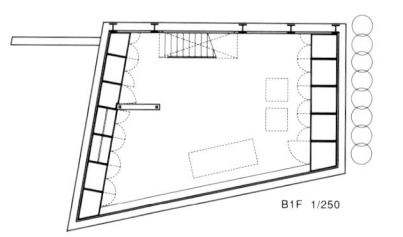

B1F 1/250

SECTION 1/150

Five-Courtyard House

ファイブコートヤードハウス　2004

The house was structured around five different courtyards, each one corresponding to a specific room.

五つ中庭のある家。
それぞれの部屋に一つずつ中庭がある。

27

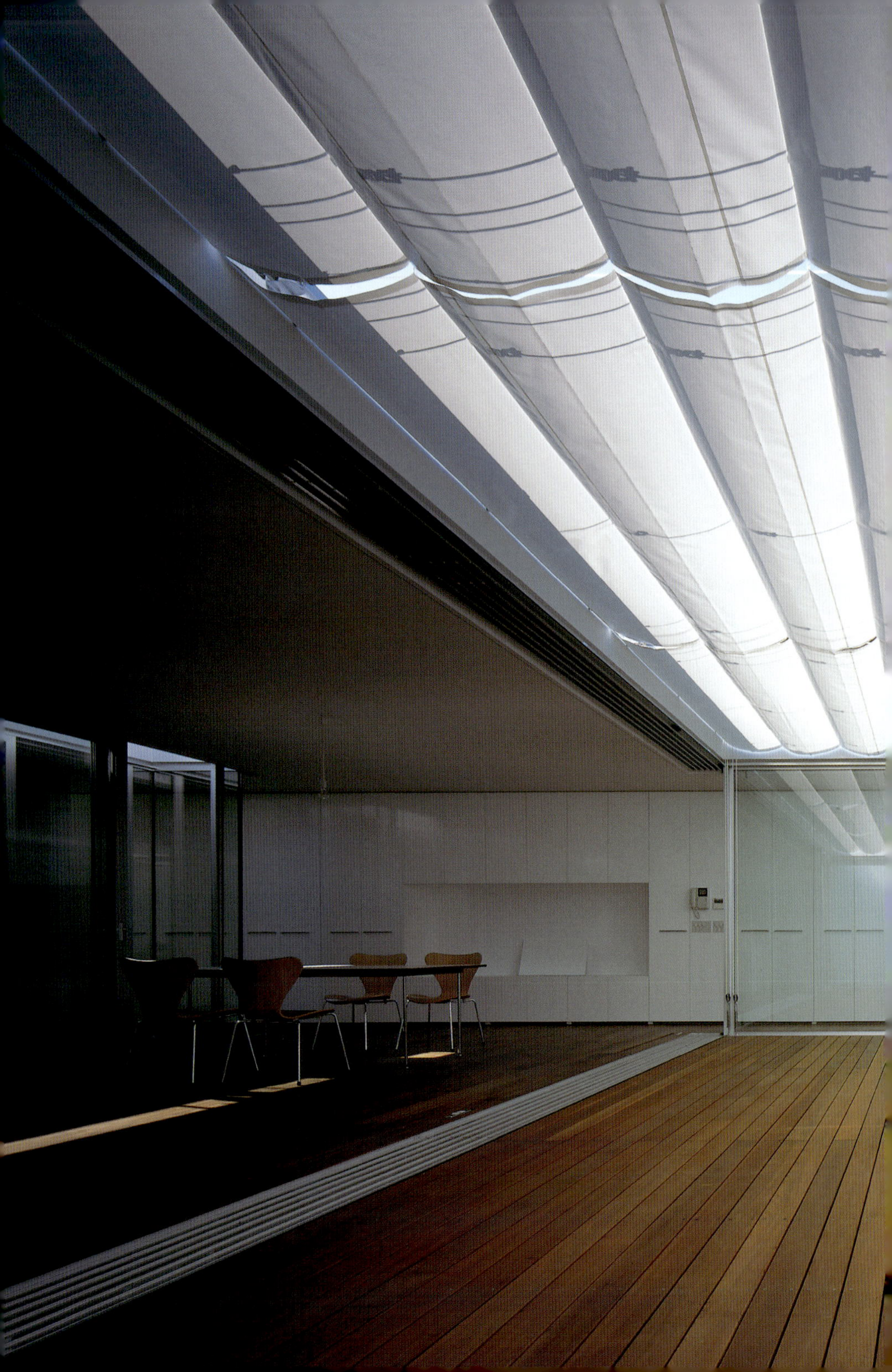

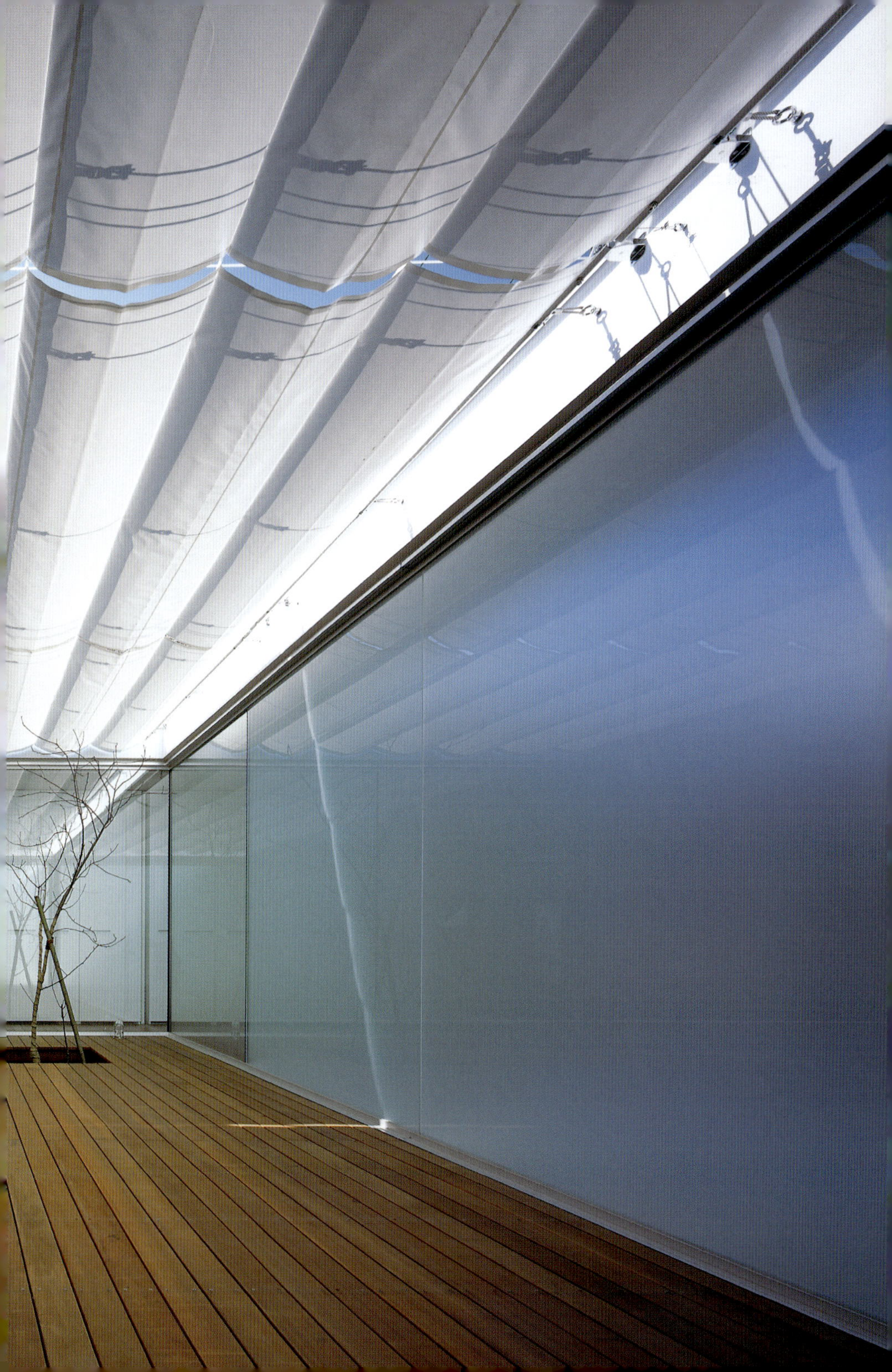

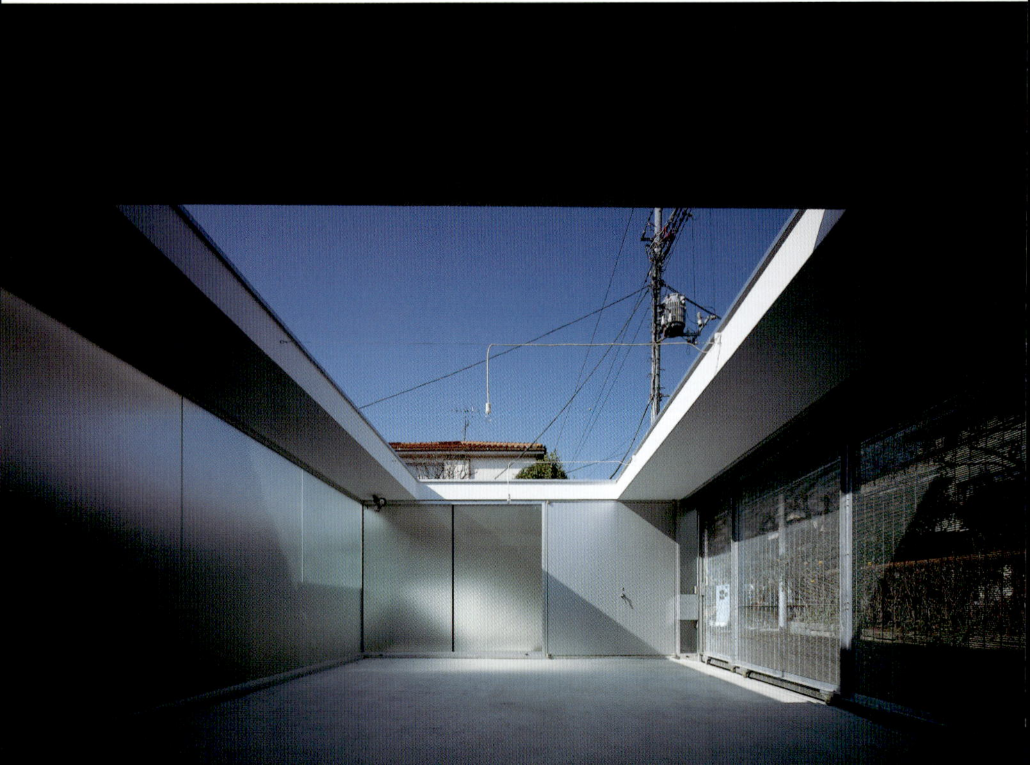

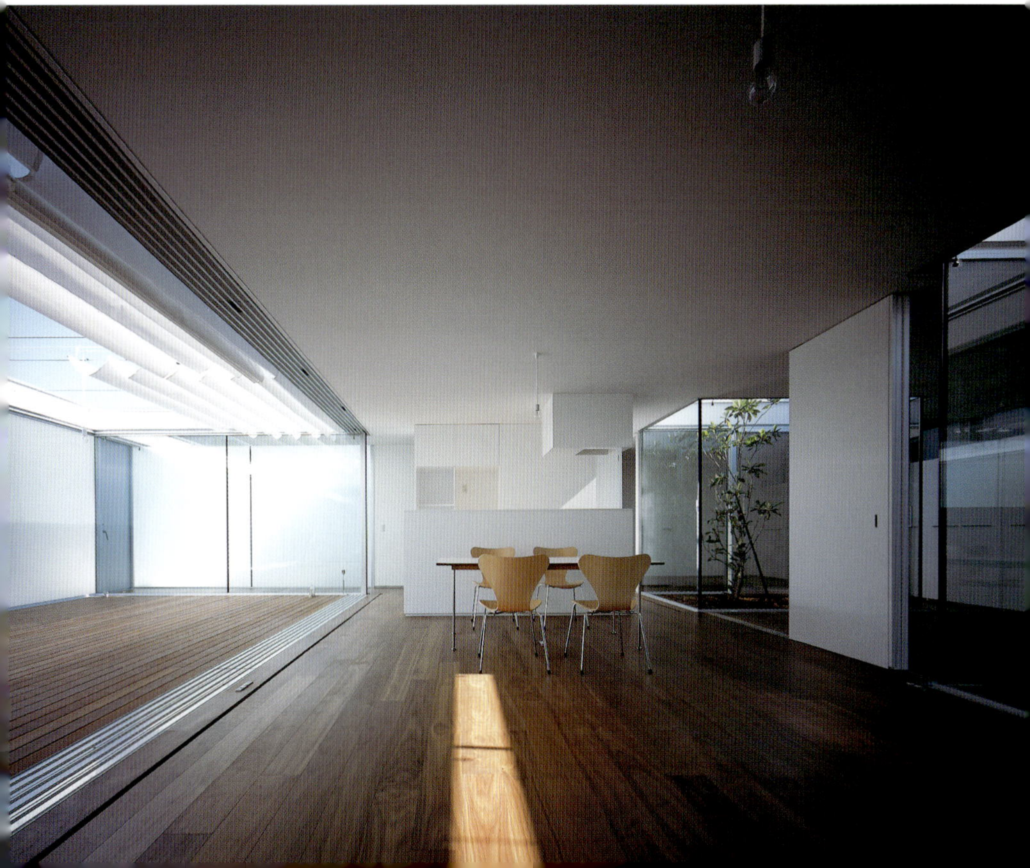

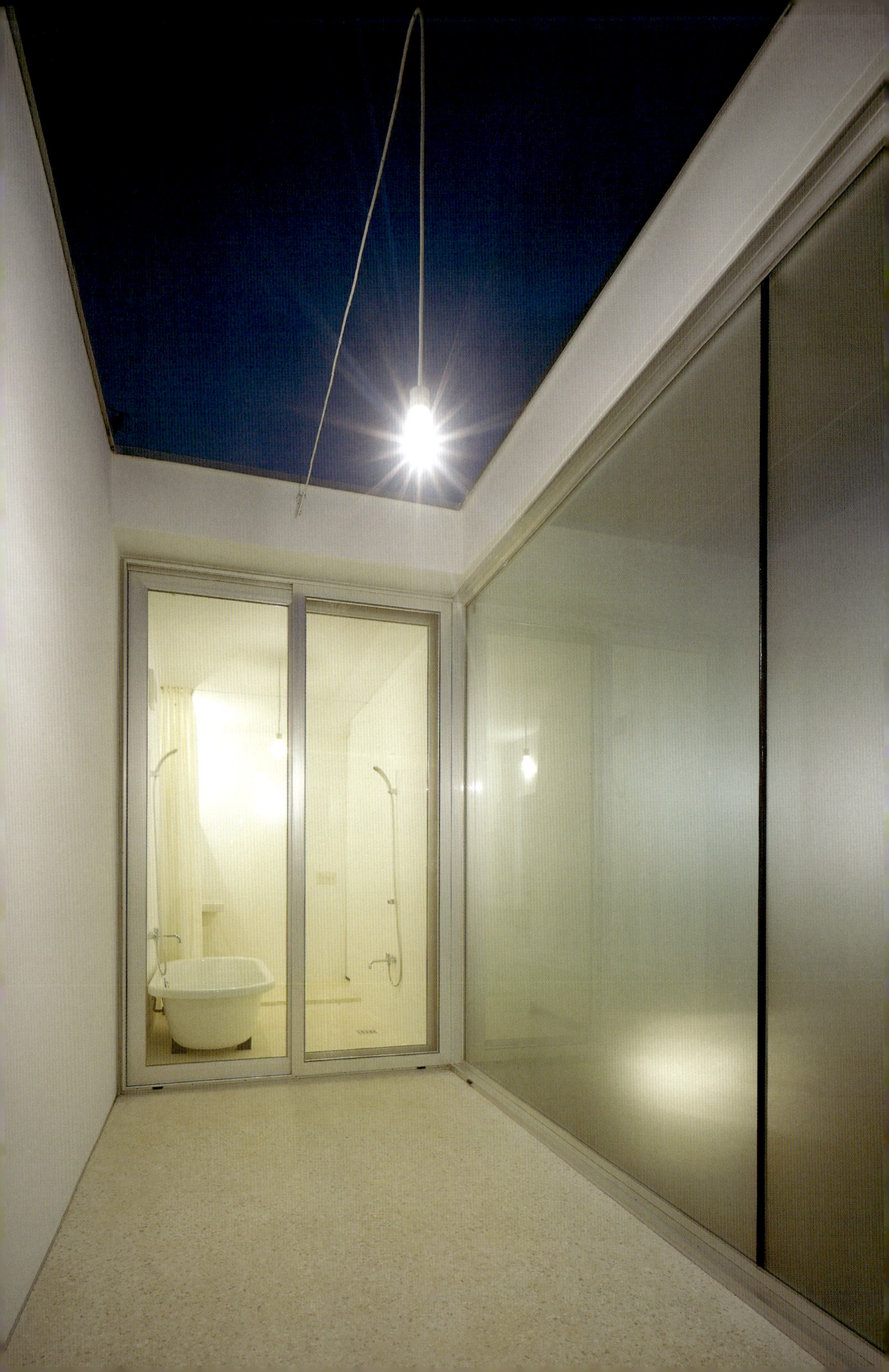

1F 1/250

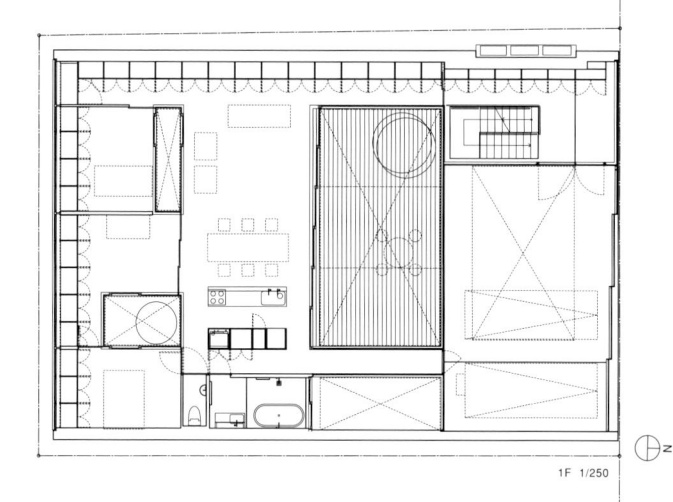

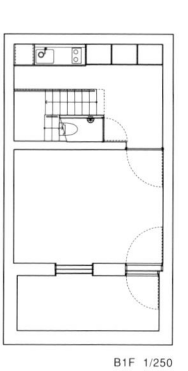

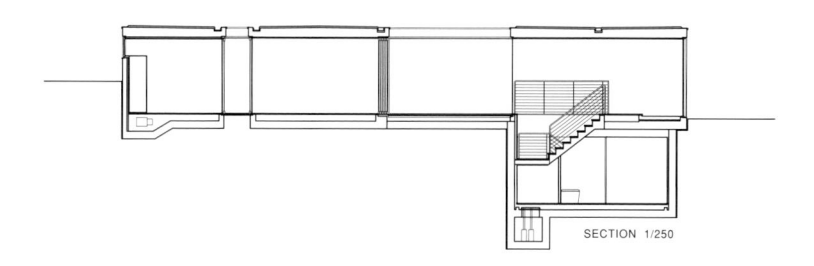

B1F 1/250

SECTION 1/250

Thin Wall Office

壁の薄いオフィス　2004

This office building is exclusively composed of 9mm steel plates and 125mm x 25mm steel flat bars.

鉄板だけで出来ている事務所ビル。
9mmの鉄板に630mm間隔で125mm×25mmのフラットバーが並ぶ。

28

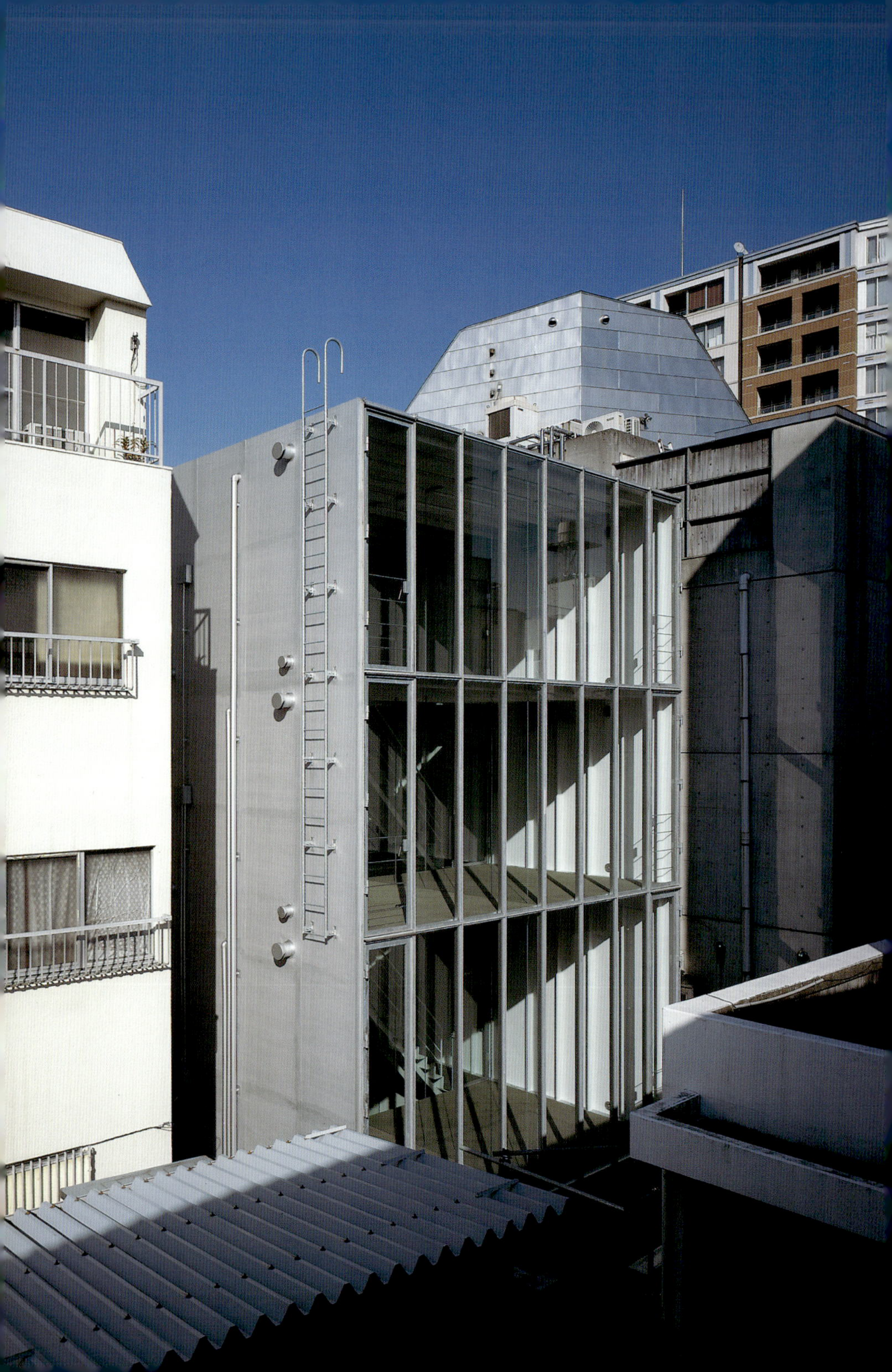

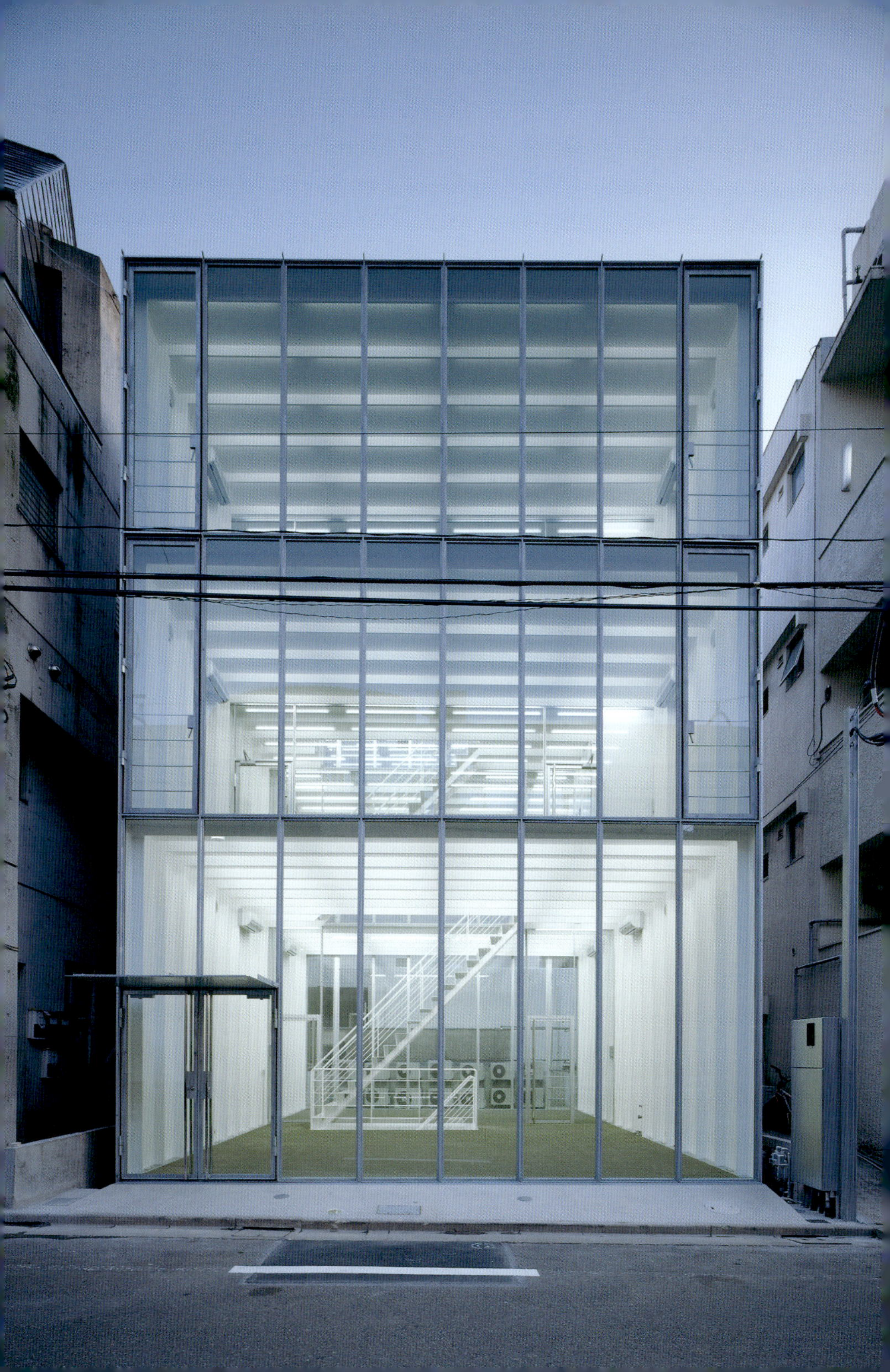

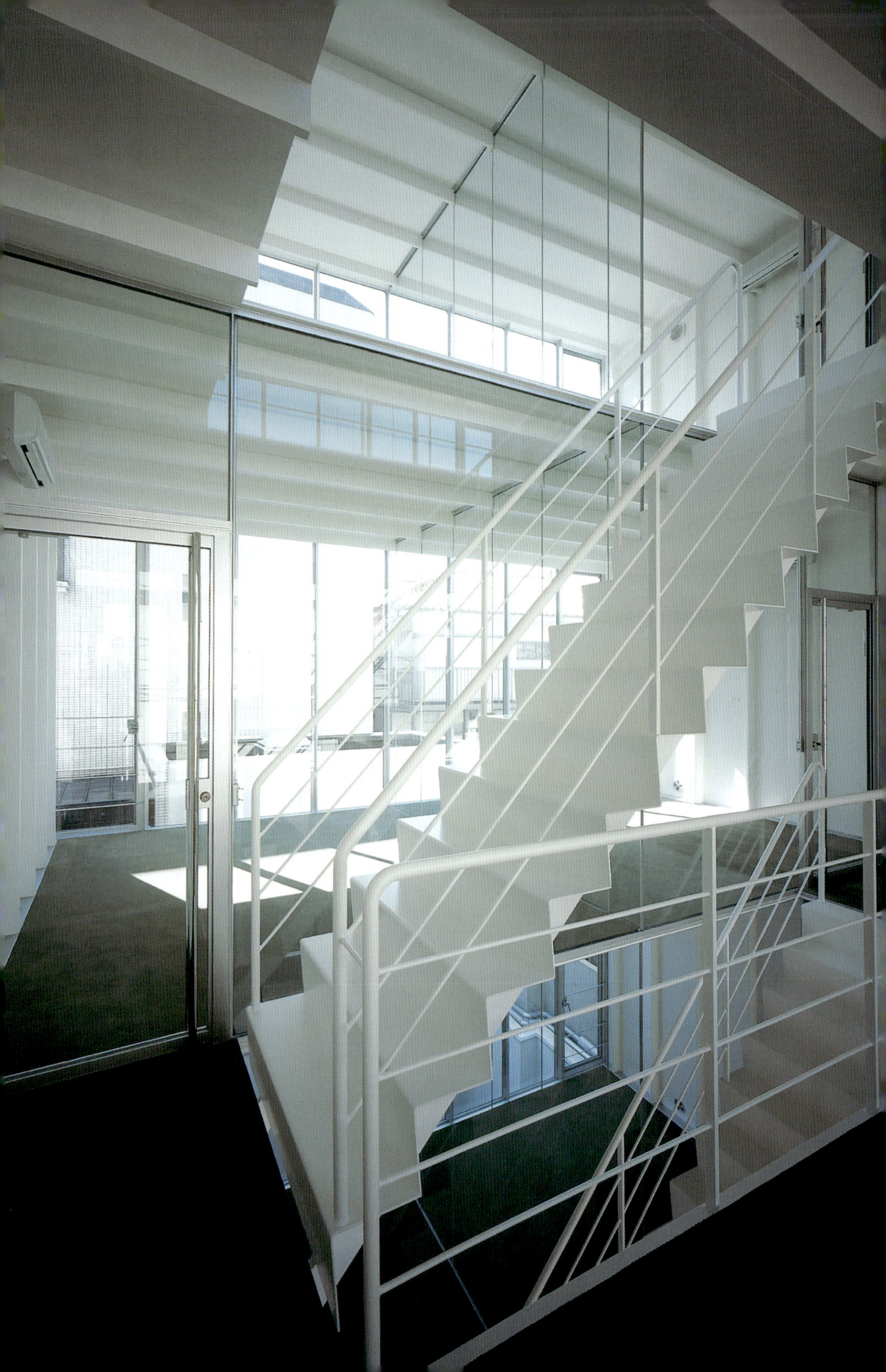

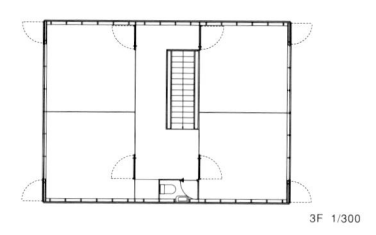

3F 1/300

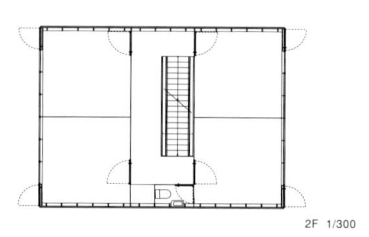

2F 1/300

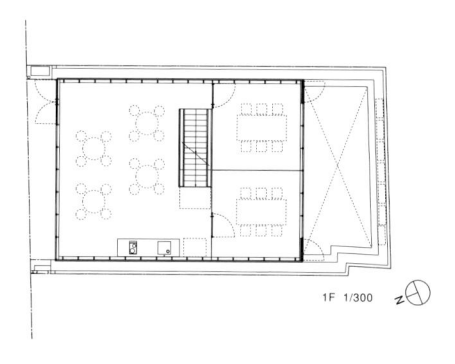

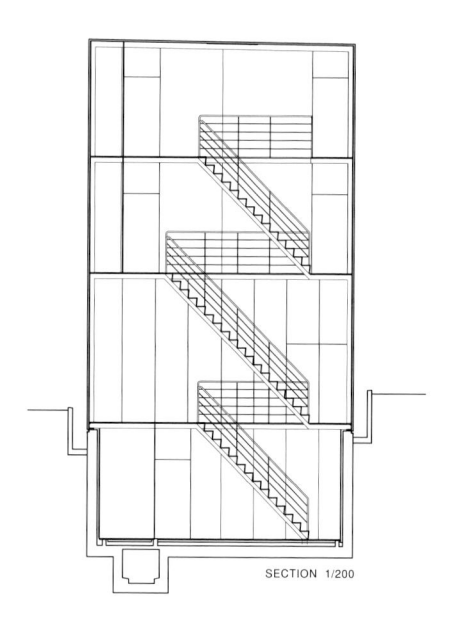

1F 1/300

SECTION 1/200

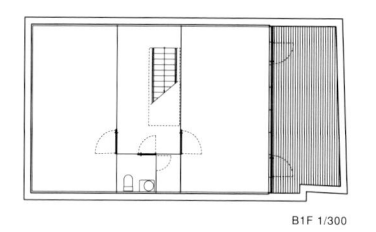

B1F 1/300

Clipping Corner House

隅切りの家　2004

The building design follows the peculiar shape of this lot, with one the corners clipped off the house's rectilinear plan. The interior was designed as a monolithic space where sliding doors can be used to create partitions.

住宅地のグリッドの一角に食い込んだ谷に隅を切り取られた建物。

29

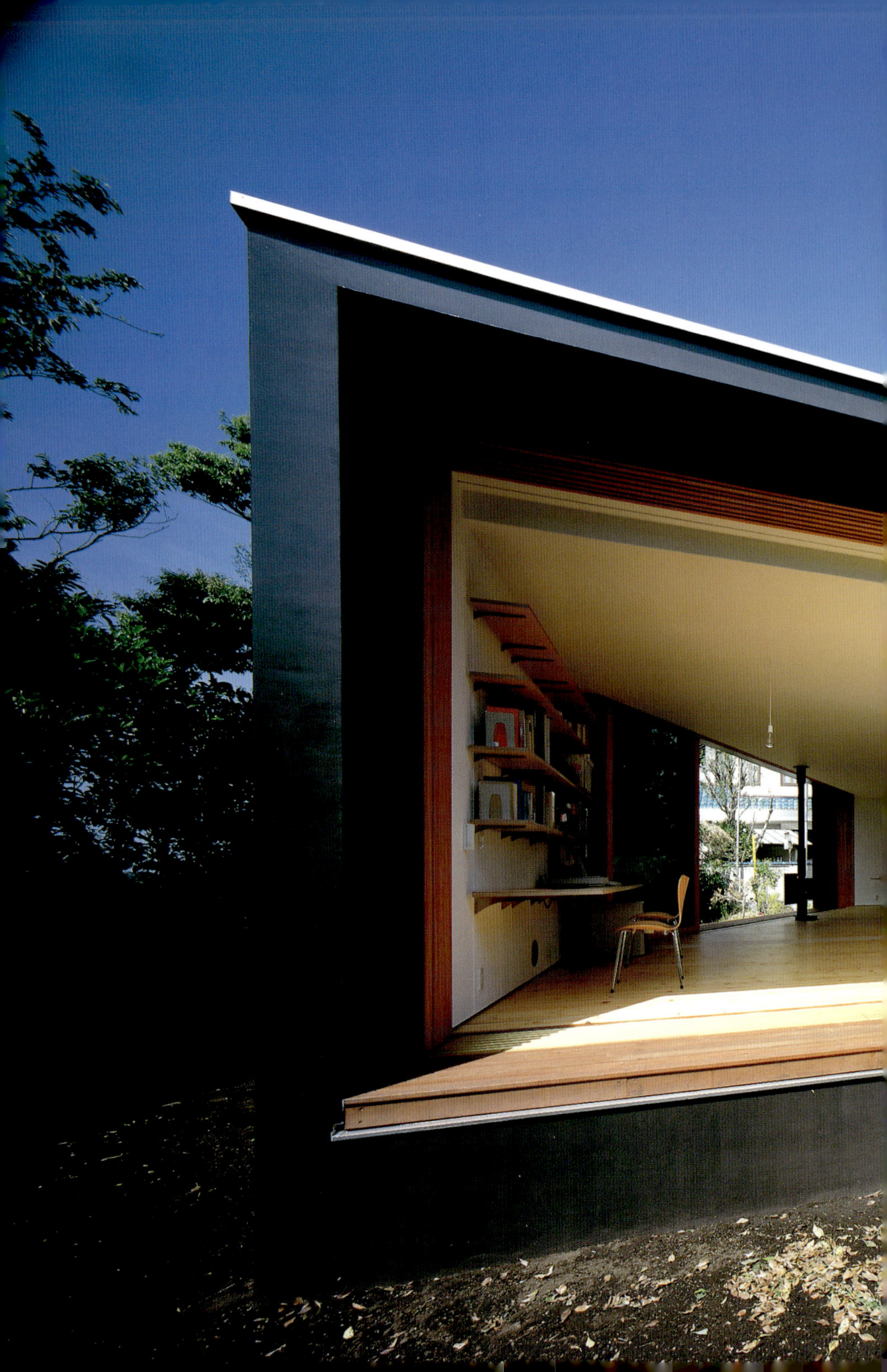

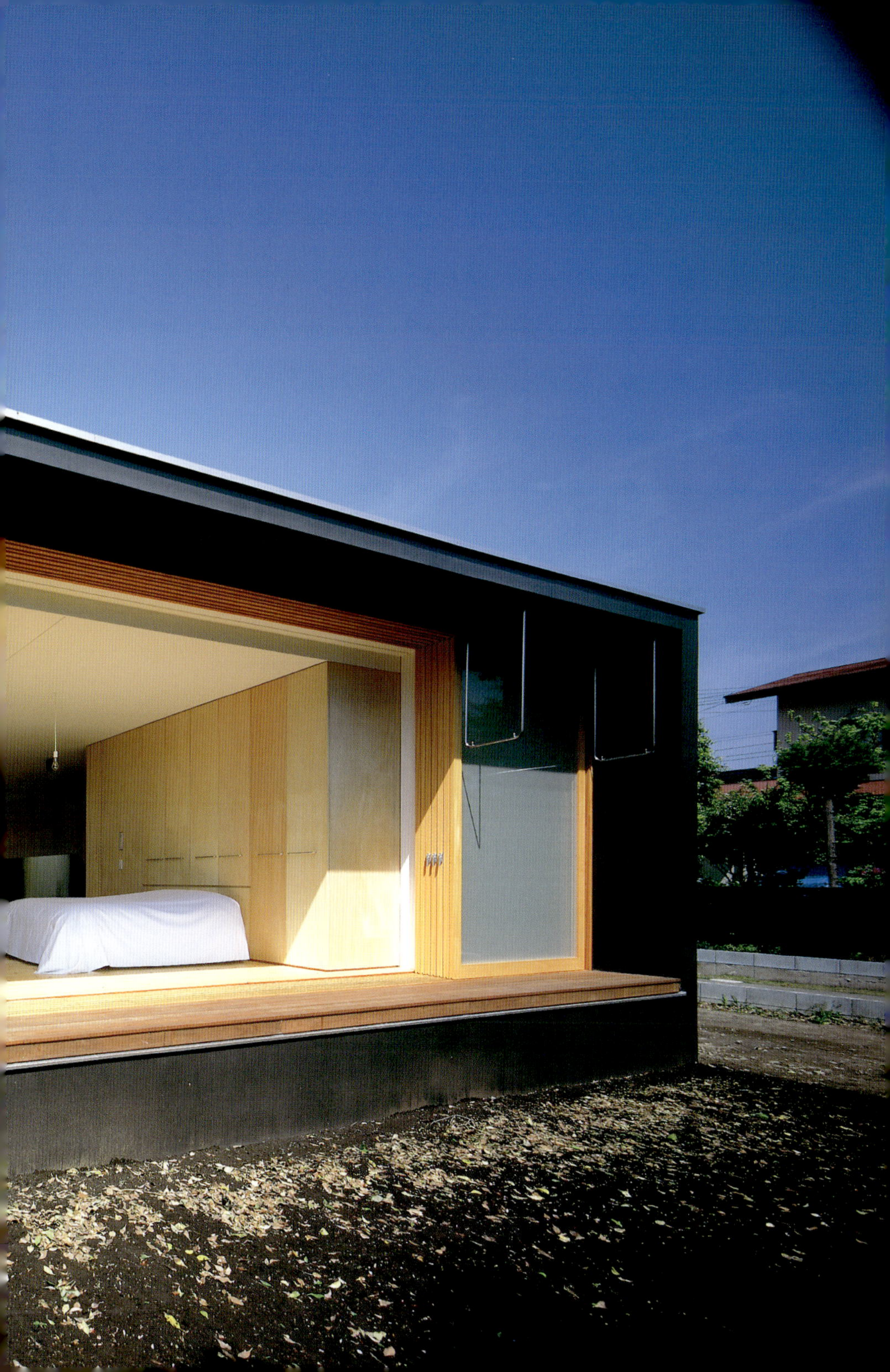

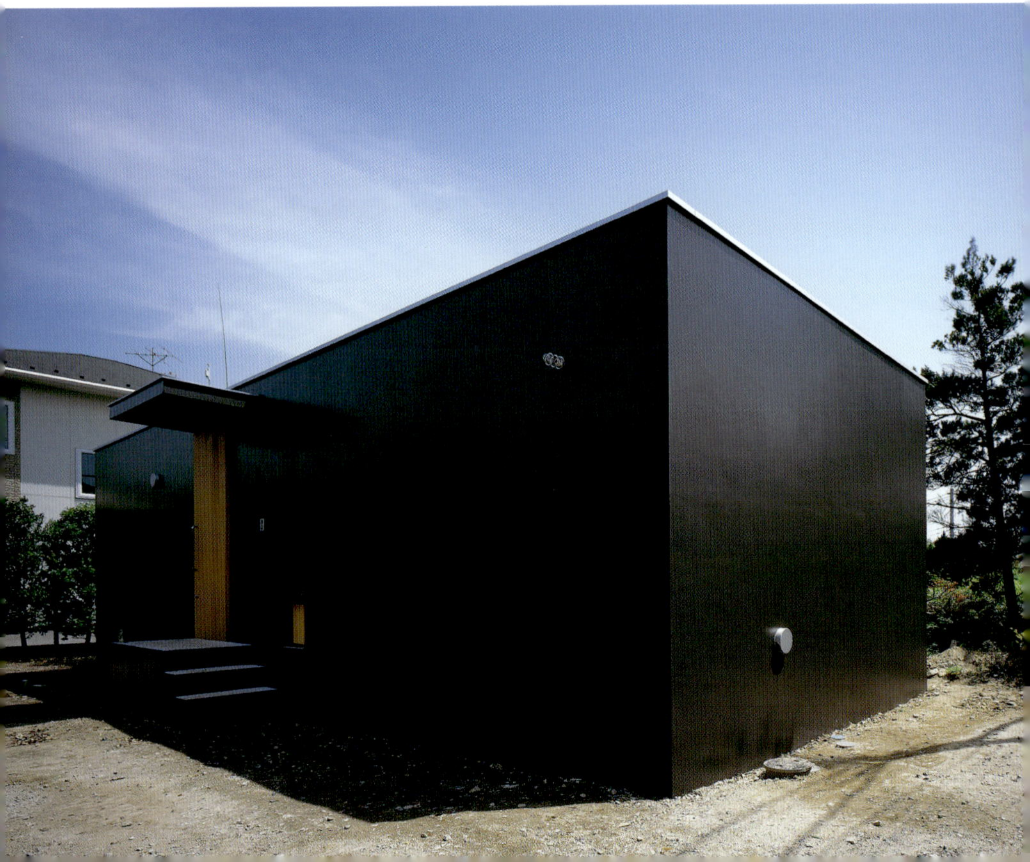

1F 1/200

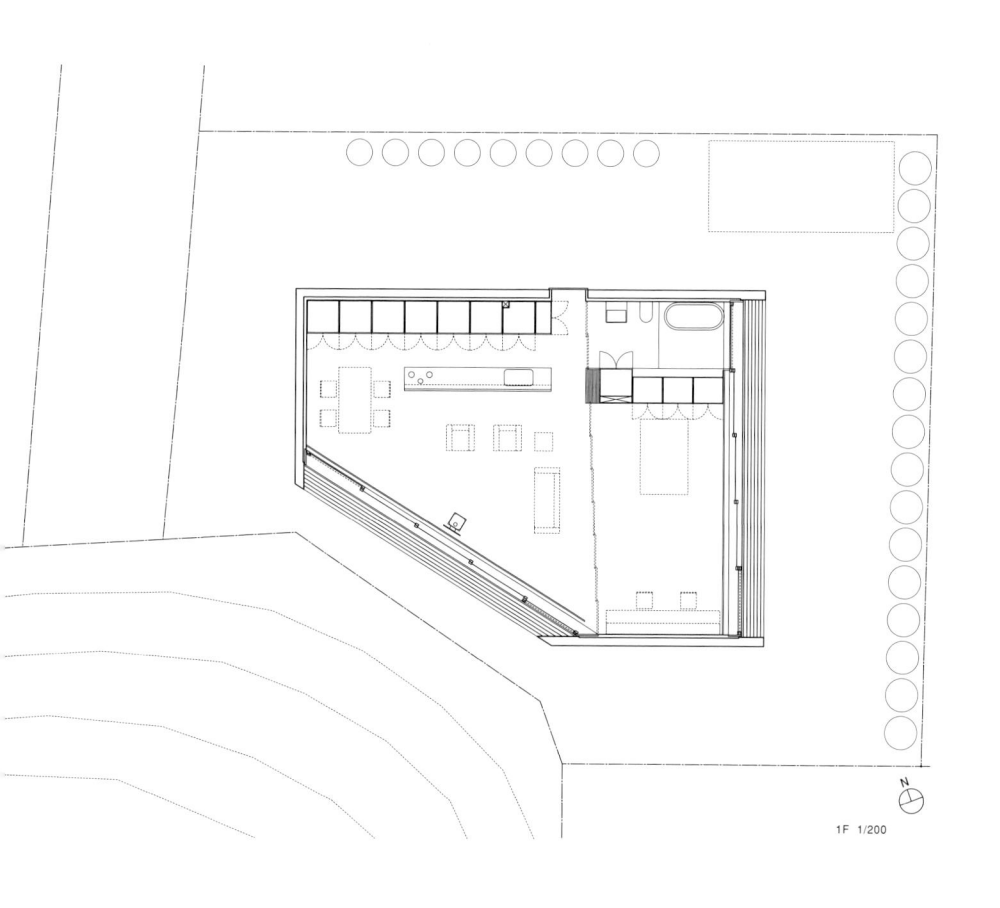

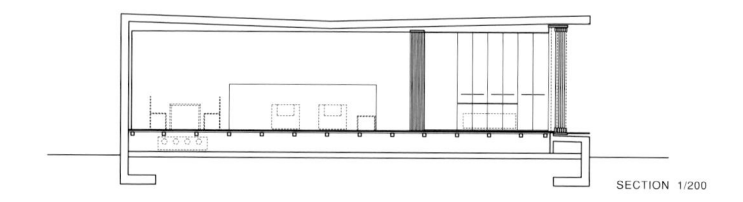

SECTION 1/200

Double Courtyard House

ダブルコートヤードハウス　2004

Zigzag-shaped house with two courtyards. The whole interior is open to the outside on two sides.

ジグザグ型の家。
空間が常に二方向に開いていて風が抜ける。

30

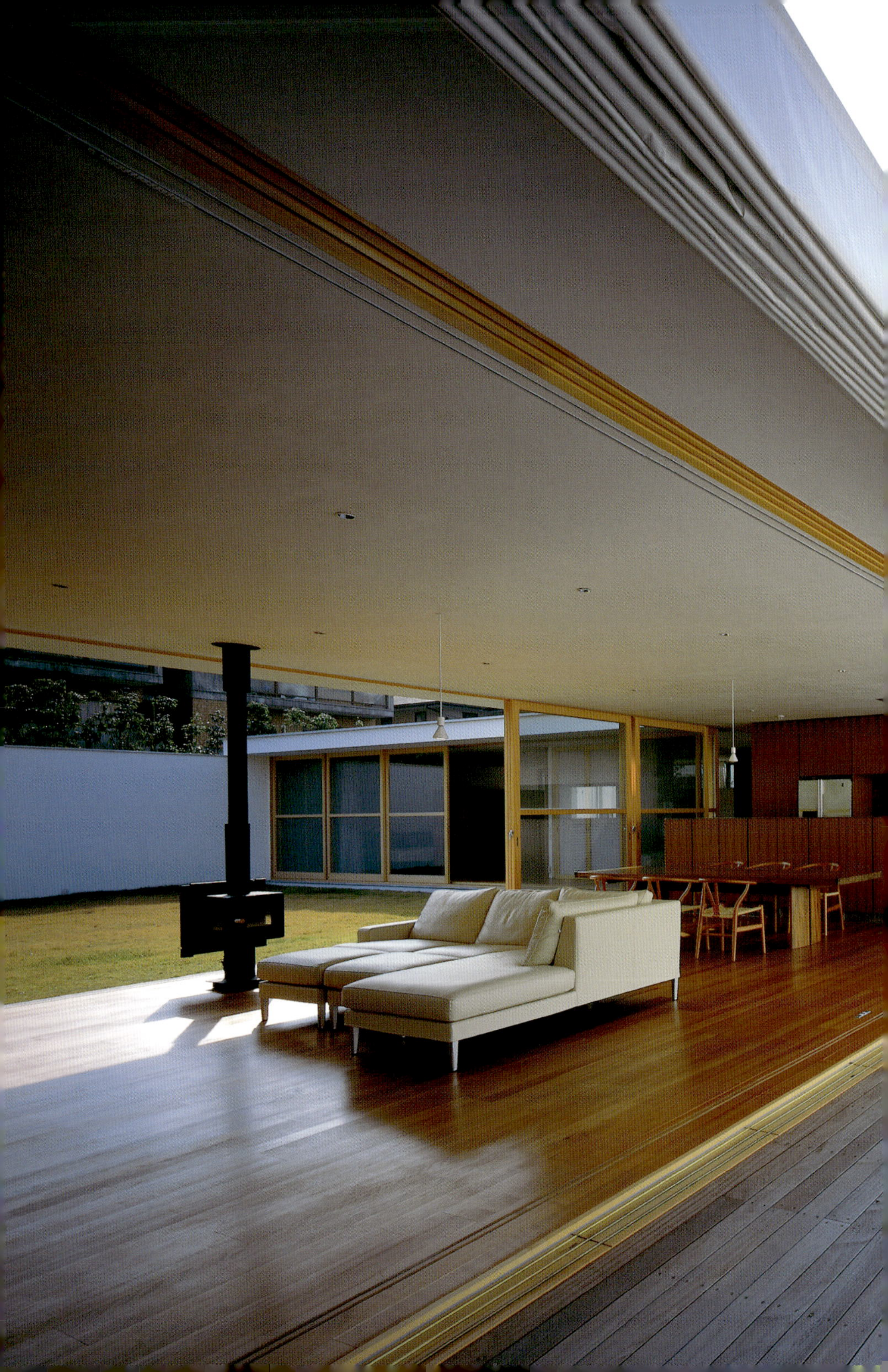

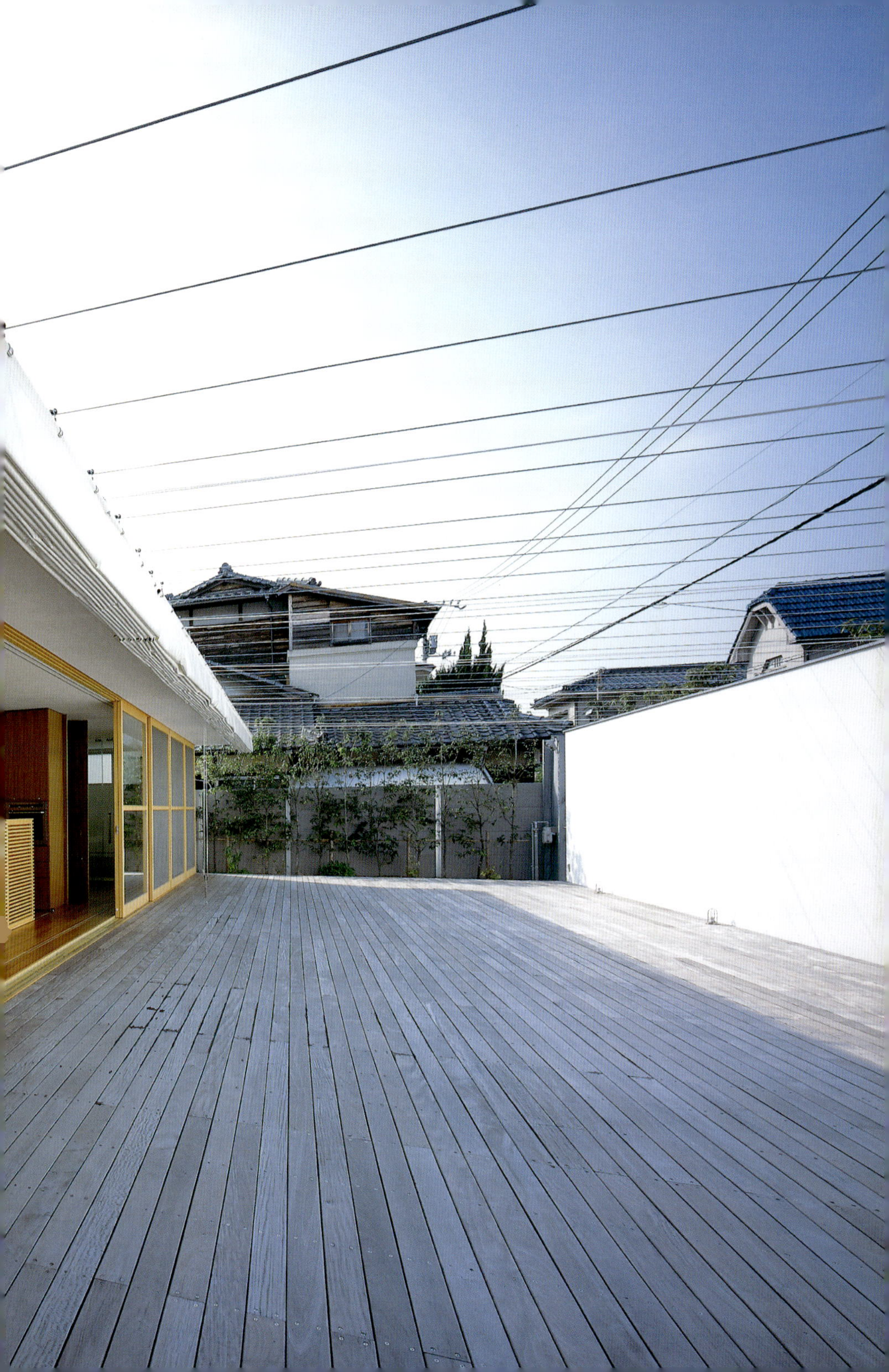

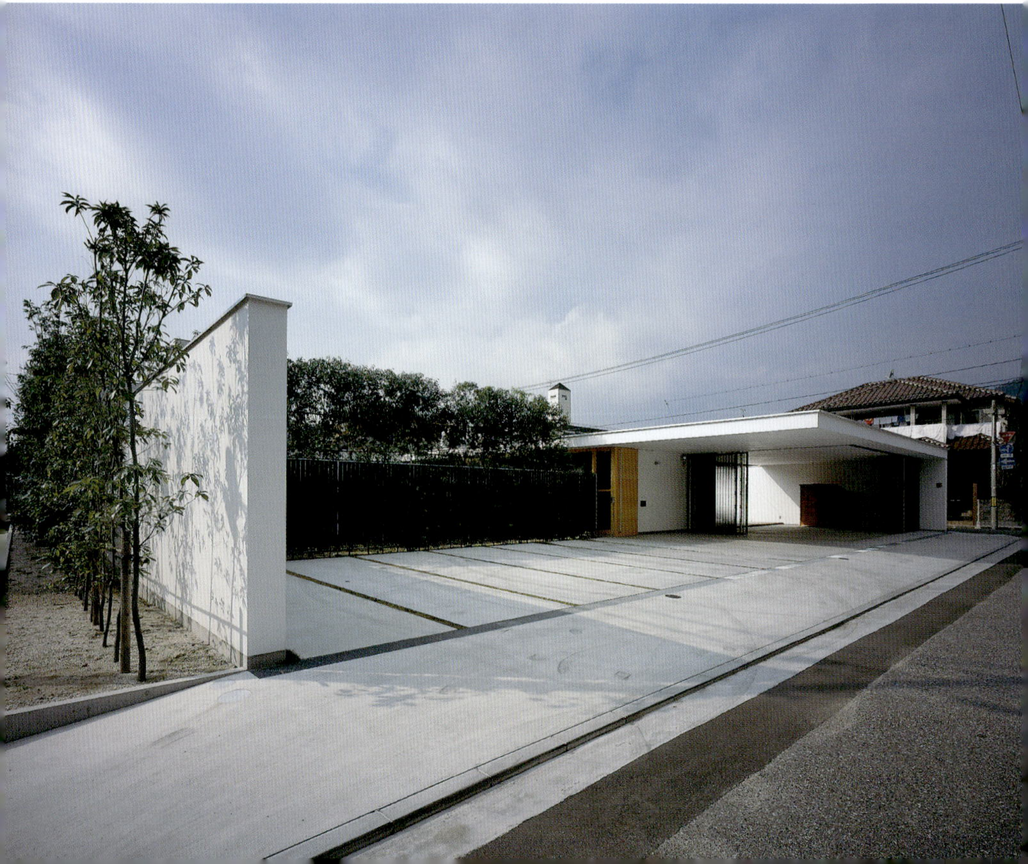

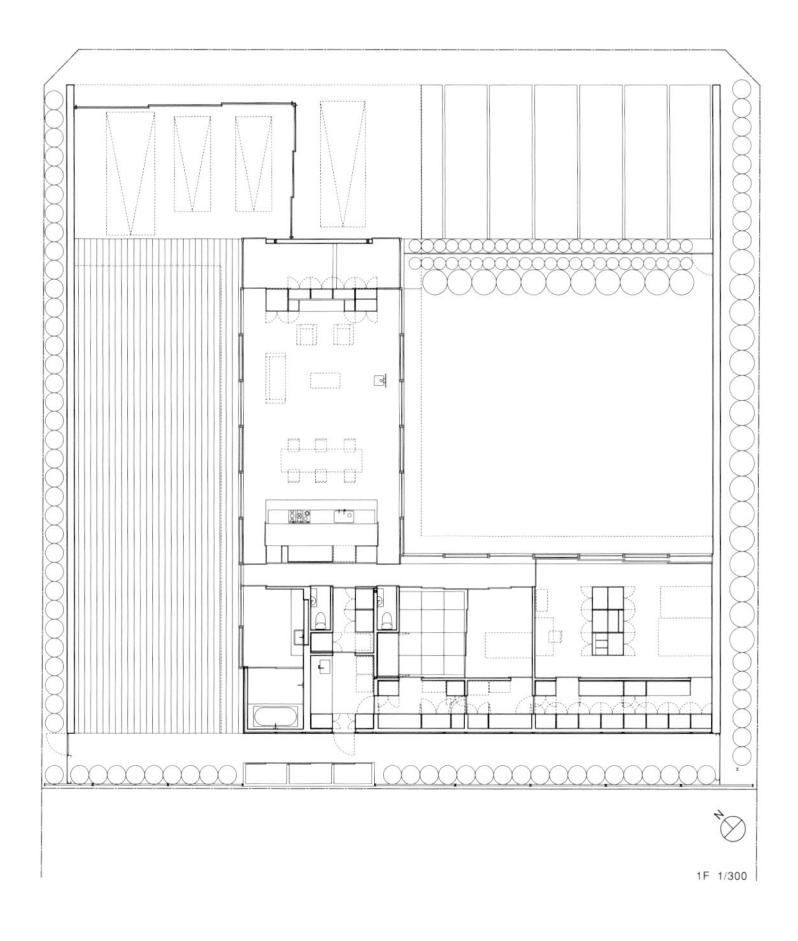

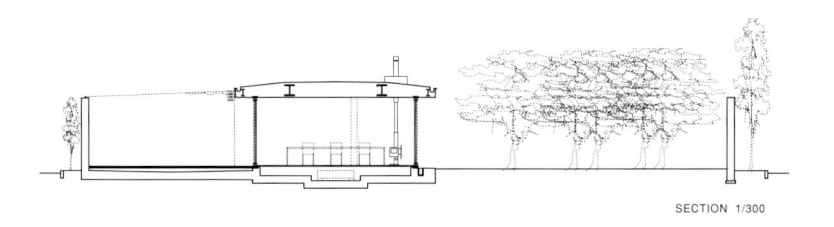

1F 1/300

SECTION 1/300

House to Catch the Forest

森を捕まえる家　2004

This cottage floats in the forest, its roof tilted to optimise the view over the treetops. The differences in ceiling heights were used to match the different purposes of the room.

森の景色を切り取るために設定された屋根と壁が
不定形の空間をつくっている。様々の天井高が変化のある
ワンルーム空間をつくり出している。

31

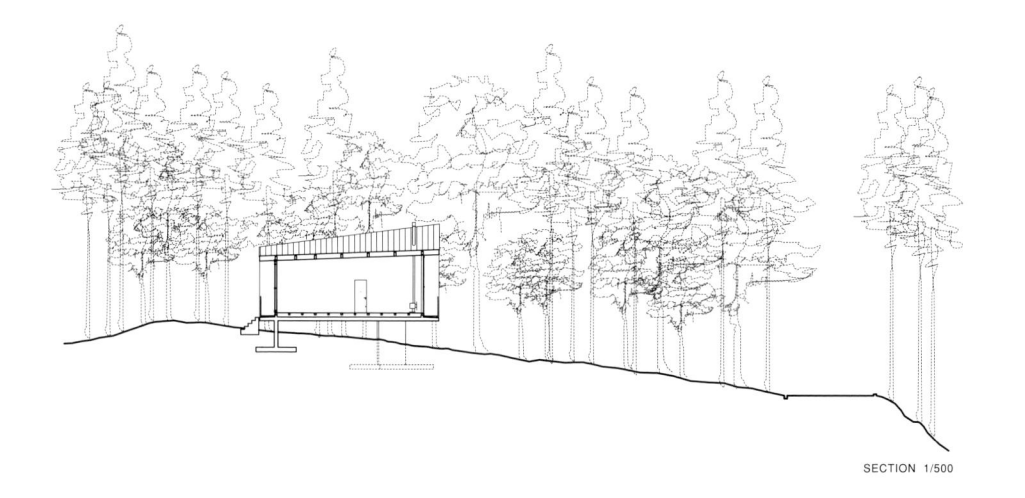

SECTION 1/500

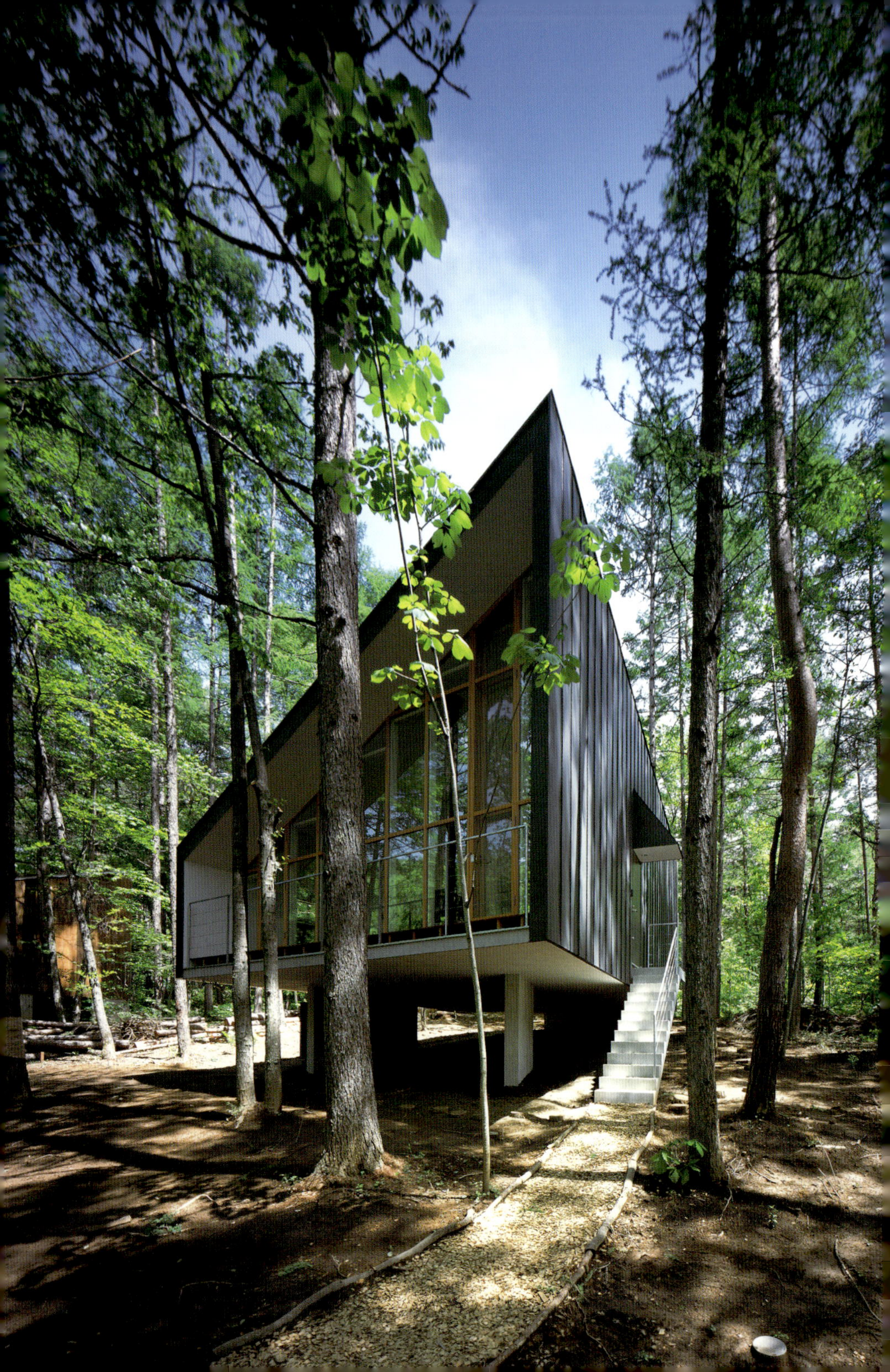

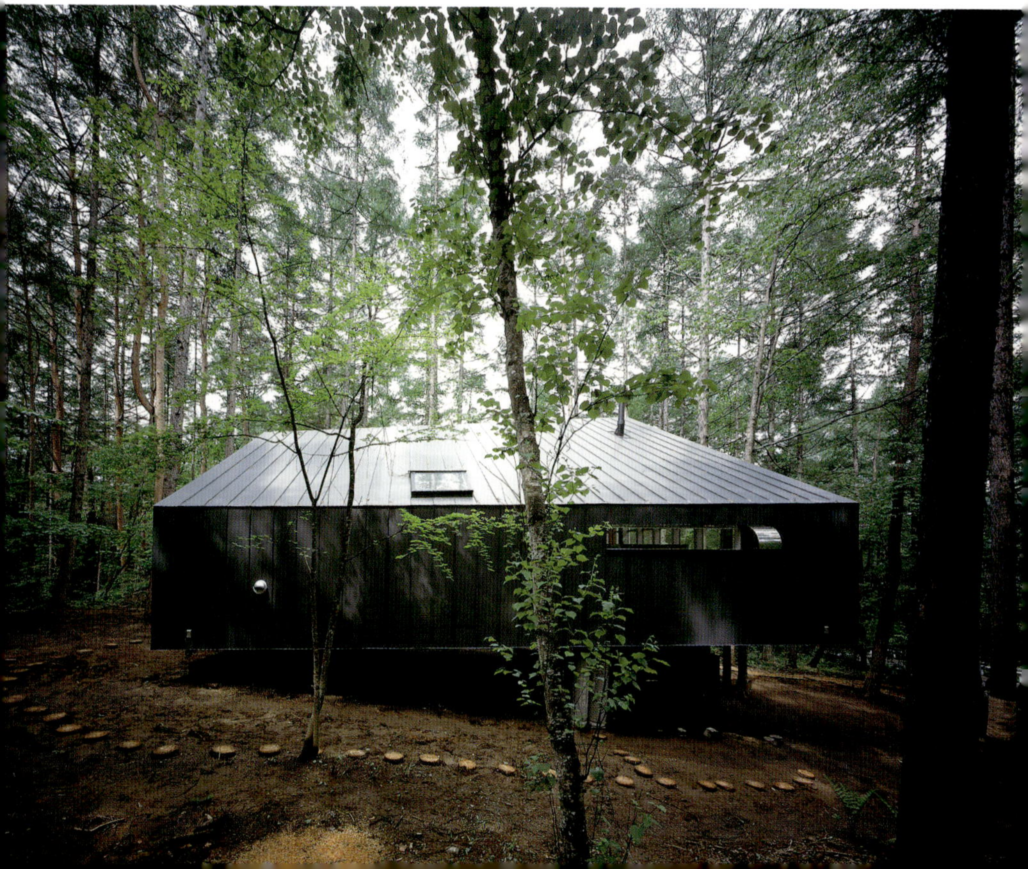

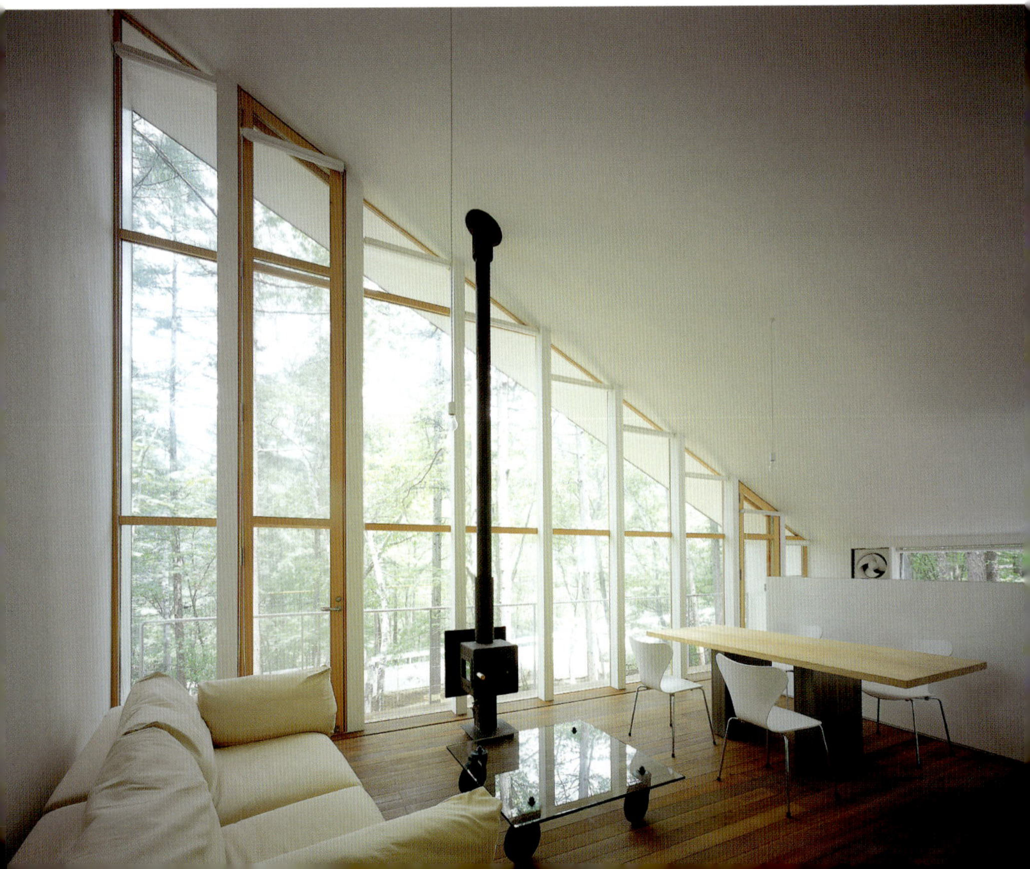

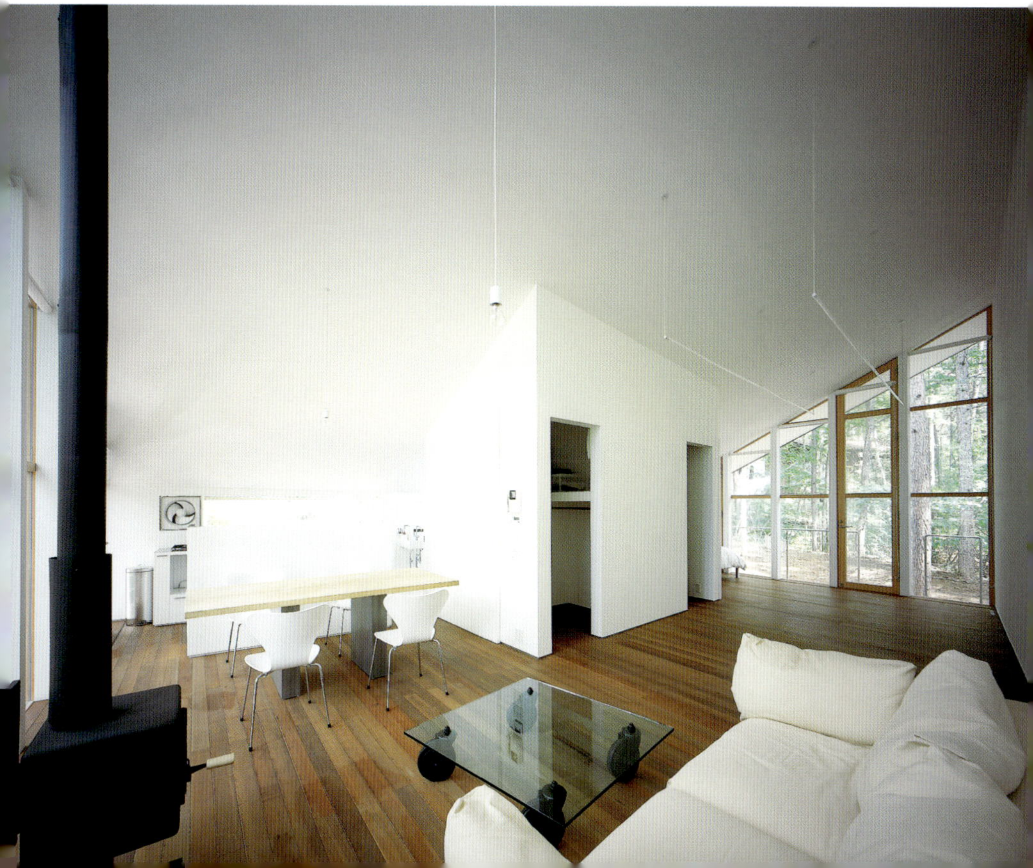

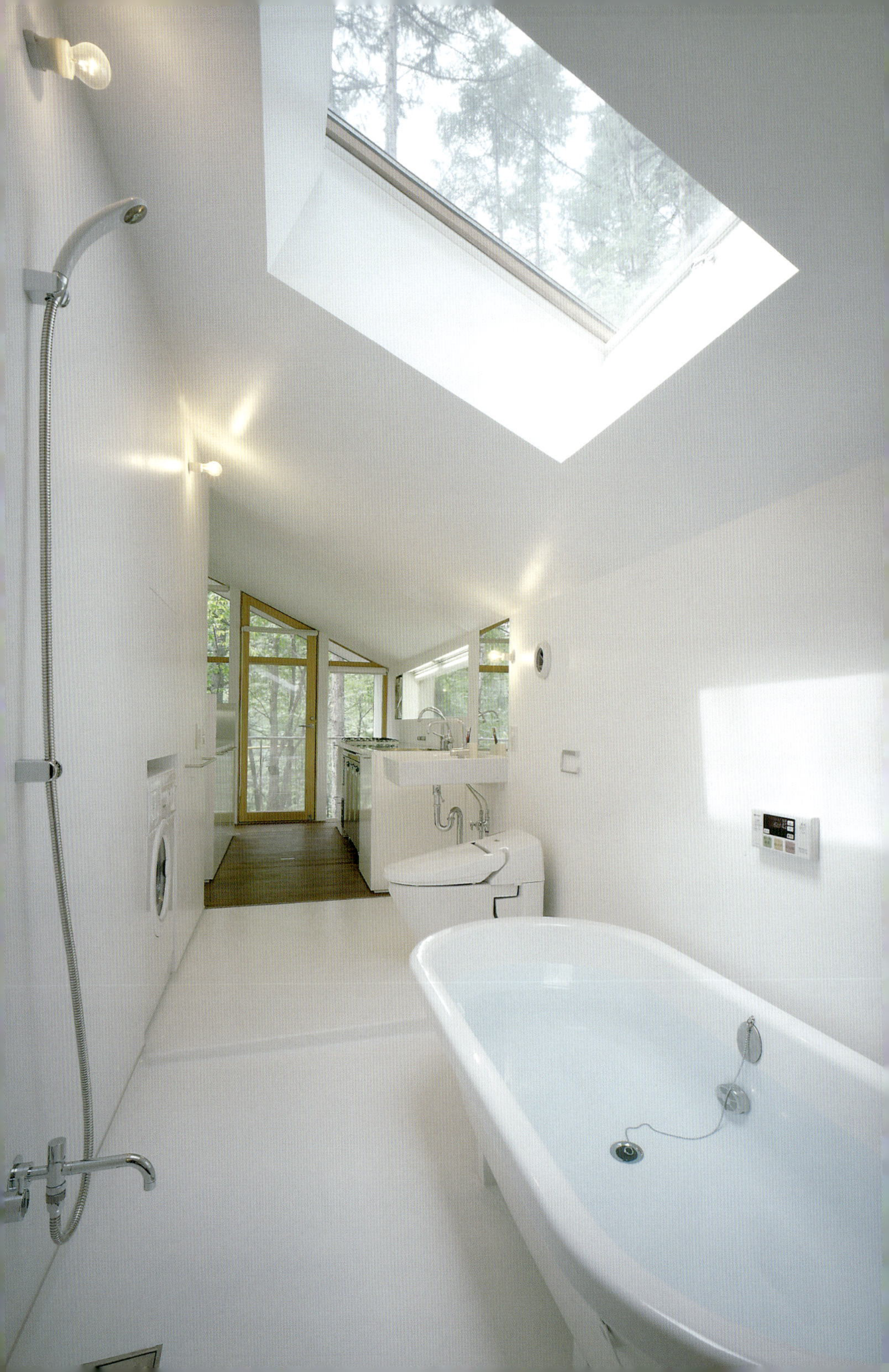

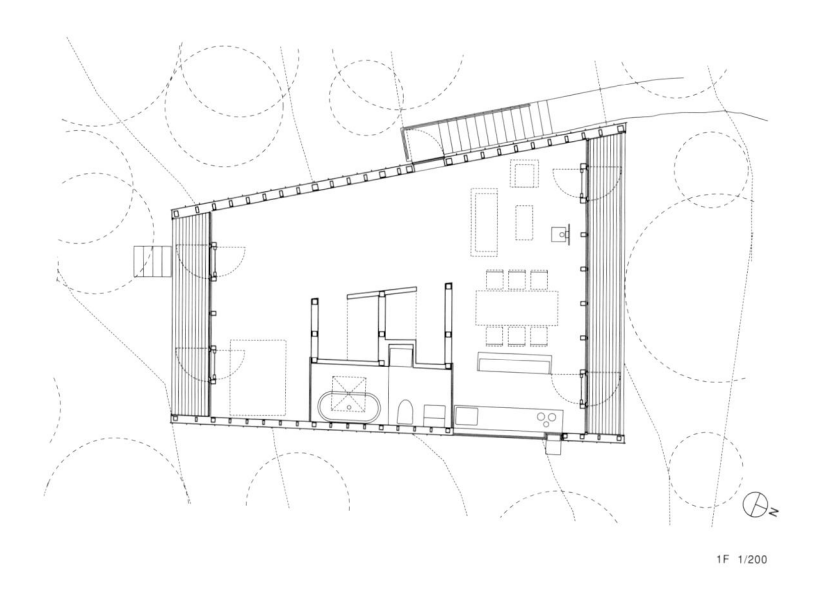

1F 1/200

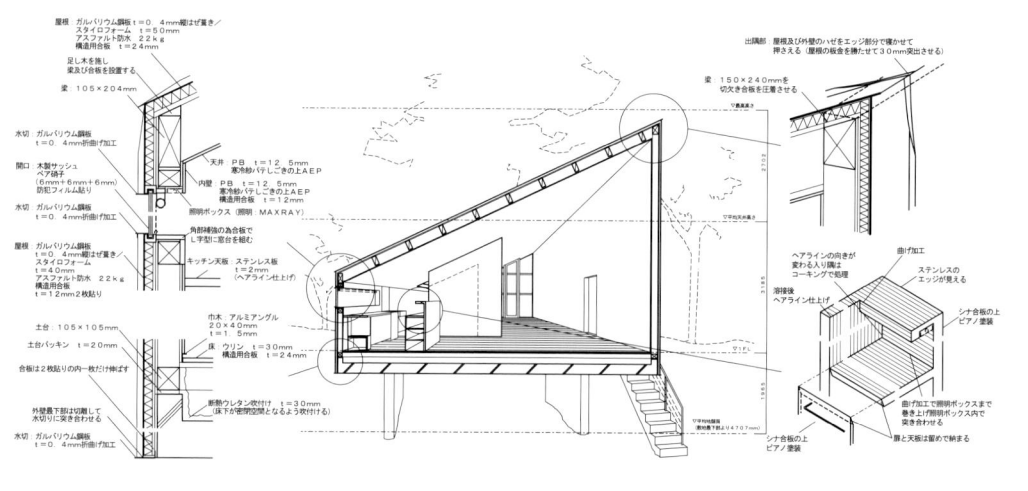

DETAIL

屋根：ガルバリウム鋼板 t=0.4mm 瓦はぜ葺き／
スタイロフォーム 22kg
アスファルト防水 22kg
構造用合板 t=12mm 2枚貼り

足し木を施し、
梁及び合板を設置する。
梁：105×204mm

水切 ガルバリウム鋼板
t=0.4mm 折曲げ加工

開口 木製サッシュ
ペア硝子
(6mm+6mm+6mm)
防露フィルム貼り

水切 ガルバリウム鋼板
t=0.4mm 折曲げ加工

屋根：ガルバリウム鋼板
t=0.4mm 瓦はぜ葺き／
スタイロフォーム
t=40mm
アスファルト防水 22kg
構造用合板 t=12mm 2枚貼り

土台：105×105mm
土台パッキン t=20mm
合板は2枚貼りの内一枚だけ突出す

外壁見下げ切断して
水切の内に突き合わせる

水切 ガルバリウム鋼板
t=0.4mm 折曲げ加工

天井 PB t=12.5mm
寒冷紗パテしごきの上AEP
内壁 PB t=12.5mm
寒冷紗パテしごきの上AEP
構造用合板 t=12mm
照明ボックス（照明 MAXRAY）

角部補強の為合板で
L字型に混合台を組む

キッチン天板：ステンレス板
t=2mm
（ヘアライン仕上げ）

巾木：アルミアングル
20×40mm
床 クリン t=30mm
構造用合板 t=24mm

断熱ウレタン吹付け t=30mm
（床下が密閉空間となるよう吹付ける）

出隅根：屋根及び外壁のハゼをエッジ部分で寝かせて
押さえる（屋根の板金を勝たせて30mm突出させる）

梁：150×240mm
を切欠き合板を圧着させる

ヘアラインの向きが
変わる入り隅を
コーキングで処理

曲げ加工

溶接後
ヘアライン仕上げ

ステンレスの
エッジが見える

曲げ加工

シナ合板の上
ピアノ塗装

曲げ加工で照明ボックスまで
巻き上げ照明ボックス内で
突き合わせる

扉と天板は嵌めて納まる

シナ合板の上
ピアノ塗装

Observatory House

展望台の家　2004

This 3-storey structure is based on an elevated concrete platform supporting two steel-frame levels. The house was designed to view the regular firework displays above the sea.

由比ヶ浜の花火を湾岸線沿いの建物を越えて展望するための家。
一本のコアで支えられた台の上に建物全体が載せられている。

32

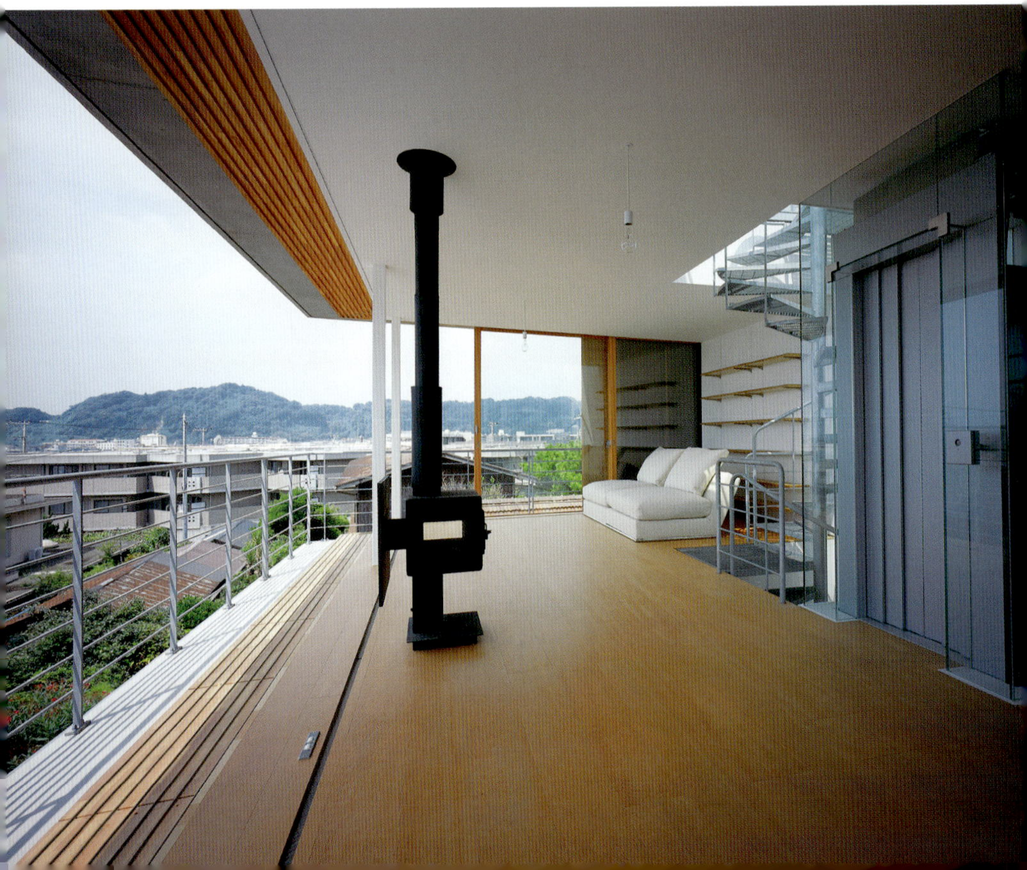

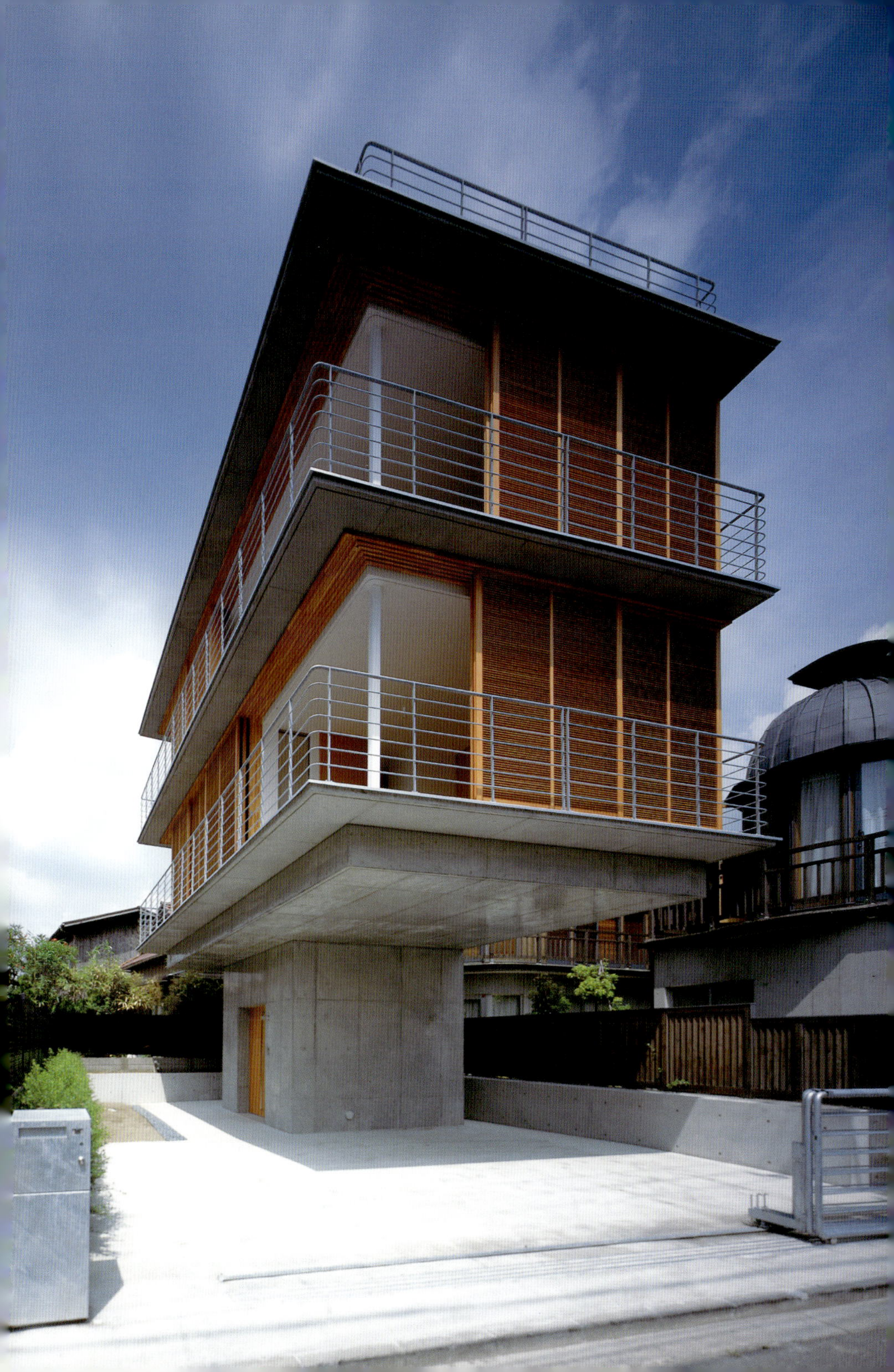

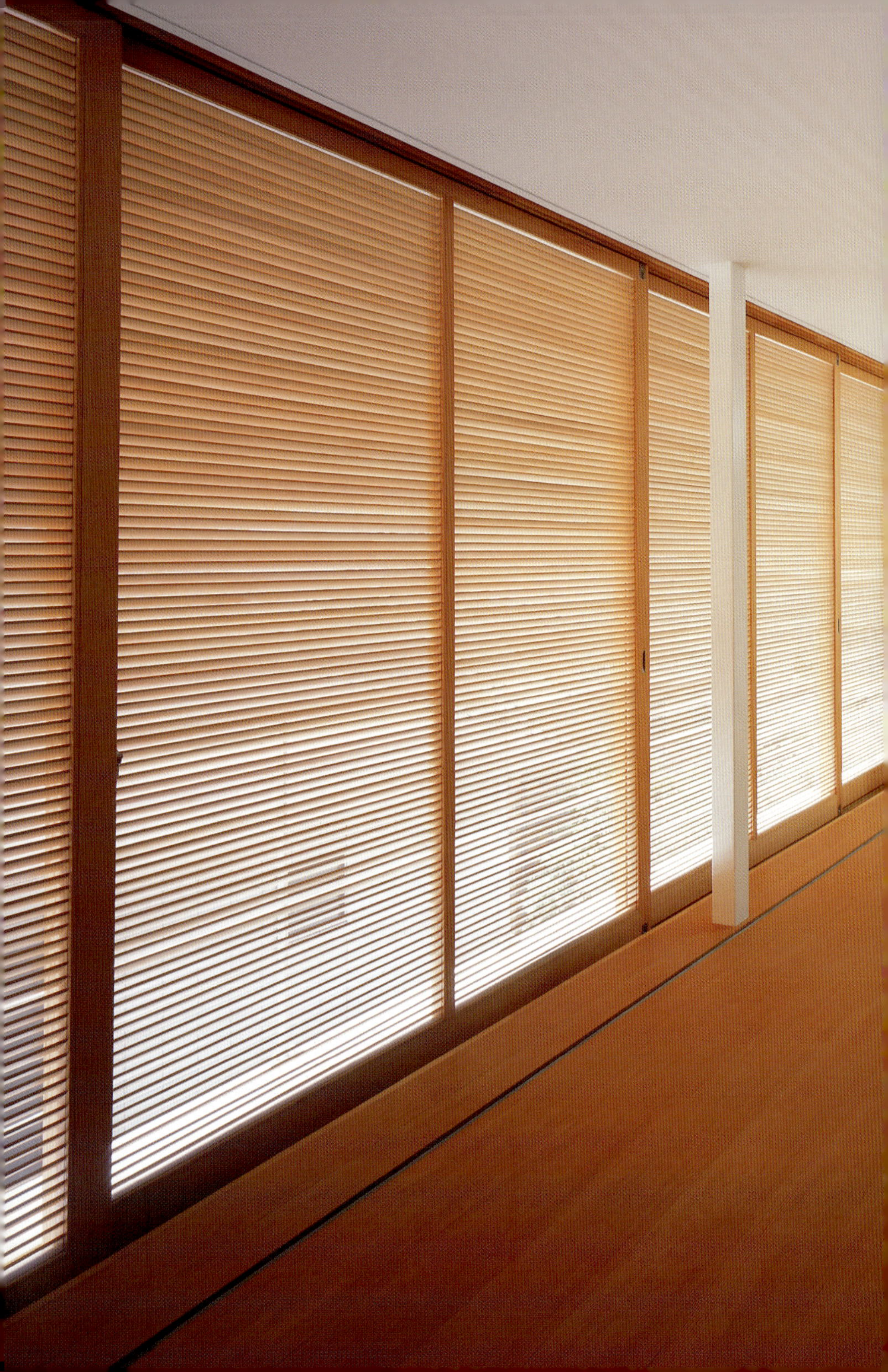

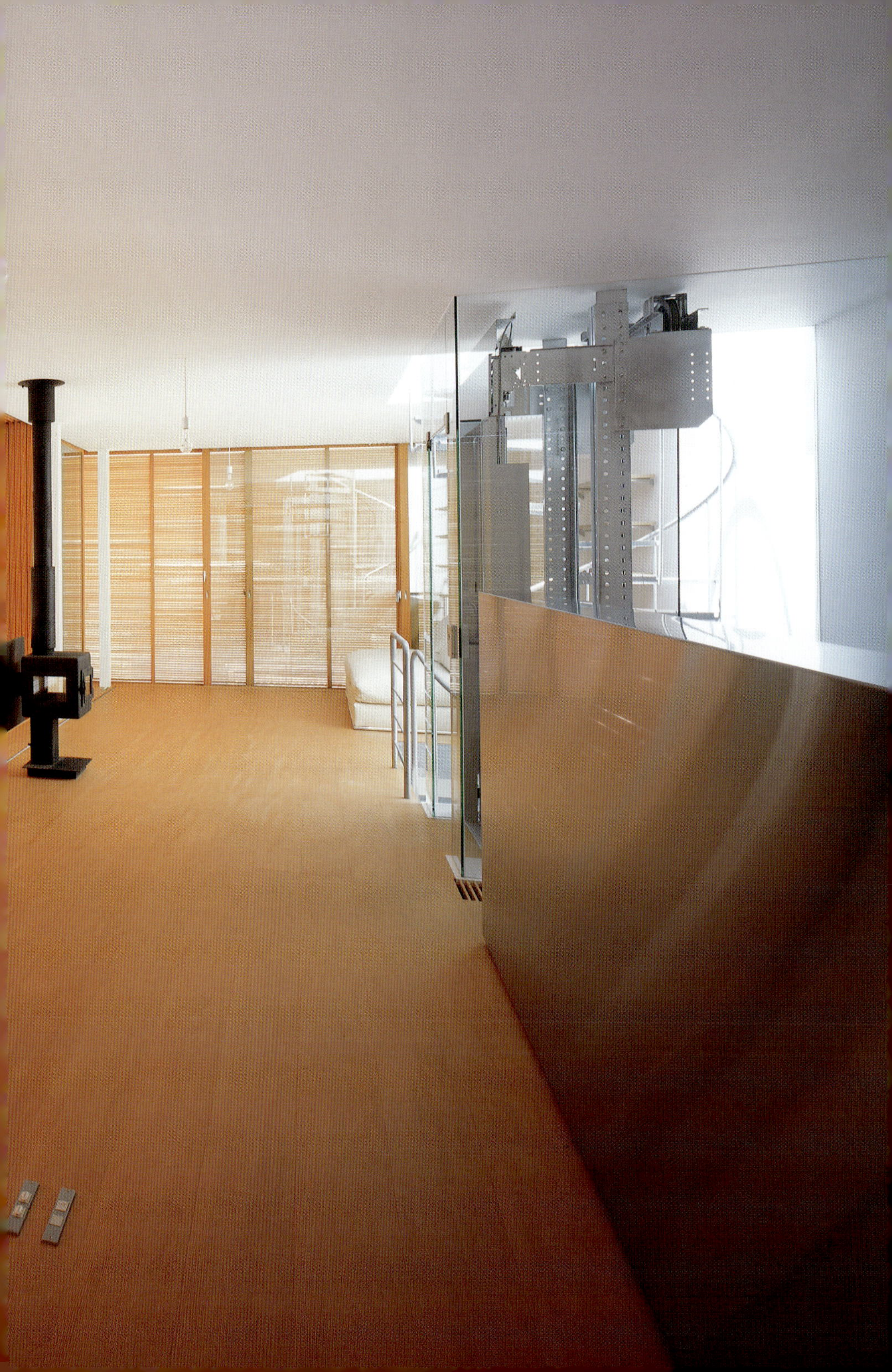

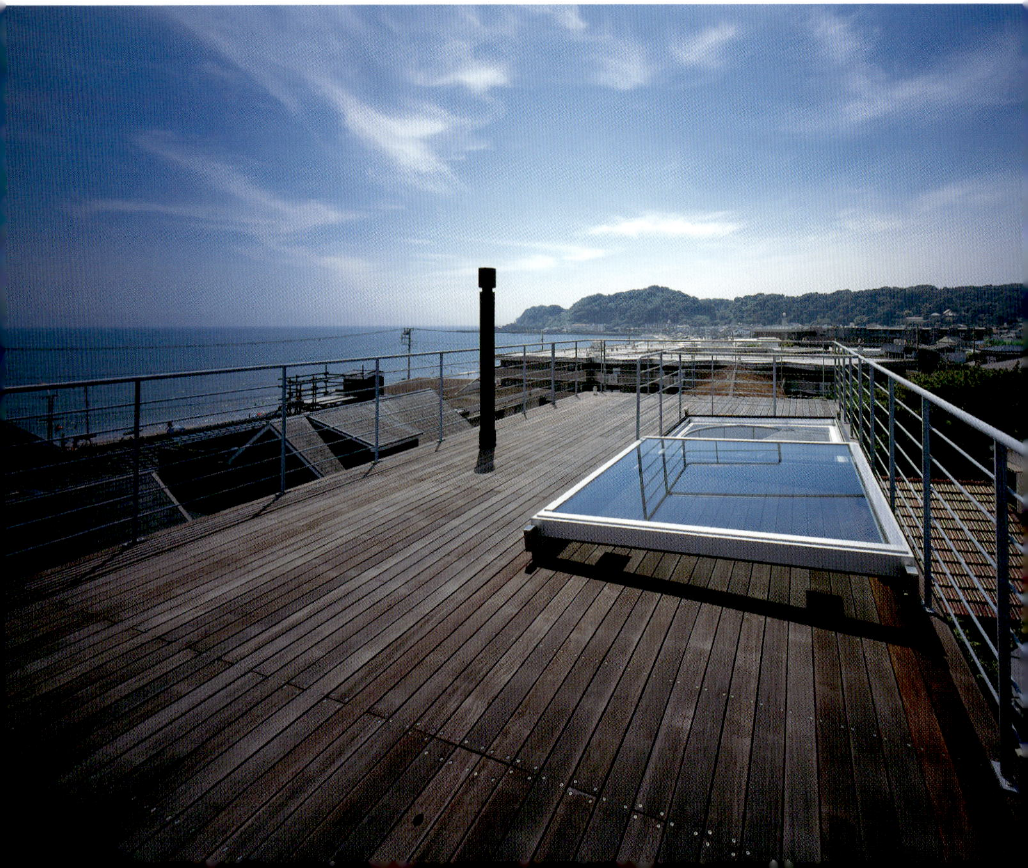

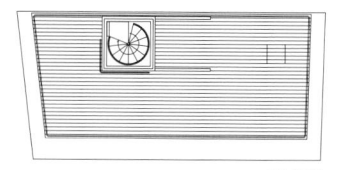

RF 1/300

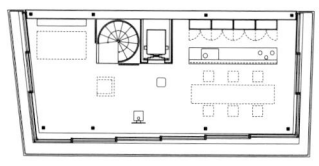

3F 1/300

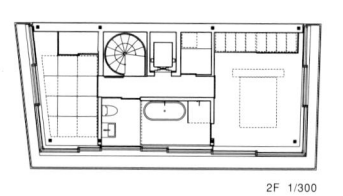

2F 1/300

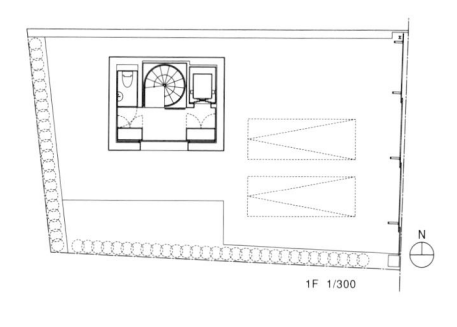

1F 1/300

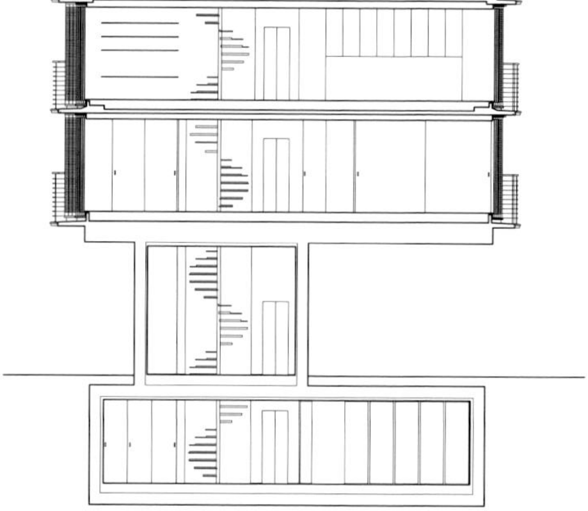

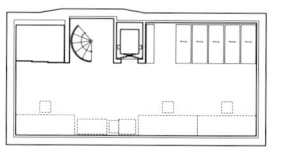

B1F 1/300

SECTION 1/250

Jyubako House

重箱の家　2004

Located in a dense residential area, this compact house has only a bathroom on its top floor. The middle level enjoys maximum ceiling height and great luminosity due to the presence of a large skylight. The ground level fully opens on a small courtyard.
The *jyubako* is a Japanese-type lunch box holding different kinds of food on several layers.

密集した住宅地に建つ家。
三階には空へと開いた浴室がある。
二階の天井高は高く、天窓からの光が溢れる。
一階は庭に向かって開いている。

33

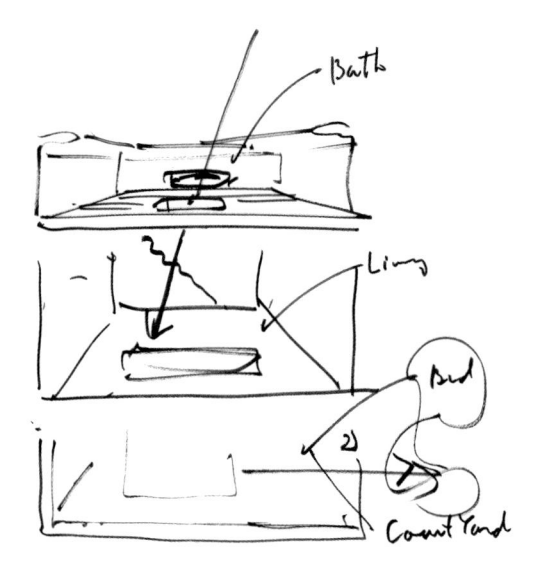

Bath

Living

Bed

Court Yard

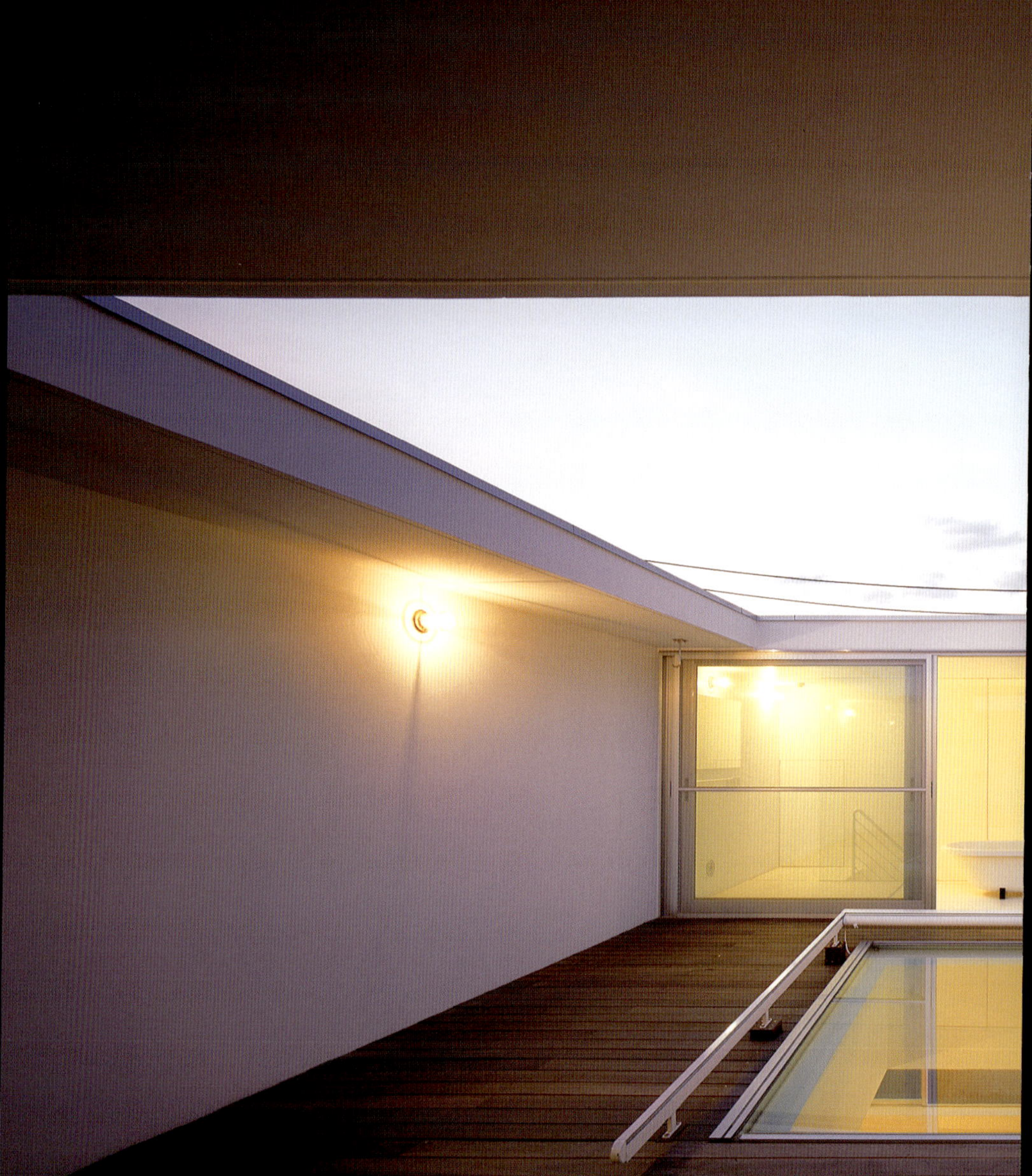

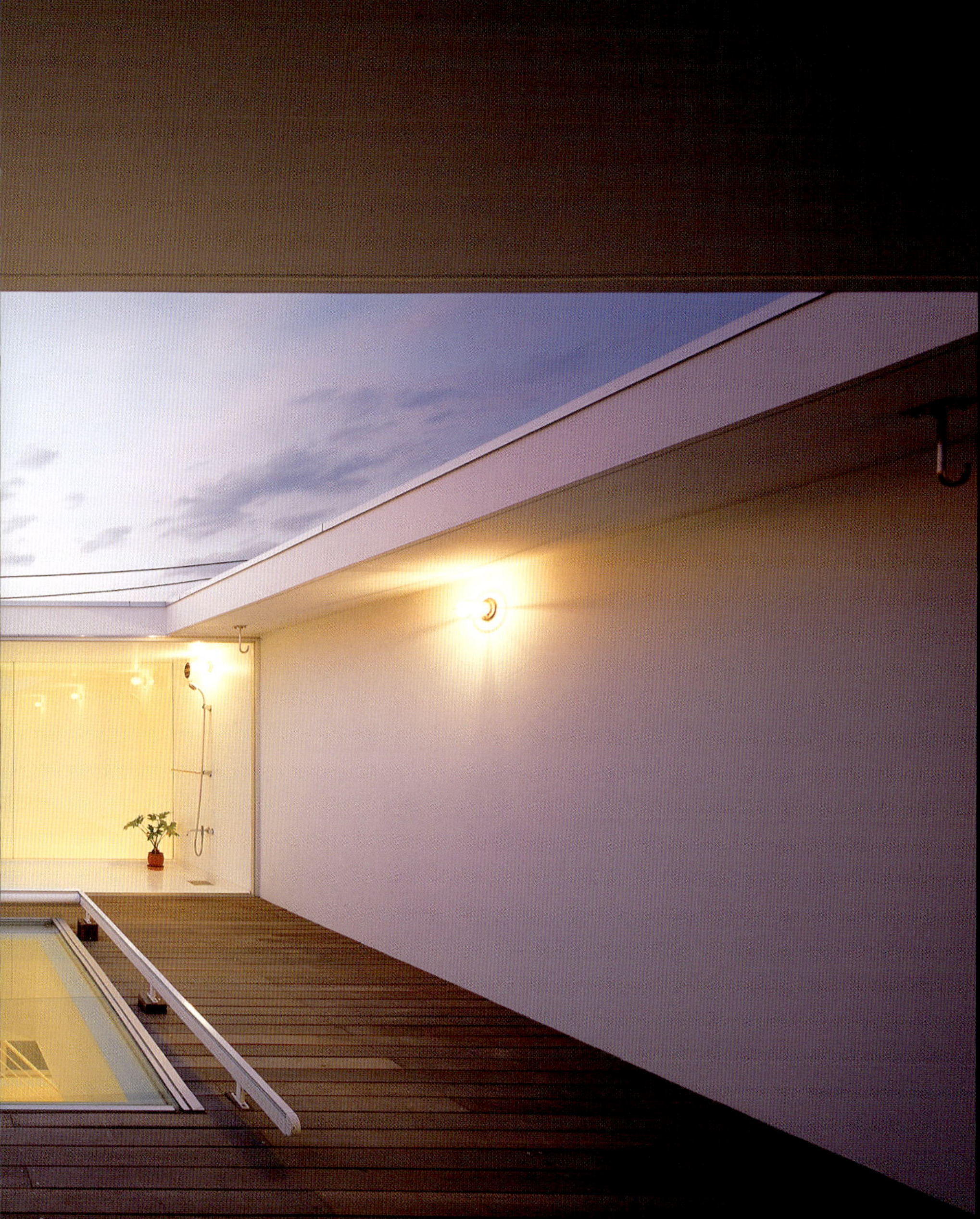

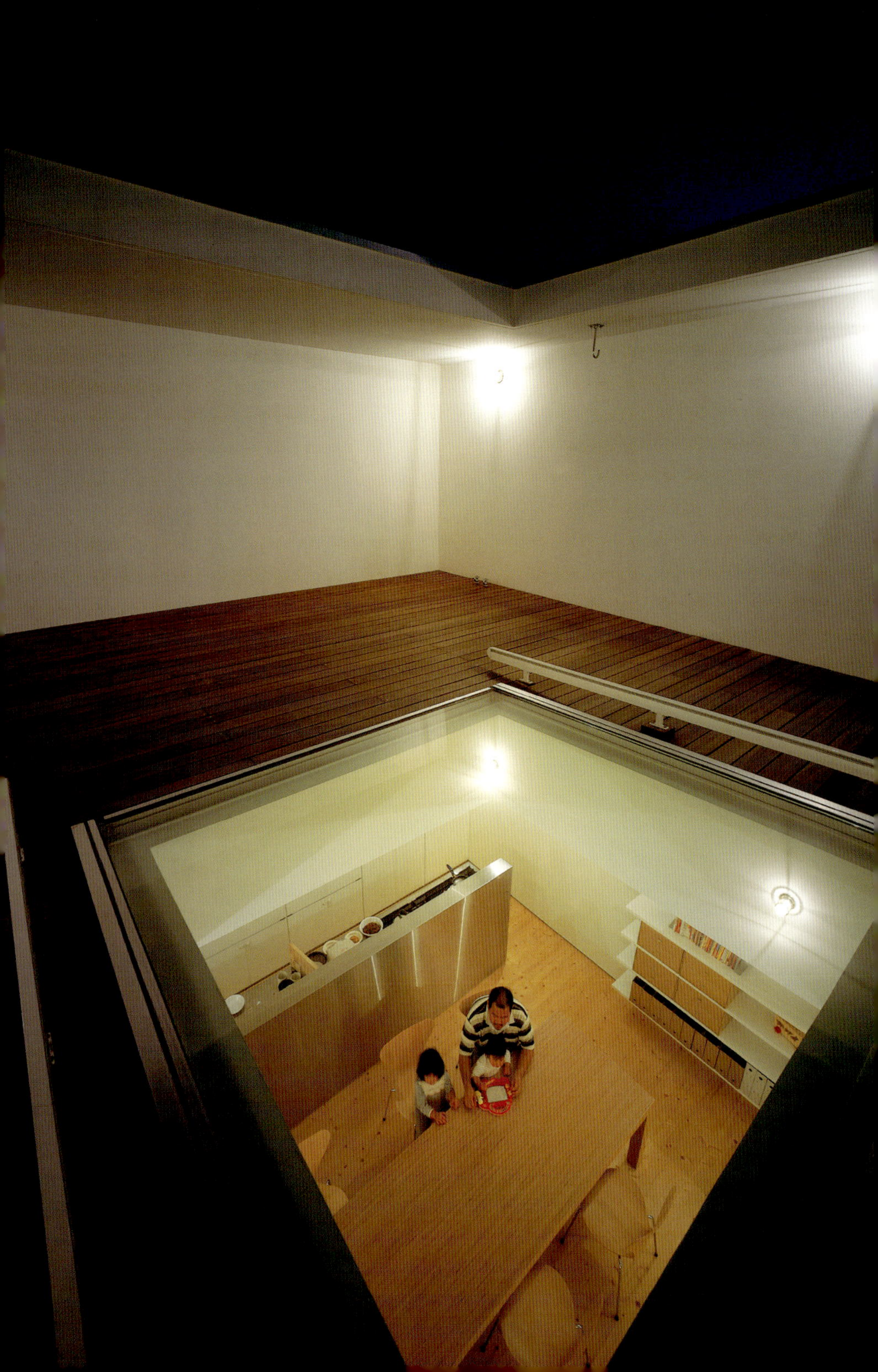

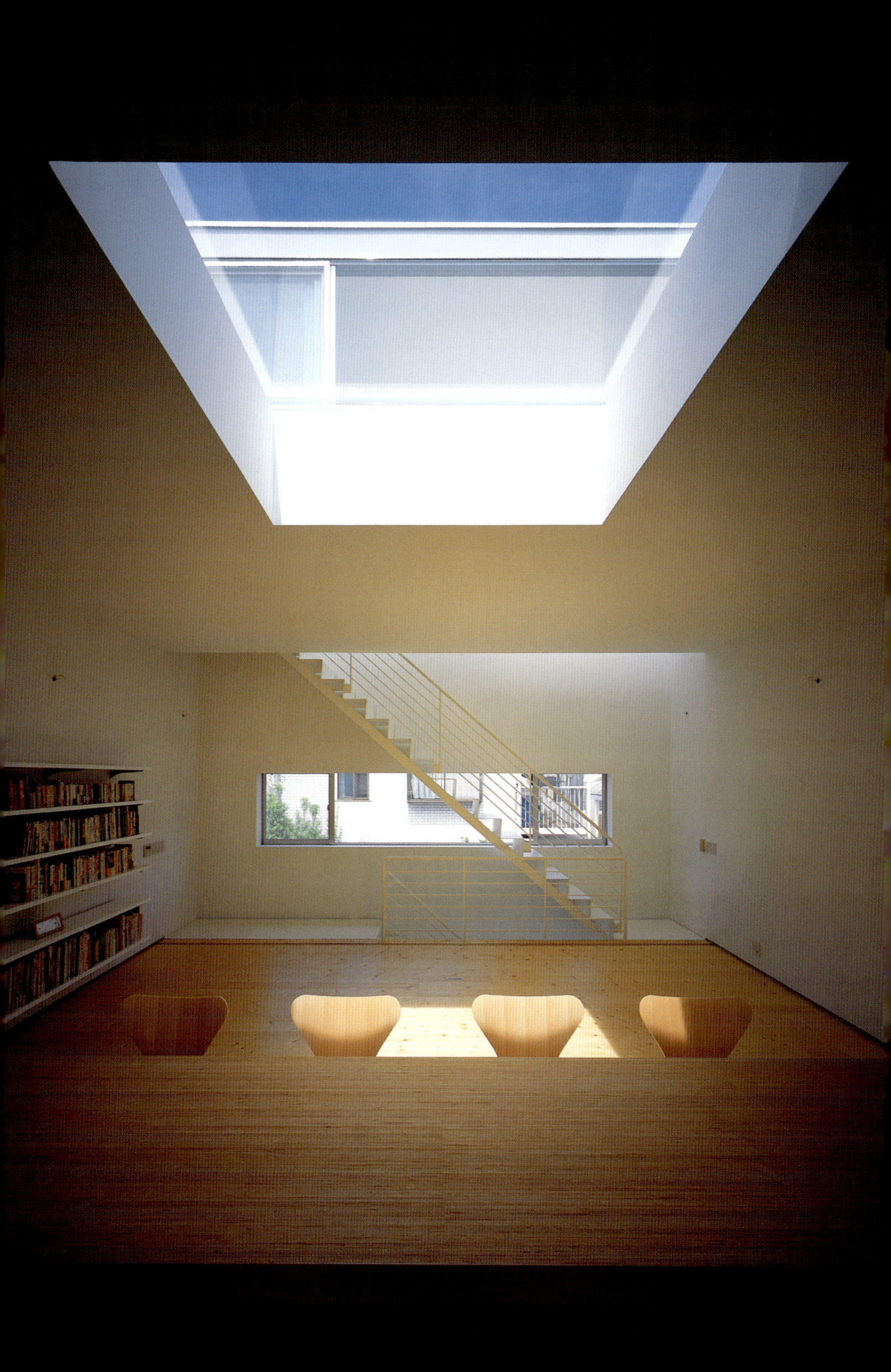

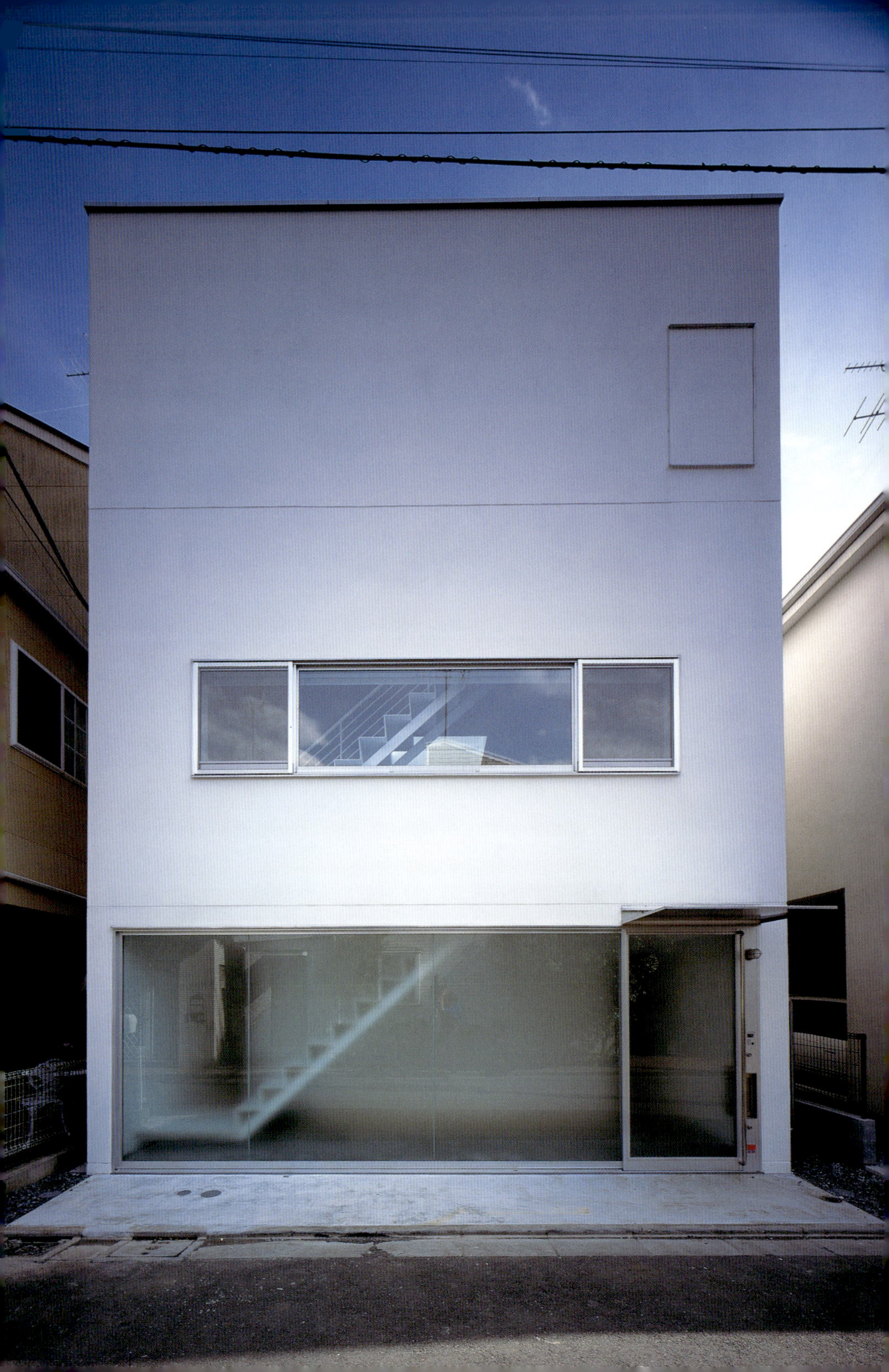

3F 1/200

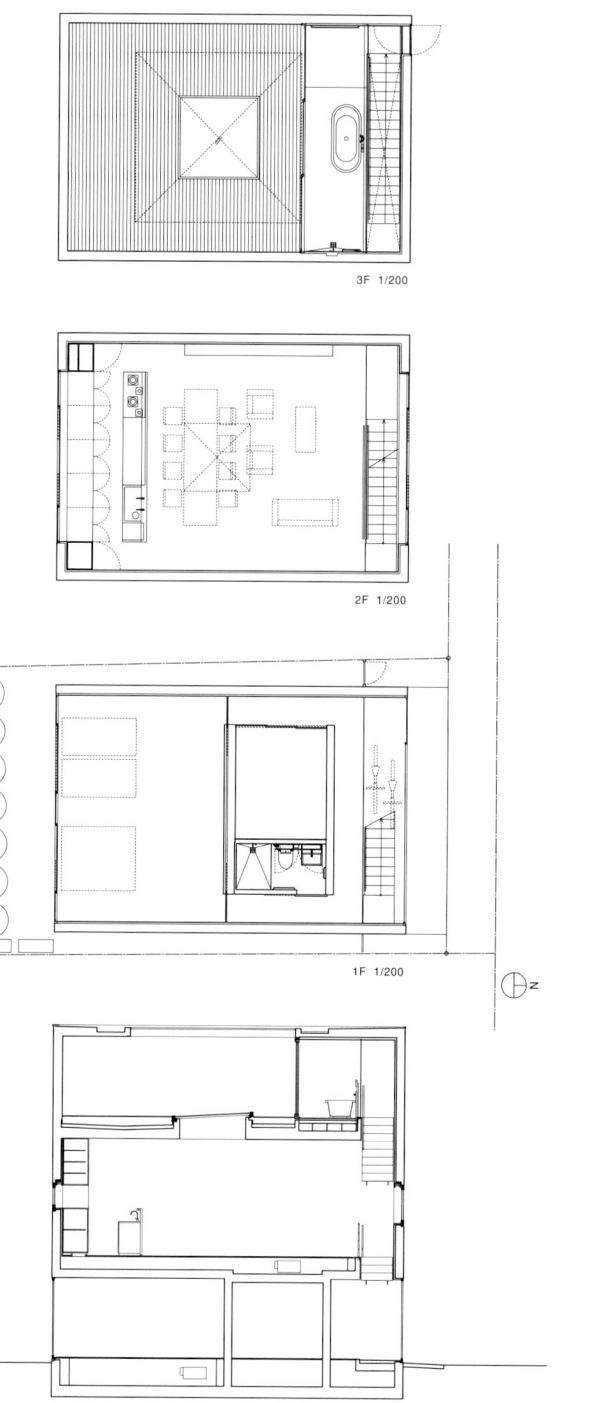

2F 1/200

1F 1/200

SECTION 1/200

Big Window House

大窓の家　2004

Located next to a park in an urban environment, this tiny house accommodates unifunctional rooms.
The large window facing the park opens fully and is electronically operated.

中心市街地の公園に面した小さな家。
電動の大窓が開くと、二階のリビング空間は一辺が完全に開いたコの字型空間となる。

34

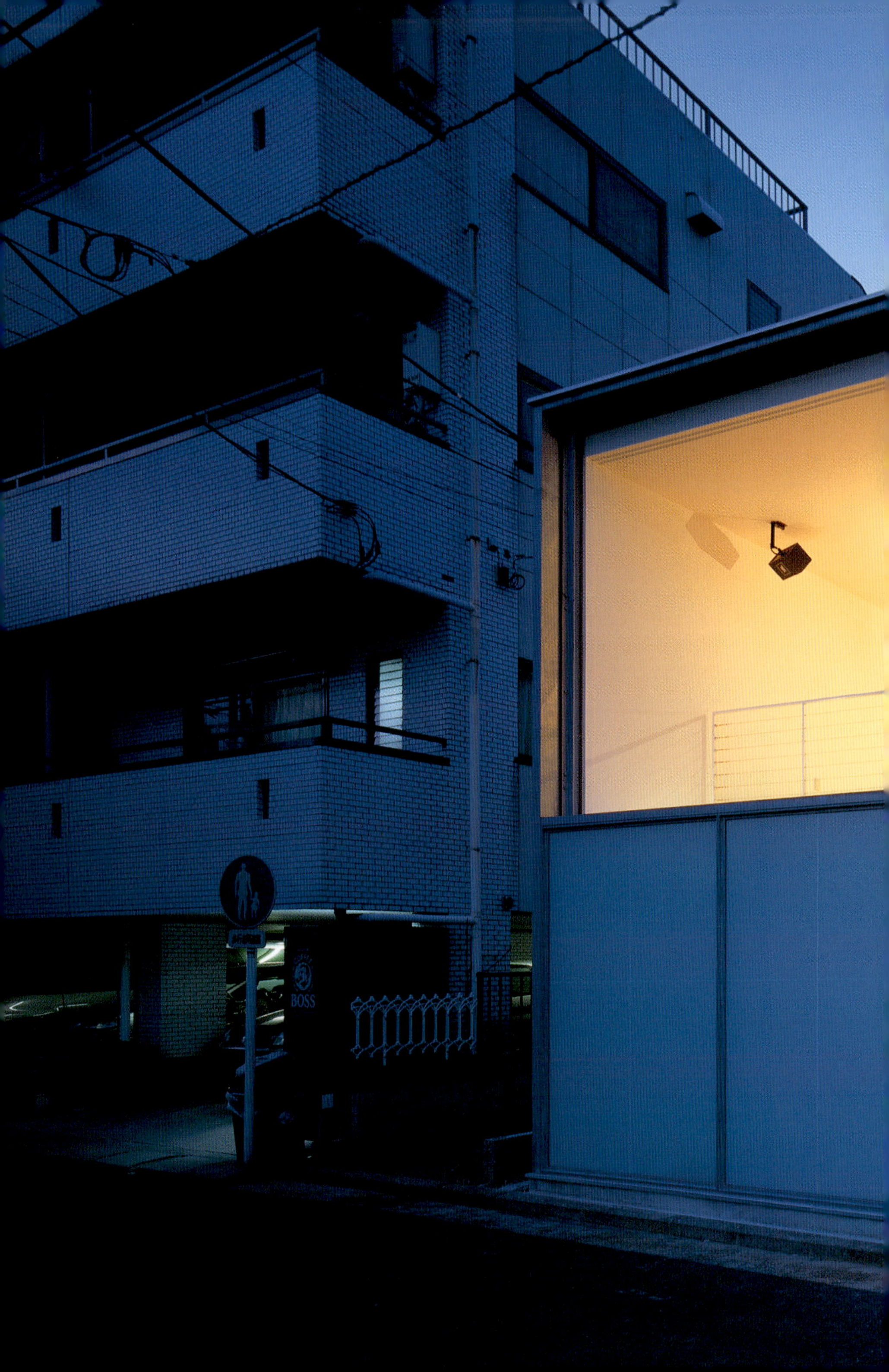
BOSS

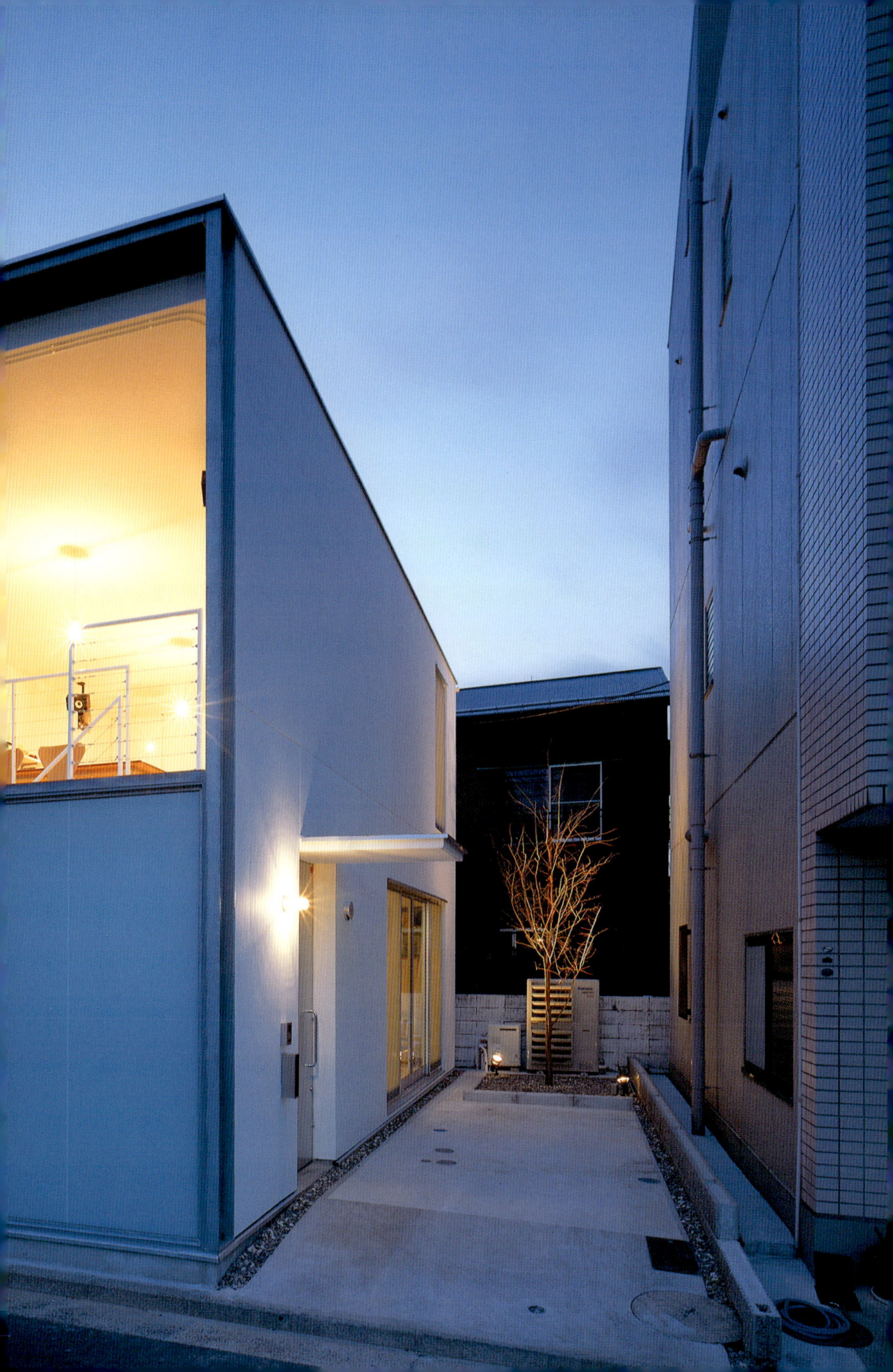

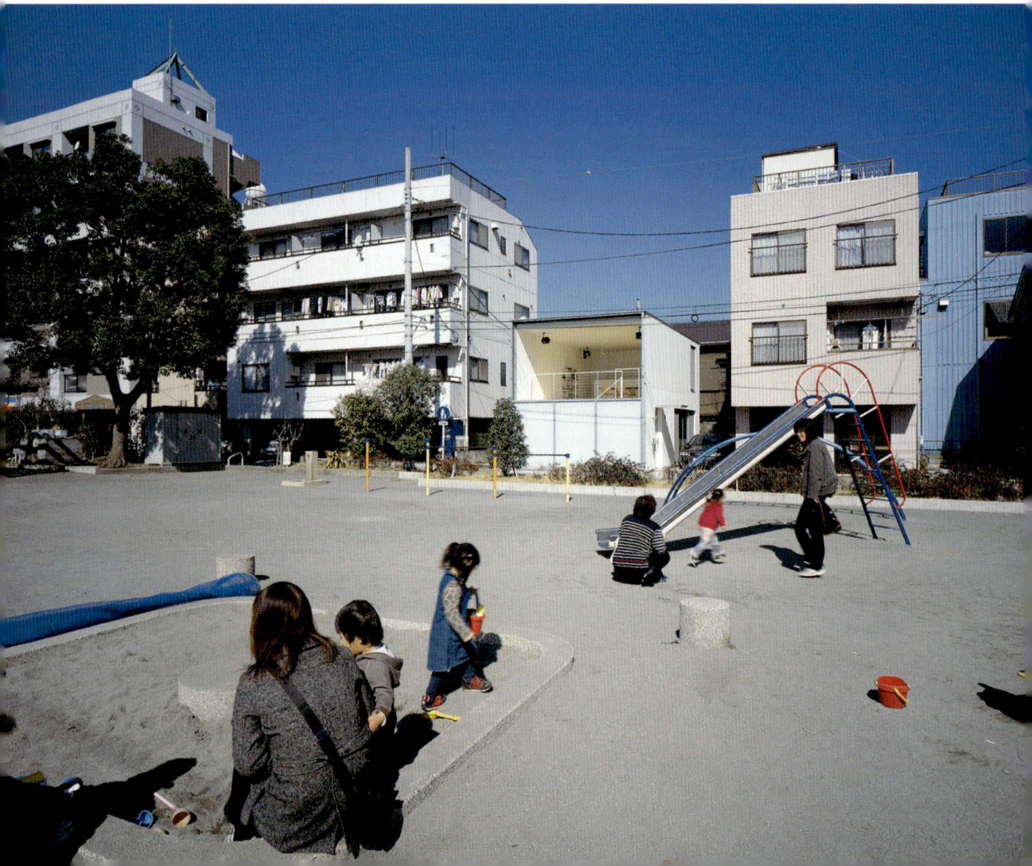

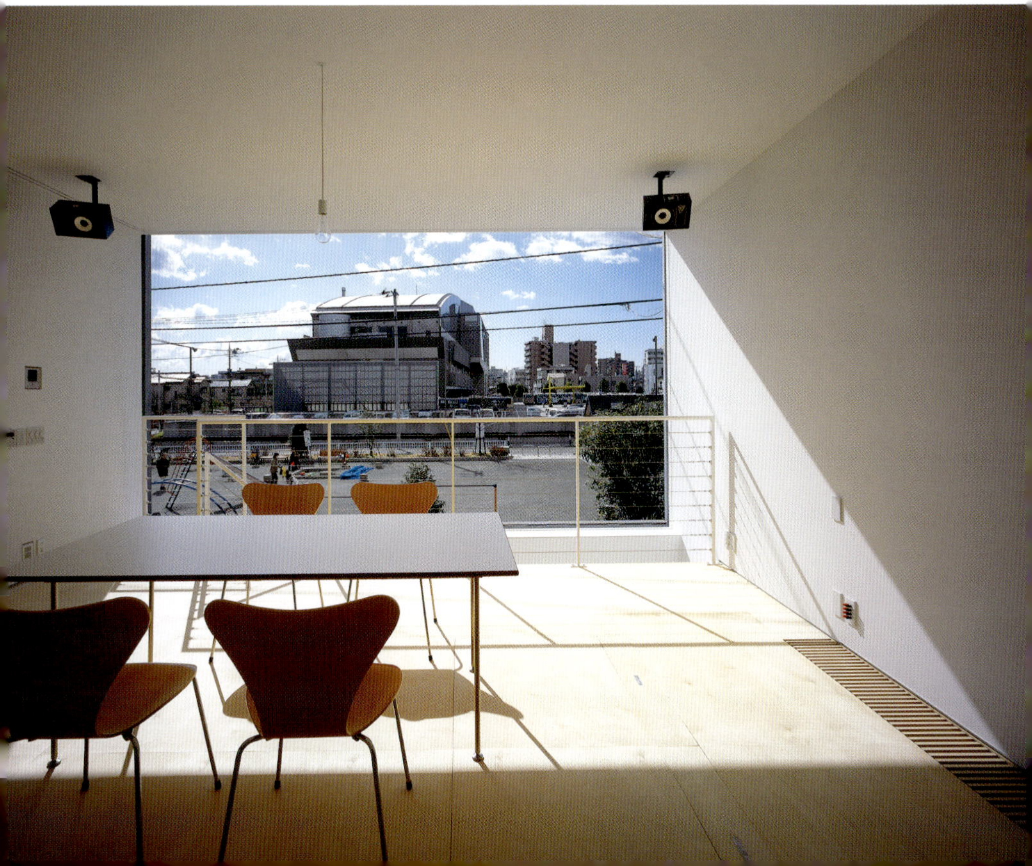

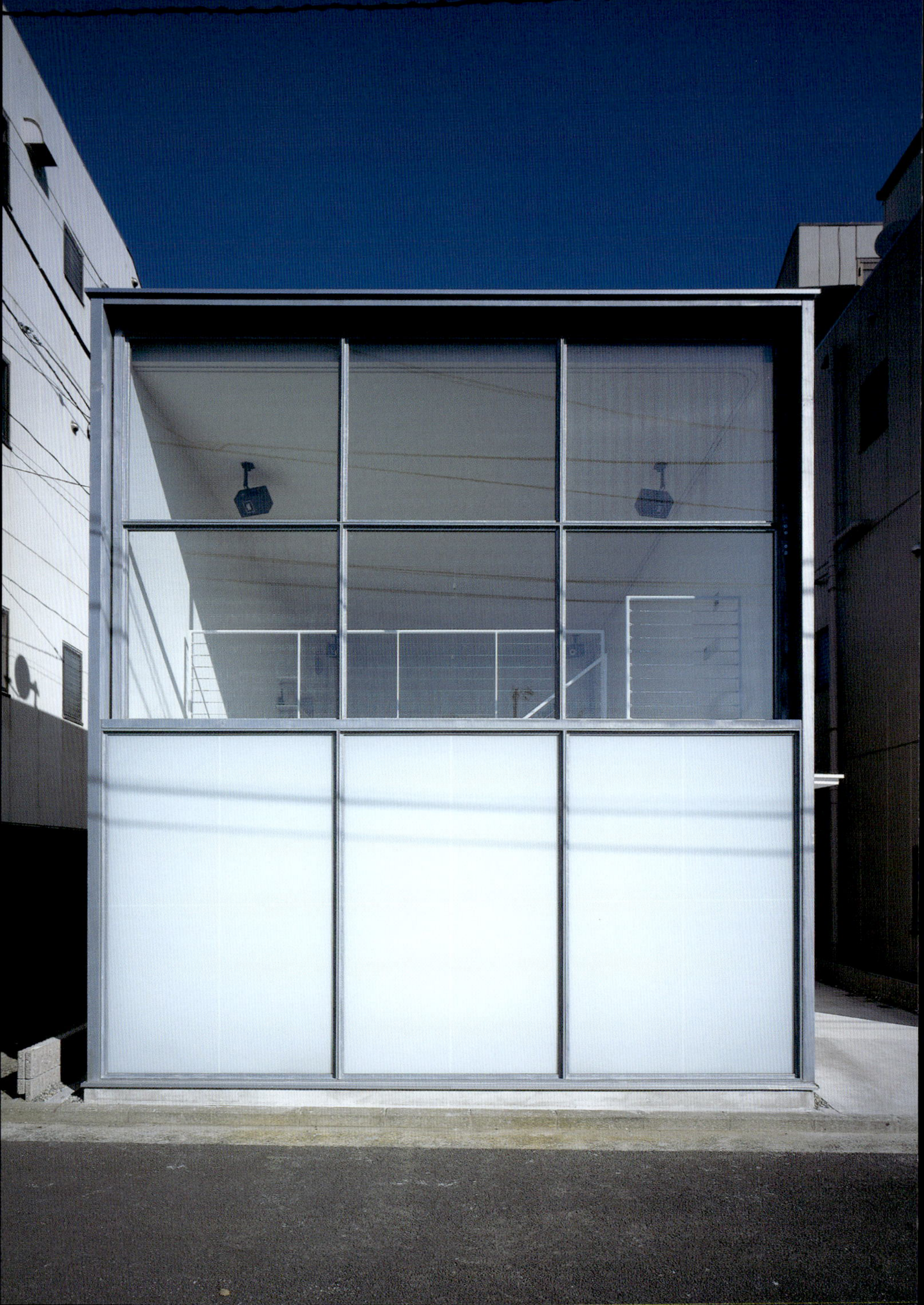

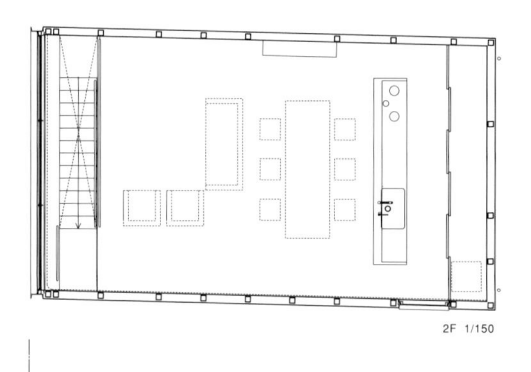

2F 1/150

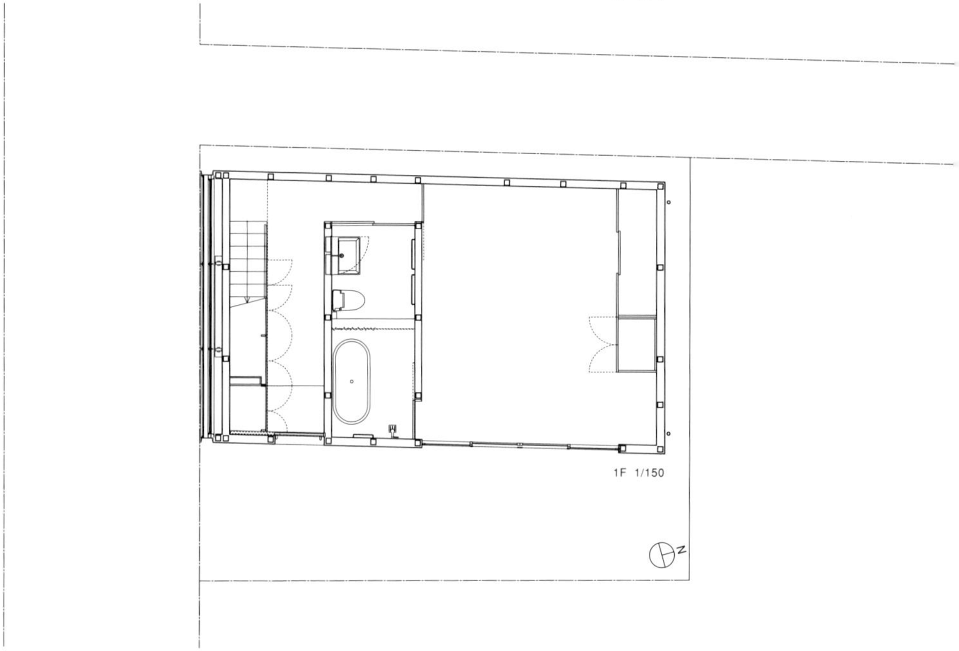

1F 1/150

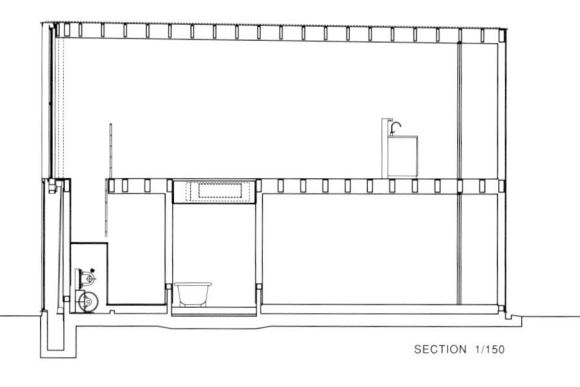

SECTION 1/150

Shoe Box House

大箱の家　2004

This large floating house is deceptively simple. In fact, the house controls its own environment. All the windows are positioned to allow light and breezes into the dwelling in ways which optimize comfort.

大きな箱が浮いた家。
それぞれの窓は光と風を得るために配置され、快適な室内環境をつくる。

35

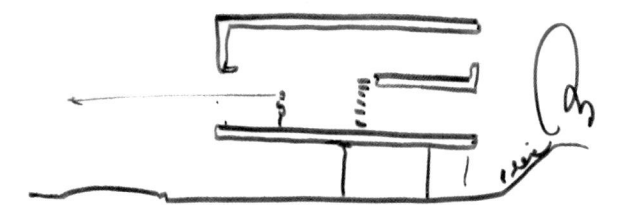

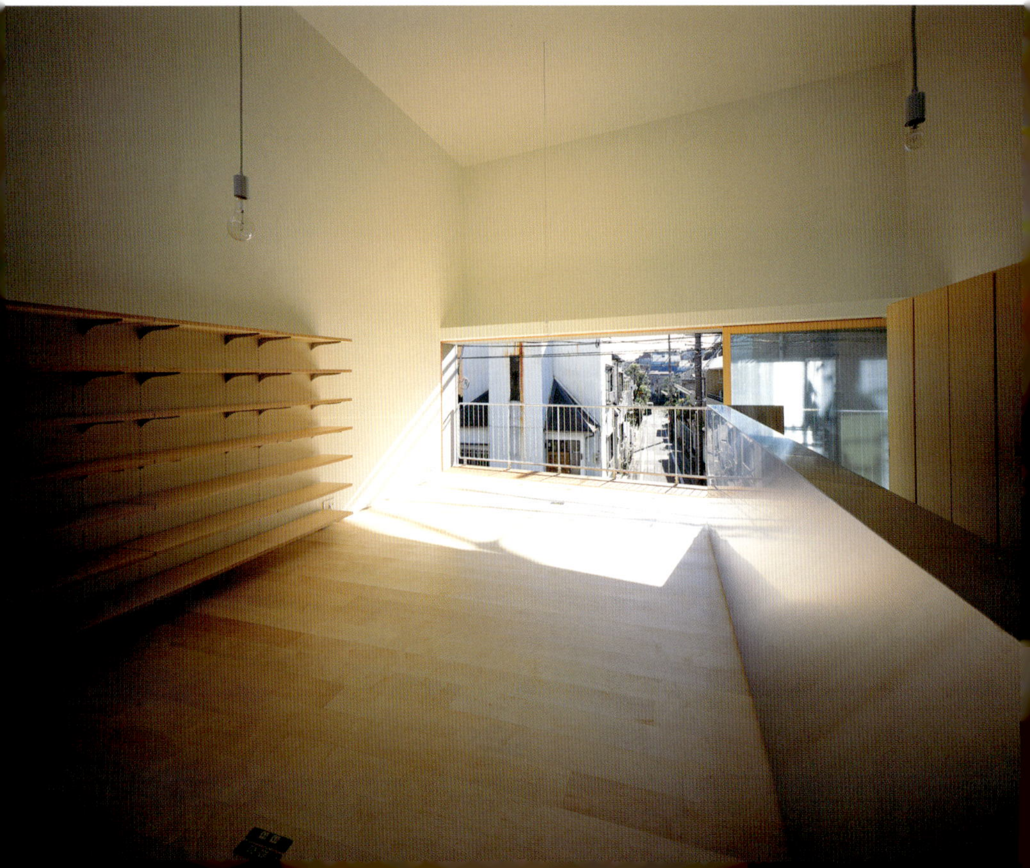

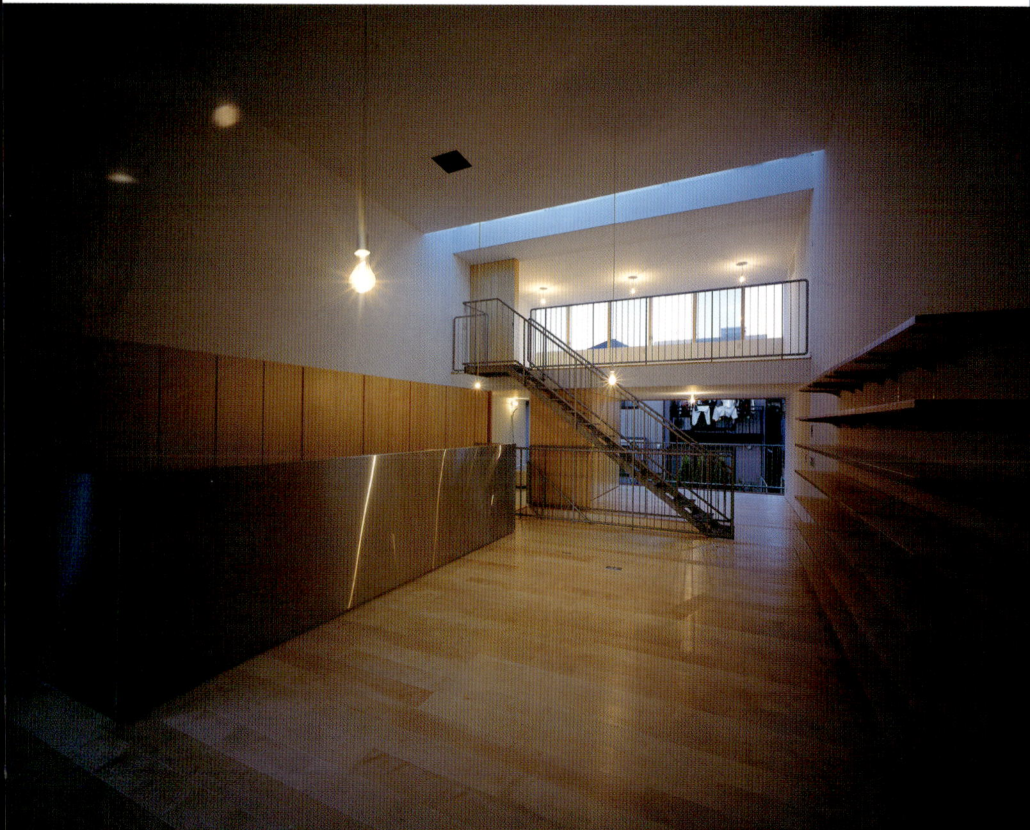

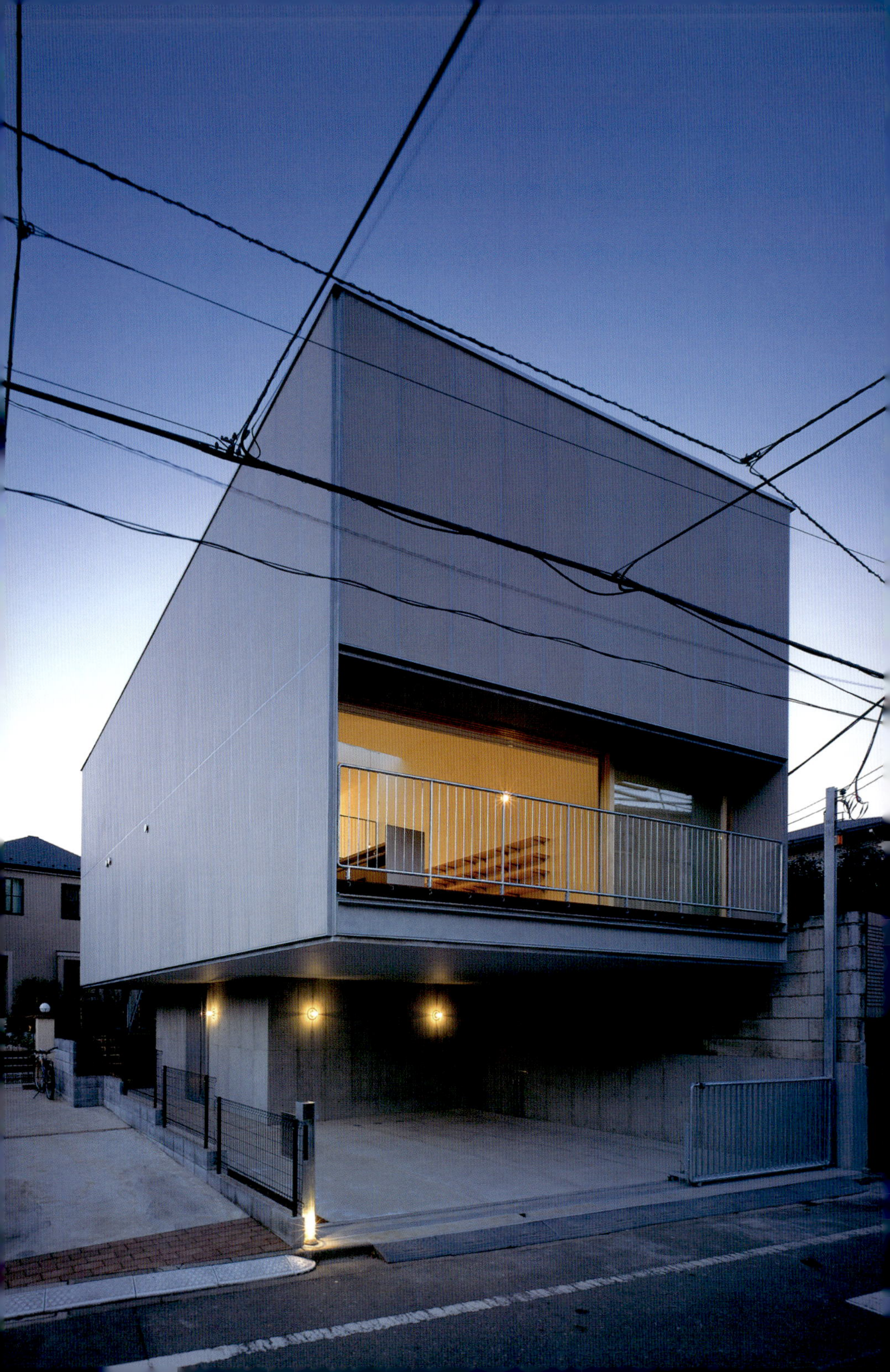

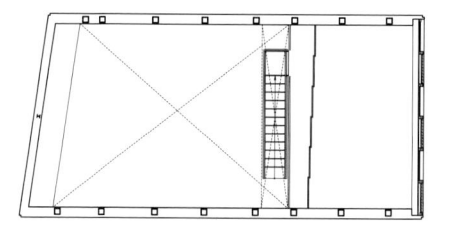

3F 1/250

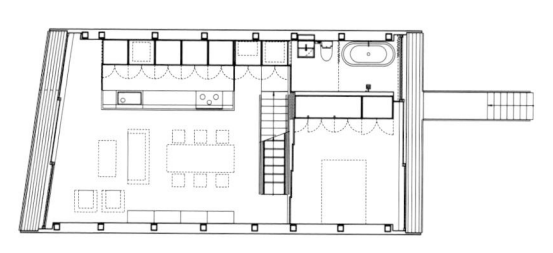

2F 1/250

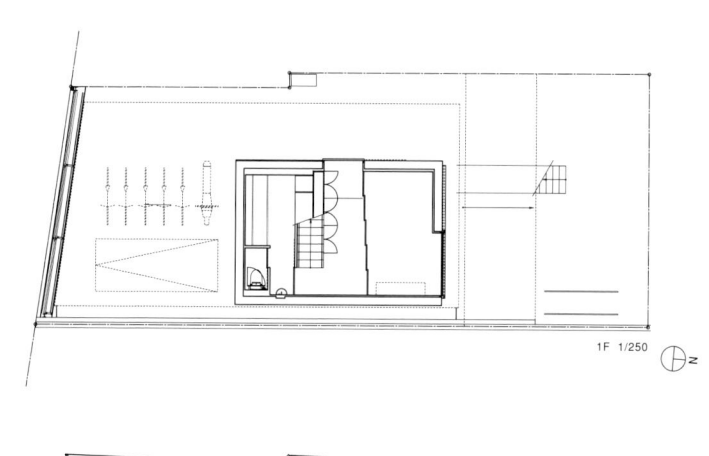

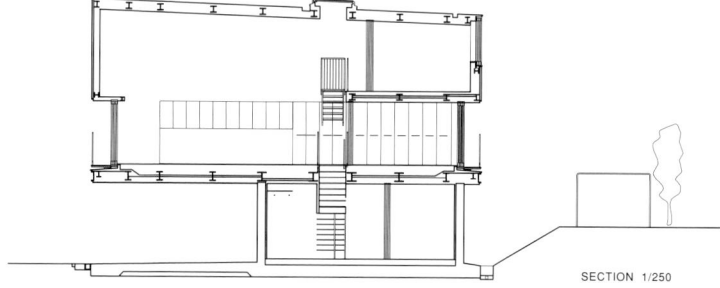

1F 1/250

SECTION 1/250

Floating Roof House

山すその家　2005

The house is located at the bottom of a hill. The floating roof allows the slope to continue through the internal space.

丘の袂に位置する家。
屋根が浮いているので、森の斜面が続いて見える。

36

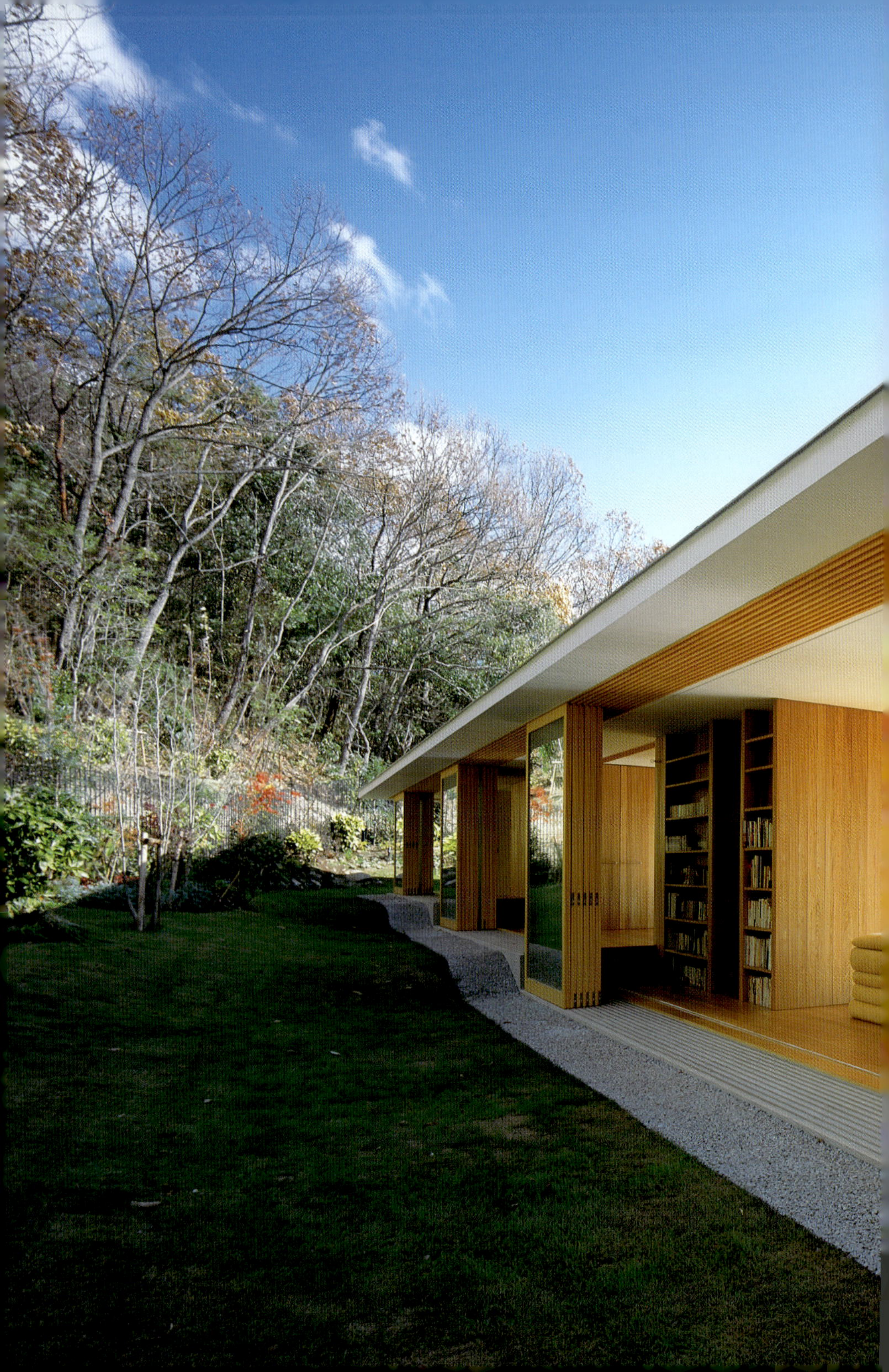

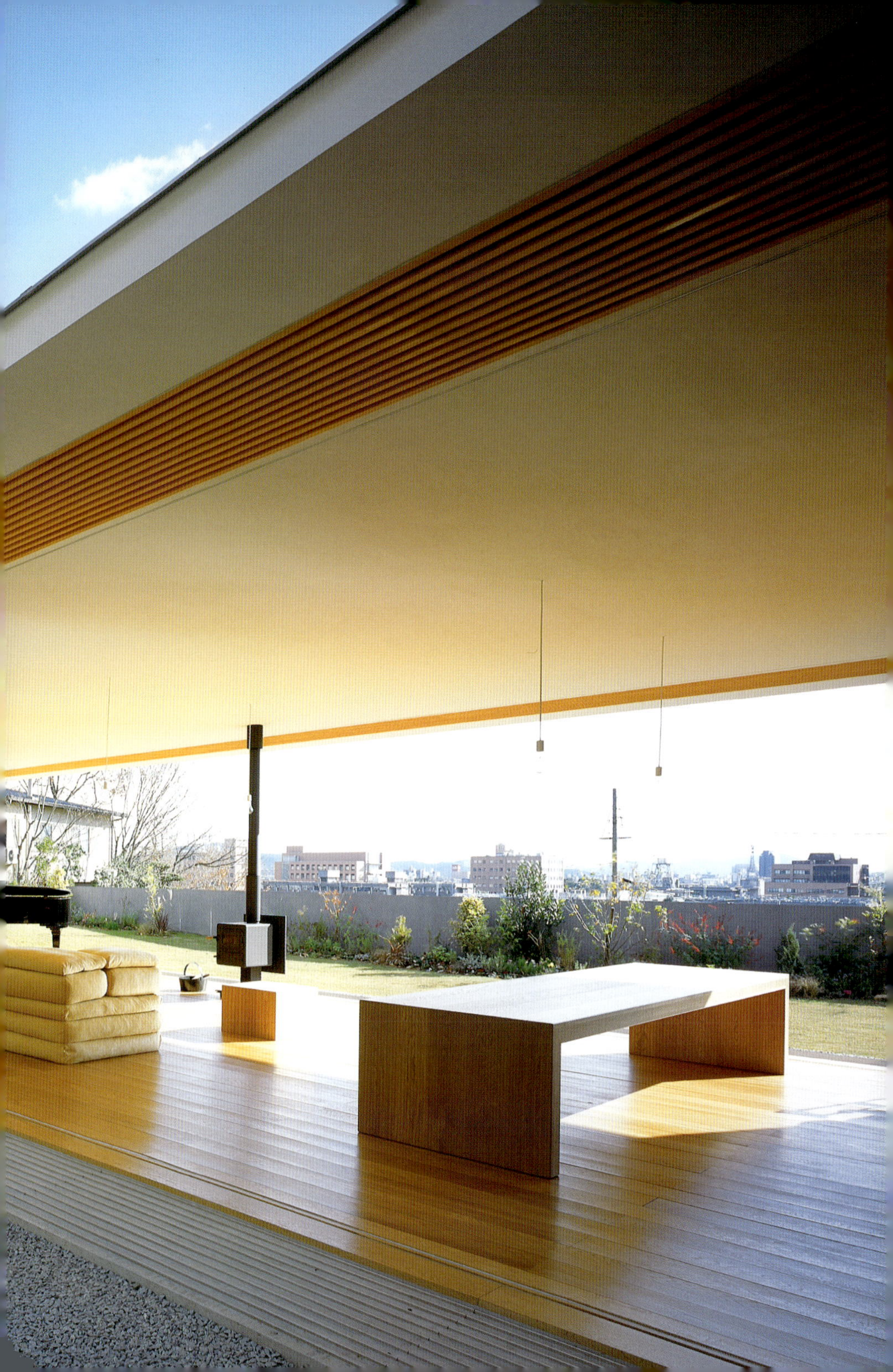

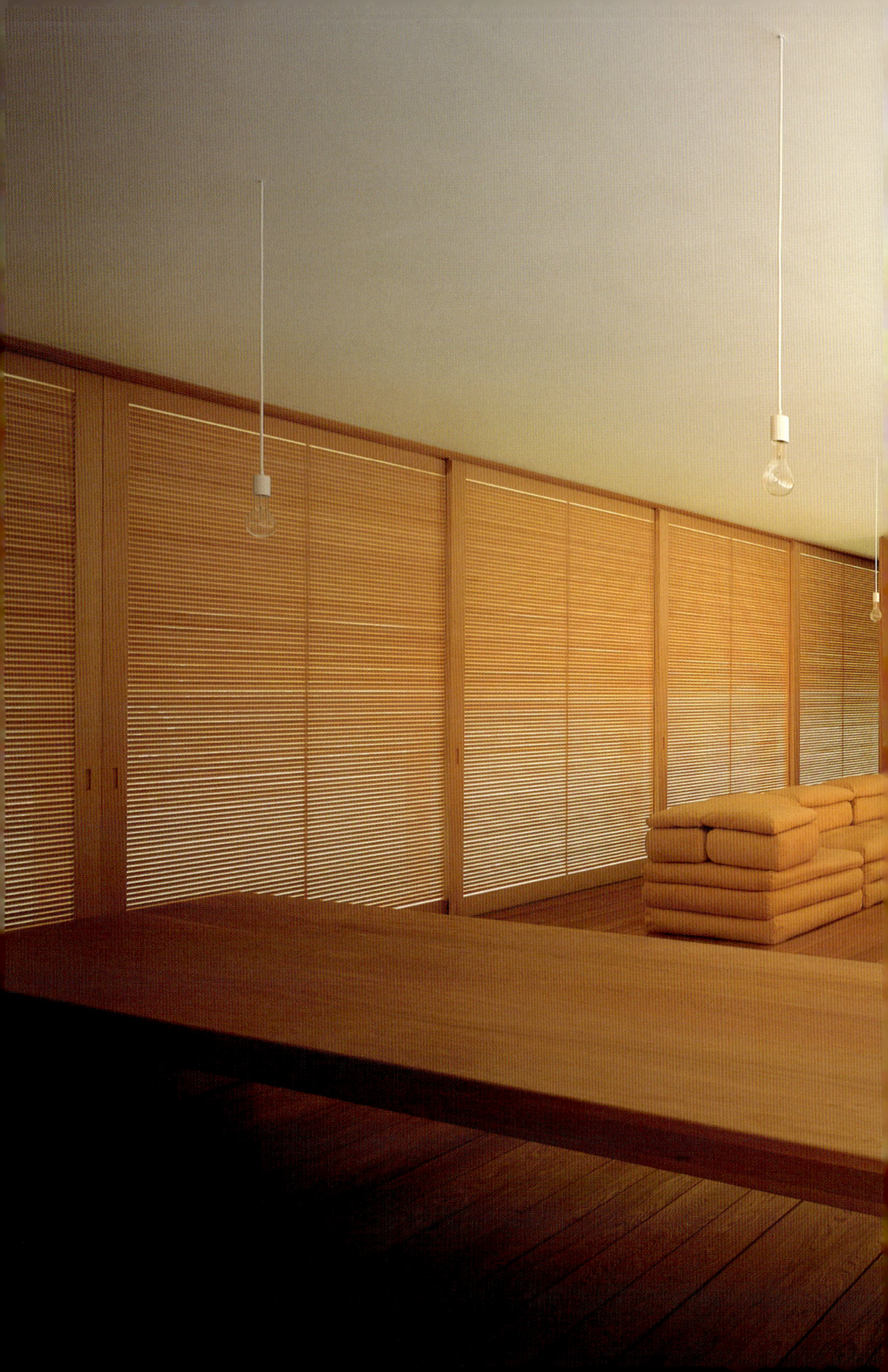

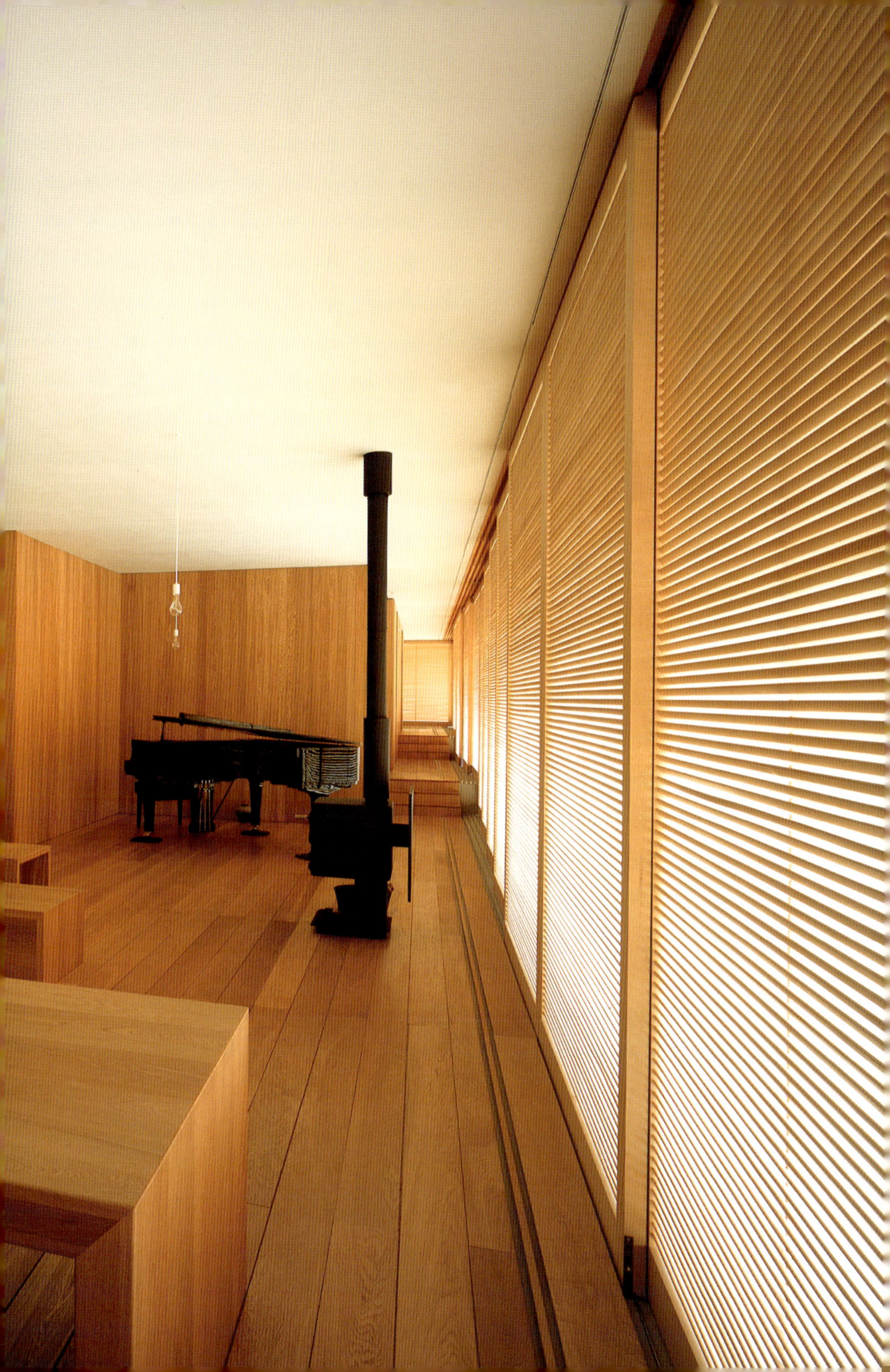

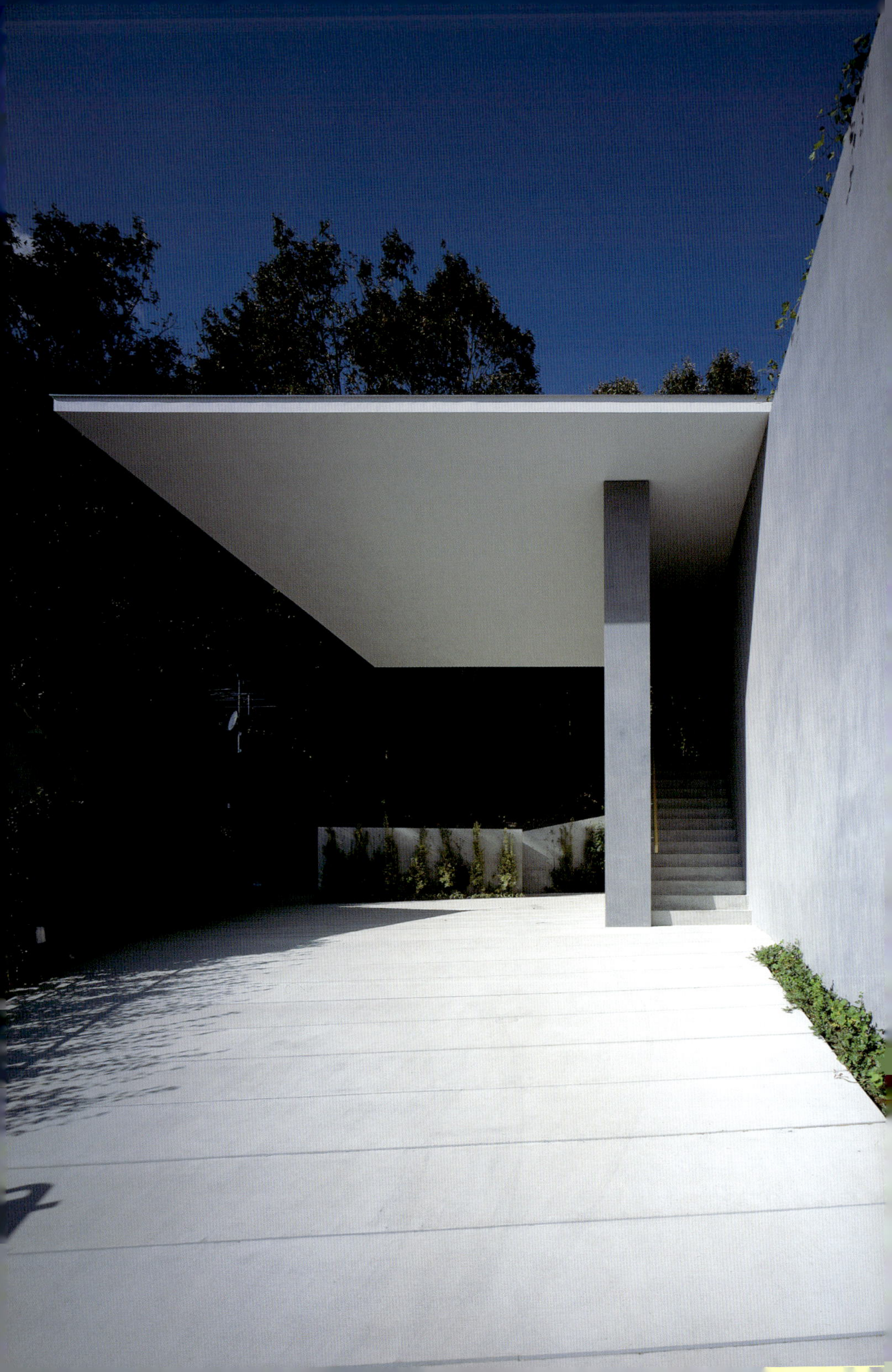

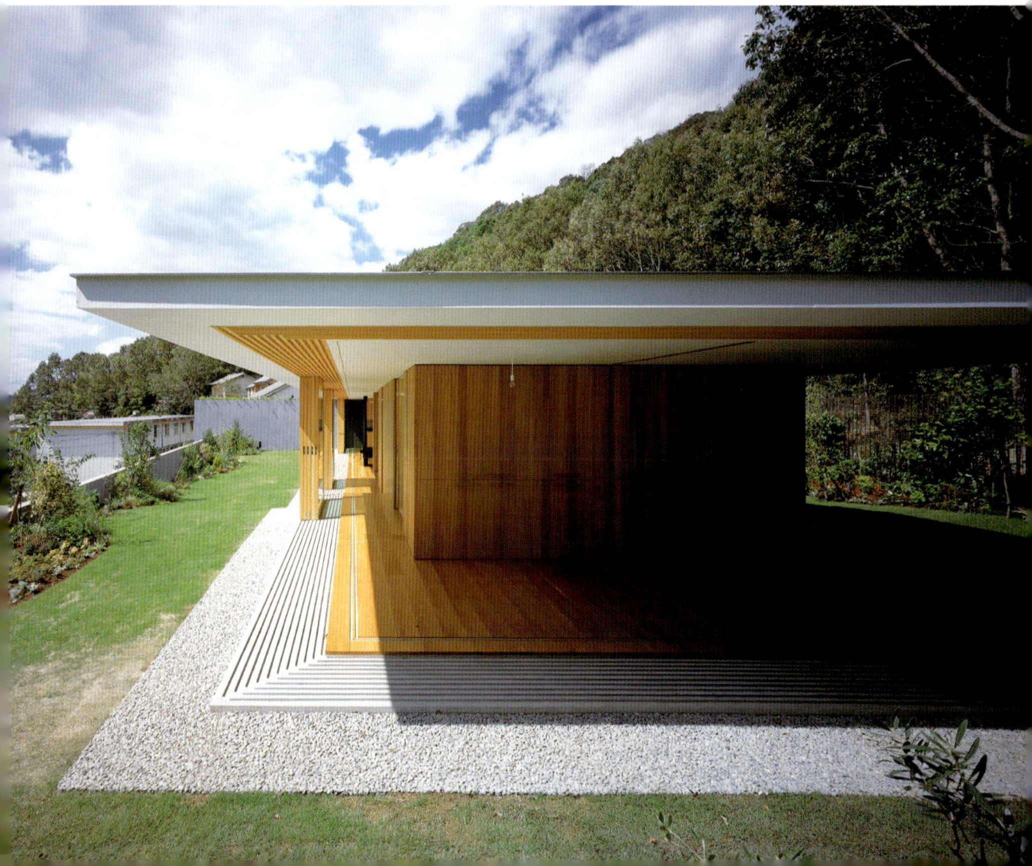

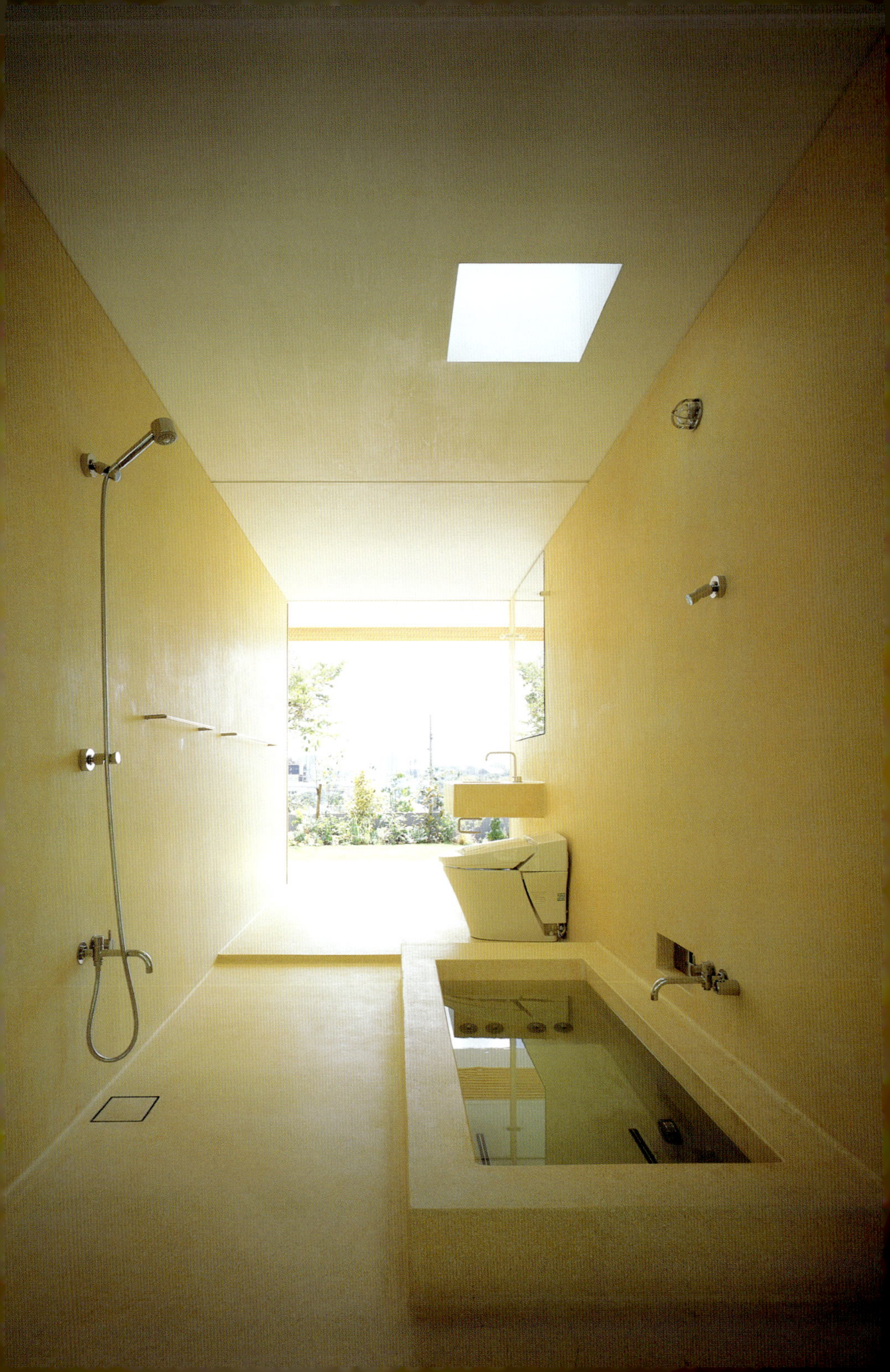

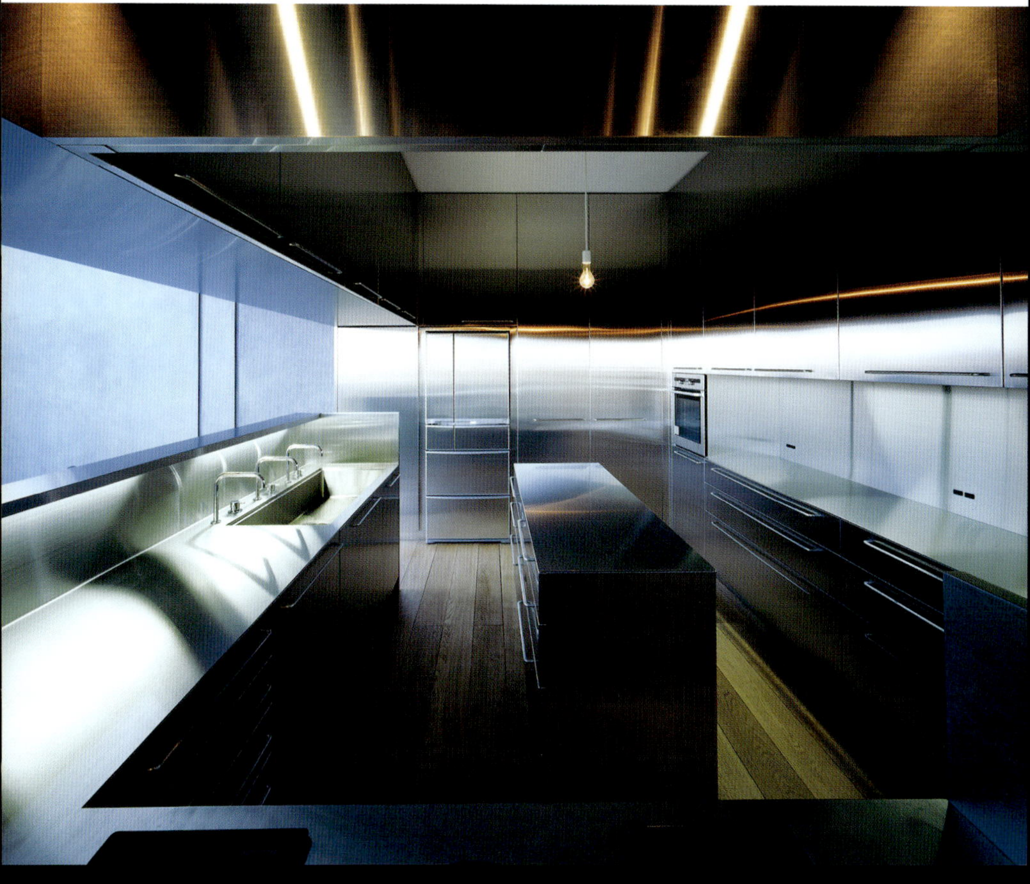

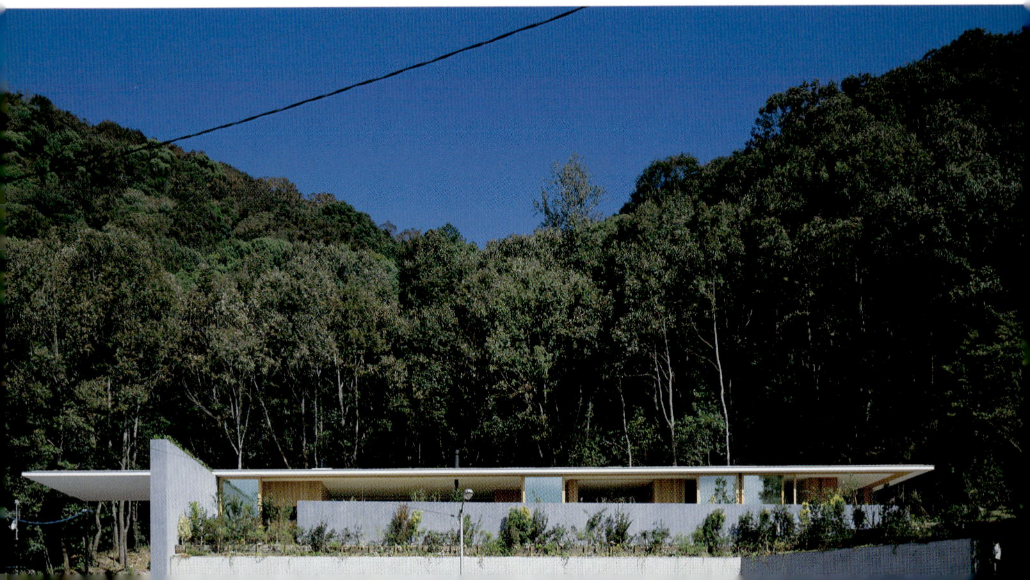

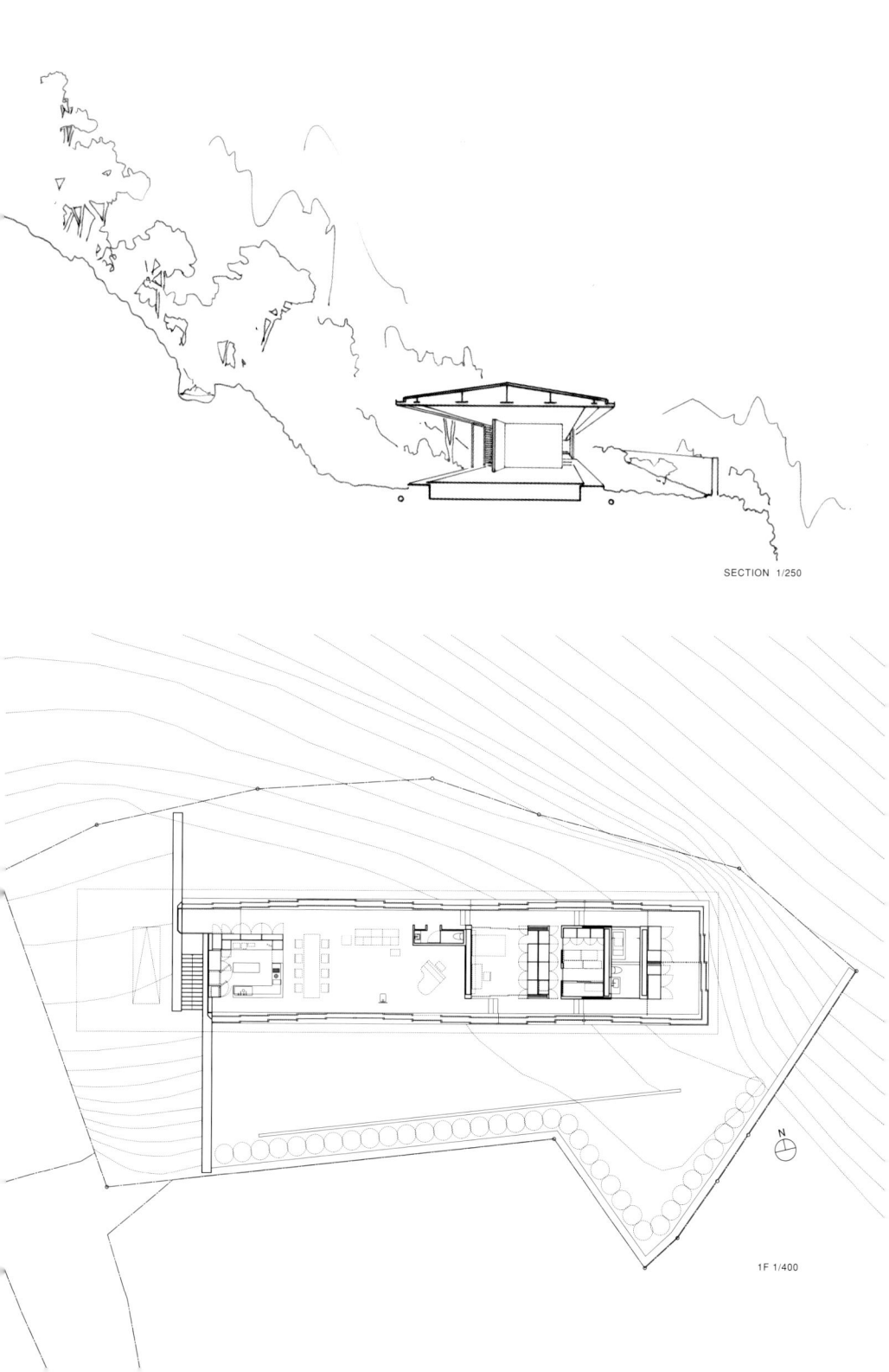

SECTION 1/250

1F 1/400

Roof Deck House

屋上の家　2005

The design of this house includes a small hut built on the roof. An 8m zelkova tree planted on the ground floor shoots up through the roof deck.

大きな屋上デッキに小屋が建っている家。
屋根を貫いて地面から高さ8mのケヤキが生えている。

37

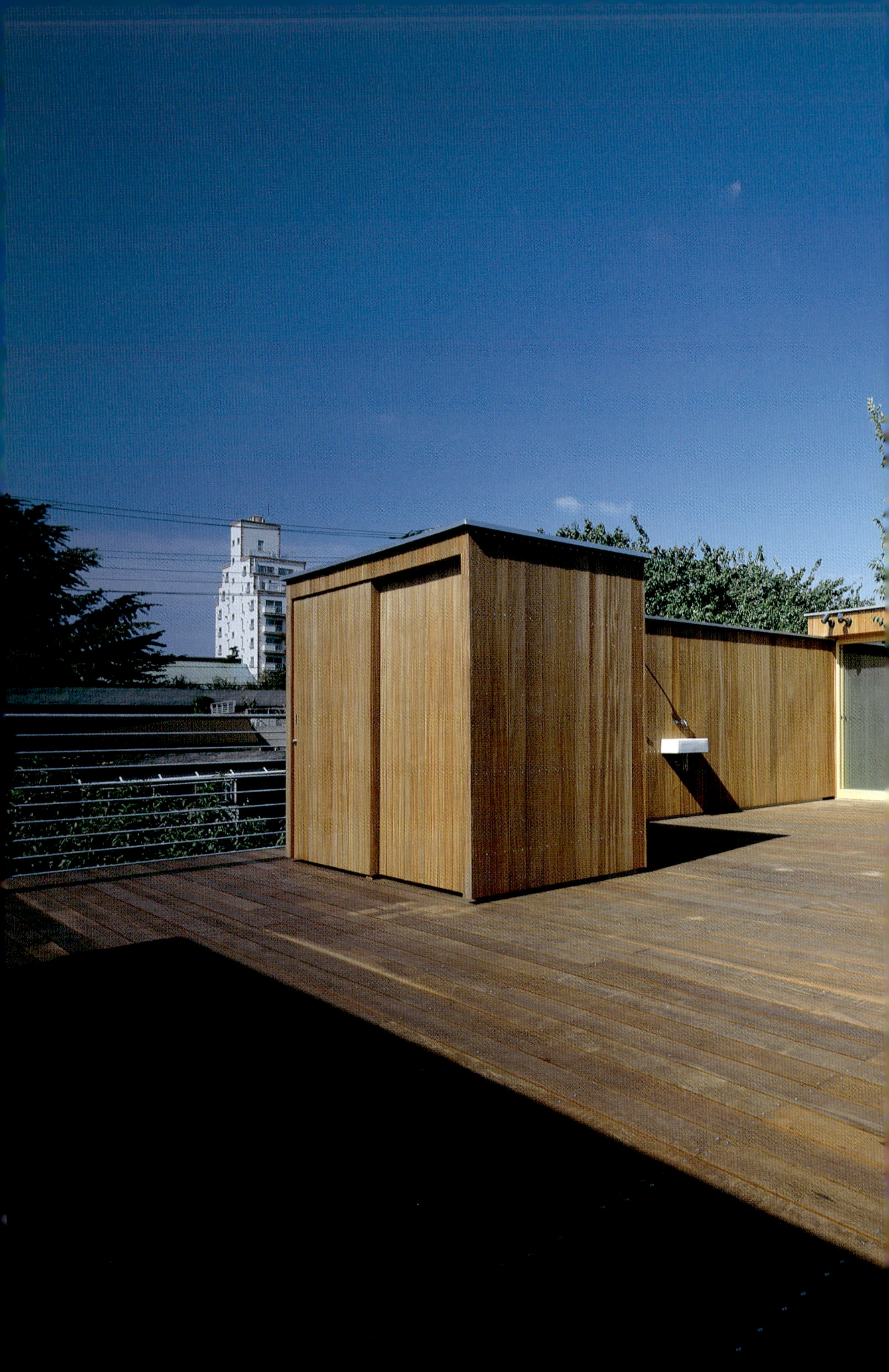

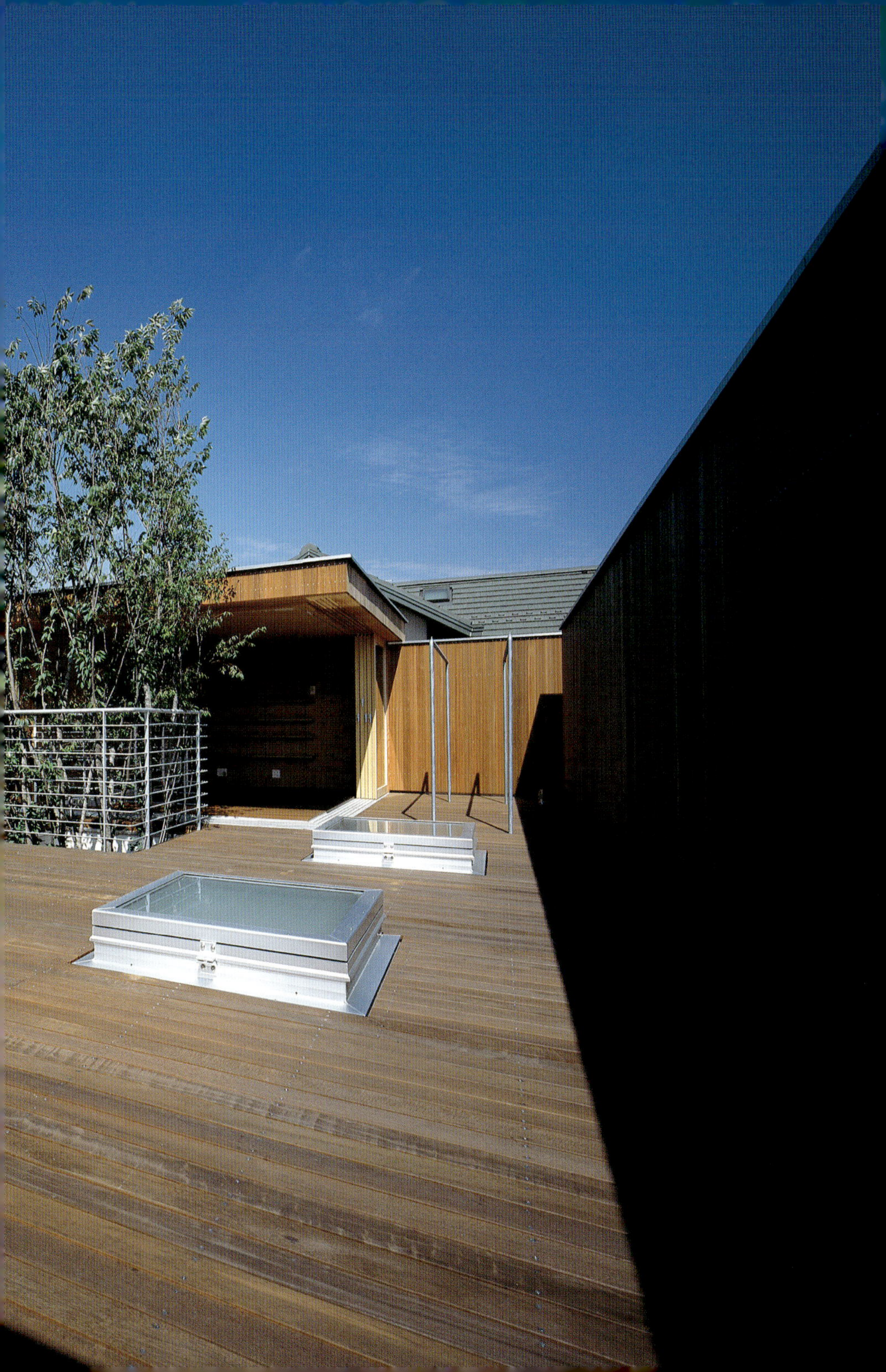

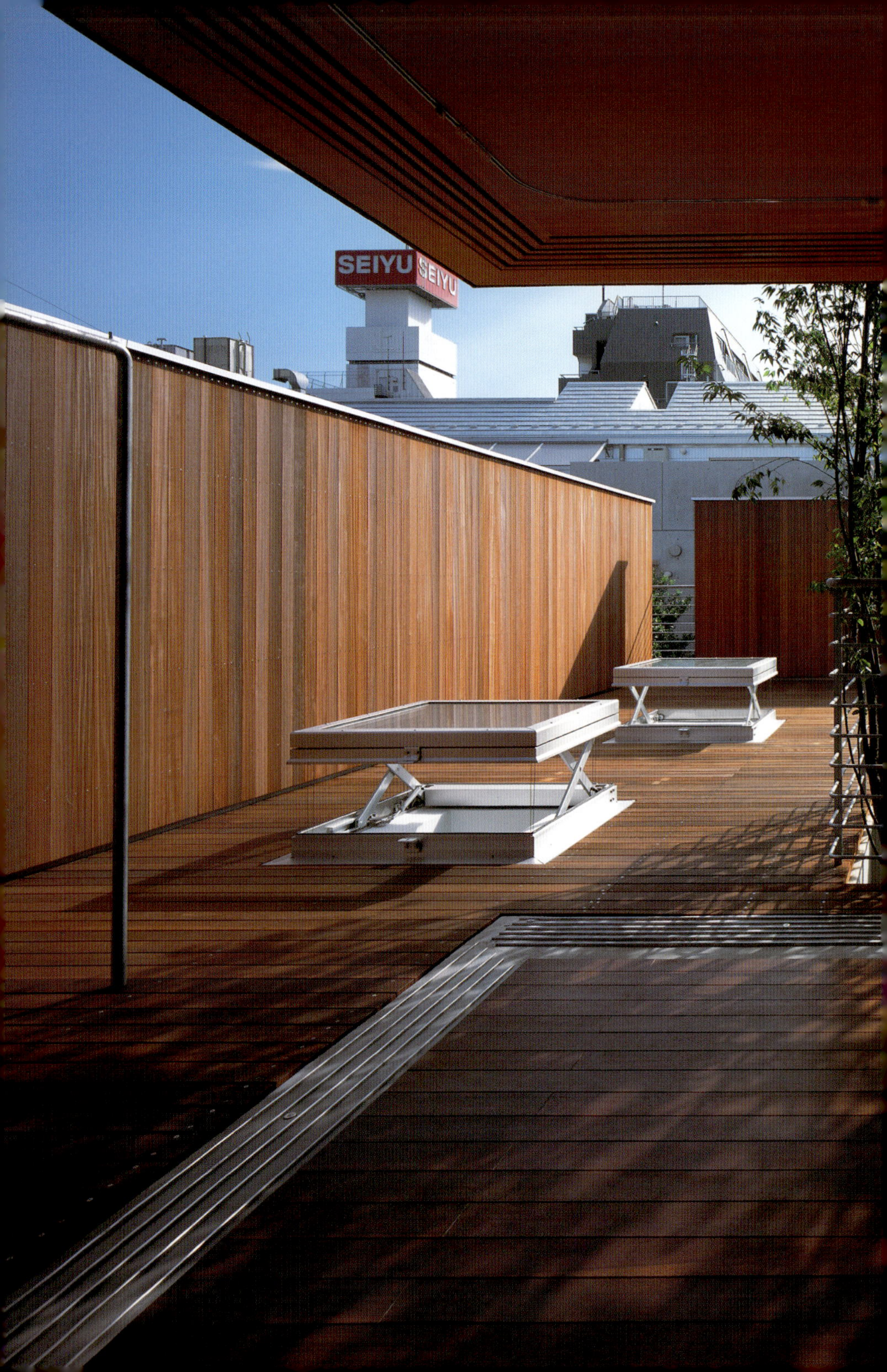
SEIYU SEIYU

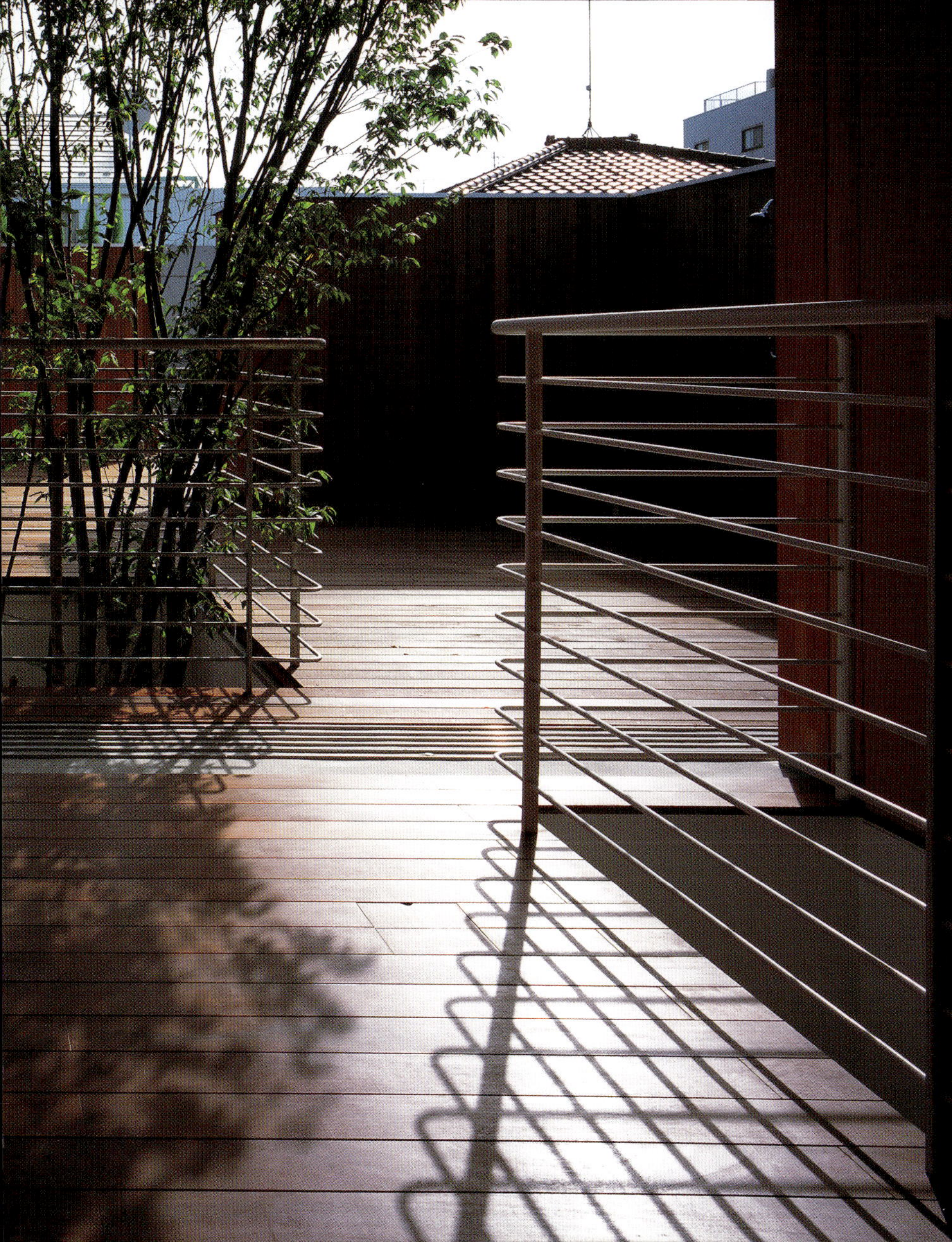

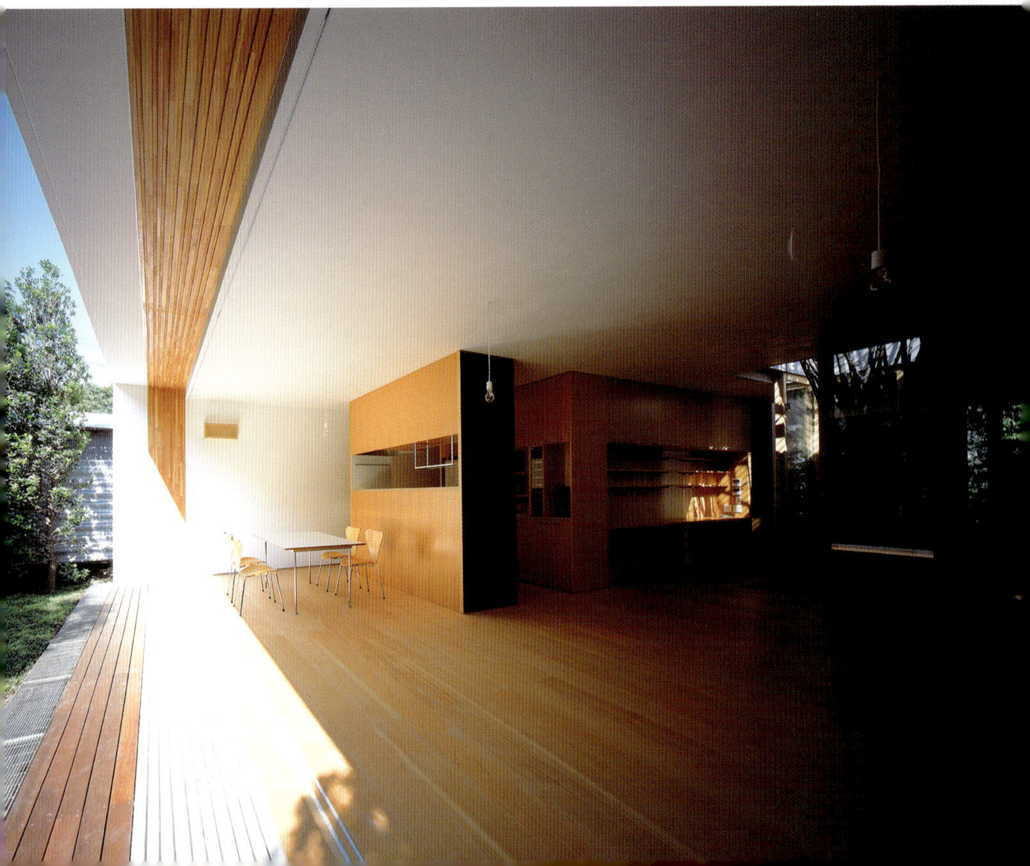

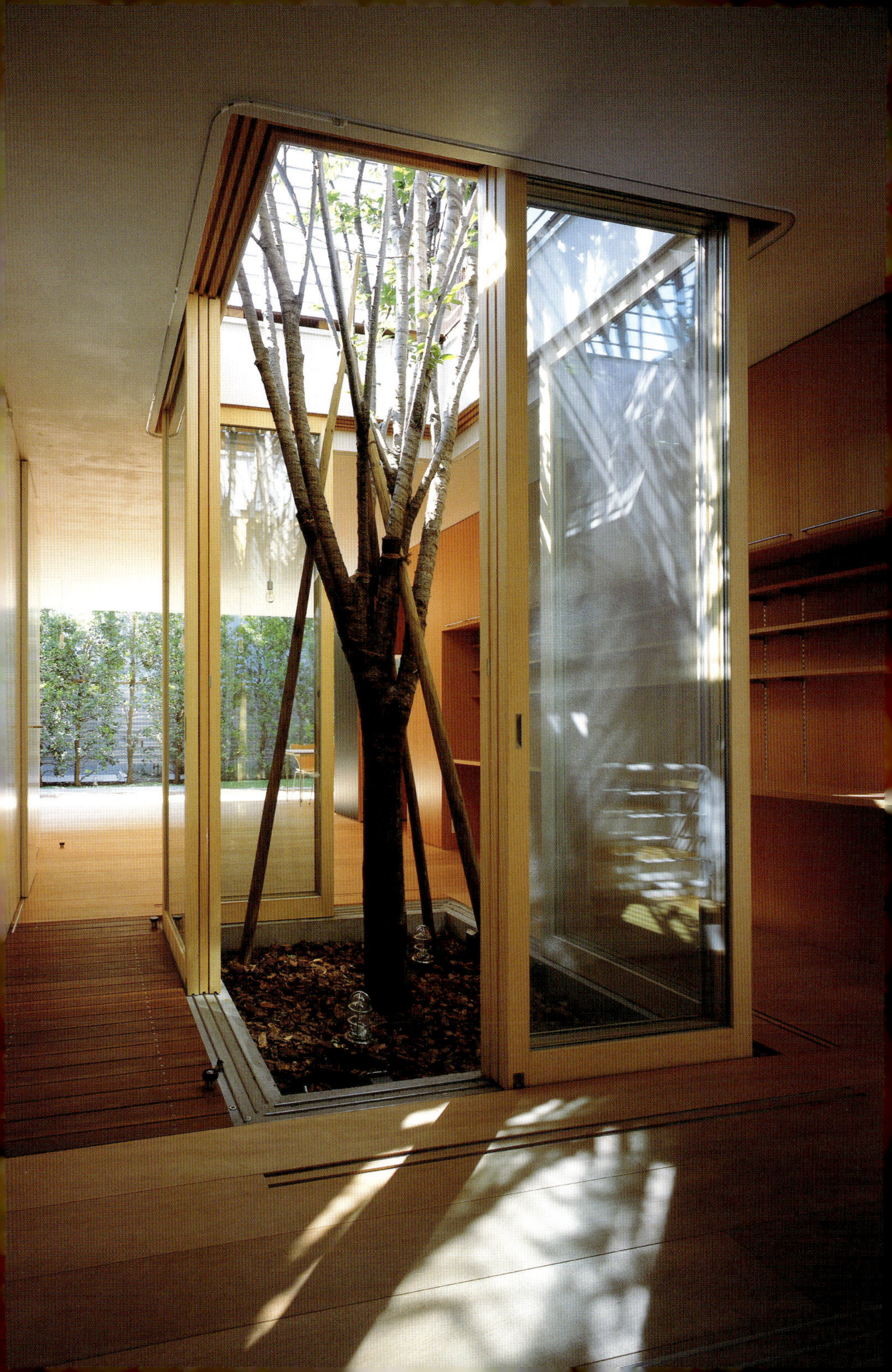

1F 1/250

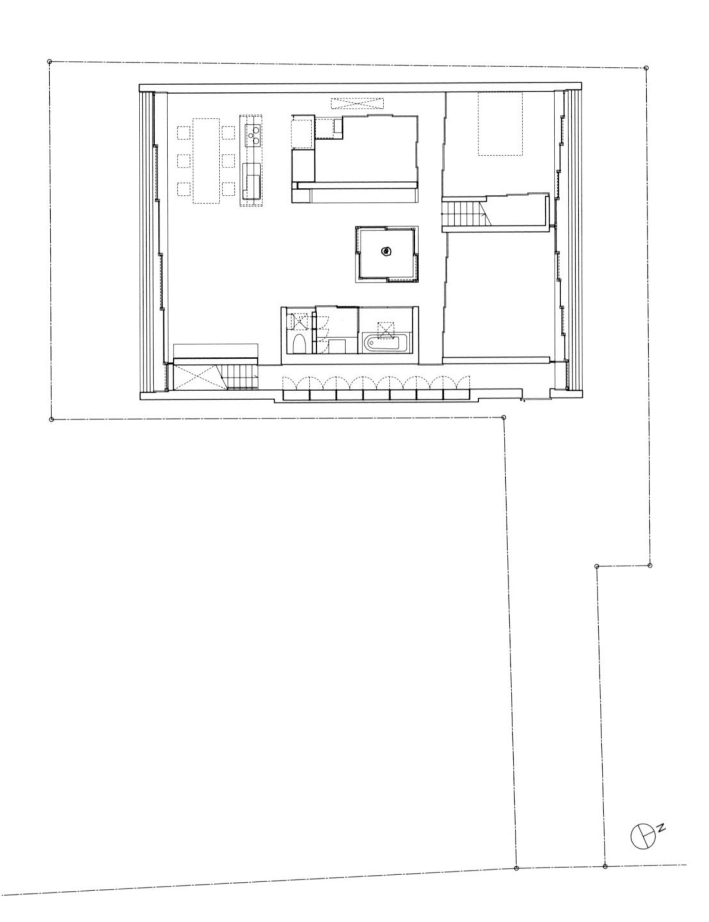

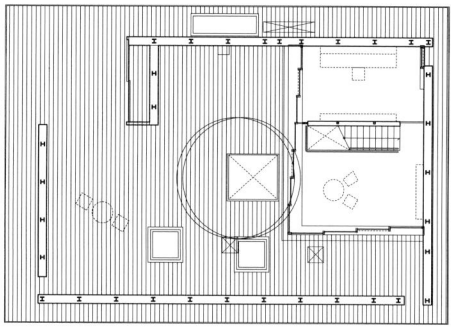

2F 1/250

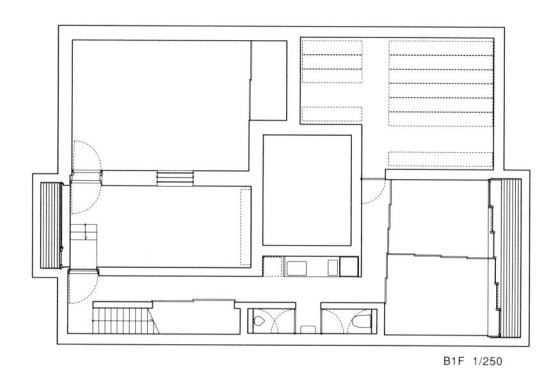

B1F 1/250

SECTION 1/250

Fuji Kindergarten

ふじようちえん　2007

This oval building, with a 200m circumference, was designed as a village for 500 children. The interior is a single large volume loosely divided by the furniture. Final plans are set to include three 25m trees shooting up through the roof deck.

500人の子供のためにつくられた、外周200mの楕円形の幼稚園。
一つの村になるように想定されている。
内部は家具で緩やかに仕切られた一体空間。
高さ25mのケヤキが3本屋上デッキを貫いて残る予定。

38

1F 1/1000

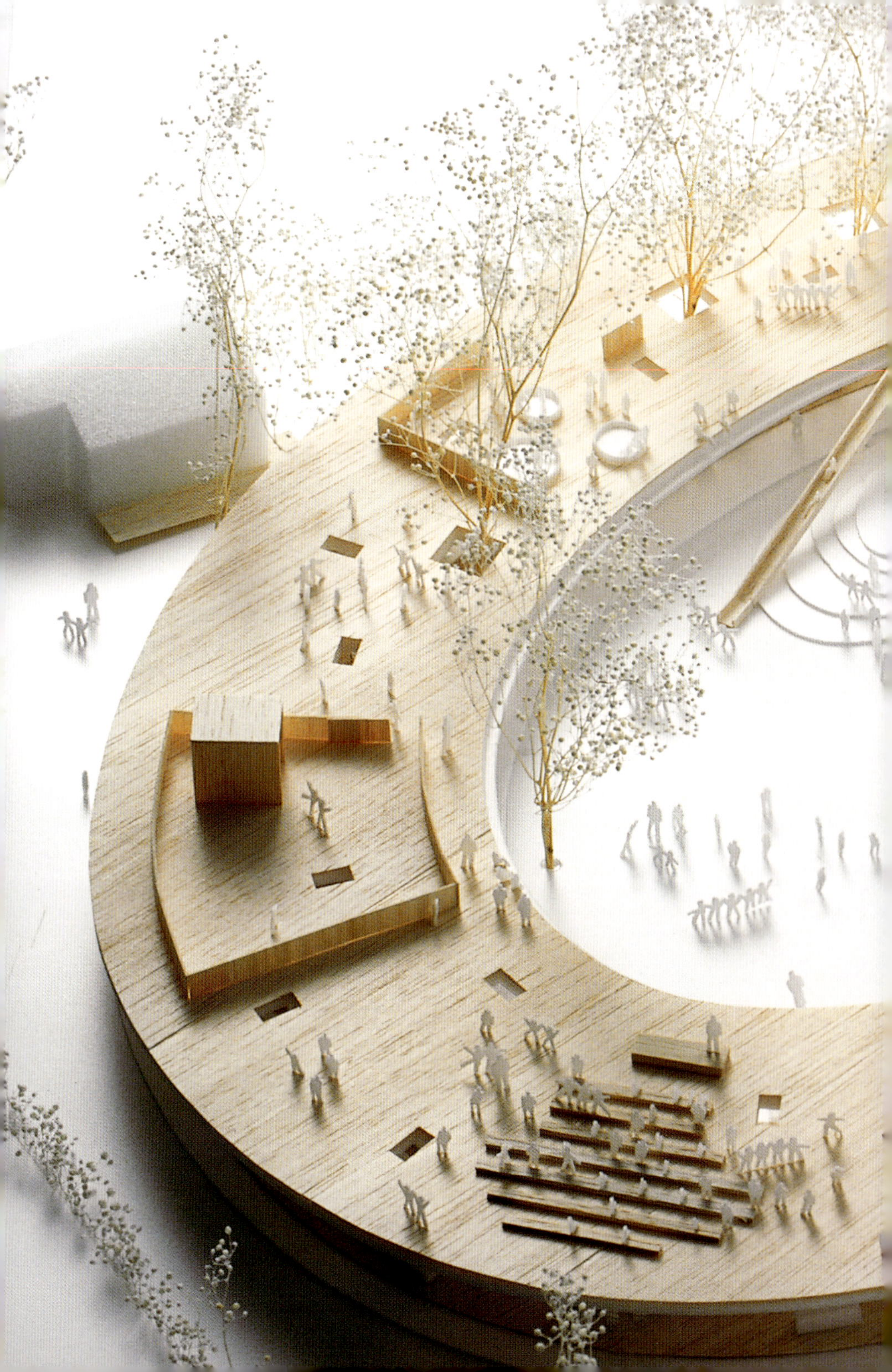

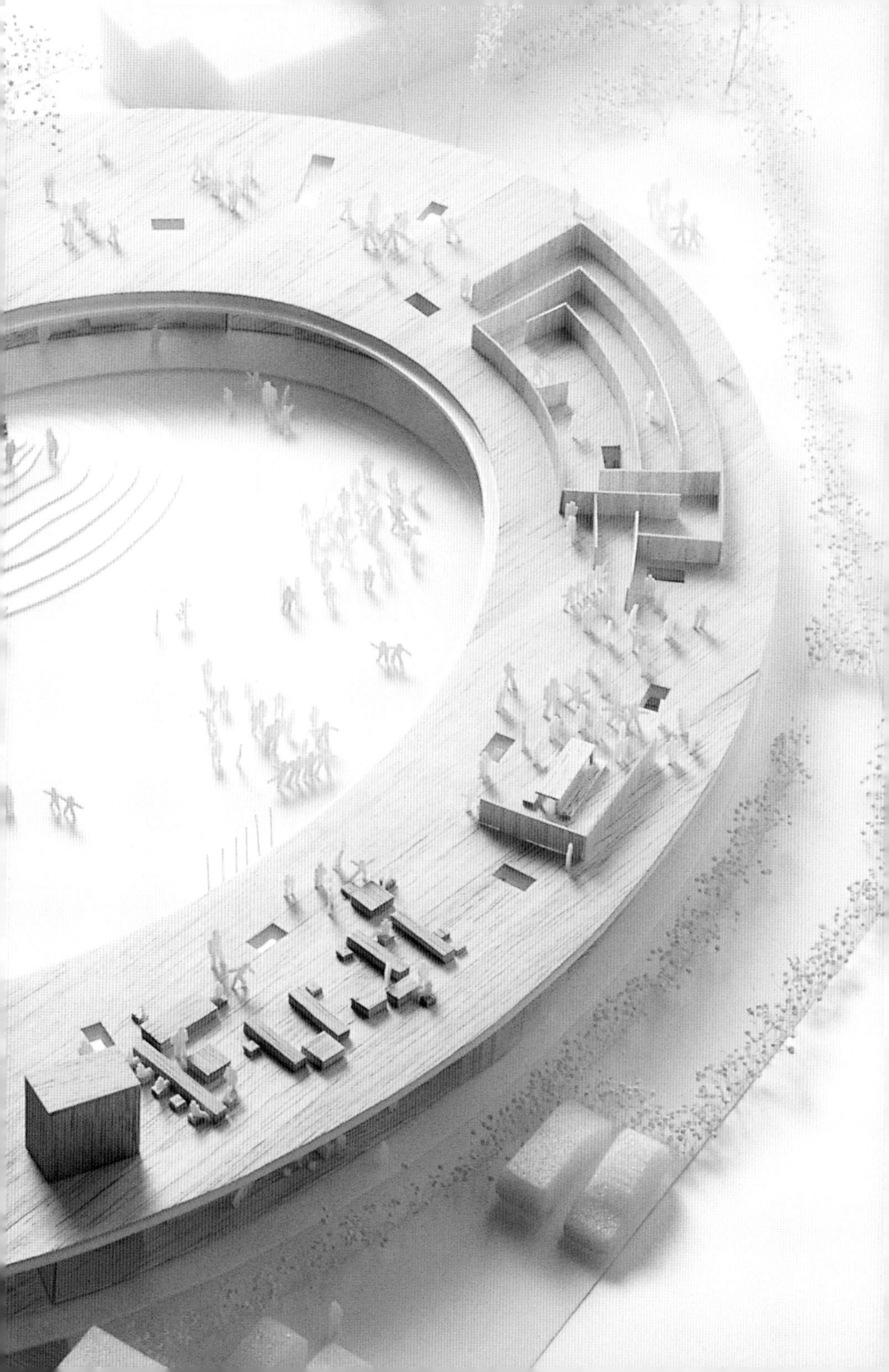

TIME-LESS 変わらないもの
Takaharu + Yui Tezuka 手塚貴晴＋手塚由比

Time-less

Regardless of changes in era and fashion, in architecture there are elements that do not change. Things such as roofs, walls, floors, and columns. These comprise the essence of architecture, which humanity has become accustomed to over a long period of time. Architecture does not progress. It changes. When designing, one is driven by the desire to test various ideas from the infinite number that will appear. Even so, among those ideas, very few are worthy of surviving beyond their own era. Unlike automobiles, the essence of architecture does not undergo dramatic improvements due to technological progress. Architecture with state-of-the-art air-conditioning may still be inferior to the seaside houses of fishermen. It is entirely possible that three-dimensionally shaped avant-garde buildings are no different from works of a century ago. Today's state-of-the-art becomes tomorrow's precedent. No matter how the era progresses, the relationship between people and architecture does not change. In any era, as things shift, the simple desires of people will not change, such as the desire for a family to sit around the dining table, or the desire to open a window and see greenery. We wish to attempt applying our hand to these fundamental things.

The primordial elements are easily found by attempting to put the "~" part into the phrase "house without ~" or "architecture without ~." The elements of architecture with a high degree of necessity are those that may be inserted in this title with very little sense of incompatibility. In the act of saying "architecture without ~" the speaker cannot avoid pursuing the meaning of "~." We have also noticed that own work often contains the title "house without walls." This comment inverts the supposition that there must be walls in architecture.

A house without a roof is rare. We think such a house probably still does not exist as a built work. This implies that, in most regions of the world, it is precisely the roof that is the origin of architecture itself. A roof shelters from rain and blocks the sun, yet this is almost identical to the word "architecture."

The *Roof House* is also a house without a roof. There are many people who misunderstand the *Roof House* as being a "house with a roof," but actually this is a reversal of the illusion that "this house has no roof." When guiding visitors up on the roof, we are often asked, "where in this house do people sleep?" This is also a strange question, as the rooms are definitely below the roof. The people being guided on the roof have forgotten the lower level that they walked through just a moment previously, and the only thing left in their minds is being up on the roof. Mr and Mrs Takahashi, who live in the *Roof House*, will try to explain that, "there is a wonderful lower level down below," but this lower level becomes no more than an appendage. The architecture itself is only on top of the roof. Naturally, on top of the roof is roofless. Therefore, the *Roof House* is "architecture without a roof."

Fondness

The longevity of architecture is determined according to the user's fondness for it. In today's technologically advanced society, it is not especially difficult to make a structure robust enough to last a century or more. The beautiful Kyoto townscape survived the war unscathed, but was destroyed by the Japanese themselves. Due to our defeat, the spirit of admiration for Japanese tradition was lost, and so fondness for the town also died. Although most houses in Japan are rebuilt after about thirty years, this is a postwar phenomenon. Houses have not become disposable because their structures are weak or because of the cold. The inhabitants of postwar houses thought of them as "apparatuses in which to somehow try and get on with life," for which they had no fondness.

Our aspiration is for the ideas of a house to be extracted from its inhabitants. Although basically an amateur, the ideas of a client conceal treasures in an interwoven bundle of idle thoughts of various sizes. To search among these idle thoughts for a strong clue that may define the entire building is an enjoyable task.

The *Roof House* is located at a fairly early stage within our body of work. Our point of departure was the ready-built house in which this family had previously lived. We had very little work at that time, so having received the commission by telephone, a few days later we excitedly imposed ourselves at their house. When visiting the house of a new client, we observe their living conditions as much as possible. Although it sounds bad to talk of observation, our purpose is to look for clues. In the case of the *Roof House*, we were suddenly given a meal. They also asked many questions, and it seemed that not only were we observing them, but we ourselves were being observed. The house itself was an old wooden house built immediately after the war, and in fairly good taste. It was a formidable opponent. Then the husband happened to say, "our family likes to climb onto the roof." We looked incredulous as the couple guided us to a narrow stair on the second floor. We arrived at a sliding window about 600mm in height and 1,200mm in width. Opening the screen entirely, they said, "the four of us eat rice balls out here." The small roof above the entrance hall was a tiled area of no more than four *tatami* mats (6.5m²) in size. It also had a fairly steep slope. At this point, our minds were made up.

The roof of the ready-built house in which this family used to live was reached by passing through a sliding window at the top of a small stair. If this is had been a door, it would have been utterly uninteresting. To forcibly pass through a small window is like the pleasure of plucking forbidden fruit. We therefore decided to make a skylight on the roof that one is forced to wrench open in order to exit. There is no handrail on the roof of the *Roof House*. You might say that the lack of a handrail reveals an adventurous spirit, but to tell the truth, achieving this was a convoluted process. As we are ostensibly a first-class licensed architect office, we are required to put a handrail on the roof. We depicted a 1.1m-high handrail in the drawings, but the husband said, "surely you won't be putting in a handrail." He went on to say, "look around the neighborhood — there is not a single house with a handrail on the roof." Indeed, the issue was settled: this *Roof House* was not to have an ordinary roof deck.

An idea drawn from the users' daily life will be strong. It will invariably be used as expected. It will not become an empty theory. This rooftop is used frequently every week. In the heat of summer, they ascend during the cool mornings and evenings, and in winter they ascend when the deck gets warm during the afternoon. For the clients, using the roof is an idea they thought of themselves. Their fondness for it is strong.

The *Roof House* is a puzzle that is incomplete without the Takahashi family. The *Roof House* is the first project ever published in the magazine *Shinkenchiku* to have included the clients in the photographs. In order to distinguish themselves from general house magazines, a specialist magazine like *Shinkenchiku* will avoid introducing the grinning faces of the clients, and focus only on the architecture. However, the *Roof House* cannot be explained without its clients. The arrangement on top of the roof is not a design, but a device.

The family of the *Roof House* is frequently compared with the *Megaphone House*, which we designed concurrently with the *Roof House*. Why does the area under the eaves of the *Roof House* suit radishes, and why does the living room of the *Megaphone House* suit a Le Corbusier sofa? Why does the *Megaphone House* have maple flooring and mortar walls whereas the walls and floors of the *Roof House* are plywood? "A house like the *Megaphone House* appeared in my dreams," is what the wife has said. What is important is to preface this with, "for us, it is good that..." It is good because this is the Takahashi family, and ultimately, it is good because of the Takahashi family. Regarding their own home, the Takahashi family uses the expression, "a house without excess or deficiency." The phrase "for our family" is concealed within the words "excess and deficiency."

Easily Understood

A while ago, the magazine *Architectural Review* published the *Roof House*. Because it is such a small project, we were truly delighted for it to be published, but when we excitedly opened to the right page, we found a strange title. "Up On The Roof." Although other works from Japan are published under their given project names, this editor had renamed it without permission. Reading on, it was apparently seen as an example of architects having interesting ideas because the sites in Tokyo are small: "Topped by a roof deck that doubles as an external room, this family house is an inventive if vertiginous response to Tokyo's lack of space." To a large extent, what was interesting about the article was an unexpected question from London: "about how many roof houses are there in Tokyo?" In fact, the *Roof House* is not located within a densely built residential district, much less the heart of Tokyo. As shown in photographs (Project No 08_), a green valley spreads out in front of the site. However, what is important here is that the meaning of the *Roof House* was disseminated to overseas readers with a definite impact. It is unnecessary to explain the *Roof House*. When giving a lecture in Bordeaux, we asked, "those people who have enjoyed the experience of climbing up onto a roof please raise your hand," and more than 80 percent of the people present raised their hands. Incidentally, when we showed the *Roof House* to a friend from India, he told us that in his hometown everyone had a roof house. It seems that in India, our *Roof House* is too ordinary to be considered a work of architecture.

Getting up onto the roof is fun. Everyone understands the reasons that it is fun. The roof is not a roof deck. Because it is a roof, it is necessary to give it a slope. Many families on outings can be seen strolling along the dry riverbed of the Tamagawa River on a weekend with good weather.

However, in most cases couples will sit on the sloping ground. There are very few couples relaxing on the flat ground in the center. The merits of the slope are, firstly, you face in the same direction, so that even if there is a lull in conversation things do not become awkward. Secondly, you look at the same scenery, so that an event as trivial as a leaping fish will become a topic of conversation. Thirdly, you are always higher than people in front, so the outlook is good, for the same reasons as with theater seating. Above all, the slope makes it easy to sit down or sprawl out. There many cases where a slope attracts people. For instance, the *Piazza del Campo* in Siena is sloped, and the plaza in front of the Pompidou Center also has a considerable incline.

Easily understood architecture has a universality. The universality we are discussing here means only that an idea will be comprehended, not that everybody will consent to it. Much less is it a universal style. To be comprehended, an easily understood device is necessary. The average user comprehends very few elements of architecture. For the average user, the elements of architecture that come to mind are the obvious parts that lie around everywhere, and have an ongoing existence unrelated to their era. The average user comprehends architecture through the everyday. A roof is understood according to its setting together with its necessary purpose, in statements such as, "rain will not blow under a roof with deep eaves," and "a thatched roof is cool even in summer." In the case of the *Roof House*, the appropriate phrase is, "when going up onto the roof to eat, the food is delicious." Architecture is no more than a setting to stimulate activity. Rather than analyze this phenomenon, our theme is to directly answer the simple question, "why is going up on the roof so comfortable?" Architecture is not established by architecture alone. Architectural elements are in an interdependent relationship with the phenomena that surround architecture. The phenomena surrounding architecture comprise everyday life. To comprehend architecture is to comprehend society based on this everyday life.

Opening Possibilities

The completion of construction is no more than the birth of a building. Architecture is a living thing that matures as it is used over time. Regrettably, it is rare for the architects, as its parents, to be involved in this growth process. It is basically the clients or other users that will raise architecture.

It is important to make it possible for the users to become involved. Put another way, architecture without a margin for the user to become involved is unlikely to be loved. Most of the architecture that has survived over the centuries is not used according to its initially intended function. We want to design architecture that does not change in quality, even if the interior is slightly altered or the furniture is replaced. Design that opens possibilities rather than closing possibilities. Beyond just being architects, we really want to have control, even just a little, but too much control will close the possibility of events beyond our own intentions. Like playing cards, the ideal is a game in which infinite possibilities are opened by a simple device. The simplicity of four suits, each with thirteen cards, produces an infinite number of games. However, it is difficult to open possibilities. To open possibilities is not to do nothing. To not do anything is merely being irresponsible. The device of the *Roof House* is a roof. Just to simply cause people to go up onto the roof is the same as casting them out into a field. Having envisioned various possibilities, the task is to distil their essence. A device is essential.

In the *Megaphone House*, possibilities are opened by the window and the large space behind it. Although it would sound good to say that we had absolutely no control over the furniture of the *Megaphone House*, actually, the real situation is that our control was rejected by the client. Just prior to the completion of construction, before the furniture was brought in, despite our assumptions we felt very anxious standing before the large vacant space. It is often said that the *Megaphone House* is not easy to photograph. We did our best to find good angles to take, but because only the sea and the window frames show up, it was said that this would not be enough to explain it to other people. We think it is good that some things do not show up in the photographs. By not showing up in the photographs, the device is not conspicuous. When we go to the *Megaphone House*, gazpacho is brought out. It is arrayed on top of a table made from a recycled old Chinese gate. The usually sordid character of recycled antiques is completely absent. There is just the inhabitant's struggle in importing it from China, and no sense of incompatibility. There is harmony between each piece of furniture selected. They suit the white plaster walls. Most of the furniture is from a collection that had been assembled over many years, before we were selected as designers. Perhaps the client chose the designers to suit this furniture.

A large table, 4m in length, opens possibilities. If a place is made that can allow children to study and work at the same time as the evening meal is being set out, the family will gather together. It fosters the wisdom to live unconcerned about bothering each other, yet without secluding each person in their own place. If it is sufficiently large, study can be done while one member takes a tiny corner to watch television. It is good if there are only four table legs, one in each corner. It is good if the 4m span can be freely divided in any way, and the four corners can be used. If there are about ten people, a full course dinner can be held, and if there are as many as fourteen people, a relaxed meeting can be held. Plywood has been laminated in vertical lengths perpendicular to the floor, making a wooden block like a *baumkuchen*, which will age beautifully without any concern for damage. Even if it is scratched, the same surface will appear in the cross-section. The engraved scratches honor its history. There is no concern about scratches. The block of wood is heavy right to its core. Even if it is tapped, sound does not reverberate.

A chair is very similar to architecture. The selection of shapes is infinite, but it must meet the condition of a person sitting on it. A chair on which it is easy to sit is ideal, but people are unlikely to sit according to ergonomics. Sofas are often used for sleeping. When guests come, we sit up with good manners, but when alone, we just want to sprawl out. The ideal depth is different for each person. With the sofa in the *Floating Roof House*, the way of sitting can be chosen. By slightly shifting the cushions of differing softness and five layers of thickness, it is possible to adjust it to your own shape and purpose.

The structural scheme is one means of opening the possibilities of a space. The column span will open possibilities. The scale of a building is often limited for constructional reasons. However, in practice, there are no physical limitations to structure. Even a 2000m span is possible in the world of engineering. A big space is attractive. Rather than minor manipulations of the shape, a space is given a far greater power just by slightly changing the scale. All the spaces in the *Megaphone House* are larger than a usual residence. The ceiling height is a little over 6m, and the span is a little over 8m. The roof of the *Floating Roof House* has a 16m span. *Toyota L&F Hiroshima* has a 45m span. The office spaces also have a ceiling height of 9m. With no extra manipulation, possibilities are anticipated in these spaces simply by implementing a large scale. A large space can hold bigger furniture than a small space, and it satisfies the simple desire for comfort just by having a large volume of air. We do not believe in using a sense of scale suitable for each purpose. Large can embrace small. If a bedroom is big, it can be used expansively, and a high ceiling feels good.

Through Rationality

We want to be rational. The comprehension of people will not be achieved without rationality. In the artifacts that exceed their era, there should be a rationality that exceeds that era. To be rationalist is not to be functionalist. Function is a criterion reduced to a measurable objective judgment. For instance, the function of how many seconds is required to accelerate to 100km per hour. However, like reading words, rationality means whether or not something fits a theory. Architecture cannot be measured by function. Being measurable by function is only a part of the architectural whole. A functionalist viewpoint cannot even give a simple explanation as to why a naturally open 200m passage is preferable to a pitch-dark 100m passage. In any context, functionality engages the established paradigm, whereas rationality is a logic system that oscillates according to the conditions. For us, rational architecture is not minimalism. Individuality arises from taking a great diversity of contexts as starting points. Therefore, if the client is different, the answer is different, from being input into the context as a pattern. Even in the same logic circuit, if the input changes, the answer will also change.

When constructing a theory, we use the word "diagram." A diagram is not a milieu. The milieu could be described as a visa required in order to cross the barrier of judgment as to whether a theory may pass as architecture. Perhaps it may be a clue for making architecture. However, the word "milieu" is not accompanied by a theory of form. Done only halfway, it also contains the risk of being trapped in a pattern. Put directly, "a diagram is a system established between elements regardless of scale."

By taking the roof as the clue to the *Roof House*, the system has been established with a one-to-one correspondence. There is an owner for each skylight in the *Roof House*. Every room has its own skylight. The skylight above the child bedroom is the younger sister's. The skylight in the study room is the elder sister's. The bedroom skylight is the father's. The skylight in the kitchen, where cooking takes place. The skylight that allows viewing the night sky from the bath.

It is possible to enjoy cool evenings on the roof by ascending the ladder in the washroom. A lantern is attached to each skylight. There are naked light bulbs below the roof. Each light bulb hangs in correspondence with each function. A light bulb for the table. A light bulb for the living room where people gather.

In Conclusion

We are architects who have returned home. From 1990 to 1994, Takaharu Tezuka was employed at the Richard Rogers Partnership, and we thoroughly enjoyed the London lifestyle. If our work permits still allowed, we might still be in London. The greatest asset we gained from living in London is an understanding of the qualify of life. During Takaharu Tezuka's internship, to be honest, the office of Richard Rogers was not in an affluent condition. Naturally, it was indeed luxurious for Takaharu Tezuka to be in the circumstances of avoiding being fired, or being unaware that he might be fired. Given the small number of staff, there were more opportunities to speak with Richard Rogers, and more chances to find projects. However, naturally the salary was low. Having paid for lodging, we were in the wretched condition of having only about 40,000 yen (400 US dollars) per month for living expenses. Incidentally, you could say that the cost of living in London then was little different from Tokyo here in 2006. However, we were superbly satisfied with life. Our apartment in London was a single room of 50m^2 with a ceiling height of 4m. This was superbly easy to live in. We could call about ten friends and have a party without any trouble. On weekends we could go cycling in nearby Richmond Park. The route to the park was pleasant. We would order a baked potato in the park teahouse, and the two of us would happily just watch the evening sun sink over the River Thames. Takaharu Tezuka will never forget the times he spent having afternoon tea with his colleagues, each day at about 3pm on the balconies that project from Richard Rogers's office out over the River Thames. Probably if we were still in London, we might have become somewhat dissatisfied, but for now these are entirely happy thoughts. We think how wonderful it would be if such everyday happiness was directly transformed into architecture.

変わらないもの

　時代や流行の変化に関わらず、建築には変わらない要素がある。屋根や壁や床や柱等である。これらは長い間、人間が慣れ親しんできた建築の本質である。建築は進歩するものではない。変化するものである。設計に携わっていると、アイデアが無限に出てきていろいろと試してみたい欲求に駆られる。しかしながら、そのアイデアの中で時代を経て生き残る価値のあるものは僅かである。建築の本質は車のように技術の進歩で劇的に改善されるものではない。空調の効いた最先端の作品が、海辺の漁民の家にかなわないこともある。三次元形態のアバンギャルドな建物が、100年前の作品と何も変わらなかったということも平気でありうる。今日の最先端は明日には先例となる。時代はどんなに進んでも人と建築との関係は変わらない。どんなに時代が進もうと人は家族で食卓を囲むであろうし、窓を開けて緑を見たいという単純な欲求は変わらない。我々はこの根本的な部分に手を加えてみたいと考えている。

　これら初源的な要素は「〜の無い家」あるいは「〜の無い建築」というフレーズの「〜」という部分に当てはめてみると見つかりやすい。入れてみてタイトルとして違和感が少ないほど、建築にとって必要性が高い要素である。「〜の無い建築」と言った途端に、発言者は「〜」の意味の探求を余儀なくされる。我々の作品も含め、「壁の無い家」というタイトルをよく見掛ける。このコメントは建築には壁があるはずだという前提条件の裏返しでもある。

　屋根の無い家は珍しい。多分まだ作品としては存在していないのではないかと思う。これは地球上のほとんどの地域で、屋根こそが建築そのものの始まりであることを意味している。屋根は雨を凌ぎ、日を遮るためのものであるが、これはほとんど建築という言葉と同意であると言ってよい。

　屋根の家は屋根の無い家でもある。「屋根の家」のことを「屋根のある家」と勘違いする人も多いが、これは「あの家には屋根が無い」との錯覚の裏返しでもある。見学者を案内すると、「この家は何処に寝るのですか」と屋根の上で質問されることが多い。これもおかしな質問で、部屋は屋根の下にあるに決まっている。屋根の上に案内された人は、今しがた通ったばかりの一階を忘れてしまって、脳裏には屋根の上しか残っていない。「屋根の家」に住まわれている高橋夫妻が「素敵な一階が下にあります」と弁明しようがしまいが、一階は付属物でしかなくなってしまっているので

ある。屋根の上こそが建築そのものなのである。当然のことながら屋根の上には屋根が無い。よって屋根の家は「屋根の無い建築」である。

思い入れ

　建築の寿命は使用者の思い入れで決まる。技術の進んだ現代社会で、100年以上壊れない構造をつくることはさほど難しいことではない。戦時をくぐり抜けて生き残ってきた美しい京都の街並みを破壊したのは、日本人である。日本の伝統を愛でる心が敗戦を通して失われたとき、街への思い入れが死んだからである。日本の住宅はほとんどが30年程度でつくり直されてしまうが、これは戦後の現象である。住宅が使い捨てになるのは、構造が弱いからでも寒いからでもない。住み手にとって、戦後の住宅には「工夫して何とか住みこなしてみたい」と思わせるだけの思い入れが無かったのである。
　住宅のアイデアは住み手から引き出すのが理想である。基本的に素人である施主のアイデアは、大小織り交ぜた雑念の固まりではあるが、宝が隠されている。この雑念の中から、建物全体をつかさどれるような強い手掛かりを探し出すのは楽しい作業である。

　「屋根の家」は我々の作品の中で、かなり初期に位置する。出発点はかつて、このご一家が暮らしていた建売住宅である。当時あまり仕事の無かった我々は依頼の電話を受けるなり、いそいそと2〜3日後には、お宅へお邪魔することになった。我々は新しい施主のお宅へお邪魔する場合、生活の具合をできる限り観察する。観察というと聞こえは悪いが、手掛かりを探すためである。屋根の家の場合は、いきなりつくね汁をごちそうになった。いろいろと質問されて、観察するどころか、どうやら我々が観察される側のようである。住宅自体は古い戦後まもなくの木造住宅で、結構味がある。かなりの強敵である。すると、ふとご主人が「我々一家は屋根の上に登るのが好きなんです」と語った。どうも半信半疑の我々を見て、ご夫婦は二階の狭い階段へと我々を案内した。行き着いた先は、高さ600mm幅1,200mm程度の引き違い窓。そこをガラリと開けて「ここで四人でおにぎりを食べるんです」とのこと。玄関の上にあたるその小さな屋根の大きさは、せいぜい畳4枚程度の瓦葺。勾配も結構急である。この時点で我々の心は決まった。
　ご家族が住まわれていた昔の建売住宅の屋根は、小さな階段上の引き違い窓をくぐり抜けた先にあった。これが扉であったら少しも

面白くない。小さな窓を無理やり通り抜けるところに、禁断の果実をもぐ喜びがあったのだと思う。よって屋根の上には天窓をこじ開けて無理やり出ていただくことにした。屋根の家の屋根には手すりが無い。手すりが無いところに冒険心があったと言いたいところであるが、これに関して実は紆余曲折がある。一応一級建築士事務所である以上は、屋上には手すりを付けなければならない。そこで1.1mの高さの手すりを図面に描いておいたところ、ご主人より「まさか手すりは付けませんよね」とのお話があった。「辺りを見渡して一軒も屋根の上に手すりのある家は無いですよ」とのこと。なるほど、この屋根の家は屋上ではないのだということで一件落着となった。

　使い手の日常から引き出したアイデアは強い。必ず予想通りに使われることになる。空論にはならない。屋根の上は毎週何度も使われている。暑い夏は涼しい朝と夜に上がり、冬はデッキが暖まった昼ごろに上がる。施主にとって屋根を使うということは、自分で考えたアイデアである。思い入れは強い。

　屋根の家は高橋一家がいなければ完成しないパズルである。屋根の家は『新建築』史上初めて施主が写真に登場した作品。『新建築』のような専門誌は一般住宅誌と一線を画すため、施主がニッコリ笑って案内するような紹介は避け、建築のみにフォーカスを当てる。ところが屋根の家は施主がいなければ説明できない。屋根の上のしつらえは、意匠ではなく仕掛けである。

　しばしば屋根の家のご家族は屋根の家を、同時期に我々が設計した「メガホンハウス」と比較する。屋根の家の軒下には何故大根が似合って、メガホンハウスのリビングにはコルビュジエのソファーが似合うのか？ 何故屋根の家の床も壁もベニヤ板なのに、メガホンハウスはメープルのフローリングで漆喰壁なのか。「私が夢描いていたのはメガホンハウスのような家」とは奥さんの弁。大切なのはこの先で「うちはこれで良いのよ……」がつく。高橋家だからこれで良い、結局のところ、高橋家だからこれが良いのである。高橋一家は自宅に対して「過不足の無い家」との表現を使う。過不足という言葉の裏には、「我が家族にとって」という一節が隠されている。

わかりやすいこと

　以前、アーキテクチャーレビュー誌が屋根の家を取り上げたことがあった。小さな作品なので取り上げてもらったことを実に喜んで、いそいそとページを開けてみると、タイトルがおかしい。Up on the roof。他の日本の作

品が作品名で取り上げられているにも関わらず、この編集者が勝手にネーミングしている。読んでみると「東京は土地が狭いので面白いことを考えた建築家がいる」との趣旨でまとめてある。よほど記事が面白かったのか、ロンドンから「東京には屋根の家は何軒ぐらいあるのか?」との質問まで舞い込んだ。実は屋根の家の周辺は住宅密集地でもなければ、ましてや東京の中心部でもない。敷地の前面には写真のとおり（作品 08_）緑の谷が広がっている。しかしここで重要なのは、海外の読者に「屋根の家」の意味が確実にインパクトをもって伝わったということである。屋根の家に説明は要らない。ボルドーで講演会をした折に「屋根の上に登って楽しかった経験のある方手を挙げて下さい」と問い掛けたところ、80パーセント以上の出席者が手を挙げた。ちなみにインドの友人に屋根の家を見せたところ、彼の町は全部屋根の家だそうである。どうも我々の「屋根の家」はインドで作品として通用しそうもない。

　屋根には登ると楽しい。その楽しさには誰にでもわかる理由がある。屋根は屋上ではない。屋根であるからには傾いていなければならない。多摩川の河川敷を良い季節の週末に散歩すると、たくさんの家族連れを見掛ける。しかしカップルが座っているのは、大抵の場合斜面である。平らのグラウンドの真ん中でくつろいでいるカップルは少ない。斜面の良いところは、第一に、同じ方向を向いているので、話題が途切れても気まずくならない。第二に、同じ景色を見ているので、魚が跳ねた程度の些細な出来事が話題につながる。第三に、いつでも前の人より高いので、劇場の客席と同じ理屈で眺望が良い。そして何より、傾いていると座りやすいし寝そべりやすい。斜面が人を呼び込む事例は多い。たとえばシエナのカンポ広場も斜面であるし、ポンピドーセンター前の広場もかなりの傾きである。

　わかりやすい建築は普遍性がある。ここで語る普遍性とは、アイデアを理解してもらえるという意味であって、決して万民に了解してもらえるということではない。ましてやユニバーサルスタイルではない。理解してもらうためには、わかりやすい仕掛けが必要である。一般の使用者にとって理解できる建築の要素は少ない。一般の使用者が思い浮かべる建築の要素とは、時代に関わらず存在し続けている、何処にでも転がっている当たり前の部位である。一般の使用者は日常を通して建築を理解する。「軒が深い屋根は雨が吹き込まない」、「茅葺の屋根は夏でも涼しい」といった具合に、屋根は必ず目的とセットで理解されている。屋根の家の場合は「屋根に上がっ

て食べるにぎり飯は旨い」というフレーズがふさわしい。建築は行動を励起するためのセッティングにすぎない。「屋根に上がると何故気持ちが良いのか」といった単純な疑問を、現象を分解することなく、そのまま解いていくのが我々のテーマである。建築は建築だけで成立しないのである。建築の要素は建築を取り巻く現象と相互依存関係にある。建築を取り巻く現象は日常である。建築の理解はこの日常に基いて社会に理解される。

可能性を開く

　竣工は建築物の生誕にすぎない。建築は使われる間、時間を経て成長する生き物である。残念ながら、親である建築家がこの成長過程に関われる機会はまれである。基本的に建築を育てるのは、施主あるいはその他の使用者である。

　使用者が入り込む可能性をつくることは大切なことである。逆に言えば使用者が入り込む余地の無い建築は、なかなか愛されない。世紀を超えて生き残ってきた建築のほとんどは、当初の予定通りの機能で使われていない。我々は内部が少々変更され家具が入れ替わろうと質の変わらない建築を設計したい。可能性を閉じるのではなく、可能性を開く設計。

我々も建築家である以上、少しでもコントロールしたいのは山々であるが、コントロールし過ぎると、自分の意図した以上の出来事が起こる可能性を閉じてしまう。理想はトランプのような、単純な仕掛けで無限の可能性を開くゲームである。単純な13枚×4種類のカードが、無限のゲームをつくり出す。しかし、可能性を開くことは難しい。可能性を開くということは何もしないことではない。何もしないことは単なる無責任である。屋根の家の仕掛けは屋根である。単に屋根に上がらせるだけでは、野原に人を放り出すことと同じになってしまう。様々な可能性を想定した上で、エッセンスを蒸留抽出する作業である。仕掛けが肝心である。

　メガホンハウスの可能性を開いたのは、窓とその後ろの大空間である。メガホンハウスの家具はまったくコントロールしなかったと言えば聞こえが良いが、実は我々のコントロールが施主から断られたのが真相である。竣工直前、予期していたこととはいえ、家具が入る前のガランとした大きな空間を前にかなりの不安感を覚えた。メガホンハウスは写真に撮りにくいと言われることが多い。良いアングルを懸命に撮ったが、海とサッシしか写っていなかったので第三者に説明がつかないと言うのである。写真に写らないことは良いこ

とであると思う。写真に写らなかったということは、仕掛けが目立たなかったということである。メガホンハウスに行くとガスパッチョが出てくる。それが中国の古い門扉を再利用したテーブルの上にポンと載って出てくる。まったくアンティークの再利用特有のいかがわしさが無い。住み手が苦労して中国から輸入しただけのことはあって、違和感が無い。一つ一つ選んだ家具が調和している。白い漆喰の壁と似合う。ほとんどの家具は我々が設計者として選定される以前から、長年に渡って集められたコレクションである。多分施主が家具に合わせて設計者を選んだからであろう。

　長さ4mの大きなテーブルは可能性を開く。夕食を並べている横で子供の勉強と仕事を同時にこなせる場をつくれば家族が集まる。自分の場所に閉じこもらず、互いの迷惑を気にしつつ暮らす知恵が育つ。十分に大きければ少々片隅でテレビを見ているメンバーがいようと勉強はできる。テーブルの足は角に4本あるだけが良い。4mのスパンの間は自由で、どう分けても良いし、四隅が使える。十人程度ならフルコースディナーをこなせるし、十四人までならゆったりと会議をこなせる。合板を床と垂直方向縦に貼り積層したバームクーヘンのような木の塊は、傷が気にならず美しく年をとる。傷がついても出てくるのは同じ断面である。歴史として刻まれる傷は勲章である。傷など気にしないのである。すべて芯まで塊の木は重い。少々たたいても音さえ返ってこない。

　椅子は建築とよく似ている。形の選択は無限であるが、人が座るという条件がついている。座りやすい椅子は理想であるが、人はなかなか人間工学通りに座ってくれない。ソファーは寝て使うことも多い。客が来たときには行儀良く浅く腰掛けるであろうが、一人のときは崩れて乗りたい。人によって理想的な奥行きは違う。「山すその家」のソファーは座る側が座り方を選べる。五層に重ねられた厚みや柔らかさの違うクッションを少しずつ動かせば、自分の形と目的に合わせることができる。

　構造の工夫は空間の可能性を開くための手段である。柱のスパンは可能性を開く。建物のスケールは構造上の理由から制限されている場合が多い。ところが実際に構造には物理的な制限は無い。土木の世界では二千mのスパンさえ可能である。大きな空間は魅力的である。空間はスケールを少し変えるだけで少々の形態操作より遥かに強い力をもつ。メガホンハウスはすべてが通常の住宅空間より大きい。天井高は6m強、スパンは8m強で

ある。「山すその家」の屋根は16mスパンである。「トヨタL＆F広島」は45mスパン。オフィス空間の天井高も9mをとった。これらの空間にはあえて操作を加えず、単純で大きなスケールがもたらす可能性に期待している。大きな空間は小さな空間よりも大きな家具を持ち込むことができるし、気積が大きいだけで気持ちが良いという単純な欲求も満たせる。我々はそれぞれの目的にふさわしいスケール感というものを信じていない。大は小を兼ねる。寝室だって大きければ大きいほど使い良いと思うし、高い天井高は気持ちよい。

理屈が通っていること

　我々は合理的でありたいと思う。合理的でなければ人の理解は得られない。時代を超える製品には必ず、時代を超えられる合理性があるはずである。合理的であるということは機能的であることではない。機能とは定量可能な客観的判断を下せる基準である。たとえば時速100キロまで加速するのに何秒要するかというのは機能である。ところが合理性とは読んで字のごとく、理屈に合っているかどうかという意味である。建築は機能で計れるものではない。機能で計れるのは建築総体のほんの一部分だけである。機能的視点では100mの真っ暗な廊下より、200mの自然に開かれた廊下のほうがよいという単純な説明さえ簡単には成し得ない。機能性はどのコンテクストでも成立するパラダイムであるのに対して、合理性は条件によって揺れ動く論理体系である。我々にとって合理的建築はミニマリズムではない。多種多様なコンテクストを出発点とした個別性である。よって施主が違えば回答は違ってくる、我々は関数でコンテクストは入力である。同じ論理回路でもインプットが変われば回答も変わる。

　我々は理屈を構築するときダイアグラムという言葉を使う。ダイアグラムは文脈ではない。文脈というと、建築として理屈が通っているかを判断する関所を通過するための通行手形とでも言ってよいであろうか。何を手掛かりとして建築をつくるかということであろうか。ところがこの文脈という単語は、形態論を伴わない。ややもすると図式に陥る危険性も含んでいる。端的に言えば「ダイアグラムとはスケールに関わらず要素の間に成立する系」である。

　屋根の家は屋根を手掛かりとして一対一対応の系が成立している。屋根の家の天窓にはそれぞれオーナーがいる。すべての部屋には一つずつ天窓がある。子供寝室の上の天窓は妹さん。勉強部屋の天窓はお姉さん。寝室の

天窓はお父さん。料理を持ち上げるキッチンの天窓。風呂から夜空を眺める天窓。

　洗面所のはしごを上がると屋根の上で夕涼みができる。それぞれの天窓には一つ一つランタンがついている。屋根の下には裸電球が下がっている。一つ一つの電球は、一つ一つの機能に対応して下げられている。テーブルのための電球。人が集まるリビングのための電球。

おわりに

　我々は帰国建築家である。1990年から1994年までリチャード・ロジャース・パートナーシップに勤務したが、そのロンドン生活がかなり気に入っていた。労働許可証さえ許せば、まだロンドンにいたのではないかと思う。ロンドン暮らしで我々の得た最大の財産は、生活の質を知ることであろう。手塚貴晴が修行時代、正直なところリチャード・ロジャースの事務所は裕福な状態ではなかった。もっとも、首を免れたのか、あるいは首になったことに気がつかなかった手塚貴晴にとっては実に贅沢な境遇であった。所員が少ないということは、憧れのリチャード・ロジャース氏と話す機会も増えるし、プロジェクトにありつくチャンスも増える。しかし当然のことながら給料は安い。宿代を払うと一月4万円程度しか生活費が無かった窮状であった。ちなみに当時のロンドンの生活費は、2006年現在の東京とほとんど変わらないと言ってよい。ところが結構我々は生活に満足していたのである。我々の住んでいたロンドンのアパートは天井高4m、50m²ほどのワンルーム。これが結構住みやすい。十人程度友人を呼んでパーティを開いて何の不自由も無い。週末ともなると近くのリッチモンド公園までサイクリング。公園まで行く道筋も楽しい。公園のティーハウスでベイクドポテトセットを頼んで、テムズ河に沈む夕日を二人で眺めるだけで幸せであった。午後3時ごろになると、リチャード・ロジャースの事務所からテムズ河に突き出したバルコニーへ同僚と繰り出し過ごしたアフタヌーンティーのひとときも忘れ得ない。多分現在もロンドンにいるとそれなりの不満はあるのかもしれないが、ひたすら楽しかった思いしかない。あの日常の楽しさをそのまま建築にできたら、どんなに素敵だろうと思う。

Project Data 作品データ

Project Name 作品名
① Principal use / 主要用途
② Building site / 所在地
③ Site area / 敷地面積
④ Building area / 建築面積
⑤ Total floor area / 延床面積
⑥ Number of stories / 規模
⑦ Structure / 構造・構法
⑧ Architects / 設計担当
⑨ Architectural and Structural design / 建築構造設計
⑩ Structural design / 構造設計
⑪ Facility design / 設備設計
⑫ Lighting design / 照明計画
⑬ Acoustical design / 音響監修
⑭ Landscape design / 外構監修
⑮ Art (total produce) / アート (統括)
⑯ Art (artist) / アート (アーティスト)
⑰ Art Director / アートディレクター
⑱ Contractors / 施工
⑲ Design period / 設計期間
⑳ Construction period / 施工期間

01_ Soejima Hospital 副島病院
① Hospital / 病院
② Saga-shi, Saga / 佐賀県佐賀市
③ 2227.01m^2
④ 1415.62m^2
⑤ 4079.48m^2
⑥ 4F
⑦ S
⑧ Takaharu + Yui Tezuka / 手塚貴晴＋手塚由比
⑩ Kajima Corporation, Kyushu / 鹿島建設九州支店
⑪ Kajima Corporation, Kyushu / 鹿島建設九州支店
⑫ LD Yamagiwa / LDヤマギワ研究所
⑱ Kajima Corporation, Matsuo Corporation JV / 鹿島建設 松尾建設JV
⑲ 1994.7-1995.5
⑳ 1995.3-1996.3

02_ Cherry Blossom House 花見の家
① Residence / 住宅
③ 82.54m^2
④ 40.42m^2
⑤ 40.42m^2
⑥ 1F
⑦ RC
⑧ Takaharu + Yui Tezuka / 手塚貴晴＋手塚由比
⑲ 1996.8

03_ Wood Deck House 鎌倉山の家
① Residence / 住宅
② Kamakura-shi, Kanagawa / 神奈川県鎌倉市
③ 269.15m^2
④ 67.28m^2
⑤ 128.45m^2
⑥ 3F
⑦ S

⑧ Takaharu + Yui Tezuka, Masahiro Ikeda, Kentaro Shono, Makoto Takei / 手塚貴晴＋手塚由比、池田昌弘、庄野健太郎、武井誠
⑨ Tezuka Architects + MASAHIRO IKEDA co., ltd / 手塚建築研究所＋MASAHIRO IKEDA co., ltd
⑪ ES Associates / イーエスアソシエイツ
⑫ LD Yamagiwa / LDヤマギワ研究所
⑱ Kikushima / 株式会社キクシマ
⑲ 1998.1-1998.12
⑳ 1999.2-1999.8

04_ Light Gauge Steel House 辻堂の家
① Residence / 住宅
② Fhujisawa-shi, Kanagawa / 神奈川県藤沢市
③ 112.90m^2
④ 46.37m^2
⑤ 139.11m^2
⑥ 3F
⑦ S (LGS)
⑧ Takaharu + Yui Tezuka, Masahiro Ikeda, Kentaro Shono, Makoto Takei / 手塚貴晴＋手塚由比、池田昌弘、庄野健太郎、武井誠
⑨ Tezuka Architects + MASAHIRO IKEDA co., ltd / 手塚建築研究所＋MASAHIRO IKEDA co., ltd
⑱ Kikushima / 株式会社キクシマ
⑲ 1998.4-1998.12
⑳ 1999.6-1999.10

05_ Kawagoe Music Apartment 川越の音楽マンション
① Collective Housing / 集合住宅
② Kawagoe-shi, Saitama / 埼玉県川越市
③ 522.55m^2
④ 326.69m^2
⑤ 2532.22m^2
⑥ B1F, 14F

⑦ SRC + RC
⑧ Takaharu + Yui Tezuka, Makoto Takei, Chie Nabeshima, Hiroshi Hibio, Tetsuya Yamazaki / 手塚貴晴＋手塚由比、武井誠、鍋島千恵、日比生寛史、山崎徹也
⑩ Ove Arup & Partners Japan Limited / オーヴアラップアンドパートナーズ
⑪ ES Associates / イーエスアソシエイツ
⑫ Masahide Kakudate (Masahide Kakudate Lighting Architect & Associates, Inc.) / 角舘政英（ぼんぼり光環境計画）
⑱ Satohide Corporation / 株式会社佐藤秀
⑲ 1998.4-1998.11
⑳ 1999.1-2000.2

06 _ Machiya House 八王子の家
① Residence / 住宅
② Hachioji-shi, Tokyo / 東京都八王子市
③ 227.20m²
④ 90.85m²
⑤ 90.85m²
⑥ B1F, 1F
⑦ RC + S
⑧ Takaharu + Yui Tezuka, Masahiro Ikeda, Chie Nabeshima / 手塚貴晴＋手塚由比、池田昌弘、鍋島千恵
⑨ Tezuka Architects + MASAHIRO IKEDA co., ltd / 手塚建築研究所＋MASAHIRO IKEDA co., ltd
⑫ Masahide Kakudate (Masahide Kakudate Lighting Architect & Associates, Inc.) / 角舘政英（ぼんぼり光環境計画）
⑱ Tokyo Tekkin Concrete / 東京鐵筋コンクリート株式会社
⑲ 1998.9-1999.6
⑳ 1999.12-2000.7

07 _ Megaphone House 腰越のメガホンハウス
① Residence / 住宅
② Kamakura-shi, Kanagawa / 神奈川県鎌倉市
③ 264.18m²
④ 103.96m²
⑤ 157.18m²
⑥ 2F
⑦ S
⑧ Takaharu + Yui Tezuka, Masahiro Ikeda, Makoto Takei / 手塚貴晴＋手塚由比、池田昌弘、武井誠
⑨ Tezuka Architects + MASAHIRO IKEDA co., ltd / 手塚建築研究所＋MASAHIRO IKEDA co., ltd
⑫ Masahide Kakudate (Masahide Kakudate Lighting Architect & Associates, Inc.) / 角舘政英（ぼんぼり光環境計画）
⑱ Isoda / 株式会社イソダ
⑲ 2000.1-2000.6
⑳ 2000.7-2000.11

08 _ Roof House 屋根の家
① Residence / 住宅
② Hatano-shi, Kanagawa / 神奈川県秦野市
③ 298.59m²
④ 107.65m²
⑤ 96.89m²
⑥ 1F
⑦ W
⑧ Takaharu + Yui Tezuka, Masahiro Ikeda, Daisuke Sanada / 手塚貴晴＋手塚由比、池田昌弘、眞田大輔
⑨ Tezuka Architects + MASAHIRO IKEDA co., ltd / 手塚建築研究所＋MASAHIRO IKEDA co., ltd
⑫ Masahide Kakudate (Masahide Kakudate Lighting Architect & Associates, Inc.) / 角舘政英（ぼんぼり光環境計画）
⑱ Isoda / 株式会社イソダ
⑲ 2000.3-2000.8
⑳ 2000.9-2001.3

09 _ Balcony House バルコニーの家
① Residence + Shop & Cafe / 住宅＋店舗
② Miura-gun, Kanagawa / 神奈川県三浦郡
③ 124.12m²
④ 44.26m²
⑤ 129.28m²
⑥ 3F
⑦ S
⑧ Takaharu + Yui Tezuka, Masahiro Ikeda, Chie Nabeshima / 手塚貴晴＋手塚由比、池田昌弘、鍋島千恵
⑨ Tezuka Architects + MASAHIRO IKEDA co., ltd / 手塚建築研究所＋MASAHIRO IKEDA co., ltd
⑫ Masahide Kakudate (Masahide Kakudate Lighting Architect & Associates, Inc.) / 角舘政英（ぼんぼり光環境計画）
⑱ Daido Kogyo, Shonan / 大同工業湘南支店
⑲ 2000.6-2000.12
⑳ 2001.1-2001.6

10 _ Wall-less House 壁のない家
① Residence / 住宅
② Setagaya-ku, Tokyo / 東京都世田谷区
③ 255.19m²
④ 50.84m²
⑤ 239.91m²
⑥ B1F, 3F
⑦ S
⑧ Takaharu + Yui Tezuka, Makoto Takei / 手塚貴晴＋手塚由比、武井誠
⑩ Ove Arup & Partners Japan Limited / オーヴアラップアンドパートナーズ
⑫ Masahide Kakudate (Masahide Kakudate Lighting Architect & Associates, Inc.) / 角舘政英（ぼんぼり光環境計画）
⑱ Matsumoto Corporation / まつもとコーポレーション東京支店
⑲ 2000.4-2000.12
⑳ 2000.1-2000.6

11 _ House to Catch the Sky 空を捕まえる家
① Residence / 住宅
② 神奈川県川崎市
③ 173.20m²
④ 86.58m²
⑤ 86.58m²
⑥ 1F
⑦ W + S
⑧ Takaharu + Yui Tezuka, Masahiro Ikeda, Wataru Obase / 手塚貴晴＋手塚由比、池田昌弘、小長谷亘
⑨ Tezuka Architects + MASAHIRO IKEDA co., ltd / 手塚建築研究所＋MASAHIRO IKEDA co., ltd
⑫ Masahide Kakudate (Masahide Kakudate Lighting Architect & Associates, Inc.) / 角舘政英（ぼんぼり光環境計画）
⑱ Daido Kogyo, Shonan / 大同工業湘南支店
⑲ 2000.4-2000.10
⑳ 2001.2-2001.8

12 _ Step House 熱海のステップハウス
① Residence / 住宅
② Atami-shi, Shizuoka / 静岡県熱海市
③ 386.71m²
④ 154.22m²
⑤ 205.97m²
⑥ B1F, 2F
⑦ RC + S
⑧ Takaharu + Yui Tezuka, Masahiro Ikeda, Chie Nabeshima / 手塚貴晴＋手塚由比、池田昌弘、鍋島千恵
⑨ Tezuka Architects + MASAHIRO IKEDA co., ltd / 手塚建築研究所＋MASAHIRO IKEDA co., ltd

⑫ Masahide Kakudate（Masahide Kakudate Lighting Architect & Associates, Inc.）/ 角舘政英（ぼんぼり光環境計画）
⑱ Daido Kogyo / 大同工業
⑲ 2000.4-2001.2
⑳ 2001.4-2001.12

13 _ House to Catch the Sky II　空を捕まえる家II
① Residence / 住宅
② Suginami-ku, Tokyo / 東京都杉並区
③ 74.32m²
④ 37.04m²
⑤ 74.08m²
⑥ 2F
⑦ S
⑧ Takaharu + Yui Tezuka, Masahiro Ikeda, Makoto Takei / 手塚貴晴＋手塚由比、池田昌弘、武井誠
⑨ Tezuka Architects + MASAHIRO IKEDA co., ltd / 手塚建築研究所＋MASAHIRO IKEDA co., ltd
⑫ Masahide Kakudate（Masahide Kakudate Lighting Architect & Associates, Inc.）/ 角舘政英（ぼんぼり光環境計画）
⑱ Takagi Komuten, Tezuka Architects / 高木工務店、手塚建築研究所
⑲ 2001-2001.7
⑳ 2001.8-2002.4

14 _ Anthill House　蟻塚の家
① Residence / 住宅
② Suginami-ku, Tokyo / 東京都杉並区
③ 53.75m²
④ 37.41m²
⑤ 156.43m²
⑥ B1F, 4F
⑦ SRC
⑧ Takaharu + Yui Tezuka, Masahiro Ikeda, Takashi Kobayashi, Chie Nabeshima, Mayumi Miura / 手塚貴晴＋手塚由比、池田昌弘、小林太加志、鍋島千恵、三浦真由美
⑨ Tezuka Architects + MASAHIRO IKEDA co., ltd / 手塚建築研究所＋MASAHIRO IKEDA co., ltd
⑫ Masahide Kakudate（Masahide Kakudate Lighting Architect & Associates, Inc.）/ 角舘政英（ぼんぼり光環境計画）
⑱ Fukazawa Komuten / 有限会社深澤工務店
⑲ 2000.4-2001.5
⑳ 2001.6-2002.4

15 _ Thin Roof Sukiya　屋根の薄い数寄屋
① Residence / 住宅
② Kamakura-shi, Kanagawa / 神奈川県鎌倉市
③ 250.74m²
④ 44.74m²
⑤ 44.74m²
⑥ 1F
⑦ W
⑧ Takaharu + Yui Tezuka, Masahiro Ikeda, Takashi Kobayashi, Chie Nabeshima, Mayumi Miura, Nobuyuki Honda / 手塚貴晴＋手塚由比、池田昌弘、小林太加志、鍋島千恵、三浦真由美、本多延幸
⑨ Tezuka Architects + MASAHIRO IKEDA co., ltd / 手塚建築研究所＋MASAHIRO IKEDA co., ltd
⑫ Masahide Kakudate（Masahide Kakudate Lighting Architect & Associates, Inc.）/ 角舘政英（ぼんぼり光環境計画）
⑱ Isoda / 株式会社イソダ
⑲ 2000.9-2000.12
⑳ 2001.1-2001.4

16 _ Thin Wall House　壁の薄い家
① Residence / 住宅
② Shibuya-ku, Tokyo / 東京都渋谷区
③ 187.36m²
④ 68.80m²
⑤ 217.51m²
⑥ B1F, 3F
⑦ S
⑧ Takaharu + Yui Tezuka, Masahiro Ikeda, Makoto Takei, Hiroshi Tomikawa / 手塚貴晴＋手塚由比、池田昌弘、武井誠、冨川浩志
⑨ Tezuka Architects + MASAHIRO IKEDA co., ltd / 手塚建築研究所＋MASAHIRO IKEDA co., ltd
⑫ Masahide Kakudate（Masahide Kakudate Lighting Architect & Associates, Inc.）/ 角舘政英（ぼんぼり光環境計画）
⑱ Nichinan Tekko / 日南鉄構株式会社
⑲ 2000.11-2001.11
⑳ 2001.12-2002.09

17 _ Hounancho "L" condominium　方南町L
① Residence / 集合住宅
② Suginami-ku, Tokyo / 東京都杉並区
③ 513.14m²
④ 318.97m²
⑤ 1040.34m²
⑥ B1F, 7F
⑦ RC
⑧ Takaharu + Yui Tezuka, Masahiro Ikeda, Wataru Obase, Makoto Takei, Hiroshi Tomikawa, Maya Masuda / 手塚貴晴＋手塚由比、池田昌弘、小長谷亘、武井誠、冨川浩志、増田まや
⑨ Tezuka Architects + MASAHIRO IKEDA co., ltd / 手塚建築研究所＋MASAHIRO IKEDA co., ltd
⑪ ES Associates / イーエスアソシエイツ
⑫ Masahide Kakudate（Masahide Kakudate Lighting Architect & Associates, Inc.）/ 角舘政英（ぼんぼり光環境計画）
⑱ Satohide Corporation / 株式会社佐藤秀
⑲ 2001.2-2001.9
⑳ 2001.10-2002.8

18 _ Canopy House　軒の家
① Residence / 住宅
② Chofu-shi, Tokyo / 東京都調布市
③ 187.36m²
④ 68.80m²
⑤ 116.32m²
⑥ 2F
⑦ S
⑧ Takaharu + Yui Tezuka, Masahiro Ikeda, Akiyoshi Takagi / 手塚貴晴＋手塚由比、池田昌弘、高木昭良
⑨ Tezuka Architects + MASAHIRO IKEDA co., ltd / 手塚建築研究所＋MASAHIRO IKEDA co., ltd
⑫ Masahide Kakudate（Masahide Kakudate Lighting Architect & Associates, Inc.）/ 角舘政英（ぼんぼり光環境計画）
⑱ Isoda / 株式会社イソダ
⑲ 2001.6-2002.2
⑳ 2002.4-2002.11

19 _ Saw Roof House　のこぎり屋根の家
① Residence / 住宅
② Ohta-ku, Tokyo / 東京都大田区
③ 281.25m²
④ 90.60m²
⑤ 181.20m²
⑥ 2F
⑦ S
⑧ Takaharu + Yui Tezuka, Masahiro Ikeda, Chie Nabeshima / 手塚貴晴＋手塚由比、池田昌弘、鍋島千恵
⑨ Tezuka Architects + MASAHIRO IKEDA co., ltd / 手塚建築研究所＋MASAHIRO IKEDA co., ltd

⑫ Masahide Kakudate (Masahide Kakudate Lighting Architect & Associates, Inc.) / 角舘政英（ぼんぼり光環境計画）
⑱ Isoda / 株式会社イソダ
⑲ 2001.11-2002.5
⑳ 2002.6-2002.11

20 _ Skylight House 天窓の家
① Residence / 住宅
② Kamakura-shi, Kanagawa / 神奈川県鎌倉市
③ 101.54m²
④ 60.83m²
⑤ 119.98m²
⑥ 2F
⑦ S
⑧ Takaharu + Yui Tezuka, Masahiro Ikeda, Makoto Takei, Ryuya Maio / 手塚貴晴＋手塚由比、池田昌弘、武井誠、麻殖生龍哉
⑨ Tezuka Architects + MASAHIRO IKEDA co., ltd / 手塚建築研究所＋MASAHIRO IKEDA co., ltd
⑫ Masahide Kakudate (Masahide Kakudate Lighting Architect & Associates, Inc.) / 角舘政英（ぼんぼり光環境計画）
⑱ Isoda / 株式会社イソダ
⑲ 2002.1-2002.8
⑳ 2002.9-2003.3

21 _ House to Catch the Sky III 空を捕まえる家 III
① Residence / 住宅
② Wako-shi, Saitama / 埼玉県和光市
③ 150.00m²
④ 89.27m²
⑤ 89.27m²
⑥ 1F
⑦ W
⑧ Takaharu + Yui Tezuka, Masahiro Ikeda, Wataru Obase, Daijiro Nakayama / 手塚貴晴＋手塚由比、池田昌弘、小長谷亘、中山大二郎
⑨ Tezuka Architects + MASAHIRO IKEDA co., ltd / 手塚建築研究所＋MASAHIRO IKEDA co., ltd
⑫ Masahide Kakudate (Masahide Kakudate Lighting Architect & Associates, Inc.) / 角舘政英（ぼんぼり光環境計画）
⑱ Misawaya Kensetsu Corporation / 株式会社三澤屋建設
⑲ 2002.4-2002.10
⑳ 2002.11-2003.4

22 _ Echigo-Matsunoyma Museum of Natural Science
越後松之山「森の学校」キョロロ
① Reserch facility / 研修施設
② Tokamachi-shi, Niigata / 新潟県十日町市
③ 4269.15m²
④ 997.45m²
⑤ 1248.18m²
⑥ B1F, 2F
⑦ S
⑧ Takaharu + Yui Tezuka, Masahiro Ikeda, Makoto Takei, Hiroshi Tomikawa, Ryuya Maio, Masafumi Harada, Miyoko Fujita, Mayumi Miura, Taro Suwa, Takahiro Nakano, Toshio Nishi, Tomohiro Sato / 手塚貴晴＋手塚由比、池田昌弘、武井誠、冨川浩史、麻殖生龍哉、原田将史、藤田美也子、三浦真由美、諏訪太郎、中野敬弘、西角隆、佐藤智弘
⑨ Tezuka Architects, Tezuka Lab at Musashi Institute of Technology, MASAHIRO IKEDA co., ltd / 手塚建築研究所、武蔵工業大学手塚研究室、MASAHIRO IKEDA co., ltd
⑪ ES Associates, Environmental Total Systems Corporation / イーエスアソシエイツ、環境トータルシステム
⑫ Masahide Kakudate (Masahide Kakudate Lighting Architect & Associates, Inc.) / 角舘政英（ぼんぼり光環境計画）
⑬ Nagata Acoustics, Inc. / 永田音響設計

⑭ Shunsuke Hirose / 廣瀬俊介
⑮ Furamu Kitagawa + Art Front Gallery / 北川フラム＋アートフロントギャラリー
⑯ Toshikatsu Endo, Takuro Ousaka, Yukiko Kasahara+Haruna Miyamori, Tadashi Kawamata, Taiko Shono / 遠藤利克、逢坂卓郎、笠原由紀子＋宮森はるな、川俣正、庄野泰子
⑱ Takahashigumi / 株式会社高橋組
⑲ 2001.8-2002.2
⑳ 2002.3-2003.6

23 _ Toyota L&F Hiroshima トヨタ L&F 広島本社
① Office & Maintenance Facility / 事務所兼自動車整備工場
② Hieoshima-shi, Hiroshima / 広島県広島市
③ 2965.98m²
④ 1504.28m²
⑤ 1504.28m²
⑥ 1F
⑦ S
⑧ Takaharu + Yui Tezuka, Masahiro Ikeda, Wataru Obase / 手塚貴晴＋手塚由比、池田昌弘、小長谷亘
⑨ Tezuka Architects + MASAHIRO IKEDA co., ltd / 手塚建築研究所＋MASAHIRO IKEDA co., ltd
⑪ イーエスアソシエイツ　環境トータルシステム
⑫ Masahide Kakudate (Masahide Kakudate Lighting Architect & Associates, Inc.) / 角舘政英（ぼんぼり光環境計画）
⑱ Kajima Corporation, Hiroshima / 鹿島建設広島支店
⑲ 2002.8-2003.5
⑳ 2003.5-2003.10

24 _ Engawa House 縁側の家
① Residence / 住宅
② Adachi-ku, Tokyo / 東京都足立区
③ 196.27m²
④ 74.48m²
⑤ 74.48m²
⑥ 1F
⑦ W + S
⑧ Takaharu + Yui Tezuka, Masahiro Ikeda, Chie Nabeshima, Mayumi Miura / 手塚貴晴＋手塚由比、池田昌弘、鍋島千恵、三浦真由美
⑨ Tezuka Architects + MASAHIRO IKEDA co., ltd / 手塚建築研究所＋MASAHIRO IKEDA co., ltd
⑫ Masahide Kakudate (Masahide Kakudate Lighting Architect & Associates, Inc.) / 角舘政英（ぼんぼり光環境計画）
⑱ Nitadori Komuten / 株式会社似鳥工務店
⑲ 2003.1-2003.5
⑳ 2003.5-2003.11

25 _ House to Catch the Sky IV 空を捕まえる家 IV
① Residence / 住宅
② Chigasaki-shi, Kanagawa / 神奈川県茅ヶ崎市
③ 259.04m²
④ 103.12m²
⑤ 103.12m²
⑥ 1F
⑦ W
⑧ Takaharu + Yui Tezuka, Masahiro Ikeda, Makoto Takei, Ryuya Maio / 手塚貴晴＋手塚由比、池田昌弘、武井誠、麻殖生龍哉
⑨ Tezuka Architects + MASAHIRO IKEDA co., ltd / 手塚建築研究所＋MASAHIRO IKEDA co., ltd
⑫ Masahide Kakudate (Masahide Kakudate Lighting Architect & Associates, Inc.) / 角舘政英（ぼんぼり光環境計画）
⑱ Isoda / 株式会社イソダ
⑲ 2002.7-2003.4
⑳ 2003.5-2003.12

26 _ Floating house フローティングハウス
① Residence / 住宅
② Meguro-ku, Tokyo / 東京都目黒区
③ 98.97m²
④ 51.03m²
⑤ 101.93m²
⑥ B1F, 2F
⑦ S
⑧ Takaharu + Yui Tezuka, Masahiro Ikeda, Wataru Obase, Daijiro Nakayama / 手塚貴晴＋手塚由比、池田昌弘、小長谷亘、中山大二郎
⑨ Tezuka Architects + MASAHIRO IKEDA co., ltd / 手塚建築研究所＋MASAHIRO IKEDA co., ltd
⑫ Masahide Kakudate (Masahide Kakudate Lighting Architect & Associates, Inc.) / 角舘政英 (ぼんぼり光環境計画)
⑱ Katsura Komuten co.,itd / 株式会社葛工務店
⑲ 2002.3-2002.12
⑳ 2003.4-2004.12

27 _ Five-Courtyard House ファイブコートヤードハウス
① Residence / 住宅
③ 277.22m²
④ 166.33m²
⑤ 220.91m²
⑥ B1F, 1F
⑦ RC
⑧ Takaharu + Yui Tezuka, Masahiro Ikeda, Chie Nabeshima / 手塚貴晴＋手塚由比、池田昌弘、鍋島千恵
⑨ Tezuka Architects + MASAHIRO IKEDA co., ltd / 手塚建築研究所＋MASAHIRO IKEDA co., ltd
⑫ Masahide Kakudate (Masahide Kakudate Lighting Architect & Associates, Inc.) / 角舘政英 (ぼんぼり光環境計画)
⑱ Satohide Corporation / 株式会社佐藤秀
⑲ 2001.4-2003.4
⑳ 2003.6-2004.1

28 _ Thin Wall Office 壁の薄いオフィス
① Office / 事務所
② Shibuya-ku, Tokyo / 東京都渋谷区
③ 120.40m²
④ 71.48m²
⑤ 283.51m²
⑥ B1F, 3F
⑦ S
⑧ Takaharu + Yui Tezuka, Masahiro Ikeda, Makoto Takei, Hiroshi Tomikawa, Masafumi Harada, Mayumi Miura, Muneaki Asayama / 手塚貴晴＋手塚由比、池田昌弘、武井誠、冨川浩史、原田将史、三浦真由美、朝山宗啓
⑨ Tezuka Architects + MASAHIRO IKEDA co., ltd / 手塚建築研究所＋MASAHIRO IKEDA co., ltd
⑫ Masahide Kakudate (Masahide Kakudate Lighting Architect & Associates, Inc.) / 角舘政英 (ぼんぼり光環境計画)
⑱ Nichinan Tekkou / 日南鉄構株式会社
⑲ 2002.8-2003.4
⑳ 2003.4-2004.2

29 _ Clipping Corner House 隅切りの家
① Residence / 住宅
② Kamakura-shi, Kanagawa / 神奈川県鎌倉市
③ 314.06m²
④ 106.85m²
⑤ 94.71m²
⑥ 1F
⑦ RC
⑧ Takaharu + Yui Tezuka, Masahiro Ikeda, Makoto Takei, Daijiro Nakayama / 手塚貴晴＋手塚由比、池田昌弘、武井誠、中山大二郎
⑨ Tezuka Architects + MASAHIRO IKEDA co., ltd / 手塚建築研究所＋MASAHIRO IKEDA co., ltd
⑫ Masahide Kakudate (Masahide Kakudate Lighting Architect & Associates, Inc.) / 角舘政英 (ぼんぼり光環境計画)
⑱ Isoda / 株式会社イソダ
⑲ 2003.3-2003.9
⑳ 2003.10-2004.3

30 _ Double Courtyard House ダブルコートヤードハウス
① Residence / 住宅
③ 853.96m²
④ 296.51m²
⑤ 237.21m²
⑥ 1F
⑦ S
⑧ Takaharu + Yui Tezuka, Masahiro Ikeda, Wataru Obase, Nana Nishimuta / 手塚貴晴＋手塚由比、池田昌弘、小長谷亘、西牟田奈々
⑨ Tezuka Architects + MASAHIRO IKEDA co., ltd / 手塚建築研究所＋MASAHIRO IKEDA co., ltd
⑫ Masahide Kakudate (Masahide Kakudate Lighting Architect & Associates, Inc.) / 角舘政英 (ぼんぼり光環境計画)
⑱ Kajima Corporation, Hirodhima / 鹿島建設広島支店
⑲ 2002.9-2003.8
⑳ 2003.9-2004.5

31 _ House to Catch the Forest 森を捕まえる家
① Weekend House / 別荘
② Chino-shi, Nagano / 長野県茅野市
③ 1054.10m²
④ 80.74m²
⑤ 80.74m²
⑥ 1F
⑦ W
⑧ Takaharu + Yui Tezuka, Masahiro Ikeda, Makoto Takei, Ryuya Maio / 手塚貴晴＋手塚由比、池田昌弘、武井誠、麻殖生龍哉
⑨ Tezuka Architects + MASAHIRO IKEDA co., ltd / 手塚建築研究所＋MASAHIRO IKEDA co., ltd
⑫ Masahide Kakudate (Masahide Kakudate Lighting Architect & Associates, Inc.) / 角舘政英 (ぼんぼり光環境計画)
⑱ Kitano Kensetsu / 北野建設
⑲ 2003.4-2003.9
⑳ 2003.10-2004.4

32 _ Observatory House 展望台の家
① Residence / 住宅
② Kamakrua-shi, Kanagawa / 神奈川県鎌倉市
③ 136.50m²
④ 54.45m²
⑤ 175.09m²
⑥ B1F, 3F
⑦ S + RC
⑧ Takaharu + Yui Tezuka, Masahiro Ikeda, Chie Nabeshima, Mayumi Miura / 手塚貴晴＋手塚由比、池田昌弘、鍋島千恵、三浦真由美
⑨ Tezuka Architects + MASAHIRO IKEDA co., ltd / 手塚建築研究所＋MASAHIRO IKEDA co., ltd
⑫ Masahide Kakudate (Masahide Kakudate Lighting Architect & Associates, Inc.) / 角舘政英 (ぼんぼり光環境計画)
⑱ Satohide Corporation / 株式会社佐藤秀
⑲ 2003.1-2003.9
⑳ 2003.10-2004.7

33 _ Jyubako House 重箱の家
① Residence / 住宅

② Setagaya-ku, Tokyo / 東京都世田谷区
③ 100.01m²
④ 59.72m²
⑤ 136.55m²
⑥ 3F
⑦ RC
⑧ Takaharu + Yui Tezuka, Masahiro Ikeda, Akiyoshi Takagi / 手塚貴晴＋手塚由比、池田昌弘、高木昭良
⑨ Tezuka Architects + MASAHIRO IKEDA co., ltd / 手塚建築研究所＋MASAHIRO IKEDA co., ltd
⑫ Masahide Kakudate（Masahide Kakudate Lighting Architect & Associates, Inc.）/ 角舘政英（ぼんぼり光環境計画）
⑱ MAEKAWA Co.,ltd / 株式会社前田建設
⑲ 2003.1-2003.6
⑳ 2004.3-2004.10

34 _ Big Window House 大窓の家
① Residence / 住宅
② Yokohama-shi, Kanagawa / 神奈川県横浜市
③ 85.07m²
④ 47.50m²
⑤ 95.00m²
⑥ 2F
⑦ W
⑧ Takaharu + Yui Tezuka, Masahiro Ikeda, Chie Nabeshima, Daisuke Kamijo, Nana Nishimuta / 手塚貴晴＋手塚由比、池田昌弘、鍋島千恵、上條大輔、西牟田奈々
⑨ Tezuka Architects + MASAHIRO IKEDA co., ltd / 手塚建築研究所＋MASAHIRO IKEDA co., ltd
⑫ Masahide Kakudate（Masahide Kakudate Lighting Architect & Associates, Inc.）/ 角舘政英（ぼんぼり光環境計画）
⑱ isoda / 株式会社イソダ
⑲ 2003.12-2004.4
⑳ 2004.5-2004.11

35 _ Shoe Box House 大箱の家
① Residence / 住宅
② Setagaya-ku, Tokyo / 東京都世田谷区
③ 165.31m²
④ 82.65m²
⑤ 159.38m²
⑥ 3F
⑦ S + RC
⑧ Takaharu + Yui Tezuka, Masahiro Ikeda, Akiyoshi Takagi, Masafumi Harada / 手塚貴晴＋手塚由比、池田昌弘、高木昭良、原田将史
⑨ Tezuka Architects + MASAHIRO IKEDA co., ltd / 手塚建築研究所＋MASAHIRO IKEDA co., ltd
⑫ Masahide Kakudate（Masahide Kakudate Lighting Architect & Associates, Inc.）/ 角舘政英（ぼんぼり光環境計画）
⑱ MAEKAWA Co.,ltd / 株式会社前田建設
⑲ 2003.8-2004.5
⑳ 2004.6-2004.12

36 _ Floating Roof House 山すその家
① Residence / 住宅
② Okayama / 岡山
③ 1035.92m²
④ 288.64m²
⑤ 342.70m²
⑥ 1F
⑦ RC + S
⑧ Takaharu + Yui Tezuka, Masahiro Ikeda, Chie Nabeshima, Hiroshi Tomikawa / 手塚貴晴＋手塚由比、池田昌弘、鍋島千恵、冨川浩史
⑨ Tezuka Architects + MASAHIRO IKEDA co., ltd / 手塚建築研究所＋MASAHIRO IKEDA co., ltd
⑫ Masahide Kakudate（Masahide Kakudate Lighting Architect & Associates, Inc.）/ 角舘政英（ぼんぼり光環境計画）
⑱ Kajima Corporation, Hiroshima / 鹿島建設広島支店
⑲ 2004.4-2004.12
⑳ 2005.1-2005.8

37 _ Roof Deck House 屋上の家
① Residence / 住宅
③ 290.95m²
④ 137.25m²
⑤ 307.15m²
⑥ B1F, 2F
⑦ RC + S
⑧ Takaharu + Yui Tezuka, Masahiro Ikeda, Chie Nabeshima, Asako Kompal / 手塚貴晴＋手塚由比、池田昌弘、鍋島千恵、今春麻子
⑨ Tezuka Architects + MASAHIRO IKEDA co., ltd / 手塚建築研究所＋MASAHIRO IKEDA co., ltd
⑫ Masahide Kakudate（Masahide Kakudate Lighting Architect & Associates, Inc.）/ 角舘政英（ぼんぼり光環境計画）
⑱ Satohide Corporation / 株式会社佐藤秀
⑲ 2004.2-2004.12
⑳ 2004.12-2005.10

38 _ Fuji Kindergarten ふじようちえん
① Kindergarten / 幼稚園
② Tachikawa-shi, Tokyo / 東京都立川市
③ 4791.70m²
④ 1354.51m²
⑤ 4839.61m²
⑥ 1F
⑦ S
⑧ Takaharu + Yui Tezuka, Masahiro Ikeda, Chie Nabeshima, Ryuya Maio, Asako Kompal, Kosuke Suzuki, Shigefumi Araki / 手塚貴晴＋手塚由比、池田昌弘、鍋島千恵、麻殖生龍哉、今春麻子、鈴木宏亮、荒木成文
⑨ Tezuka Architects + MASAHIRO IKEDA co., ltd / 手塚建築研究所＋MASAHIRO IKEDA co., ltd
⑪ Takenaka Corporation / 竹中工務店
⑫ Masahide Kakudate（Masahide Kakudate Lighting Architect & Associates, Inc.）/角舘政英（ぼんぼり光環境計画）
⑰ Kashiwa Sato / 佐藤可士和
⑲ 2005.1-

Publications 掲載誌一覧

※（ ）記載のないものは作品紹介記事

1995

『日本経済新聞』95.05.13（インタビュー記事）／『SD』95.12, SDレビュー1995, 副島病院

1996

『新建築』96.05, 副島病院／『GA Japan』96.05, 副島病院／『GA Japan』96.11, K-Tower Project／『JA 1996建築年鑑』副島病院

1997

『日経アーキテクチュア』97.1.13, 新世紀の100人（インタビュー記事）／『毎日新聞』97.02.14, 副島病院（紹介記事）／『GA Japan』97.03, 花見の家／『ディテール』97.04, 副島病院／『SD』97.05, アーキグラム（論文）／『JIA NEWS』97.05, 4人の30代建築家100人の仕事（記事）／『日経アーキテクチュア』97.07.28, 私の超仕事術（インタビュー記事）／『JIA NEWS』97.12, 30×100meeting（記事）／『マンスリーハウジングレポート』97.12, ウエストロンドンのテラスハウス（記事）

1998

『グッドデザイン1997-1998』(財)日本産業デザイン振興会, 副島病院／『年鑑日本の空間デザイン'98』六耀社, 副島病院／『SD』98.01, SDレビューの15年, 副島病院／『日本建築学会・建築雑誌増刊・作品選集1998』副島病院／『日本建築学会・建築雑誌』98.08, 日本建築学会作品選奨 副島病院（記事）／『新建築住宅特集』98.08, jt file 日本の建築家による椅子展 発砲スチロールソファー／『COMFORT』98.autumn34, INFORMATION 日本の建築家による椅子展 発砲スチロールソファー／『SD』98.12, SDレビュー1998, LGS構造の家／『日本建築学会・建築雑誌』98.12, プロフェッサーアーキテクトは教壇で（文）

1999

『新建築』99.01, スタンダード、若手建築家に聞く／『建築文化』9901, プロトタイプからダイアグラムへ、巻頭論文『建築の二十一世紀』（論文）／『建築東京』99.03, 合理性と機能性（記事）／『建築文化』99.05, ジャン・プルーヴェ、モダニズムの33人（論文）／『現代数寄屋のディテール こころと作法』副島病院／『建築計画設計シリーズ16』医療施設／『市ヶ谷出版社、副島病院／『ふぉれんと』99.09.08, ミュージション川越（記事）／『建築文化』99.10, 鎌倉山の家／『新建築住宅特集』99.11, 鎌倉山の家／『新建築住宅特集』99.12, 辻堂の家／『新建築住宅特集』99.12, 裏原宿のビル／『BRUTUS』99.12.01, センセイじゃない建築家リスト（建築家紹介）

2000

『TOTO通信』00.01, 建築家10人に聞く「母の家」（インタビュー記事）／『日経アーキテクチャー』00.01.24, 辻堂の家、裏原宿のビル／『Hanako』00.02.09, 建築家やデザイナーが作ったアパート・マンション賃貸情報 ミュージション川越／『ニューハウス』00.02, 鎌倉山の家／『日経アーキテクチャー』00.03.06, クレインズⅤ（裏原宿のビル）／『週刊宝島』00.03.15, 超わがまま賃貸物件30 ミュージション川越／『建築技術』00.04, 辻堂の家、裏原宿のビル／『建築知識』00.05, LGSパネル工法（記事）／『ディテール』00春号, 辻堂の家、裏原宿のビル／『e-box 1999 Vol.21』日本オーチスエレベーター株式会社（インタビュー記事）／『新建築』00.03, 裏原宿のビル／『新建築』00.04, 川越の音楽マンション／『図2 建築模型の表現』図研究会 東海大学出版会、花見の家／『CAR magazine 262』00.04, 新クルマ居住学②（プロジェクト）／『住宅建築』00.05, 鎌倉山の家、辻堂の家／『室内』00.05, 裏原宿のビル／『建築東京』00.06, 住宅建築賞 鎌倉山の家／『ニューハウス』00.06, 辻堂の家／『建築文化』00.07, ガラスアトリウムが生まれた '80年代「特集 東京」（論文）／『新しい住まいの設計』00.07, 鎌倉山の家／『CAR magazine 262』00.07, 新クルマ居住学⑤（プロジェクト）／『ソトコト』00.08, 鎌倉山の家、プラモデルハウス／『Casa BRUTUS』00.07.10, Pla-model House／『30代建築家30人による30の住宅地展』ギャップ出版、

00.08、バタフライハウス ／『BRUTUS』00.09.01、ブルータス不動産 ミュージション川越 ／『CREATORS FILE ―for living― vol.2』ギャップ出版、00.10、 ／『住宅論―12のダイアローグ』青木淳、INAX出版、00.10、(対談) ／『一個人』00.10、"小さな家で、いい"鎌倉山の家 ／『FIGARO』00.10.05、デザイナーが造るマンション、ミュージション川越 ／『ニューハウス』00.10、鎌倉山の家 キッチン ／『新建築住宅特集』00.11、八王子の家 ／『住宅建築』00.11、八王子の家 ／『新しい住まいの設計』00.11、建築家名鑑（建築家紹介）／『室内』00.12、八王子の家

2001

『グッドデザイン 2000-2001』クレインズＶ、川越の音楽マンション ／『ディテール』01.01、WIRED DINER、川越の音楽マンション ／『AUSTRALIAN STYLE』01.01、八王子の家 ／『クロワッサン特大号』01.01.10、八王子の家 ／『すまいろん』01.01、街並み計画とパネル工法（論文）／『ニューハウス』01.02、"この建築家に会いたい"手塚貴晴＋手塚由比（インタビュー記事）／『ニューハウス』01.02、八王子の家 ／『ライフスタイルで決める住まい』ニューハウス出版、鎌倉山の家 ／『MEMO男の部屋』01.02、辻堂の家 ／『ニューハウス』01.03、PLAY BACK 2000 鎌倉山の家 ／『pen』01.02.15、人気建築家が設計した美しいマンション、ミュージション川越 ／『モダンリビング』01.03、鎌倉山の家 ／『マンスリー・エム』01.04、自分仕様の集合住宅、ミュージション川越 ／『GA Japan』01.03、腰越のメガホンハウス ／『新建築』01.03、腰越のメガホンハウス ／『自然の中で暮らしたい』春号 VOL.4、腰越のメガホンハウス ／『日経アーキテクチュア』01.03.05、個性派アパートメント20選、ミュージション川越 ／『MADORI・日本人と住まい6「間取り」』リビングデザインセンター、01.03、八王子の家 ／『INAX REPORT』01.03、アンベール城、ジャイ・マンディル殿（記事）／『わが家は3階建て・ニューハウスムック66』ニューハウス出版、01.04、辻堂の家 ／『日経アーキテクチュア』01.04.30、CLOSE-UP住宅、腰越のメガホンハウス ／『ニューハウス』01.06、エリア別建築家・設計事務所紹介 ／『新建築』01.06、松之山ステージ・自然科学館「森の学校」(仮称)提案協議結果発表 ／『建築文化』01.06、ライト・アーキテクチュア、八王子の家 ／『室内』01.06、誌上建宅学会、屋根の家 ／『MONUMENT』01.06、RESIDENTIAL SPECIAL、腰越のメガホンハウス ／『2000万円で理想の家を実現する本』01.06、プラモデルハウス 山下邸 ／『狭小住宅63』01.06、辻堂の家 ／『NEW BLOOD』01.06、手塚貴晴＋手塚由比（インタビュー記事）／『planet architecture vol.4（CD-ROM）』01.06、4 Tokyo Houses、鎌倉山の家（作品＆インタビュー）／『Grazia』01.07、癒しのお風呂を我が家に！、八王子の家 ／『Lives創刊号』01.07、建築家が提案するふたりで住む家、花見の家 ／『建築知識』01.07、開口部のディテール実用図鑑、八王子の家・腰越のメガホンハウス ／『建築知識』01.07、特別企画・映画「みんなのいえ」に行こう！（対談記事）／『ニューハウス』01.08、自分流キッチンの楽しみ、腰越のメガホンハウス ／『auto fashion ORIGINAL』01.08、TEZUKA with 2CV（インタビュー記事）／『日本建築学会・建築雑誌』01.06、特集＝建築学会の新しい役割を問う『町家のすすめと三つの提言』(論文) ／『建築知識』01.08、Tシャツ建築 ／『新しい住まいの設計』01.09、屋根の家 ／『ニューハウス』01.09、屋根の家 ／『新建築住宅特集』01.08、屋根の家 ／『湘南スタイルmagazine Vol.7』01.09、腰越のメガホンハウス ／『MEMO男の部屋』01.09、楽しい発明のある家、屋根の家 ／『Esquire』01.09、注目の建築家たちが考える、夢の私的別荘プラン、腰越のメガホンハウス ／『QUA 2001 SUMMER No.20』01.09、建築人登場（インタビュー記事）／『新建築』01.09、研究室レポート、武蔵工業大学手塚貴晴研究室（記事）／『建築文化』01.10、20世紀建築モデル・カタログ リチャード・ロジャース（論文）／『新しい住まいの設計』01.10、腰越のメガホンハウス ／『テレビ朝日、渡辺篤史のたてもの探訪』01.08.04、腰越のメガホンハウス ／『こんな家に住みたい』01.08、屋根の家 ／『ひとり暮らしをとことん楽しむ』01.10、ミュージション川越 ／『すてきな家づくり 小さくても快適に住める家500の実例集』01.10、辻堂の家 ／『ニューハウス』01.11、鎌倉山の家 ／『夢田舎vol.22』01.11、鎌倉山の家 ／『ARCHITECTURE REVIEW』01.10、屋根の家 ／『DREAM』01.09、屋根の家 ／『Casa BRUTUS』01.11、武蔵工業大学手塚貴晴研究室（記事）／『pen』01.11、若手建築家が、設計する。空を捕まえる家 ／『新建築住宅特集』01.11、特集：同時に展開した家たち、対談、バルコニーの家、空を捕まえる家 ／『新建築住宅特集』01.11、壁のない家、バルコニーの家、空を捕まえる家 ／『新建築住宅特集』01.11、空を捕まえる家Ⅱ、熱海のステップハウス（プロジェクト）／『建築文化』01.11、小住宅の現在形、空を捕まえる家 ／『室内』01.11、暖炉・薪ストーブの楽しみ、屋根の家

2002

『新しい住まいの設計』02.01、腰越のメガホンハウス ／『Slow life』02.01、鎌倉山の家 ／『小さくても住み心地満点の間取りプラン』01.12、八王子の家・鎌倉山の家 ／『マンスリー・エム』02.01、ぬくもりの、モダン住宅、バルコニーの家 ／『女性にやさしい家500の実例集』01.12、鎌倉山の家 ／『自遊人』02.01、「屋外書斎」という隠れ家、鎌倉山の家 ／『モダンリビング』02.02、魅せる家、屋根の家 ／『モダンリビング』02.02、薪ストーブのある暮らし、腰越のメガホンハウス ／『はじめての家づくり便利百貨2002年度版』02.01、八王子の家 ／『DREAM DESIGN』02.01、バス＆サニタリーデザイン、屋根の家 ／『和楽』02.02、スタイルのあるバスルーム、八王子の家 ／『上海築居』02.01、副島病院、鎌倉山の家、八王子の家、腰越のメガホンハウス、屋根の家、空を捕まえる家 ／『ニューハウス』02.03、屋根の家 ／『新建築住宅特集』02.03、第18回吉岡賞発表、屋根の家 ／『新鋭建築家50人の住宅ファイル』02.03、屋根の家 ／『建築家と家を建てたい』02.02、八王子の家 ／『VA別冊建築画報』02.02、屋根の家 ／『IN-EX project 02 customize』02.03、屋根の家 ／『住まい100選No.33』02.03、鎌倉山の家 ／『こんな家に住みたい』02.04、開くか閉じるか建築家のキッチンから手法を学ぶ、屋根の家 ／『ニューハウスムック住み心地のいい品質・性能を極めた家』02.04、屋根の家 ／『週刊文春』02.03.21、八王子の家 ／『新しい住まいの設計』

02.05，私の好きな椅子（記事）／『スズキ不動産vol.2 デザイナーズマンション情報』02.04，ミュージション川越 ／『モダンリビング』02.05，Message from Next Architects（作品・インタビュー記事）／『住まいと電化』02.04，住宅の自由さと可能性、屋根の家（作品・記事）／『IKEBANA RYUSEI』02.04，場にいける・場をいける、空を捕まえる家 ／『テレビ朝日、D's Garage』02.02.08，建築家インタビュー ／『STYLE HOUSE』02.05，空を捕まえる家 ／『建設ジャーナル第734号』02.05，松之山ステージ・自然科学館「森の学校」（仮称）／『都市 この小さな惑星の』02.05，リチャード・ロジャース著（翻訳）／『ニューハウス』02.06，空を捕まえる家 ／『MEMO男の部屋』02.06，屋根の家、腰越のメガホンハウス、八王子の家、バルコニーの家 ／『建築文化』02.06，アトリエ派のミニマル・プレゼンテーション（作品＆インタビュー）／『こんな家に住みたい』02.05，第18回吉岡賞受賞、屋根の家（記事）／『建築グルメマップ2 九州・沖縄を歩こう！』02.06，副島病院 ／『ソトコト』02.07，アーキテクツ・イレブン、手塚貴晴＋手塚由比（記事）／『lives』02.07，東京・大阪デザイン物件レビュー、方南町L／『週刊現代』02.06.29，渡辺篤史「住みたい家はここが違う」屋根の家 ／『ARCHILAB ORLEANS 2002』02.06，壁のない家、松之山ステージ・自然科学館「森の学校」（仮称）、屋根の家 ／『Beaux Arts magazine』02.06，ARCHILAB 2002，壁のない家、屋根の家（記事、作品）／『建築文化』02.08，カ・イ・カン住宅、空を捕まえる家Ⅱ ／『建築文化』02.08，住宅、その多様なカイカンの創出へ向けて（座談会記事）／『料理好きのためのキッチン実例200』02.07，眺めのいいキッチン、屋根の家 ／『MONUMENT』02.07，副島病院、屋根の家、八王子の家、松之山ステージ・自然科学館「森の学校」（仮称）／『DETAIL』02.08，屋根の家 ／『新建築住宅特集』02.08，熱海のステップハウス、バタフライハウス ／『person』02.09，おじゃまします！達人の「工房」、手塚貴晴＋手塚由比（インタビュー記事）／『モダンリビング』02.09，海山暮らしという生活、熱海のステップハウス ／『CONFORT』02.09，建具自由自在、壁のない家 ／『d＋a』02.07，屋根の家、鎌倉山の家、腰越のメガホンハウス、松之山ステージ・自然科学館「森の学校」（仮称）／『architecture interieure cree』02.08，屋根の家、空を捕まえる家、空を捕まえる家Ⅱ ／『THE GOLD』02.09，屋根の家 ／『室内』02.09，空を捕まえる家Ⅱ ／『室内』02.09，分離発注方式でその場を切抜いた例（記事）／『CONFORT』02.10，ライティングアーキテクト・角舘政英の仕事、屋根の家、空を捕まえる家Ⅱ ／『ハウスナリー福井』02.09，渡辺篤史さん「感動の家」鎌倉山の家 ／『ディテール』02.10，境界のうつろい、屋根の家、腰越のメガホンハウス ／『CASA BRUTUS』02.10，なんてったて建築家！建築家紹介 ／『X-knowledge HOME』02.10，新世代のカケラ、建築家紹介、屋根の家、方南町の分譲マンション ／『こすもす』02.10，快適LIFE・省エネ上手、空を捕まえる家 ／『男の隠れ家』02.11，デザインコンシャスな家、八王子の家 ／『マンスリー・エム』02.11，オフィスを頼むなら、この建築家＆デザイナー、手塚建築研究所（建築家紹介）／『小さくても庭のある住宅成功例64』02.11，バルコニーの家 ／『Grazia』02.11，いちばんの贅沢は家にある、腰越のメガホンハウス ／『マイホームプラン』02.11，建築からあなたへ、屋根の家 ／『Esquire』02.12，日本の住宅の新スタンダード、壁のない家、方南町L ／『Tokyo Houses』02.11，鎌倉山の家、八王子の家、腰越のメガホンハウス、屋根の家 ／『BRUTUS』02.11.1，21世紀、日本の集合住宅はどうなる!?、ミュージション川越、方南町L ／『BRUTUS』02.11.15，ブルータス不動産、方南町の分譲マンション ／『日経アーキテクチュア』02.11.11，9坪ハウス、LGS Kit House（プロジェクト）／『渡辺篤史のこんな家でくらしたい』02.11，鎌倉山の家 ／『住宅情報STYLE』02.11.20，やっぱりメゾネットが好き、方南町L ／『ニューハウス』03.01，空間 見えるものも見えないもの、方南町L（作品＆インタビュー）／『SOLID』03.01，シェアリングオフィスの新常識って何だ、Thin Wall Office（プロジェクト）／『住宅建築』02.12，最小限住宅の可能性—9坪ハウスシンポジウムより、LGSキットハウス（プロジェクト）／『日本経済新聞』02.11.21，住宅も構造に注目、バルコニーの家 ／『ARCHITECTURAL RECORD』02.12，DESIGN VANGUARD 2002，副島病院、壁のない家、屋根の家、蟻塚の家、松之山ステージ・自然科学館「森の学校」（仮称）／『TITLE』02.12，デザインびいきの物件探し、方南町L

2003

『日経アーキテクチュア』03.01.06，今年前半に竣工する主なプロジェクト、「森の学校」キョロロ ／『ニューハウス』03.03，空を捕まえる家Ⅱ ／『木の家に暮らす』03.01，手塚貴晴＋由比を知る6つのキーワード、屋根の薄い数寄屋（作品＆インタビュー）／『クロワッサン』03.01，小さくても常識やぶりの住みやすい家、屋根の家 ／『建築家』03.02.15，サステイナブルへの挑戦（記事）／『週刊文春』03.02.27，環境性能という研ぎすまされた技術、屋根の家（インタビュー記事）／『ニューハウス』03.04，大きな工夫のある小さな家、蟻塚の家 ／『ニューハウス』03.04，自宅にカフェをオープンしました!、バルコニーの家 ／『DAIKEN NEWS』03.01，スローライフな住まい、住まい方、八王子の家、熱海のステップハウス、屋根の家 ／『Technique et architecture』03.01，In the slope，屋根の家 ／『HaWaYu』03.03，室内と中庭が、ゆるやかに優しくつながる家、八王子の家 ／『日経アーキテクチュア』03.03.31，「(仮称)鬼石町屋内広場」設計競技最終審査結果、佳作（記事）／『日経アーキテクチュア』03.03.31，勝手にClose Up建築第4回、屋根の家 ／『わかはNo.347』03.03，時代をうけつぎ、次代をになう⑥（建築家インタビュー）／『新建築』03.04，鬼石町多目的ホール「(仮称)鬼石町屋内広場」設計競技結果発表、佳作（記事）／『白と茶色のインテリア』03.04，腰越のメガホンハウス ／『HaWaYu』03.04，光と風を招き、空をひとり占めにする家、空を捕まえる家Ⅱ ／『日経アーキテクチュア』03.04.28，建て主の琴線に触れた建築、六本木フォトスタジオ ／『モダンリビング』03.05，集合住宅新基準、ミュージション川越 ／『HaWaYu』03.05，海を眺めて暮らしたいその想いとこだわりを体現する家、腰越のメガホンハウス ／『木の家に暮らす』03.06，理想の木の家を建ててくれる建築家＆メーカーガイド、手塚貴晴＋手塚由比（建築家紹介）／『ABSTRACT MAGAZINE』03.05，壁のない家 ／『新建築住宅特集』03.06，キッチン・水回りSELECTION2003，熱海のステップハウス ／『建築雑誌増刊 作品選集2003』03.03，2003年日本建築学会作品選奨、屋根の家 ／『こんな家に住みたい』03.09，建築家file 08，手塚貴晴＋手塚由比（建築家紹介）／『MONITOR』03.05，屋根の家、壁のない家、空を捕まえる家Ⅱ ／『ぐっすり』03.05，建築家手塚貴晴、由比夫妻の考える寝室、副島病院、腰越のメガホンハウス、熱海のステップハウス ／『住宅情報STYLE』03.06.18，建築家に聞く「窓」の意味、空を捕

まえる家Ⅱ、川越の音楽マンション ／『HOME CLUB』03.06, 建築家インタビュー／『新建築住宅特集』03.07, のこぎり屋根の家、空を捕まえる家Ⅲ ／『BRUTUS』03.07.01, クルマと建築、多機能ぶりを比べると?、バルコニーの家 ／『Casa BRUTUS』03.07, Japan travel special, 越後松之山「森の学校」キョロロ ／『都心に住む』03.08, 気鋭建築家インタビュー(建築家紹介)／『Arigatt』03.08, Daidokoro File, 蟻塚の家 ／『CONFORT』03.08, SKETCH OF ARCH-WORKS, ヴェニス(水彩画・文)／『CONFORT』03.08, 浴室空間、くつろぎのメソッド、天窓の家 ／『新潟発』03.08, いざ、アート大陸妻有へ!、越後松之山「森の学校」キョロロ ／『空間要素』03.07, 移動する・昇降する ロイズ・オブ・ロンドン(解説文)／『新建築住宅特集』03.08, 近作訪問、空を捕まえる家Ⅱ ／『日経アーキテクチュア』03.08.04, さびが守る全長160mの鉄のヘビ、越後松之山「森の学校」キョロロ ／『Asian Interior Design』03.08, 空を捕まえる家Ⅲ、蟻塚の家 ／『新建築』03.08, 越後松之山「森の学校」キョロロ ／『建築MAP東京・2』03.08, 裏原宿のビル ／『建築MAP東京・2』03.08, のこぎり屋根の家 ／『CONFORT』03.09, SKETCH OF ARCH-WORKS, タージマハル(水彩画・文)／『新建築住宅特集』03.09, 近作訪問、のこぎり屋根の家 ／『美術手帖』03.09, メイキング・オブ・"キョロロ"、越後松之山「森の学校」キョロロ ／『新しい住まいの設計』03.10, キッチン&ダイニングの「賢い」プランニング、腰越のメガホンハウス ／『GA JAPAN』03.09, 越後松之山「森の学校」キョロロ ／『建築文化』03.10, 越後松之山「森の学校」キョロロ ／『日経アーキテクチュア』03.09.01,「対話力」で選別される住宅設計者、手塚貴晴+手塚由比(建築家紹介)／『日経アーキテクチュア』03.09.01, 勝手にClose Up建築第7回、越後松之山「森の学校」キョロロ ／『CONFORT』03.10, SKETCH OF ARCH-WORKS, プラハ(水彩画・文)／『ディテール』03.10, 住宅のディテールファイル、屋根の家 ／『ペチャクチャナイト6』03.08.28, 講演会CD-ROM ／『CONFORT』03.11, SKETCH OF ARCH-WORKS, エグゼター(水彩画・文)／『DETAIL』03.10, 越後松之山「森の学校」キョロロ ／『Esquire』03.12, のこぎり屋根の家 ／『CONFORT』03.12, 生活スタイルから導かれる現代住宅のあかり、八王子の家、熱海のステップハウス、のこぎり屋根の家 ／『CONFORT』03.12, SKETCH OF ARCH-WORKS, ジャイサルメール(水彩画・文)／『厳選|建築家名鑑』03.11, 建築家紹介(作品・アンケート)／『pen』03.12, 建築家が選ぶ、構造美の家具100点

2004

『ニューハウス』04.01, インテリアを楽しむシンプルな家、空を捕まえる家Ⅲ ／『CONFORT』04.01, SKETCH OF ARCH-WORKS, テーベ(水彩画・文)／『モダンリビング』04.01, 大きな開口部を持つ住まい、のこぎり屋根の家、熱海のステップハウス ／『ELEVATOR NEWS』03.12, 越後松之山「森の学校」キョロロ ／『JA YEAR BOOK 2003』04.01, 越後松之山「森の学校」キョロロ ／『新建築住宅特集』04.01, 縁側の家 ／『ディテール』04.01, 越後松之山「森の学校」キョロロ ／『新しい住まいの設計』04.02, 都市型2世帯快適生活、のこぎり屋根の家 ／『東京カレンダー』04.02, トイレ空間進化論、のこぎり屋根の家 ／『家庭画報』04.02,「暖」に集う、腰越のメガホンハウス ／『TORONTO STAR』03.11.29, 新聞記事、屋根の家、壁のない家、軒の家 ／『CONFORT』04.02, SKETCH OF ARCH-WORKS, ソールスベリ(水彩画・文)／『らしく』04.01, 建築家紹介、のこぎり屋根の家、空を捕まえる家Ⅱ ／『VA』03.12, ファサードエンジニアリング、越後松之山「森の学校」キョロロ ／『ARCHITECTURAL RECORD』04.01, MUSEUM MANIA, 越後松之山「森の学校」キョロロ ／『Inside minimalist interior』04.01, 壁のない家 ／『新建築住宅特集』04.02, 近作訪問、篠原聡子・縁側の家 ／『現代日本の建築1』04.01, 越後松之山「森の学校」キョロロ、屋根の家、壁のない家 ／『設計道場Report vol.33』04.01, 講演レポート／『Techniques & architecture』04.01, 越後松之山「森の学校」キョロロ ／『CONFORT』04.03, SKETCH OF ARCH-WORKS, セナンク修道院(水彩画・文)／『MEN'S EX』04.03, 実現住宅、のこぎり屋根の家 ／『モダンリビング』04.03, 空を捕まえる家Ⅲ ／『メトロポリターナ』04.02, ふたりで夢を描いてみたら、建築家紹介 ／『Casa BRUTUS』04.03, この先の住宅、最新情報。屋根の家 ／『TITLE』CASUAL HOUSE 2004, 縁側の家 ／『TITLE』CASUAL HOUSE 2004, 9坪ハウスLoft LGS Kit ／『新建築』04.03, HQ#01ビル ／『新建築』04.03, トヨタL&F広島 本社 ／『新建築』04.03, 薄い壁の家 ／『MONUMENT』04.03, 越後松之山「森の学校」キョロロ ／『CONFORT』04.04, SKETCH OF ARCH-WORKS, ロスアンゼルス(水彩画・文)／『Verb』04.04, STOVE, 腰越のメガホンハウス、屋根の家 ／『ABSTRACT MAGAZINE』04.01, 越後松之山「森の学校」キョロロ ／『快楽住宅』04.04, STOVE, 腰越のメガホンハウス ／『pen+』04.03, 若手建築家が考える、人にやさしい家、空を捕まえる家 ／『ホームシアターファイル』03.7, 照明もまたコンテンツである2、屋根の家、腰越のメガホンハウス ／『積算資料SUPPORT』04.04, 注目の建設資材「対候性鋼板」、越後松之山「森の学校」キョロロ ／『新建築』04.04, エコウィルハウスコンペティション結果発表、審査委員 ／『CONFORT』04.05, SKETCH OF ARCH-WORKS, サン・マドレーヌ教会(水彩画・文)／『PASAJES』04.05, 越後松之山「森の学校」キョロロ ／『BRUTUS』04.05, CAR STYLE BOOK 2004／『THE ARCHITECTURE NEWSPAPER』04.4.6, Japan Society シンポジウム(記事)／『CITY』04.05, sheltering sky, 八王子の家 ／『CONFORT』04.06, SKETCH OF ARCH-WORKS, エローラ(水彩画・文)／『室内interior』04.05, 越後松之山「森の学校」キョロロ ／『新建築住宅特集』04.06, キッチン・水廻りSELECTION, 縁側の家 ／『a+t』04.05, 越後松之山「森の学校」キョロロ ／『家庭画報INTERNATIONAL』04.07, 八王子の家、壁のない家 ／『CONFORT』04.07, SKETCH OF ARCH-WORKS, バナラシ(水彩画・文)／『くうかん』04.06, 手塚貴晴+手塚由比、方南町6 ／『minimalism: Design Source』04.06, 越後松之山「森の学校」キョロロ ／『建設通信新聞』04.06.02, JIA新潟地域大学卒業設計コンクール(記事)／『shift001』04.06.25, 建築家手塚貴晴、インタビュー(記事)／『era31』04.03, 越後松之山「森の学校」キョロロ ／『la Repubblica delle Donne』04.06, 縁側の家 ／『pen』04.07, アウディ 哲学を持つクルマと建築物、越後松之山「森の学校」キョロロ ／『住まいの収納300の知恵』04.08, 動線スペース収納アイデア、空を捕まえる家Ⅱ ／『Latte』04.10, 気持ちのいい家とは、どんな家ですか?、のこぎり屋根の家 ／『24の家』04.10, 屋根

の家 ／『新建築住宅特集』04.10, 森を捕まえる家 ／『アイデア住宅 LIVING SPHERES Vol.21』04.09, 屋根の家 ／『JAPANESE DESIGN』04.09, 副島病院, 方南町L、薄い屋根の数寄屋、越後松之山「森の学校」キョロロ ／『ARCHITETTURA OFX』04.09, 越後松之山「森の学校」キョロロ ／『スチールデザインNo.4』04.09, トヨタL&F広島 本社 ／『日経アーキテクチュアspecial』04.10, 美しい屋根、トヨタL&F広島 本社 ／『メイプル』04.11, 縁側の家 ／『INTERNI』04.10, 越後松之山「森の学校」キョロロ ／『Icon』04.12, 越後松之山「森の学校」キョロロ ／『Domus 875』04.11, 越後松之山「森の学校」キョロロ、屋根の家、バルコニーの家 ／『ARCHITECTURAL REVIEW』04.12, 越後松之山「森の学校」キョロロ ／『MONITOR』04.12, 越後松之山「森の学校」キョロロ ／『SD 2004』04.12, 建築家たちのサスティナブル観（アンケート）／『建築家』04.12, JIA全国学生卒業設計コンクール公開審査（記事）

2005

『新建築住宅特集』05.01, 隅切りの家 ／『新建築住宅特集』05.01, 展望台の家 ／『THE VERY SMALL HOME』05.01, 縁側の家 ／『TITLE』05.02, 展望台の家 ／『Casa BRUTUS』05.02, 住宅案内2005、展望台の家 ／『Casa BRUTUS』05.02, 住宅案内2005, 森を捕まえる家 ／『ViA arquitectura』05.01, 越後松之山「森の学校」キョロロ ／『BRUTUS』05.02, 佐藤可士和と手塚夫妻が創る幼稚園とは？（記事）／『5日で学ぶJW-cad4』05.02, 手塚貴晴十手塚由比の「屋根の家」を描く, 屋根の家 ／『LIVING design』05.03, やっぱりお風呂が好き, 重箱の家 ／『自分らしい住まいを建築家とつくる』05.03, 屋根の家 ／『10 x 10 _ 2』05.03, 壁のない家、トヨタL&F広島、越後松之山「森の学校」キョロロ ／『日本建築学会・建築雑誌増刊・作品選集2005』越後松之山「森の学校」キョロロ ／『僕らはこうして建築家になった。』05.03, インタビュー本 ／『新建築住宅特集』05.04, 大窓の家 ／『新建築住宅特集』05.04, 建築の基本的要素を考える（論文）／『COMPACT HOUSE』05.03, 空を捕まえる家Ⅲ ／『ニューハウス』05.05, 大窓の家 ／『MEMO男の部屋』05.05, お家ができるまで、大窓の家 ／『男の隠れ家』05.05, 至福の風呂空間、展望台の家 ／『清流』05.05, インタビュー記事 ／『Grazia』05.05, キッチンが中心の家、のこぎり屋根の家 ／『DETAIL』05.04, 越後松之山「森の学校」キョロロ ／『ARCHITECTURE REVIEW』05.04, 幼稚園プロジェクト（プロジェクト）／『DBZ』05.04, 越後松之山「森の学校」キョロロ、壁のない家、屋根の家、空を捕まえる家Ⅱ、縁側の家 ／『At the Heart of Life』05.04, 腰越のメガホンハウス、のこぎり屋根の家、屋根の家 ／『IW』05.05, 屋根の家 ／『Diseno Interior』05.04, 屋根の家 ／『モダンリビング』05.05, 重箱の家 ／『家種』05.05, 壁のない家（プロジェクト）／『MEMO男の部屋』05.07, お家ができるまで、大窓の家 ／『Dobrewnetrze』05.05, 屋根の家 ／『モダンリビング』05.06, 森を捕まえる家 ／『Casa BRUTUS』06.07, のこぎり屋根の家、屋根の家、八王子の家 ／『AW』05.06, 越後松之山「森の学校」キョロロ ／『NEW DOMESTIC INTERIORS』05.06, 空を捕まえる家Ⅲ、縁側の家 ／『東京生活』05.07, のこぎり屋根の家 ／『Icon』05.08, 大窓の家 ／『ハーフ＋アイデア』05.07, 木デッキ上の風呂小屋 ／『CASA VOGUE』05.07, 屋根の家 ／『Japan House』05.08, 縁側の家 ／『建築家の自邸2』05.08, のこぎり屋根の家 ／『Grazia』05.10, 重箱の家 ／『東京生活』05.09, 大箱の家 ／『ARCHITECTURE REVIEW』05.09, 縁側の家 ／『男の隠れ家』05.11, 森を捕まえる家 ／『LEE』05.11, 重箱の家 ／『ブレーン』05.11, 藤幼稚園（プロジェクト）／『AERA DESIGN』05.11, 壁のない家、熱海のステップハウス、屋根の家、トヨタL&F広島、越後松之山「森の学校」キョロロ ／『MAC POWER』05.11, 藤幼稚園（プロジェクト）／『階段』05.11, 腰越のメガホンハウス、空を捕まえる家Ⅱ、蟻塚の家 ／『行列のできる建築家名鑑』05.11, 展望台の家、屋根の家、鎌倉山の家 ／『はじめての家づくり便利百貨2006』05.11, 空を捕まえる家Ⅱ ／『Kierunki Directions』05.11, 屋根の家、越後松之山「森の学校」キョロロ ／『DESIGN DIFFUSION NEWS』05.11, 縁側の家 ／『デザインで選ぶ住まいの設備2006』05.11, 重箱の家 ／『きもちのいい家』05.12, 作品集 ／『THE NEW HOUSE』05.12, 屋根の家 ／『Arquitectura Viva』05.12, 屋根の家 ／『Arquitectura Viva』05.12, Extreme Eurasia展（記事）／『吉阪隆正の迷宮』05.12, 次世代からのメッセージ ／『SMALL SPACES』05.12, 空を捕まえる家Ⅱ、縁側の家 ／『建築家のメモⅡ』05.12,（文）

2006

『SPAS for your home』06.01, 八王子の家 ／『家庭画報』06.02, 腰越のメガホンハウス、のこぎり屋根の家、鎌倉山の家

Credits クレジット

Photo Credits / フォトクレジット

Katsuhisa Kida / 木田勝久　All except the photographs below. / 以下を除くすべて

GA Photographers / GA フォトグラファーズ　02_ / pp. 3-4
Hiroyuki Takahashi / 高橋宏幸　08_ / p. 5 [top]
Mitsumasa Fujitsuka / 藤塚光政　38_ / pp. 3-4
Shinkenchiku-sha / 新建築写真部　01_ / pp. 5-6, 04_ / pp. 3, 4, 05_ / p. 3, 11_ / p. 5
Tezuka Architects / 手塚建築研究所　16_ / pp. 3, 4, 22_ / pp. 3-4

English Translations / 翻訳

Thomas Daniell / トーマス・ダニエル　Preface / 序文、TIME-LESS / 変わらないもの
Miguel A. Quintana / ミゲル・クィンタナ　Project Notes / 作品コンセプト

Editing / 編集

Shuichi Sakuma (Tezuka Architects) / 佐久間周一（手塚建築研究所）

Biography 略歴

Takaharu Tezuka / 手塚貴晴

1964	Born in Tokyo
1987	B. Arch., Musashi Institute of Technology
1990	M. Arch., Architecture at University of Pennsylvania
1990-1994	Richard Rogers Partnership Ltd.
1994	Established Tezuka Architects
1996-2003	Assistant Professor, Musashi Institute of Technology
2003-	Associate Professor, Musashi Institute of Technology
2005, 06	Visiting Professor, Salzburg Summer Academy
2006	Visiting Professor, University of California, Berkeley

1964	東京生まれ
1987	武蔵工業大学卒業
1990	ペンシルバニア大学大学院修了
1990-1994	リチャード・ロジャース・パートナーシップ・ロンドン勤務
1994	手塚建築研究所を手塚由比と共同設立
1996-2003	武蔵工業大学専任講師
2003-	武蔵工業大学助教授
2005, 06	ザルツブルグ・サマーアカデミー教授
2006	UCバークレー客員教授

Yui Tezuka / 手塚由比

1969	Born in Kanagawa
1992	B. Arch., Musashi Institute of Technology
1992-1993	Bartlett School of Architecture, University College of London
1994	Established Tezuka Architects
1999-	Member, Visiting Faculty, Toyo University
2001-	Member, Visiting Faculty, Tokai University
2006	Visiting Professor, Salzburg Summer Academy
2006	Visiting Professor, University of California, Berkeley

1969	神奈川生まれ
1992	武蔵工業大学卒業
1992-1993	ロンドン大学バートレット校
1994	手塚建築研究所を手塚貴晴と共同設立
1999-	東洋大学非常勤講師
2001-	東海大学非常勤講師
2006	ザルツブルグ・サマーアカデミー教授
2006	UCバークレー客員教授

Award / 受賞歴

1995
SD Review Winner, Kajima Institute Publishing Co Ltd, Soejima Hospital

1997
JCD 2nd Award, Japanese Society of Commercial Space Designers, Soejima Hospital
Good Design Gold Prize, Japan Industrial Design Promotion Organization, Soejima Hospital
Sagacity Urban Design Award, Saga City, Soejima Hospital
Midori no Machikado Prize, Saga Prefecture, Soejima Hospital

1998
Annual Architectural Commendations, Architectural Institute of Japan, Soejima Hospital
SD Award, Kajima Institute Publishing Co Ltd, Light Gauge Steel House

2000
Housing Prize, Tokyo Society of Architects & Building Engineers, Wood Deck House
JCD 3rd Award, Japanese Society of Commercial Space Designers, Light Gauge Steel Office
Kurasikku Prize (Townscape Award), Kawagoe Kura No Kai, Kawagoe Music Apartment
Good Design Prize, Japan Industrial Design Promotion Organization, Light Gauge Steel House
Good Design Prize, Japan Industrial Design Promotion Organization, Kawagoe Music Apartment
Award for Kawagoe Landscape Design, Kawagoe City, Kawagoe Music Apartment

2002
Yoshioka Prize, Yoshioka Foundation, Roof House
JIA Prize, Japan Institute of Architects, Roof House

2003
Annual Architectural Commendations, Japan Institute of Architects, Roof House
Good Design Prize, Japan Industrial Design Promotion Organization (Styrene foam sofa)

2004
Good Design Prize, Annual Architectural Commendations - Hounancho "L" Condominium
Ecobuild Award, Ecobuild Japan, Echigo-Matsunoyama Museum of Natural Science

2005
Annual Architectural Commendations, Japan Institute of Architects, Echigo-Matsunoyama Museum of Natural Science

1995
SDレビュー入選、鹿島出版会、副島病院

1997
JCDデザイン賞優秀賞、日本商環境設計家協会、副島病院
グッドデザイン賞金賞、(財)日本産業デザイン振興会、副島病院
都市景観賞、佐賀市、副島病院
緑の街角賞、佐賀県、副島病院

1998
日本建築学会作品選奨賞、日本建築学会、副島病院
SD賞、鹿島出版会、辻堂の家

2000
東京建築士会住宅建築賞、東京建築士会、鎌倉山の家
JCDデザイン賞奨励賞、(社)日本商環境設計家協会、裏原宿のビル
蔵詩句大賞、川越蔵の会、川越の音楽マンション(ミュージション川越)
グッドデザイン賞、(財)日本産業デザイン振興会、裏原宿のビル
グッドデザイン賞、(財)日本産業デザイン振興会、川越の音楽マンション
都市景観賞、川越市、川越の音楽マンション

2002
第18回吉岡賞、財団法人 吉岡文庫育英会、屋根の家
2002年度JIA新人賞、(社)日本建築家協会、屋根の家

2003
2003年日本建築学会作品選奨、(社)日本建築家協会、屋根の家
2003年度グッドデザイン賞、(財)日本産業デザイン振興会賞、発泡スチロールソファ

2004
2004年度グッドデザイン賞、(財)日本産業デザイン振興会、方南町L
2004 Ecobuild award、エコビルド実行委員会 NPOグリーンシティー推進機構、越後松之山「森の学校」キョロロ

2005
2005年日本建築学会作品選奨、(社)日本建築家協会、越後松之山「森の学校」キョロロ

手塚貴晴＋手塚由比　建築カタログ

2006年3月15日　初版第1刷発行
2017年9月30日　初版第12刷発行

著者：手塚貴晴＋手塚由比

発行者：加藤 徹
発行所：TOTO出版（TOTO株式会社）
〒107-0062 東京都港区南青山1-24-3
TOTO乃木坂ビル2F
［営業］TEL:03-3402-7138　FAX:03-3402-7187
［編集］TEL:03-3497-1010
URL：http://www.toto.co.jp/publishing/

ブックデザイン：天木理恵

印刷・製本：図書印刷株式会社

本書はTOTOギャラリー・間（東京）にて開催された「手塚貴晴＋手塚由比展」
（2006年3月15日〜5月20日）に併せて発行されたものです。

落丁本・乱丁本はお取り替えいたします。
本書の全部又は一部に対するコピー・スキャン・デジタル化等の無断複製行為は、著作権法上で
の例外を除き禁じます。本書を代行業者等の第三者に依頼してスキャンやデジタル化することは、
たとえ個人や家庭内での利用であっても著作権上認められておりません。
定価はカバーに表示してあります。

© 2006 手塚貴晴＋手塚由比
Printed in Japan
ISBN978-4-88706-267-2